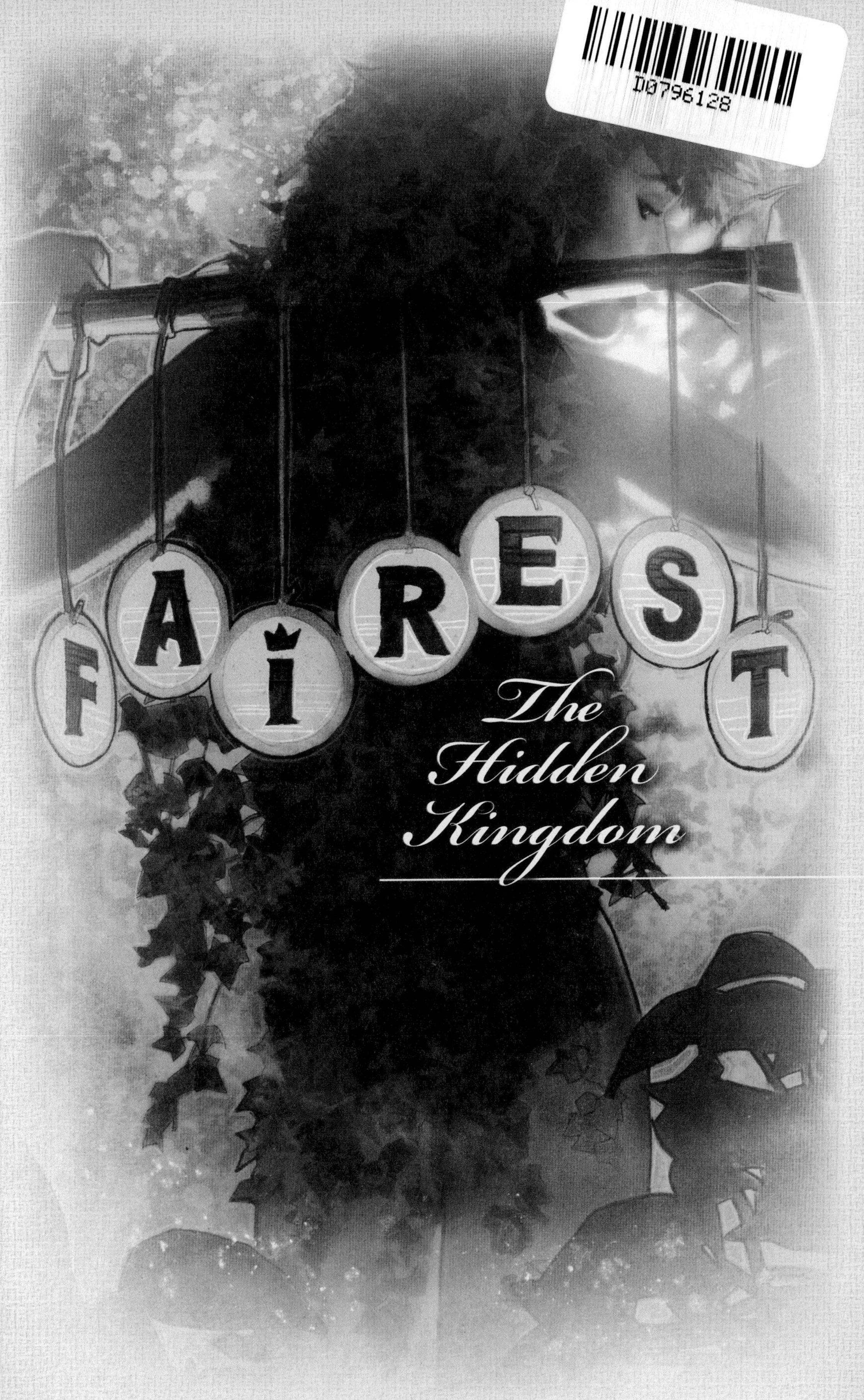
FAIREST
The Hidden Kingdom

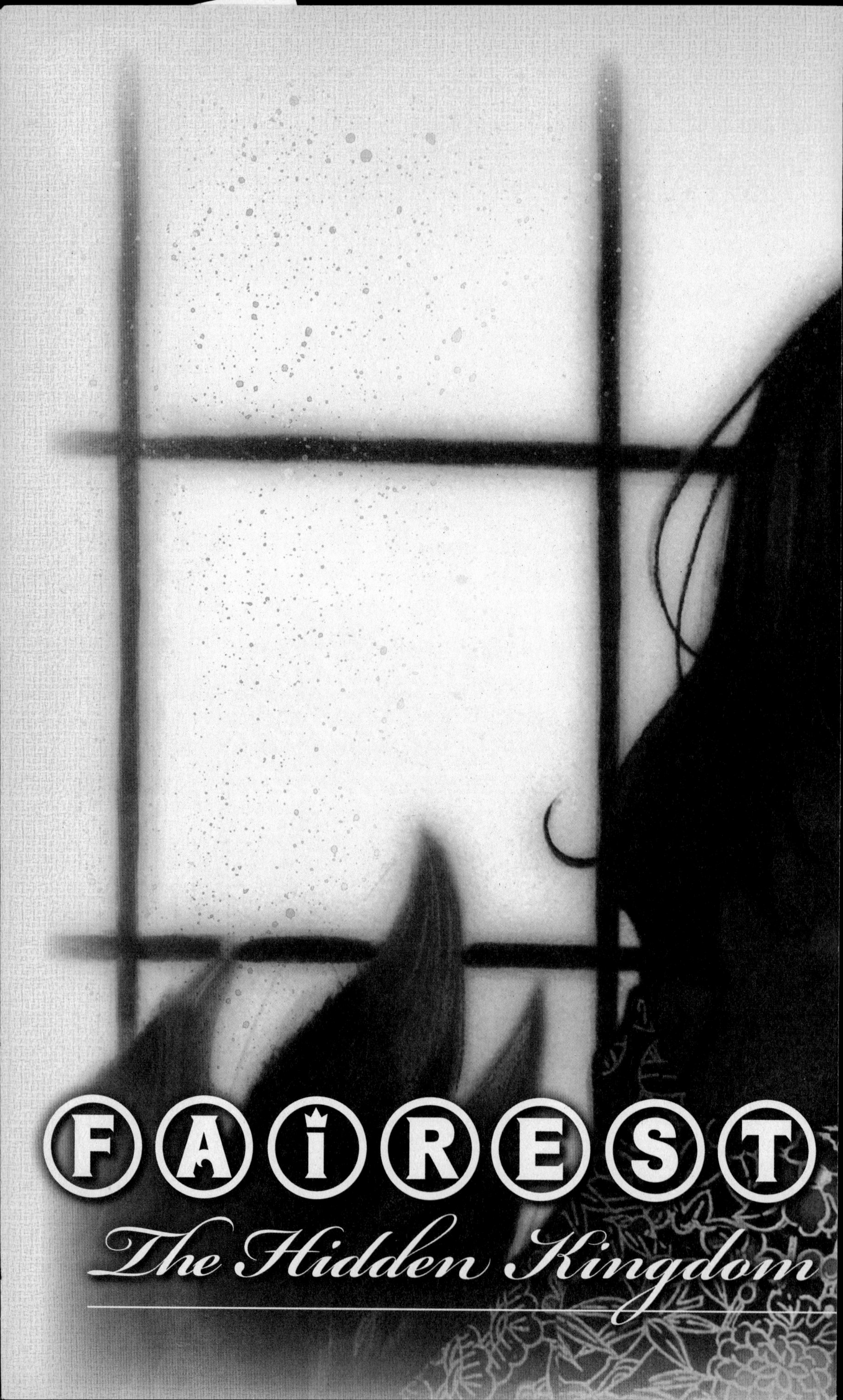
FAIREST
The Hidden Kingdom

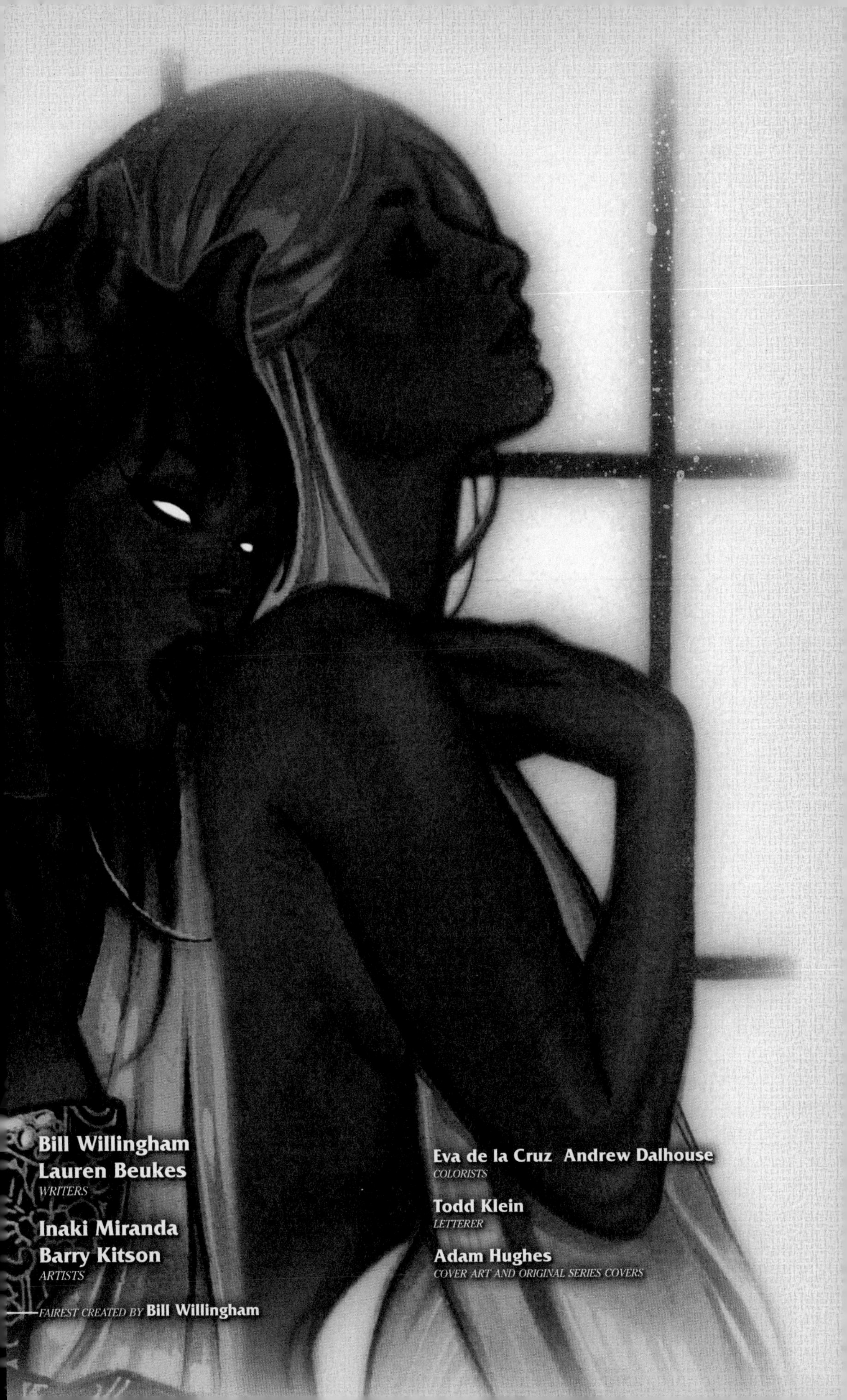

Bill Willingham
Lauren Beukes
WRITERS

Inaki Miranda
Barry Kitson
ARTISTS

FAIREST CREATED BY **Bill Willingham**

Eva de la Cruz Andrew Dalhouse
COLORISTS

Todd Klein
LETTERER

Adam Hughes
COVER ART AND ORIGINAL SERIES COVERS

FAIREST: THE HIDDEN KINGDOM
Published by DC Comics. Cover and compilation Copyright © 2013
Bill Willingham and DC Comics. All Rights Reserved. Originally published
in single magazine form in FAIREST 8-14. Copyright © 2012, 2013 Bill
Willingham and DC Comics. All Rights Reserved. All characters, their
distinctive likenesses and related elements featured in this publication
are trademarks of Bill Willingham. VERTIGO is a trademark of DC Comics.
The stories, characters and incidents featured in this publication are
entirely fictional. DC Comics does not read or accept unsolicited
submissions of ideas, stories or artwork.

DC Comics, 1700 Broadway, New York, NY 10019
A Warner Bros. Entertainment Company
Printed in the U.S.A. First Printing. ISBN: 978-1-4012-4021-9

Library of Congress Cataloging-in-Publication Data

Willingham, Bill, author.
 Fairest. Volume 2, Hidden kingdom / Bill Willingham, Lauren Beukes,
Inaki Miranda, Barry Kitson.
    pages cm
 "Originally published in single magazine form in Fairest 8-14."
 ISBN 978-1-4012-4021-9
 1. Graphic novels. I. Beukes, Lauren, author. II. Miranda, Inaki, illustrator.
III. Kitson, Barry, illustrator. IV. Title. V. Title: Hidden kingdom.
 PN6728.F255W55 2013
 741.5'973—dc23
                          2013009149

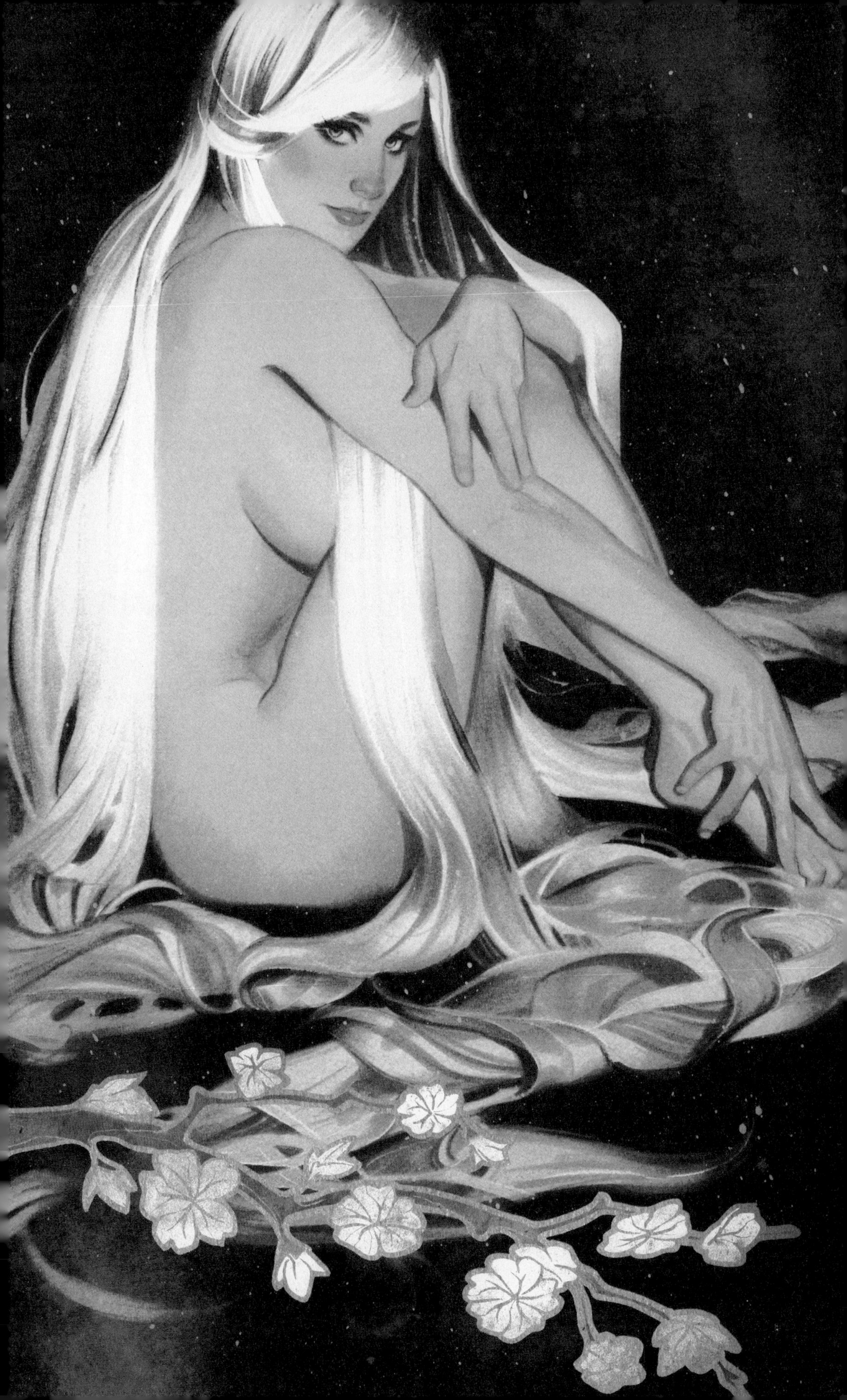

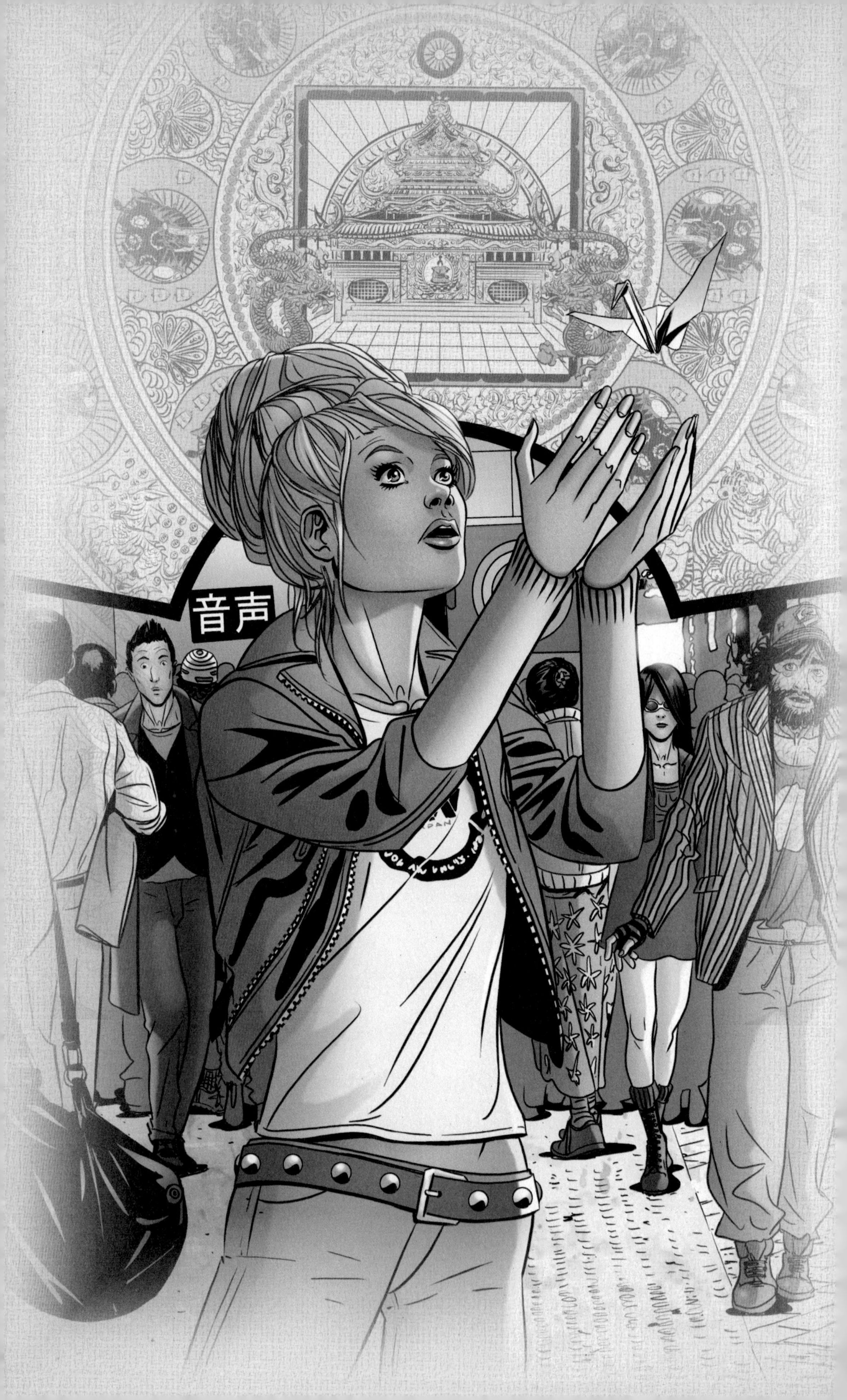
音声

THE PAST IS A DEAD DOG.

New York City. 2002. Before everything.

TRIPLE FEATURE: BUNNY LAKE IS MISSING. DON'T LOOK NOW. PICNIC AT HANGING ROCK

TRIPLE FEATURE: BUNNY LAKE IS MISSING. DON'T LOOK NOW. PICNIC AT HANGING ROCK

YOU NEED TO LEAVE IT IN THE GUTTER WITH THE WET LEAVES AND USED CONDOMS AND TRASH.

WALK AWAY. DON'T LOOK BACK.

La garrapata
HOTEL BLACKTH
BLACKTHORN

THAT WAY YOU CAN'T SEE IT PADDING AFTER YOU.

THE HIDDEN KINGDOM
CHAPTER ONE: BIG IN JAPAN

LAUREN BEUKES
writer

INAKI MIRANDA
artist

EVA DE LA CRUZ
colors

TODD KLEIN
letters

ADAM HUGHES
cover

BILL WILLINGHAM
consultant & Fables creator

GREGORY LOCKARD
assistant editor

SHELLY BOND
editor

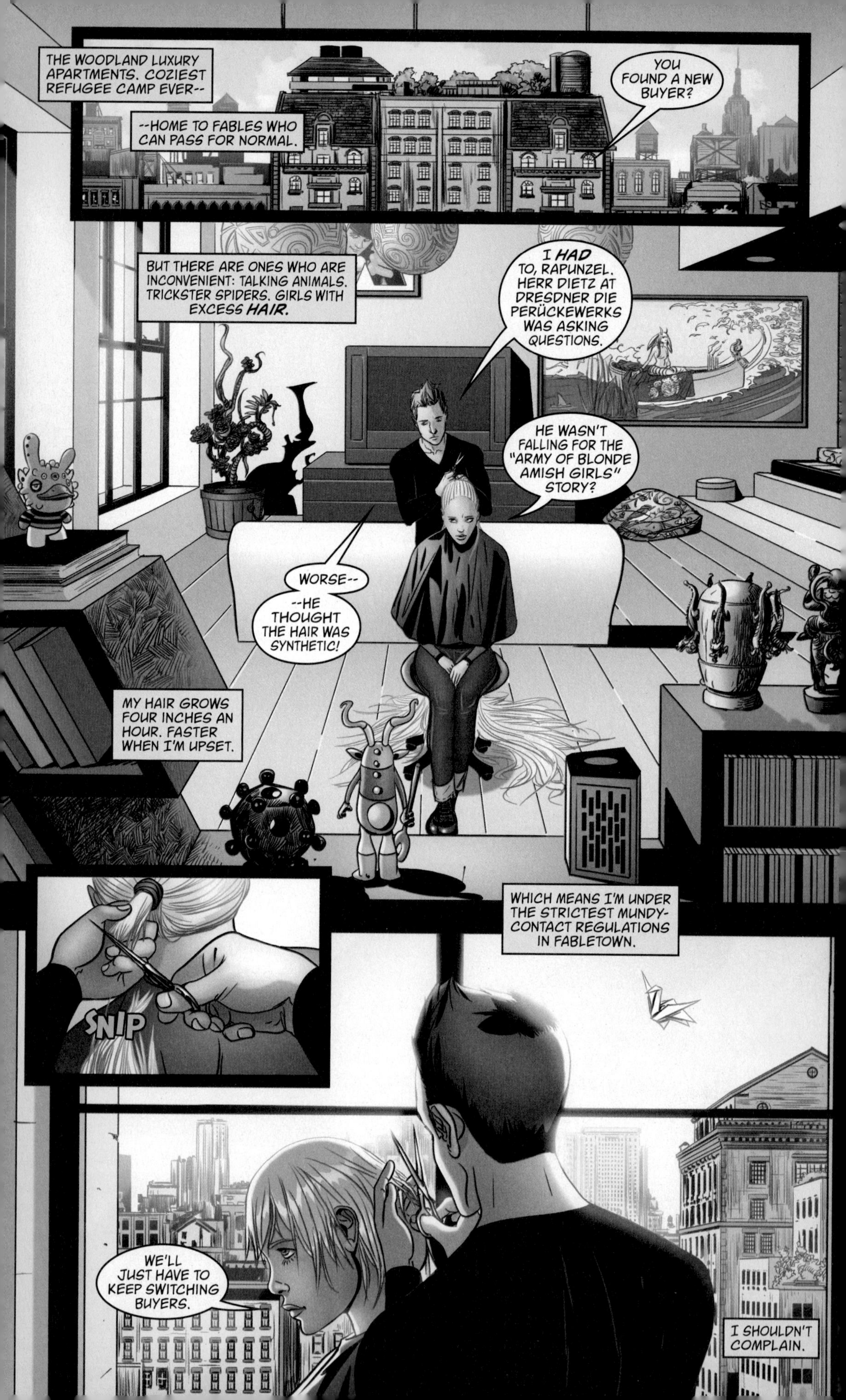
THE WOODLAND LUXURY APARTMENTS. COZIEST REFUGEE CAMP EVER--
--HOME TO FABLES WHO CAN PASS FOR NORMAL.
YOU FOUND A NEW BUYER?
BUT THERE ARE ONES WHO ARE INCONVENIENT: TALKING ANIMALS. TRICKSTER SPIDERS. GIRLS WITH EXCESS HAIR.
I HAD TO, RAPUNZEL. HERR DIETZ AT DRESDNER DIE PERÜCKEWERKS WAS ASKING QUESTIONS.
HE WASN'T FALLING FOR THE "ARMY OF BLONDE AMISH GIRLS" STORY?
WORSE--
--HE THOUGHT THE HAIR WAS SYNTHETIC!
MY HAIR GROWS FOUR INCHES AN HOUR. FASTER WHEN I'M UPSET.
SNIP
WHICH MEANS I'M UNDER THE STRICTEST MUNDY-CONTACT REGULATIONS IN FABLETOWN.
WE'LL JUST HAVE TO KEEP SWITCHING BUYERS.
I SHOULDN'T COMPLAIN.

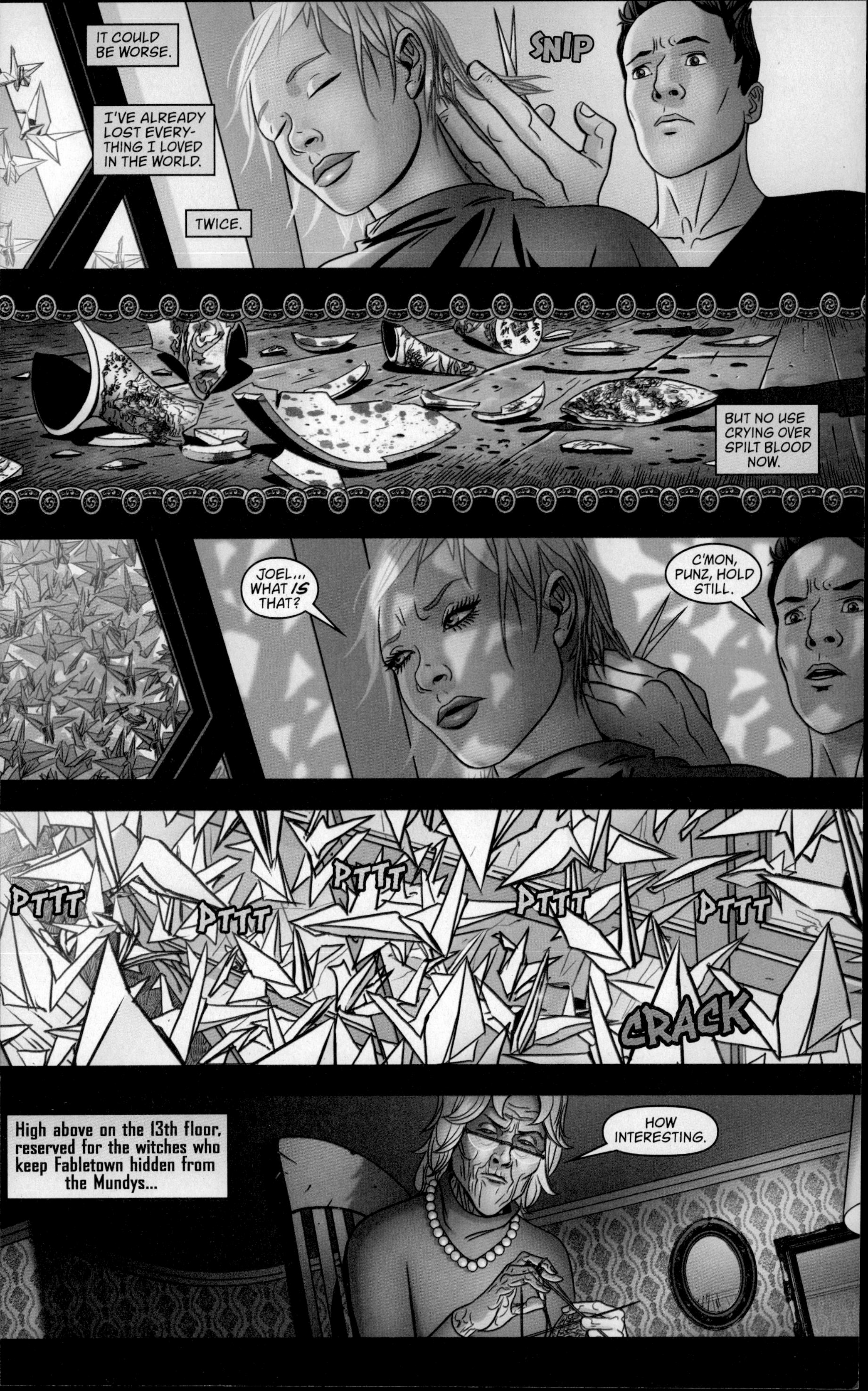
IT COULD BE WORSE.
SNIP
I'VE ALREADY LOST EVERYTHING I LOVED IN THE WORLD.
TWICE.
BUT NO USE CRYING OVER SPILT BLOOD NOW.
JOEL... WHAT IS THAT?
C'MON, PUNZ, HOLD STILL.
PTTT
PTTT
PTTT
PTTT
PTTT
CRACK
High above on the 13th floor, reserved for the witches who keep Fabletown hidden from the Mundys...
HOW INTERESTING.

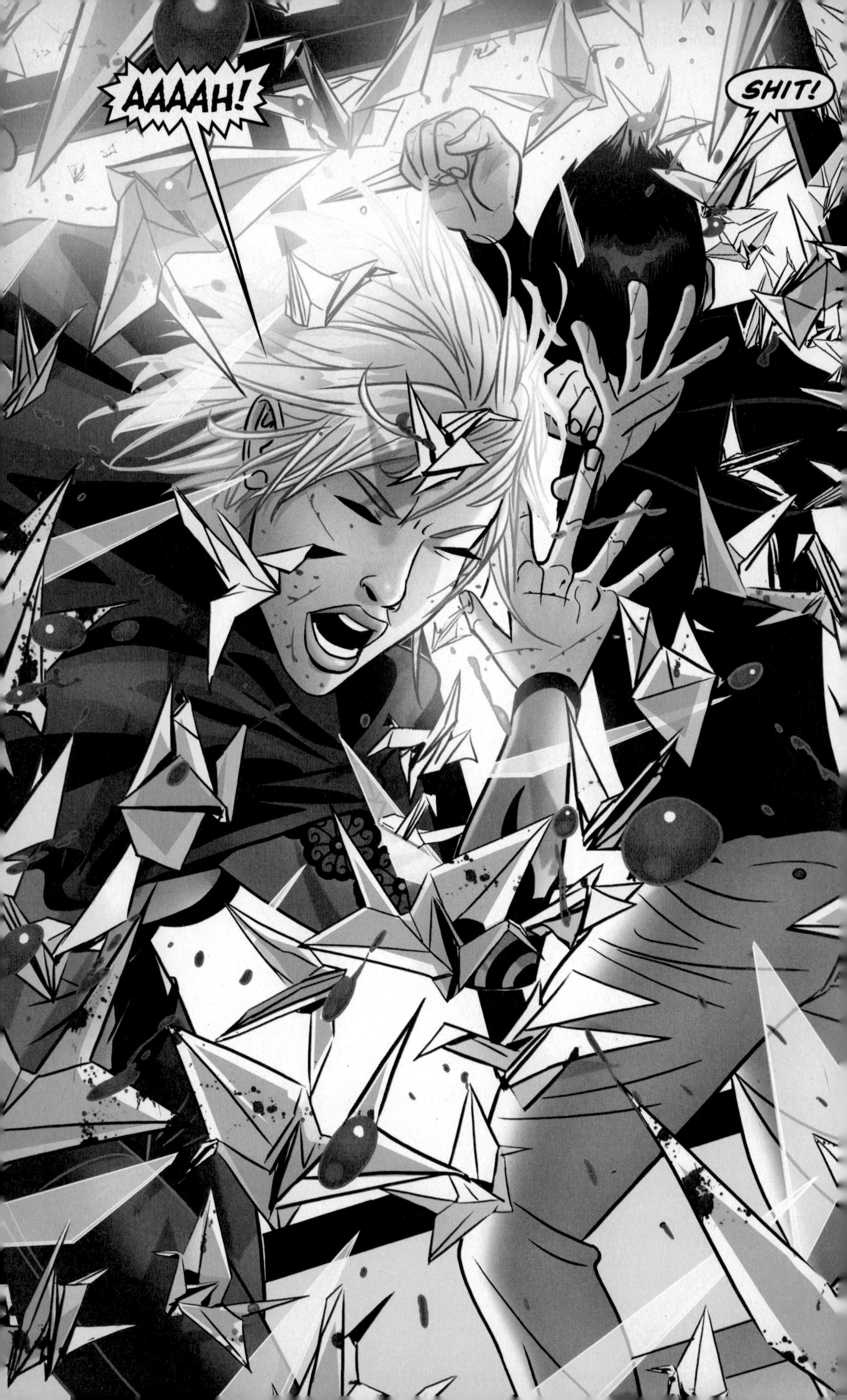
AAAAH!
SHIT!

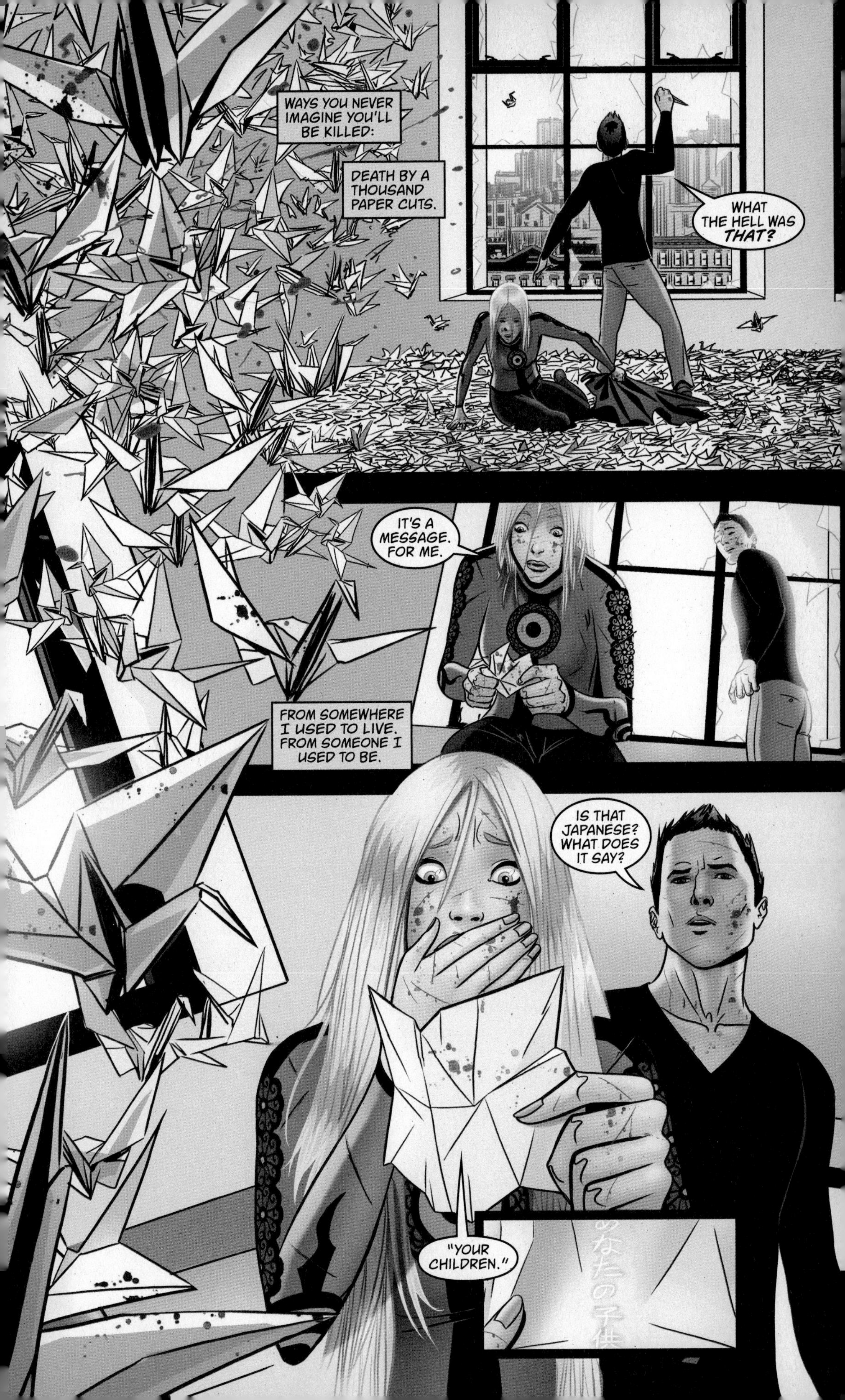
WAYS YOU NEVER IMAGINE YOU'LL BE KILLED:
DEATH BY A THOUSAND PAPER CUTS.
WHAT THE HELL WAS THAT?
IT'S A MESSAGE. FOR ME.
FROM SOMEWHERE I USED TO LIVE. FROM SOMEONE I USED TO BE.
IS THAT JAPANESE? WHAT DOES IT SAY?
"YOUR CHILDREN."
なたの子供

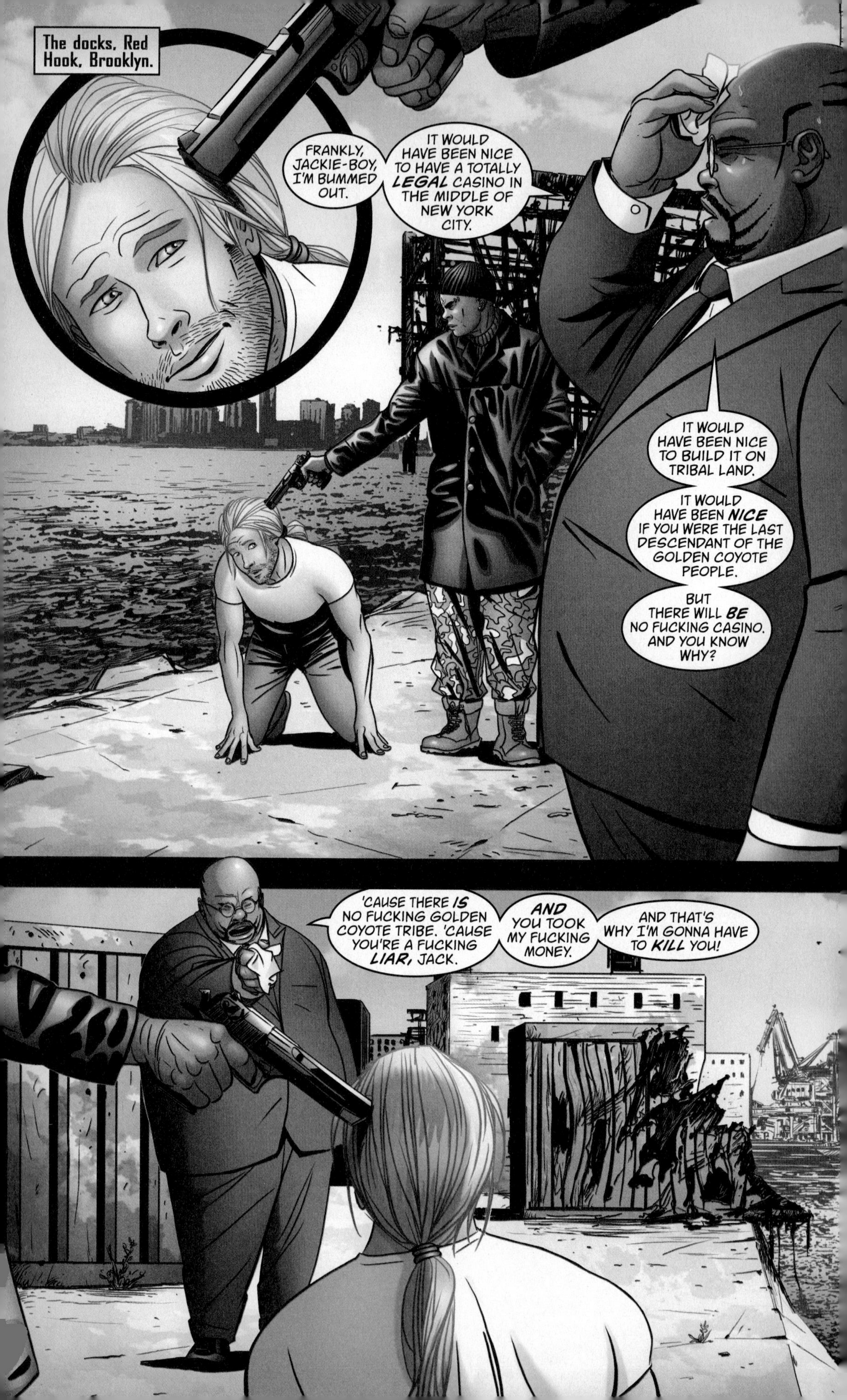
The docks, Red Hook, Brooklyn.
FRANKLY, JACKIE-BOY, I'M BUMMED OUT.
IT WOULD HAVE BEEN NICE TO HAVE A TOTALLY LEGAL CASINO IN THE MIDDLE OF NEW YORK CITY.
IT WOULD HAVE BEEN NICE TO BUILD IT ON TRIBAL LAND.
IT WOULD HAVE BEEN NICE IF YOU WERE THE LAST DESCENDANT OF THE GOLDEN COYOTE PEOPLE.
BUT THERE WILL BE NO FUCKING CASINO. AND YOU KNOW WHY?
'CAUSE THERE IS NO FUCKING GOLDEN COYOTE TRIBE. 'CAUSE YOU'RE A FUCKING LIAR, JACK.
AND YOU TOOK MY FUCKING MONEY.
AND THAT'S WHY I'M GONNA HAVE TO KILL YOU!

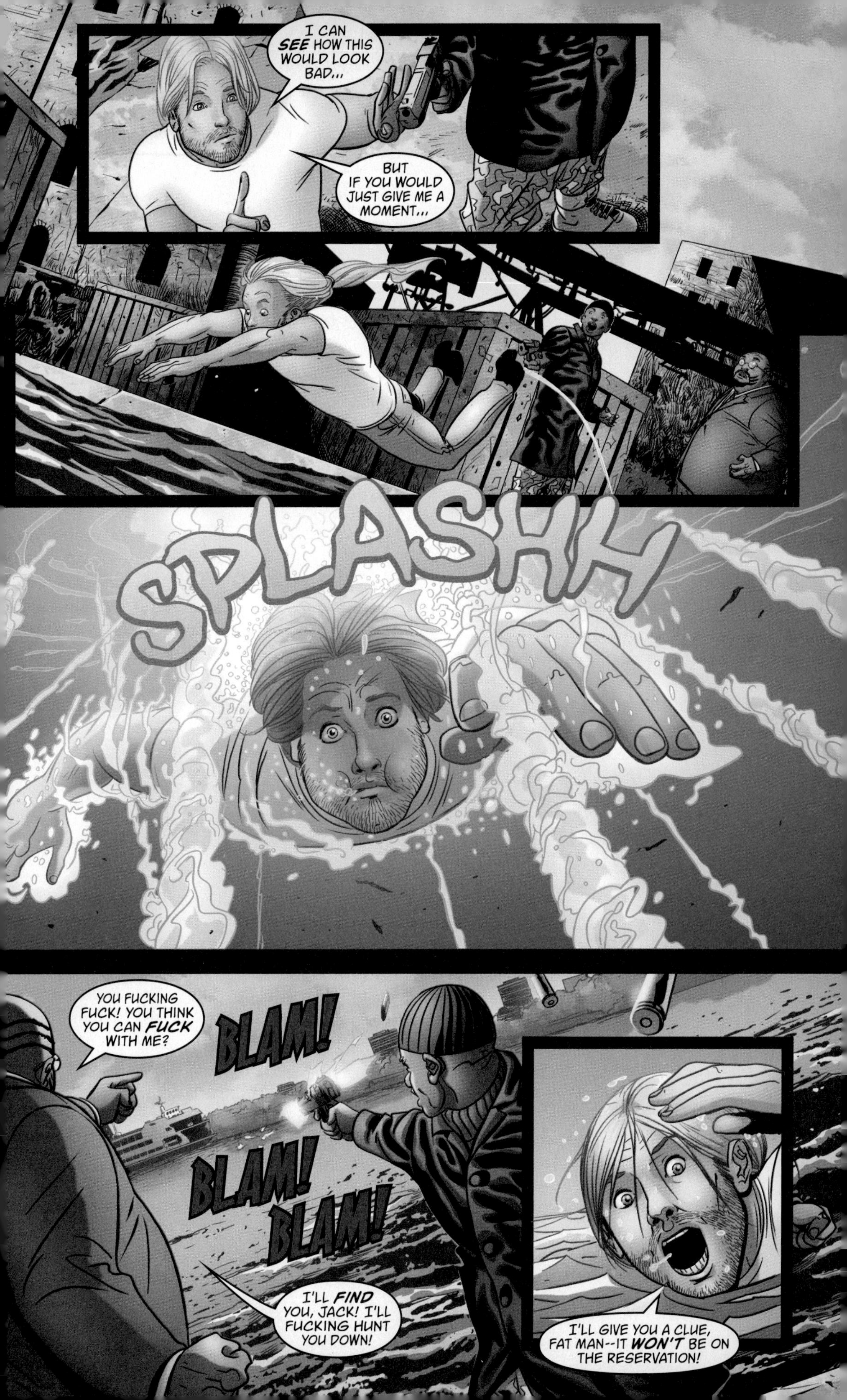
I CAN SEE HOW THIS WOULD LOOK BAD...
BUT IF YOU WOULD JUST GIVE ME A MOMENT...
SPLASHH
YOU FUCKING FUCK! YOU THINK YOU CAN FUCK WITH ME?
BLAM!
BLAM!
BLAM!
I'LL FIND YOU, JACK! I'LL FUCKING HUNT YOU DOWN!
I'LL GIVE YOU A CLUE, FAT MAN--IT WON'T BE ON THE RESERVATION!

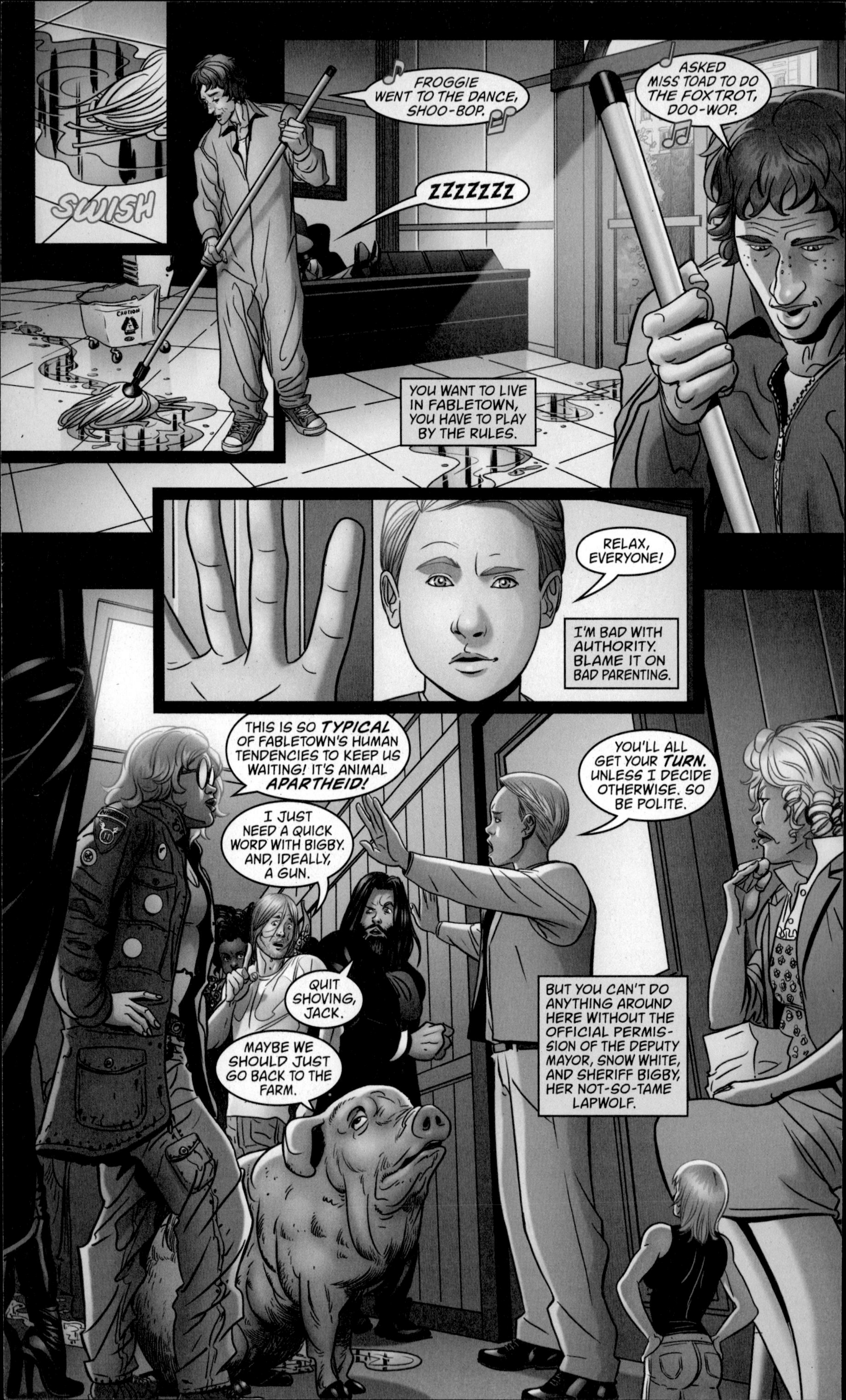
SWISH
FROGGIE WENT TO THE DANCE, SHOO-BOP.
ZZZZZZZ
ASKED MISS TOAD TO DO THE FOXTROT, DOO-WOP.
YOU WANT TO LIVE IN FABLETOWN, YOU HAVE TO PLAY BY THE RULES.
RELAX, EVERYONE!
I'M BAD WITH AUTHORITY. BLAME IT ON BAD PARENTING.
THIS IS SO TYPICAL OF FABLETOWN'S HUMAN TENDENCIES TO KEEP US WAITING! IT'S ANIMAL APARTHEID!
I JUST NEED A QUICK WORD WITH BIGBY. AND, IDEALLY, A GUN.
QUIT SHOVING, JACK.
MAYBE WE SHOULD JUST GO BACK TO THE FARM.
YOU'LL ALL GET YOUR TURN. UNLESS I DECIDE OTHERWISE. SO BE POLITE.
BUT YOU CAN'T DO ANYTHING AROUND HERE WITHOUT THE OFFICIAL PERMISSION OF THE DEPUTY MAYOR, SNOW WHITE, AND SHERIFF BIGBY, HER NOT-SO-TAME LAPWOLF.

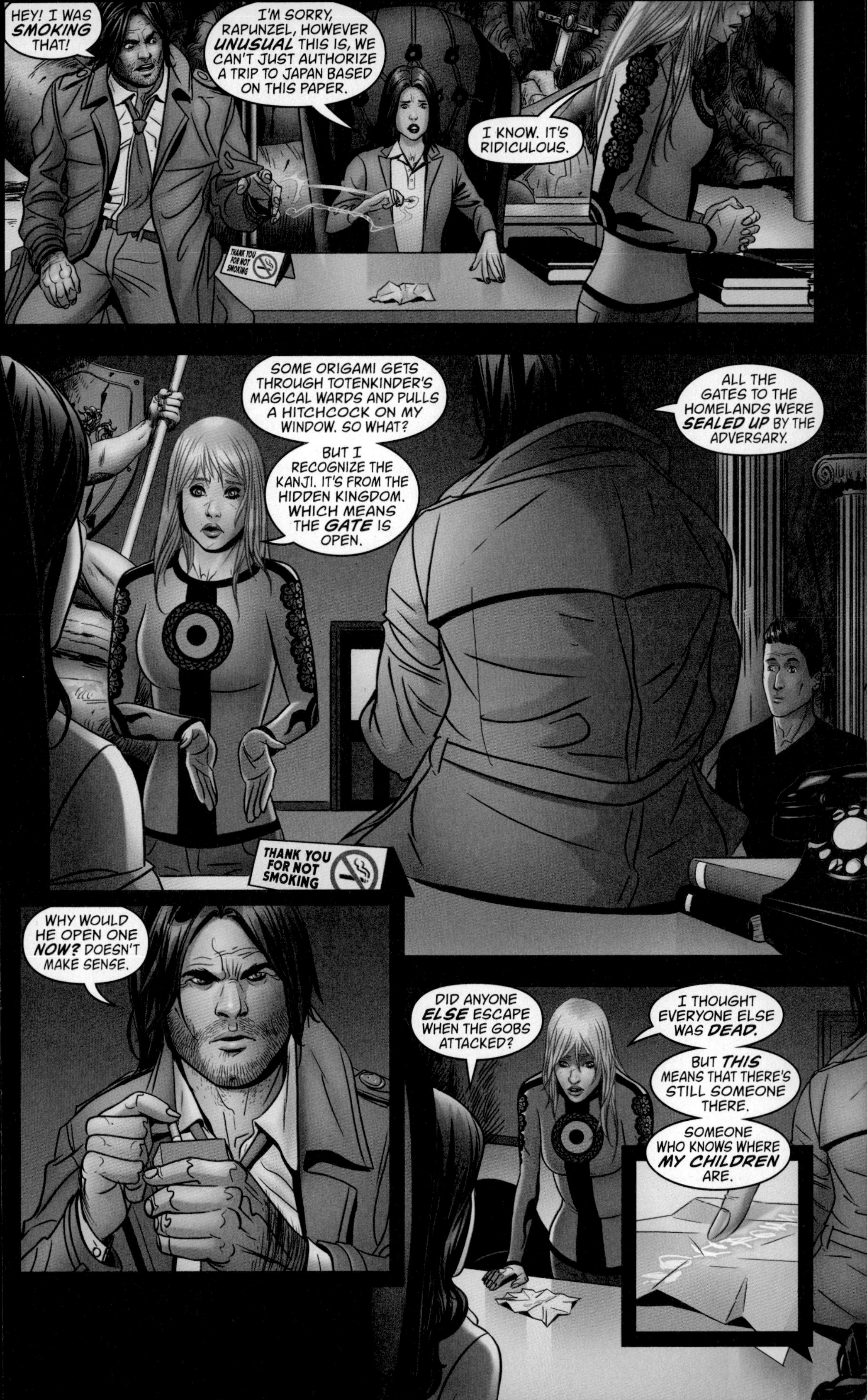
HEY! I WAS SMOKING THAT!
I'M SORRY, RAPUNZEL, HOWEVER UNUSUAL THIS IS, WE CAN'T JUST AUTHORIZE A TRIP TO JAPAN BASED ON THIS PAPER.
I KNOW. IT'S RIDICULOUS.
THANK YOU FOR NOT SMOKING
SOME ORIGAMI GETS THROUGH TOTENKINDER'S MAGICAL WARDS AND PULLS A HITCHCOCK ON MY WINDOW. SO WHAT?
BUT I RECOGNIZE THE KANJI. IT'S FROM THE HIDDEN KINGDOM. WHICH MEANS THE GATE IS OPEN.
ALL THE GATES TO THE HOMELANDS WERE SEALED UP BY THE ADVERSARY.
THANK YOU FOR NOT SMOKING
WHY WOULD HE OPEN ONE NOW? DOESN'T MAKE SENSE.
DID ANYONE ELSE ESCAPE WHEN THE GOBS ATTACKED?
I THOUGHT EVERYONE ELSE WAS DEAD.
BUT THIS MEANS THAT THERE'S STILL SOMEONE THERE.
SOMEONE WHO KNOWS WHERE MY CHILDREN ARE.

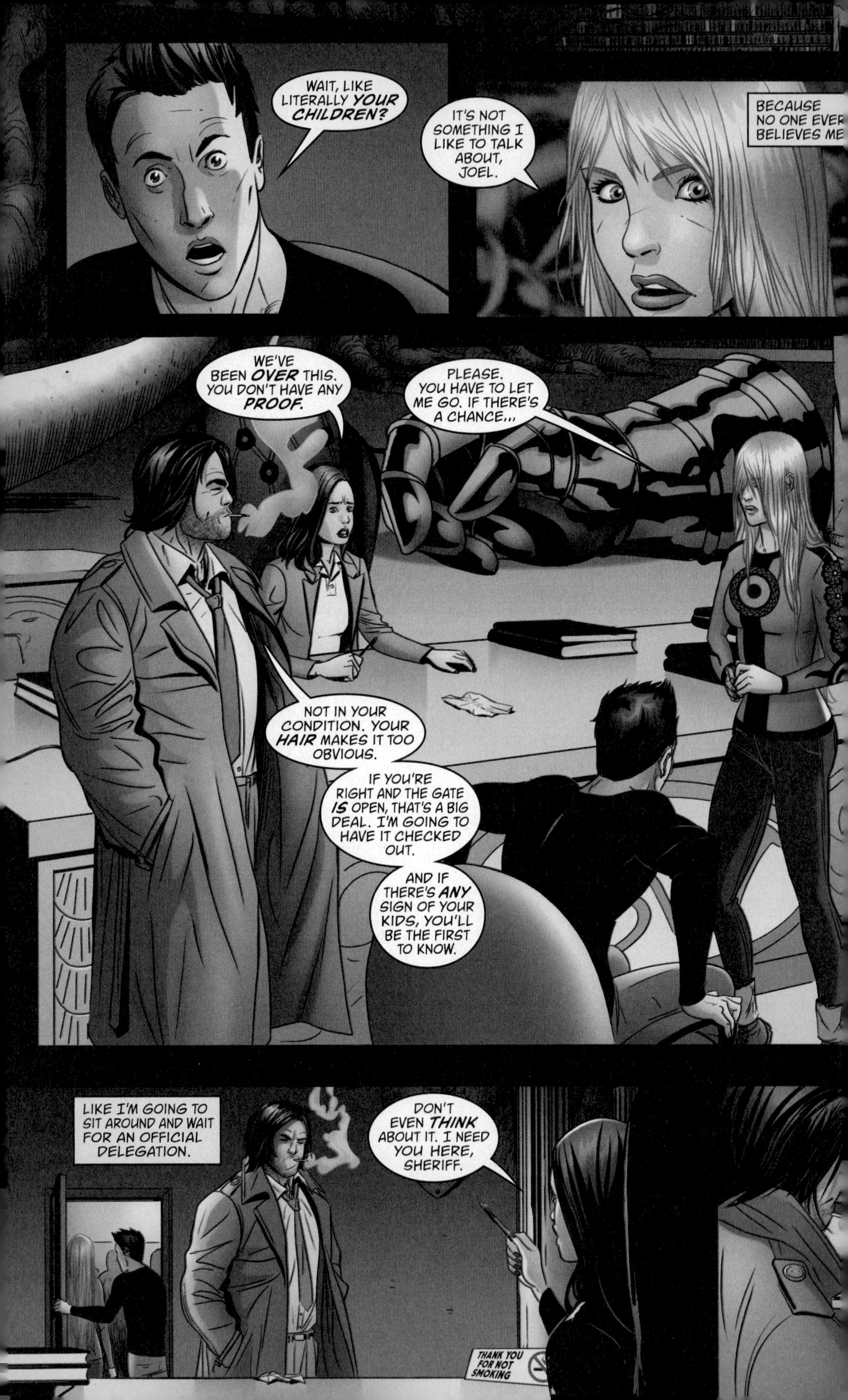
WAIT, LIKE LITERALLY YOUR CHILDREN?
IT'S NOT SOMETHING I LIKE TO TALK ABOUT, JOEL.
BECAUSE NO ONE EVER BELIEVES ME
WE'VE BEEN OVER THIS. YOU DON'T HAVE ANY PROOF.
PLEASE. YOU HAVE TO LET ME GO. IF THERE'S A CHANCE...
NOT IN YOUR CONDITION. YOUR HAIR MAKES IT TOO OBVIOUS.
IF YOU'RE RIGHT AND THE GATE IS OPEN, THAT'S A BIG DEAL. I'M GOING TO HAVE IT CHECKED OUT.
AND IF THERE'S ANY SIGN OF YOUR KIDS, YOU'LL BE THE FIRST TO KNOW.
LIKE I'M GOING TO SIT AROUND AND WAIT FOR AN OFFICIAL DELEGATION.
DON'T EVEN THINK ABOUT IT. I NEED YOU HERE, SHERIFF.
THANK YOU FOR NOT SMOKING

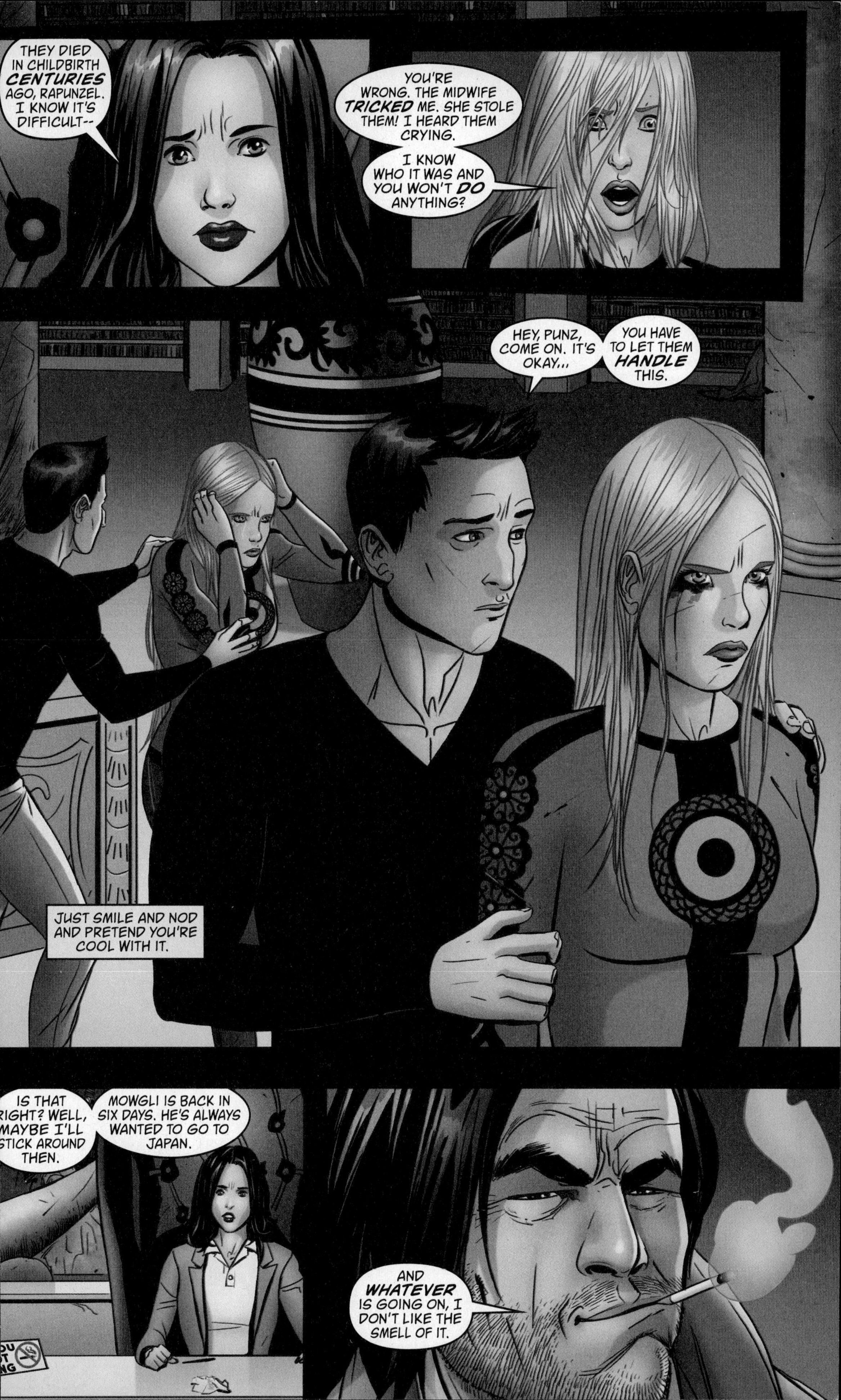

THEY DIED IN CHILDBIRTH CENTURIES AGO, RAPUNZEL. I KNOW IT'S DIFFICULT--
YOU'RE WRONG. THE MIDWIFE TRICKED ME. SHE STOLE THEM! I HEARD THEM CRYING.
I KNOW WHO IT WAS AND YOU WON'T DO ANYTHING?
HEY, PUNZ, COME ON. IT'S OKAY...
YOU HAVE TO LET THEM HANDLE THIS.
JUST SMILE AND NOD AND PRETEND YOU'RE COOL WITH IT.
IS THAT RIGHT? WELL, MAYBE I'LL STICK AROUND THEN.
MOWGLI IS BACK IN SIX DAYS. HE'S ALWAYS WANTED TO GO TO JAPAN.
AND WHATEVER IS GOING ON, I DON'T LIKE THE SMELL OF IT.

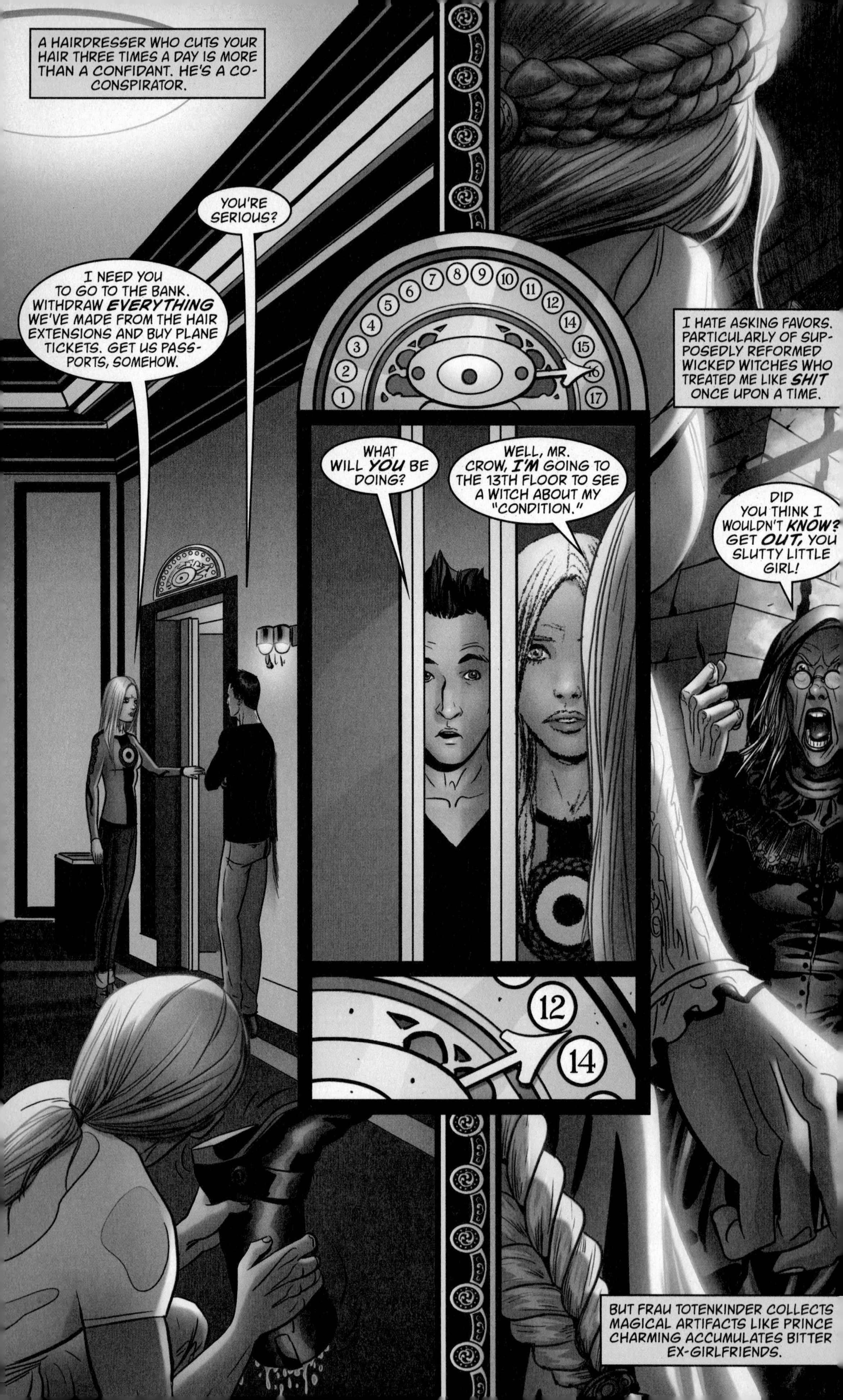
A HAIRDRESSER WHO CUTS YOUR HAIR THREE TIMES A DAY IS MORE THAN A CONFIDANT. HE'S A CO-CONSPIRATOR.
I NEED YOU TO GO TO THE BANK. WITHDRAW EVERYTHING WE'VE MADE FROM THE HAIR EXTENSIONS AND BUY PLANE TICKETS. GET US PASS-PORTS, SOMEHOW.
YOU'RE SERIOUS?
WHAT WILL YOU BE DOING?
WELL, MR. CROW, I'M GOING TO THE 13TH FLOOR TO SEE A WITCH ABOUT MY "CONDITION."
I HATE ASKING FAVORS. PARTICULARLY OF SUP-POSEDLY REFORMED WICKED WITCHES WHO TREATED ME LIKE SHIT ONCE UPON A TIME.
DID YOU THINK I WOULDN'T KNOW? GET OUT, YOU SLUTTY LITTLE GIRL!
BUT FRAU TOTENKINDER COLLECTS MAGICAL ARTIFACTS LIKE PRINCE CHARMING ACCUMULATES BITTER EX-GIRLFRIENDS.

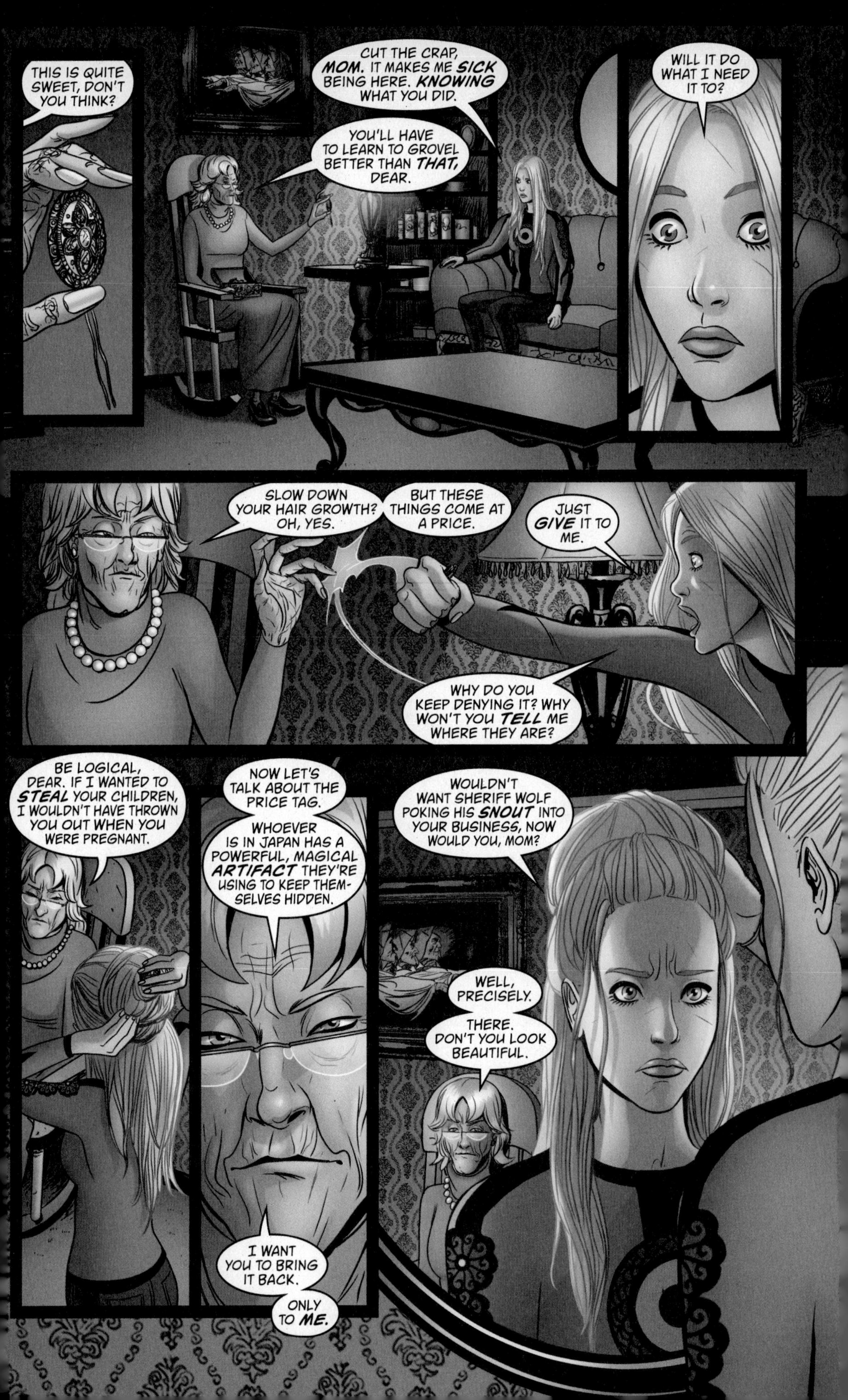
THIS IS QUITE SWEET, DON'T YOU THINK?
CUT THE CRAP, MOM. IT MAKES ME SICK BEING HERE. KNOWING WHAT YOU DID.
YOU'LL HAVE TO LEARN TO GROVEL BETTER THAN THAT, DEAR.
WILL IT DO WHAT I NEED IT TO?
SLOW DOWN YOUR HAIR GROWTH? OH, YES.
BUT THESE THINGS COME AT A PRICE.
JUST GIVE IT TO ME.
WHY DO YOU KEEP DENYING IT? WHY WON'T YOU TELL ME WHERE THEY ARE?
BE LOGICAL, DEAR. IF I WANTED TO STEAL YOUR CHILDREN, I WOULDN'T HAVE THROWN YOU OUT WHEN YOU WERE PREGNANT.
NOW LET'S TALK ABOUT THE PRICE TAG.
WHOEVER IS IN JAPAN HAS A POWERFUL, MAGICAL ARTIFACT THEY'RE USING TO KEEP THEMSELVES HIDDEN.
I WANT YOU TO BRING IT BACK.
ONLY TO ME.
WOULDN'T WANT SHERIFF WOLF POKING HIS SNOUT INTO YOUR BUSINESS, NOW WOULD YOU, MOM?
WELL, PRECISELY.
THERE. DON'T YOU LOOK BEAUTIFUL.

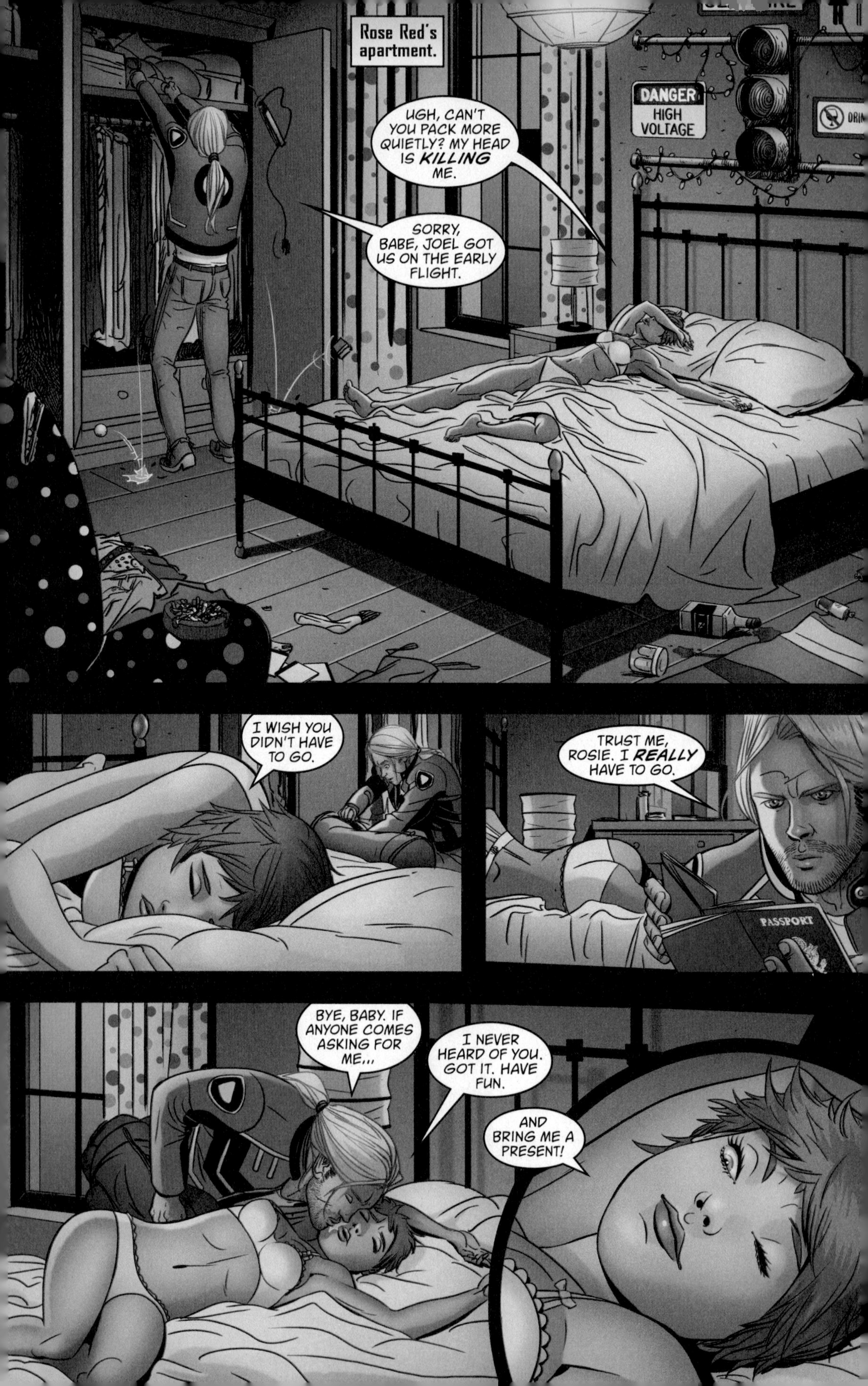
Rose Red's apartment.
DANGER HIGH VOLTAGE
UGH, CAN'T YOU PACK MORE QUIETLY? MY HEAD IS *KILLING* ME.
SORRY, BABE, JOEL GOT US ON THE EARLY FLIGHT.
I WISH YOU DIDN'T HAVE TO GO.
TRUST ME, ROSIE. I *REALLY* HAVE TO GO.
PASSPORT
BYE, BABY. IF ANYONE COMES ASKING FOR ME...
I NEVER HEARD OF YOU. GOT IT. HAVE FUN.
AND BRING ME A PRESENT!

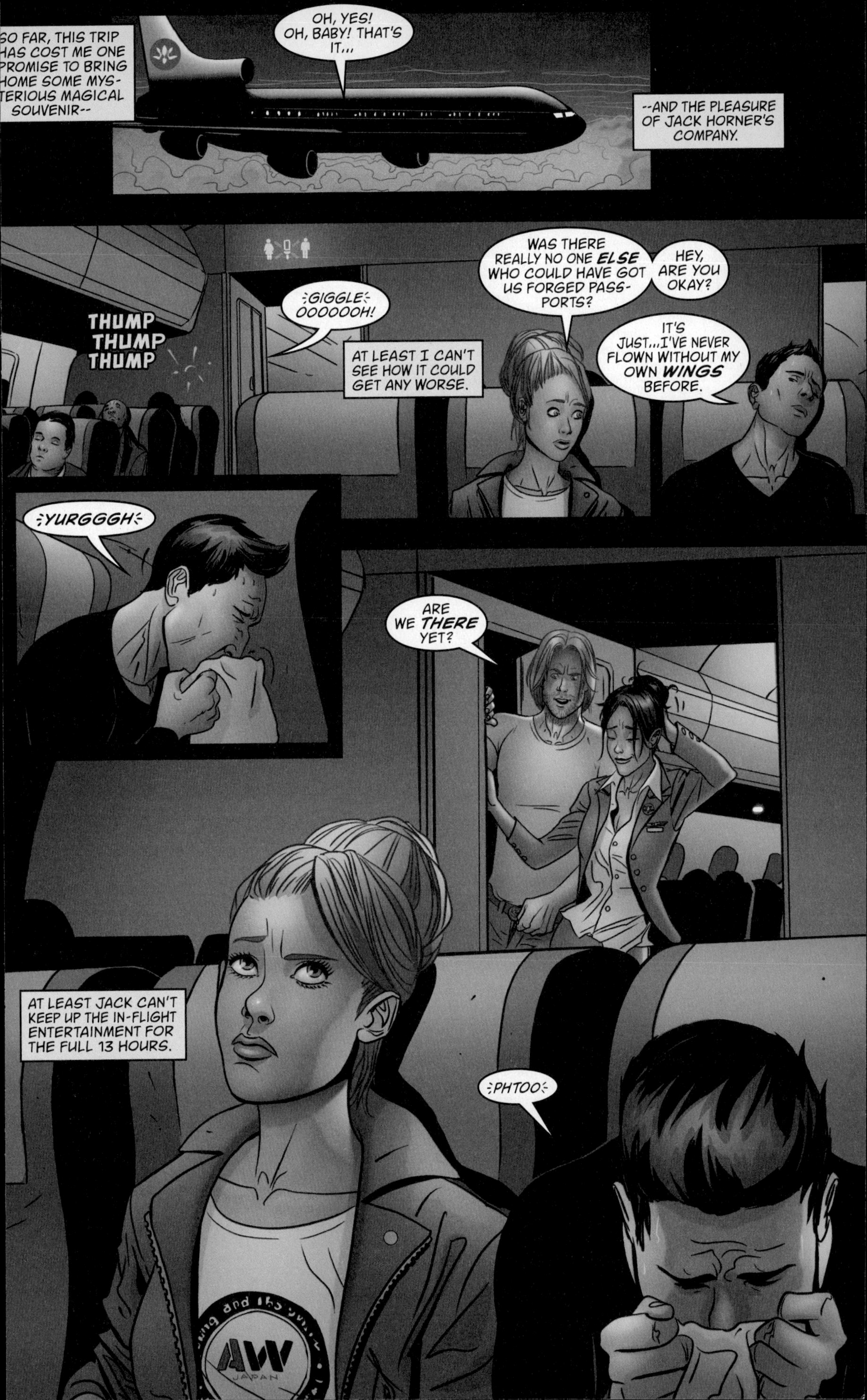
SO FAR, THIS TRIP HAS COST ME ONE PROMISE TO BRING HOME SOME MYSTERIOUS MAGICAL SOUVENIR--
OH, YES! OH, BABY! THAT'S IT...
--AND THE PLEASURE OF JACK HORNER'S COMPANY.
THUMP THUMP THUMP
GIGGLE OOOOOOH!
AT LEAST I CAN'T SEE HOW IT COULD GET ANY WORSE.
WAS THERE REALLY NO ONE ELSE WHO COULD HAVE GOT US FORGED PASSPORTS?
HEY, ARE YOU OKAY?
IT'S JUST...I'VE NEVER FLOWN WITHOUT MY OWN WINGS BEFORE.
YURGGGH
ARE WE THERE YET?
AT LEAST JACK CAN'T KEEP UP THE IN-FLIGHT ENTERTAINMENT FOR THE FULL 13 HOURS.
PHTOO

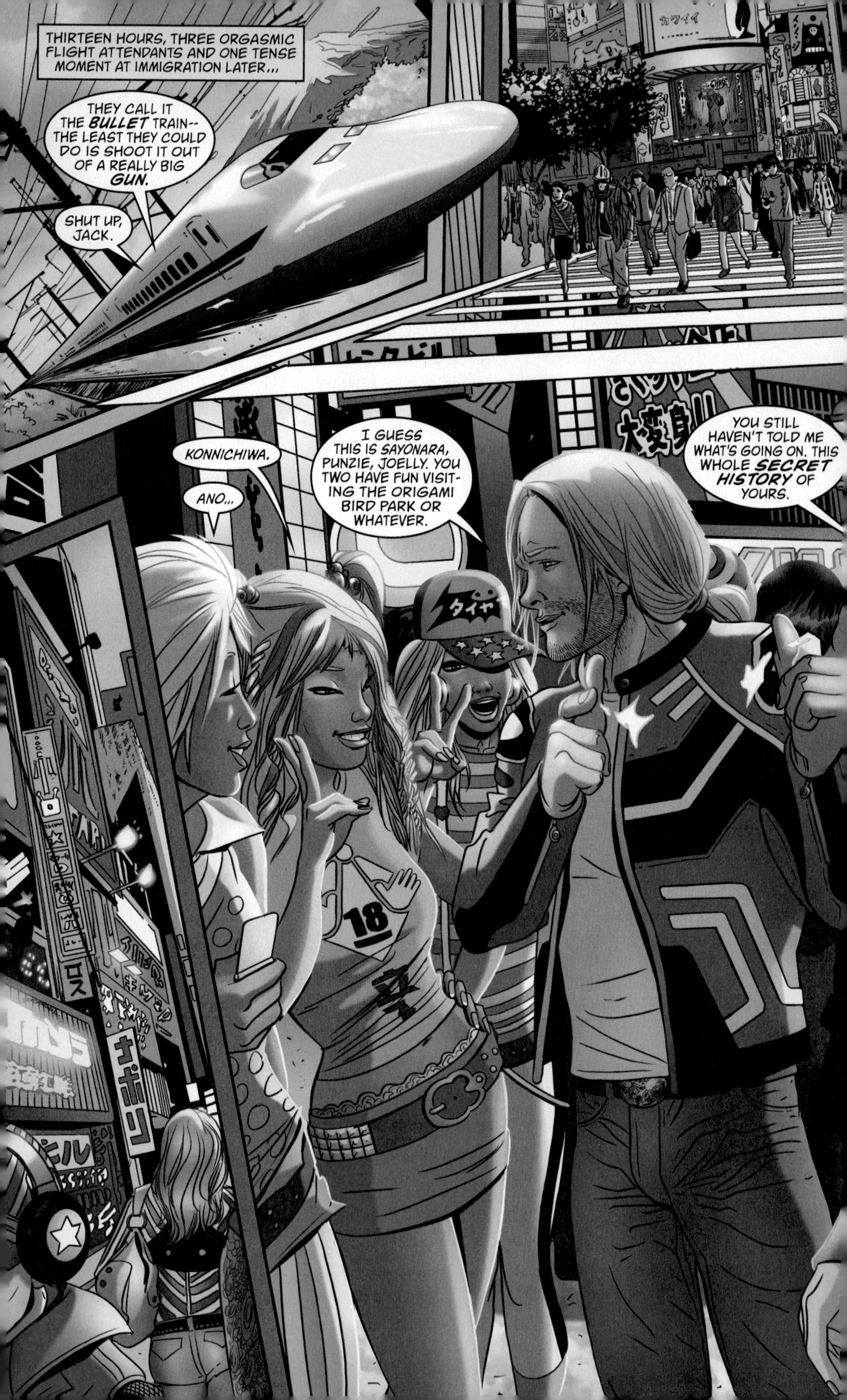

THIRTEEN HOURS, THREE ORGASMIC FLIGHT ATTENDANTS AND ONE TENSE MOMENT AT IMMIGRATION LATER...
THEY CALL IT THE **BULLET** TRAIN-- THE LEAST THEY COULD DO IS SHOOT IT OUT OF A REALLY BIG **GUN**.
SHUT UP, JACK.
KONNICHIWA.
ANO...
I GUESS THIS IS *SAYONARA*, PUNZIE, JOELLY. YOU TWO HAVE FUN VISITING THE ORIGAMI BIRD PARK OR WHATEVER.
YOU STILL HAVEN'T TOLD ME WHAT'S GOING ON. THIS WHOLE ***SECRET HISTORY*** OF YOURS.

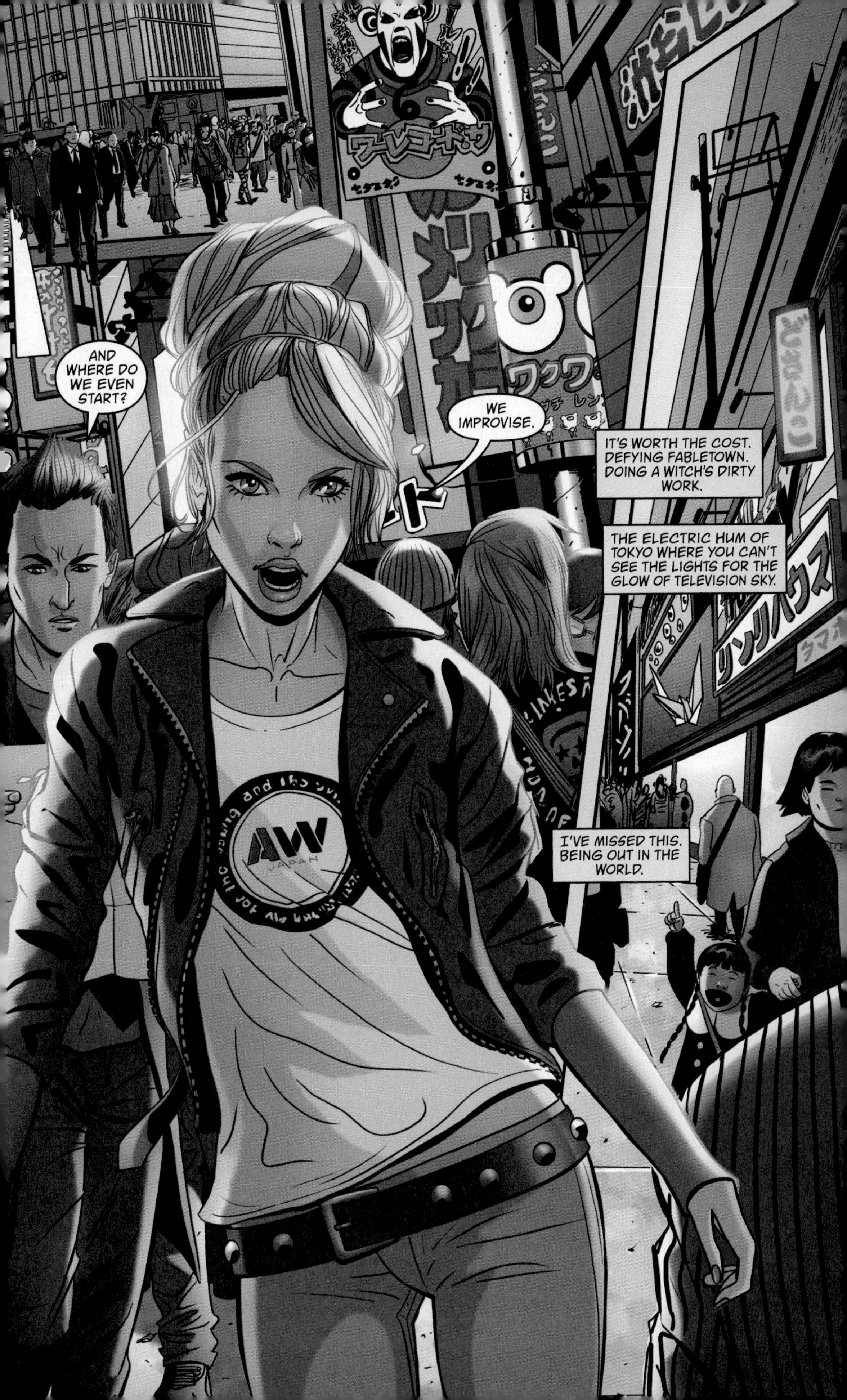
AND WHERE DO WE EVEN START?
WE IMPROVISE.
IT'S WORTH THE COST. DEFYING FABLETOWN. DOING A WITCH'S DIRTY WORK.
THE ELECTRIC HUM OF TOKYO WHERE YOU CAN'T SEE THE LIGHTS FOR THE GLOW OF TELEVISION SKY.
I'VE MISSED THIS. BEING OUT IN THE WORLD.

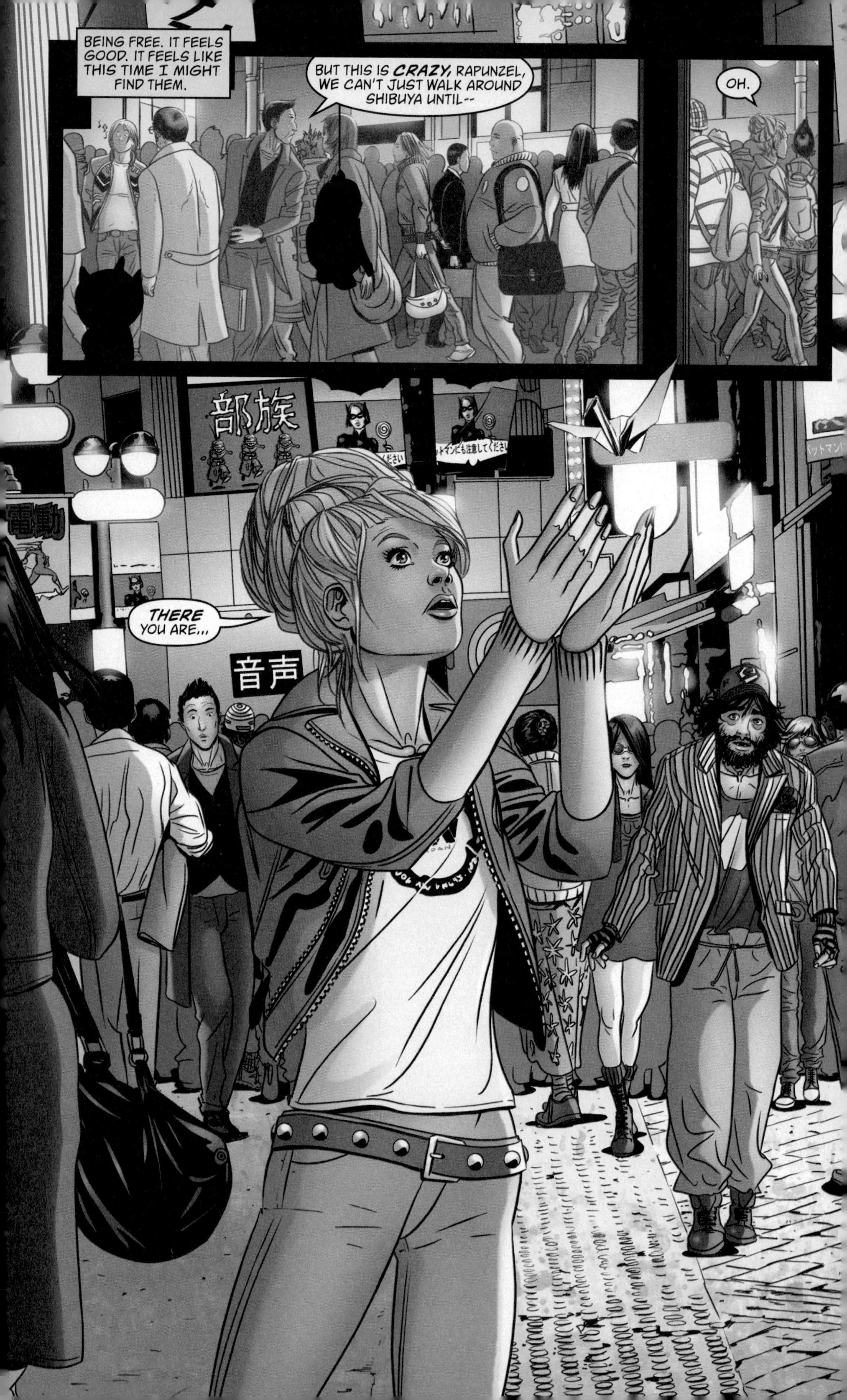
BEING FREE. IT FEELS GOOD. IT FEELS LIKE THIS TIME I MIGHT FIND THEM.
BUT THIS IS CRAZY, RAPUNZEL, WE CAN'T JUST WALK AROUND SHIBUYA UNTIL--
OH.
部族
電動
THERE YOU ARE...
音声

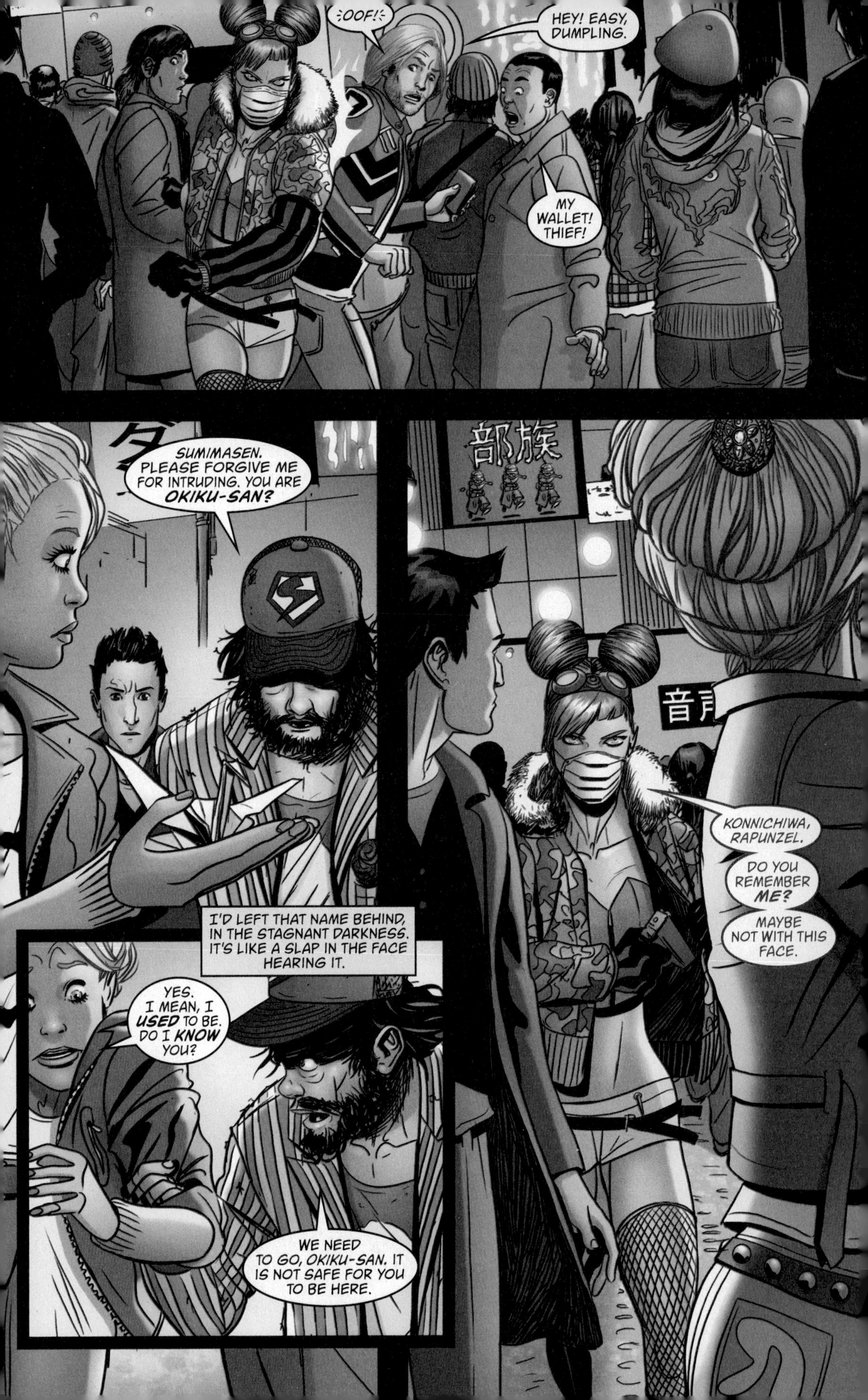

:OOF!:
HEY! EASY, DUMPLING.
MY WALLET! THIEF!
SUMIMASEN. PLEASE FORGIVE ME FOR INTRUDING. YOU ARE OKIKU-SAN?
I'D LEFT THAT NAME BEHIND, IN THE STAGNANT DARKNESS. IT'S LIKE A SLAP IN THE FACE HEARING IT.
YES. I MEAN, I USED TO BE. DO I KNOW YOU?
WE NEED TO GO, OKIKU-SAN. IT IS NOT SAFE FOR YOU TO BE HERE.
部族
音
KONNICHIWA, RAPUNZEL.
DO YOU REMEMBER ME?
MAYBE NOT WITH THIS FACE.

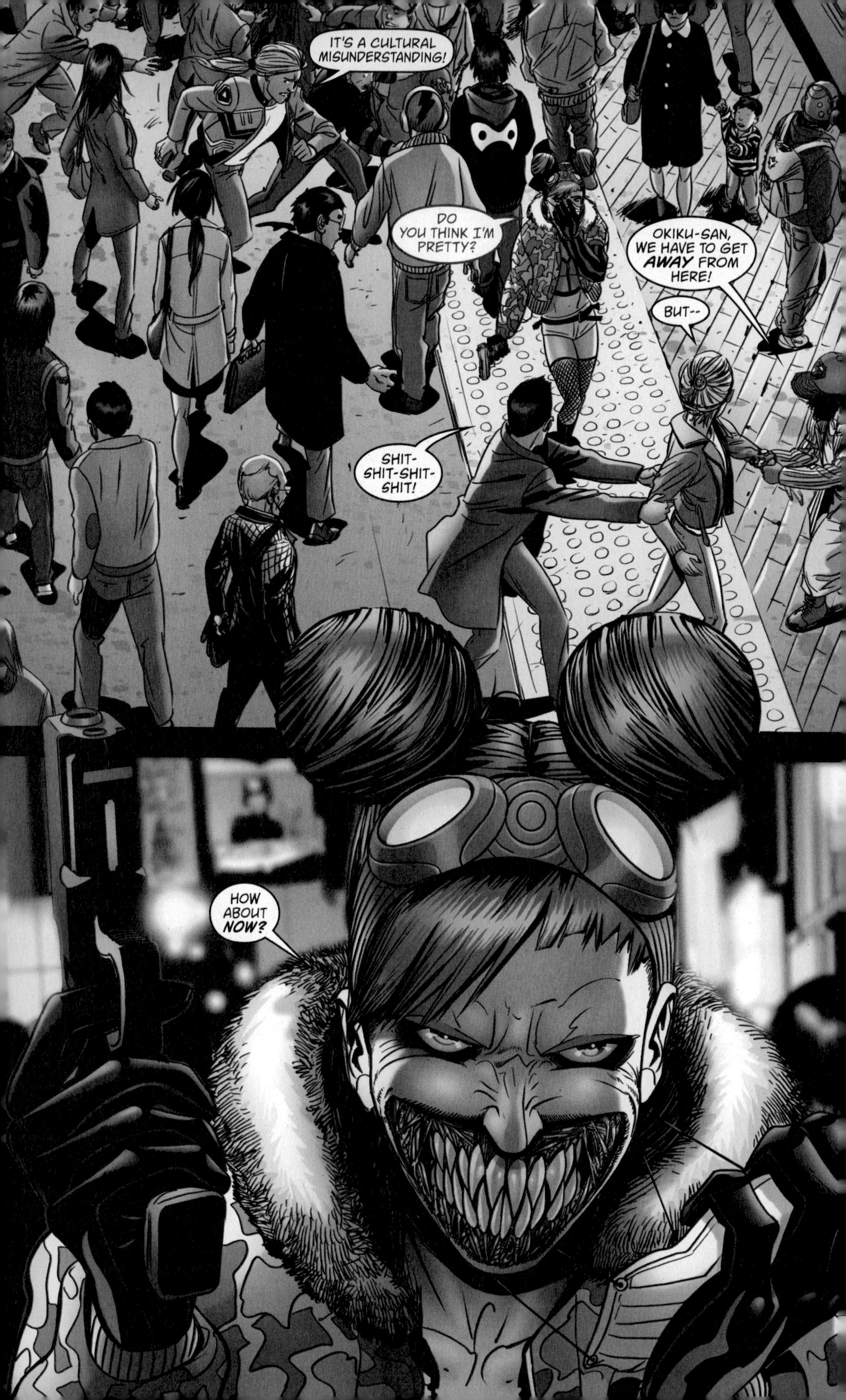
IT'S A CULTURAL MISUNDERSTANDING!
DO YOU THINK I'M PRETTY?
OKIKU-SAN, WE HAVE TO GET **AWAY** FROM HERE!
BUT--
SHIT-SHIT-SHIT-SHIT!
HOW ABOUT **NOW?**

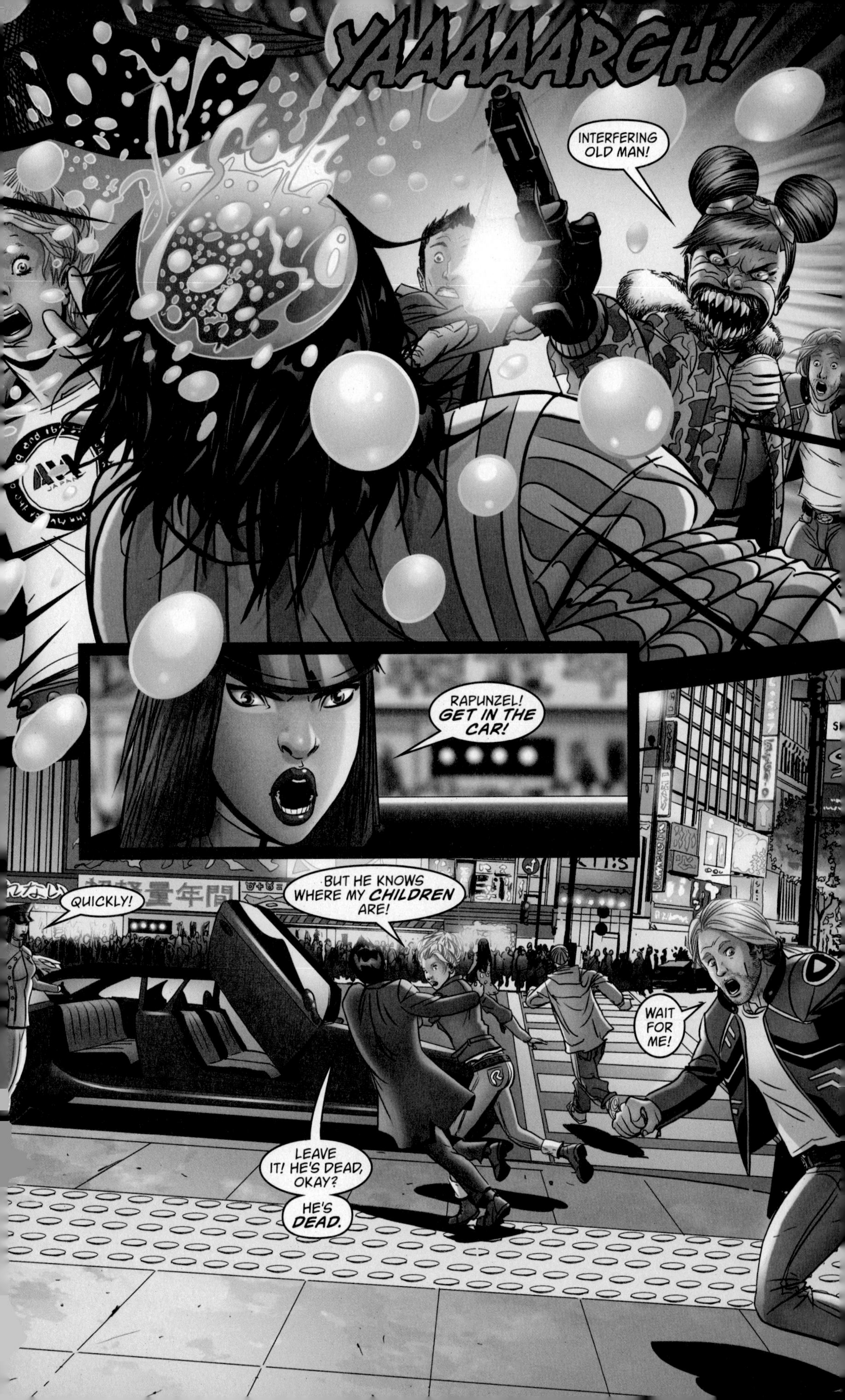
YAAAAARGH!
INTERFERING OLD MAN!
RAPUNZEL! GET IN THE CAR!
QUICKLY!
BUT HE KNOWS WHERE MY CHILDREN ARE!
WAIT FOR ME!
LEAVE IT! HE'S DEAD, OKAY?
HE'S DEAD.

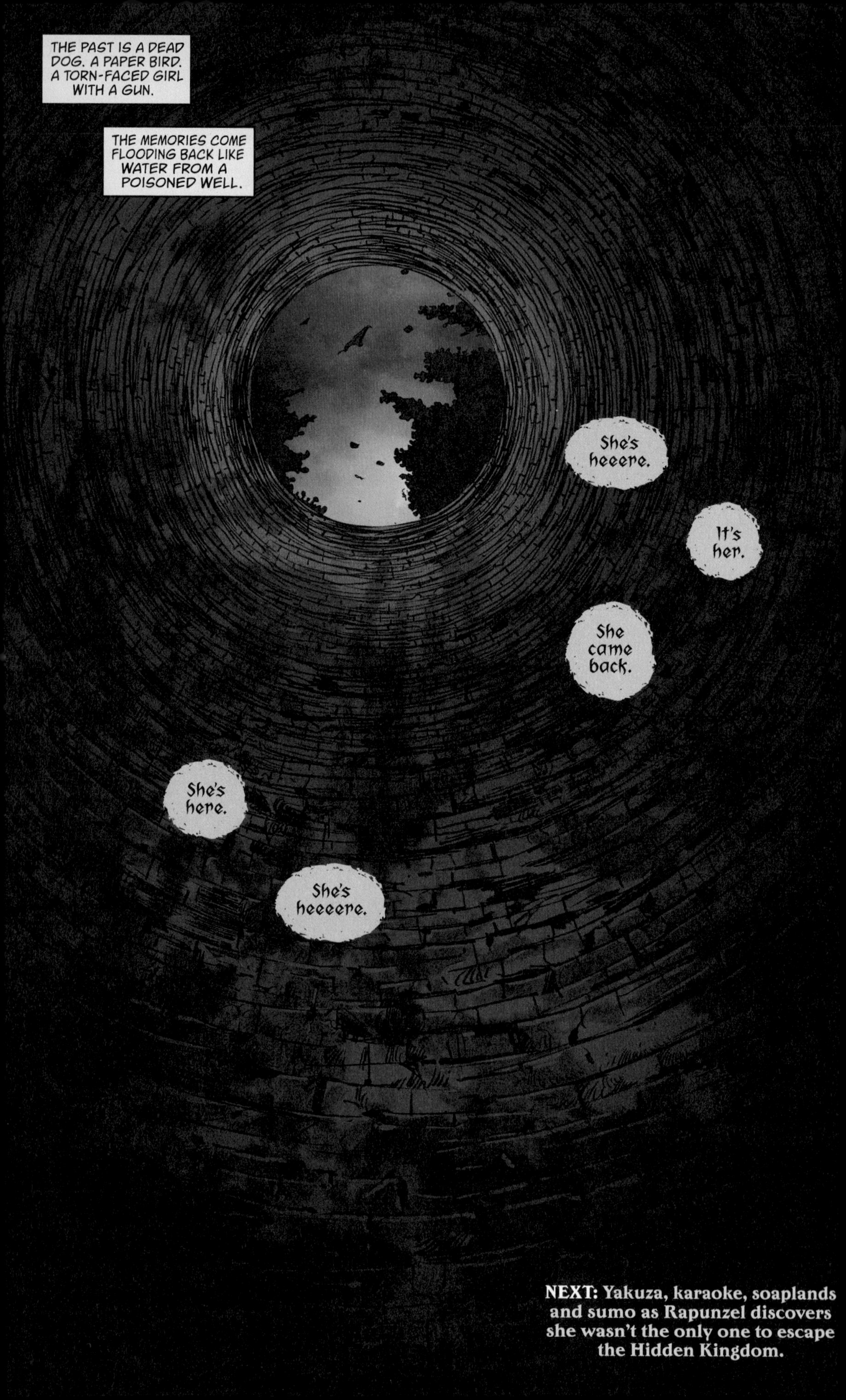
THE PAST IS A DEAD DOG. A PAPER BIRD. A TORN-FACED GIRL WITH A GUN.
THE MEMORIES COME FLOODING BACK LIKE WATER FROM A POISONED WELL.
She's heeere.
It's her.
She came back.
She's here.
She's heeeere.
NEXT: Yakuza, karaoke, soaplands and sumo as Rapunzel discovers she wasn't the only one to escape the Hidden Kingdom.

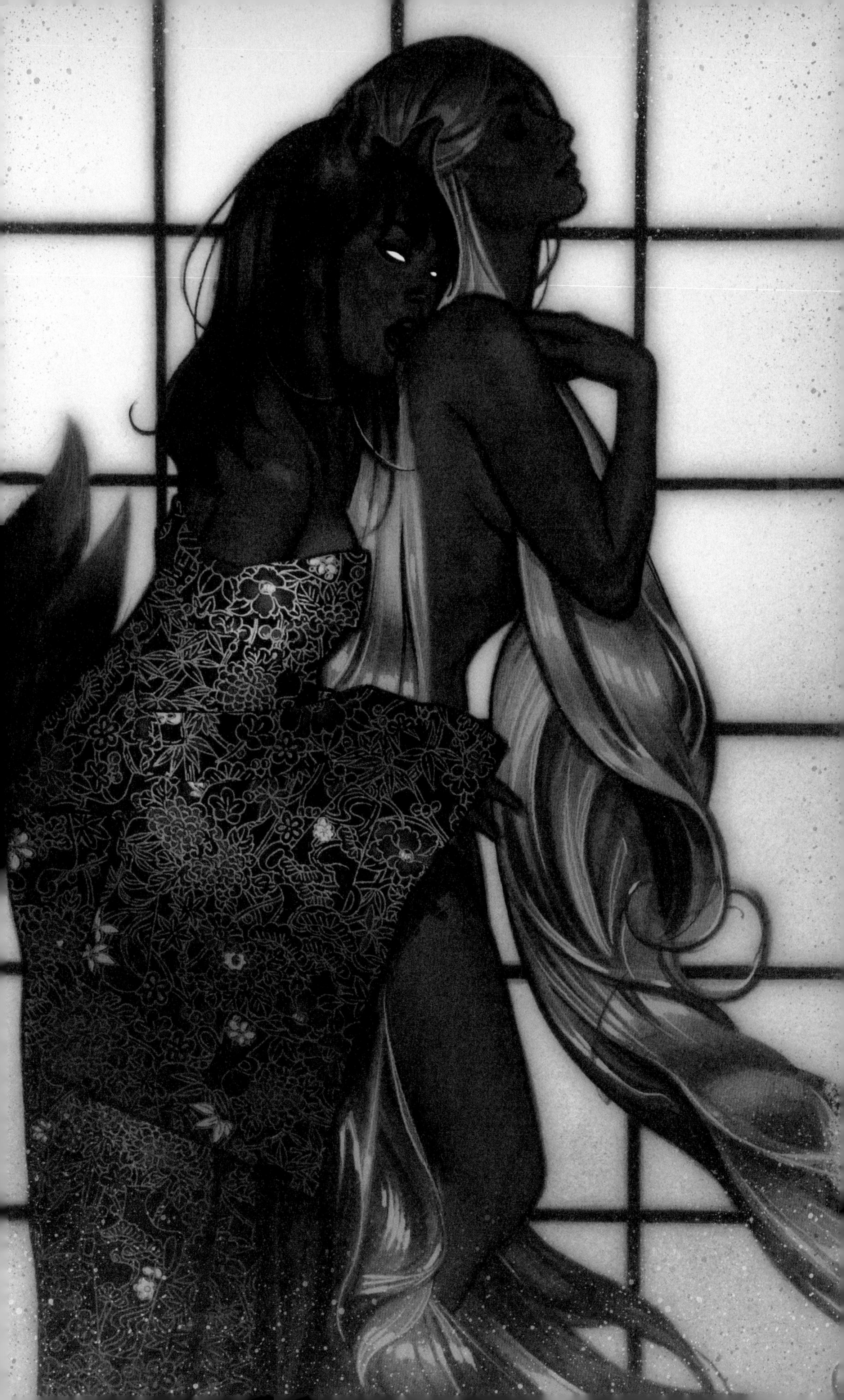

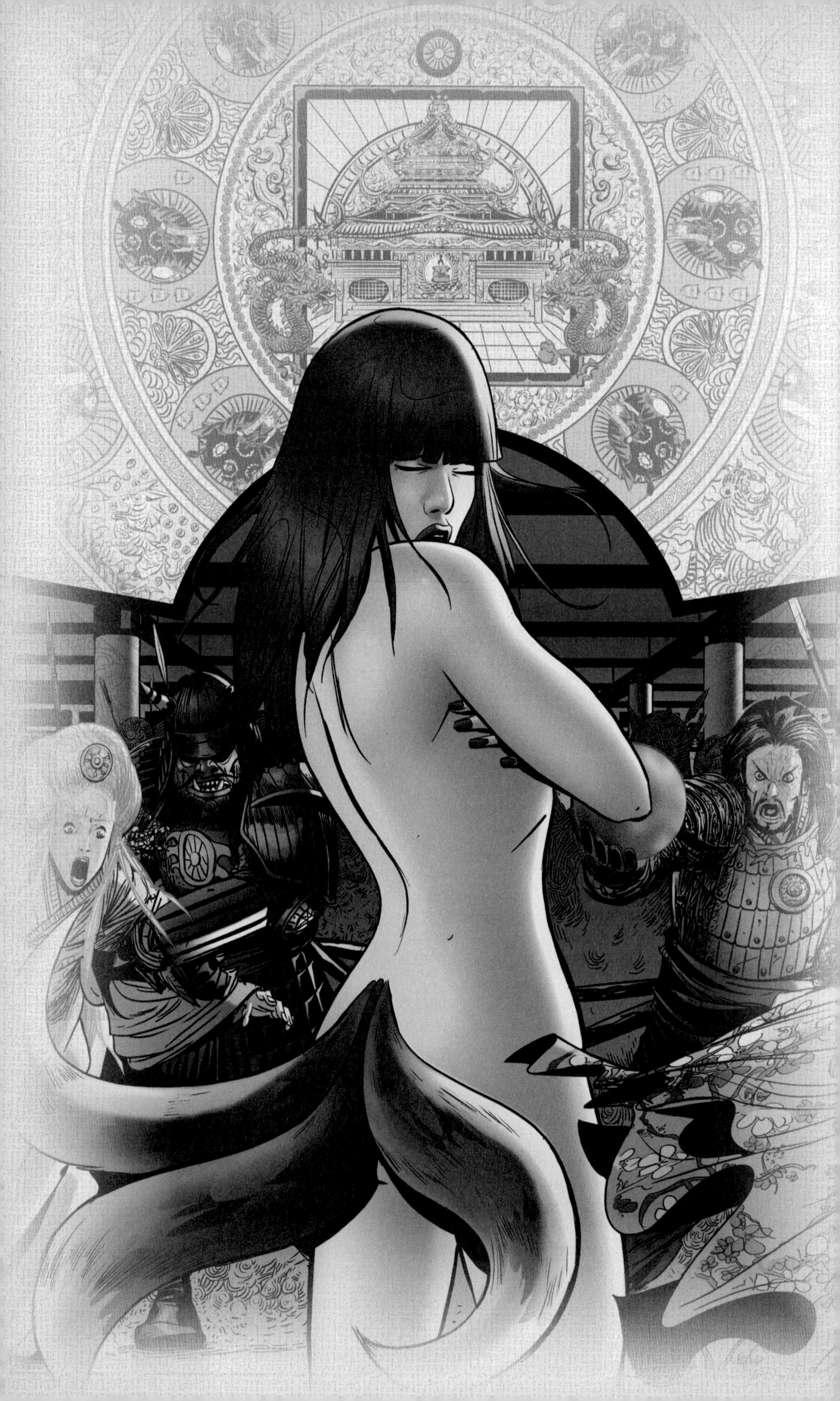

The Hidden Kingdom. 900 years ago.

I CAME HERE TO ERASE MYSELF.

I GAVE UP LOOKING FOR MY DAUGHTERS AND SAILED OFF THE EDGE OF THE WORLD.

I WAS PLANNING TO DIE.

THAT DIDN'T WORK OUT SO WELL.

I WAS WASHED UP ON THE SHORES OF ANOTHER WORLD.

THE *FUNA YUREI*, THE SPIRITS OF THE DROWNED, RESCUED ME.

THEY DRESSED ME UP LIKE A DOLL AND GOT ME THROUGH THE FORTI-FICATIONS OF THE CELESTIAL PALACE.

I WISH THEY'D LET ME JOIN THEM IN DEATH. I WOULD HAVE BEEN A GREAT GHOST.

MAYBE I DIDN'T HAVE THE RIGHT HAT.

THE HIDDEN KINGDOM
CHAPTER TWO: HARD-BOILED WONDERLAND

LAUREN BEUKES
writer

INAKI MIRANDA
artist

EVA DE LA CRUZ
colors

TODD KLEIN
letters

ADAM HUGHES
cover

BILL WILLINGHAM
consultant & **Fables** creator

GREGORY LOCKARD
assistant editor

SHELLY BOND
editor

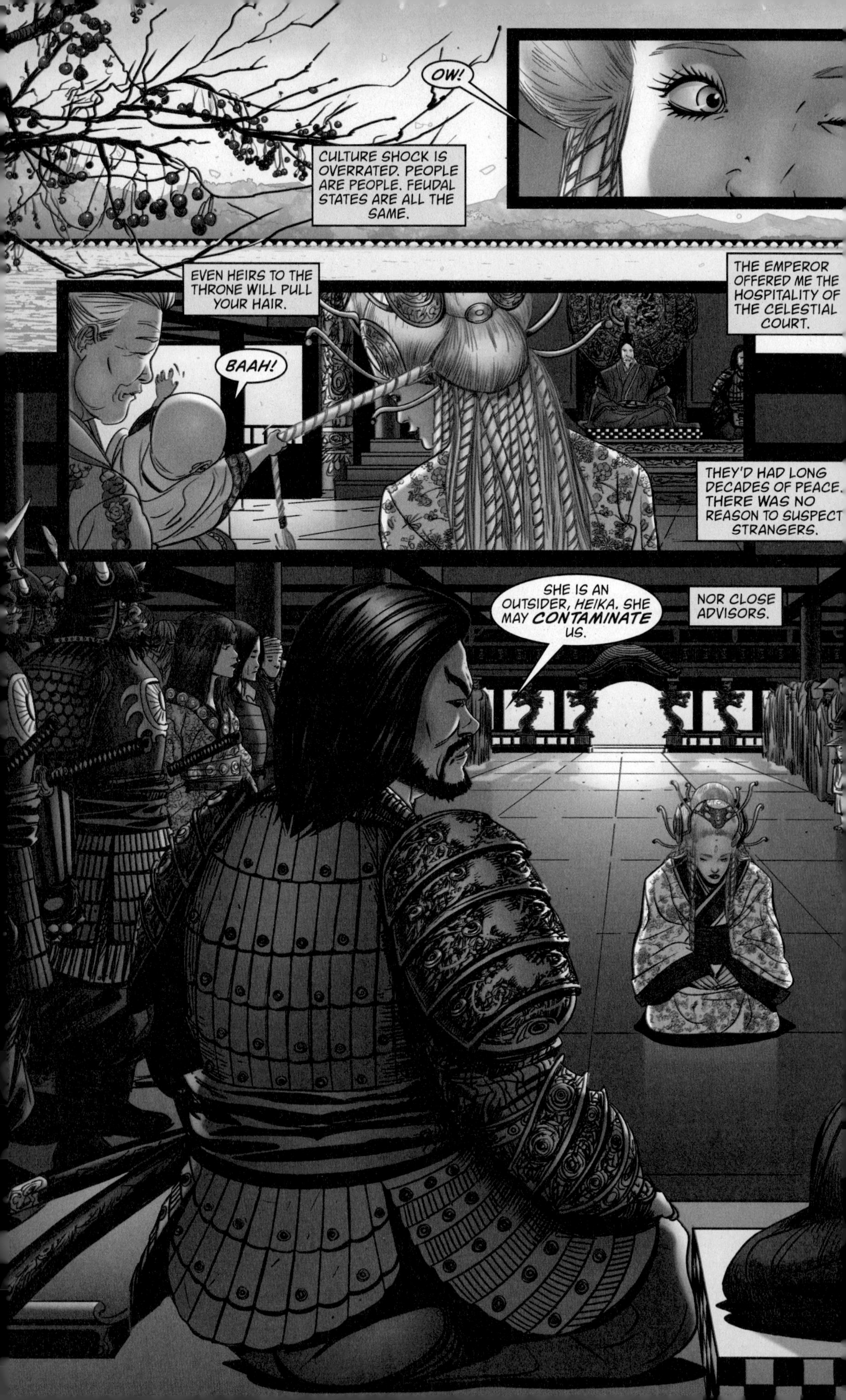
OW!
CULTURE SHOCK IS OVERRATED. PEOPLE ARE PEOPLE. FEUDAL STATES ARE ALL THE SAME.
EVEN HEIRS TO THE THRONE WILL PULL YOUR HAIR.
BAAH!
THE EMPEROR OFFERED ME THE HOSPITALITY OF THE CELESTIAL COURT.
THEY'D HAD LONG DECADES OF PEACE. THERE WAS NO REASON TO SUSPECT STRANGERS.
NOR CLOSE ADVISORS.
SHE IS AN OUTSIDER, HEIKA. SHE MAY CONTAMINATE US.

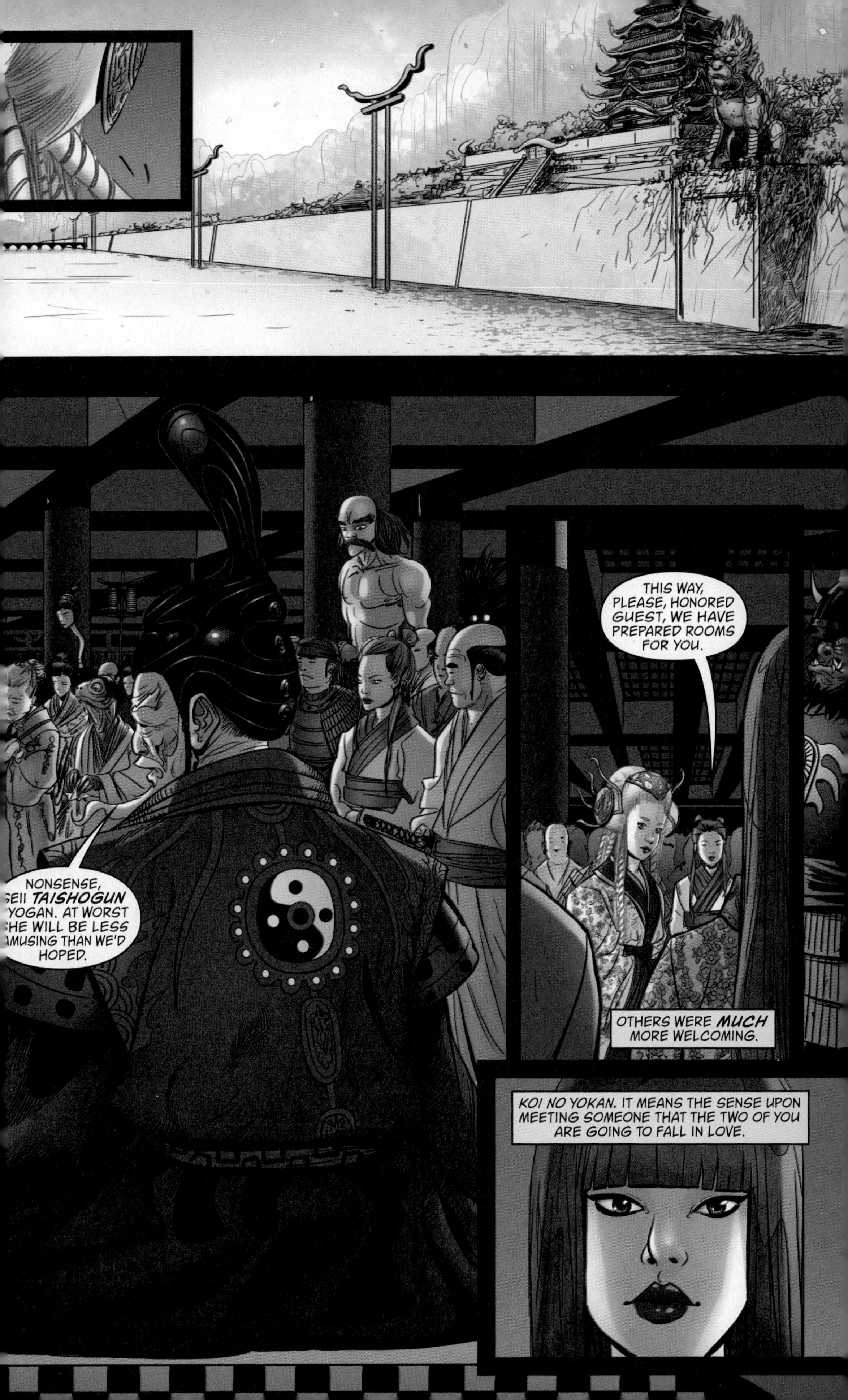

NONSENSE, SEII TAISHOGUN YOGAN. AT WORST SHE WILL BE LESS AMUSING THAN WE'D HOPED.
THIS WAY, PLEASE, HONORED GUEST, WE HAVE PREPARED ROOMS FOR YOU.
OTHERS WERE MUCH MORE WELCOMING.
KOI NO YOKAN. IT MEANS THE SENSE UPON MEETING SOMEONE THAT THE TWO OF YOU ARE GOING TO FALL IN LOVE.

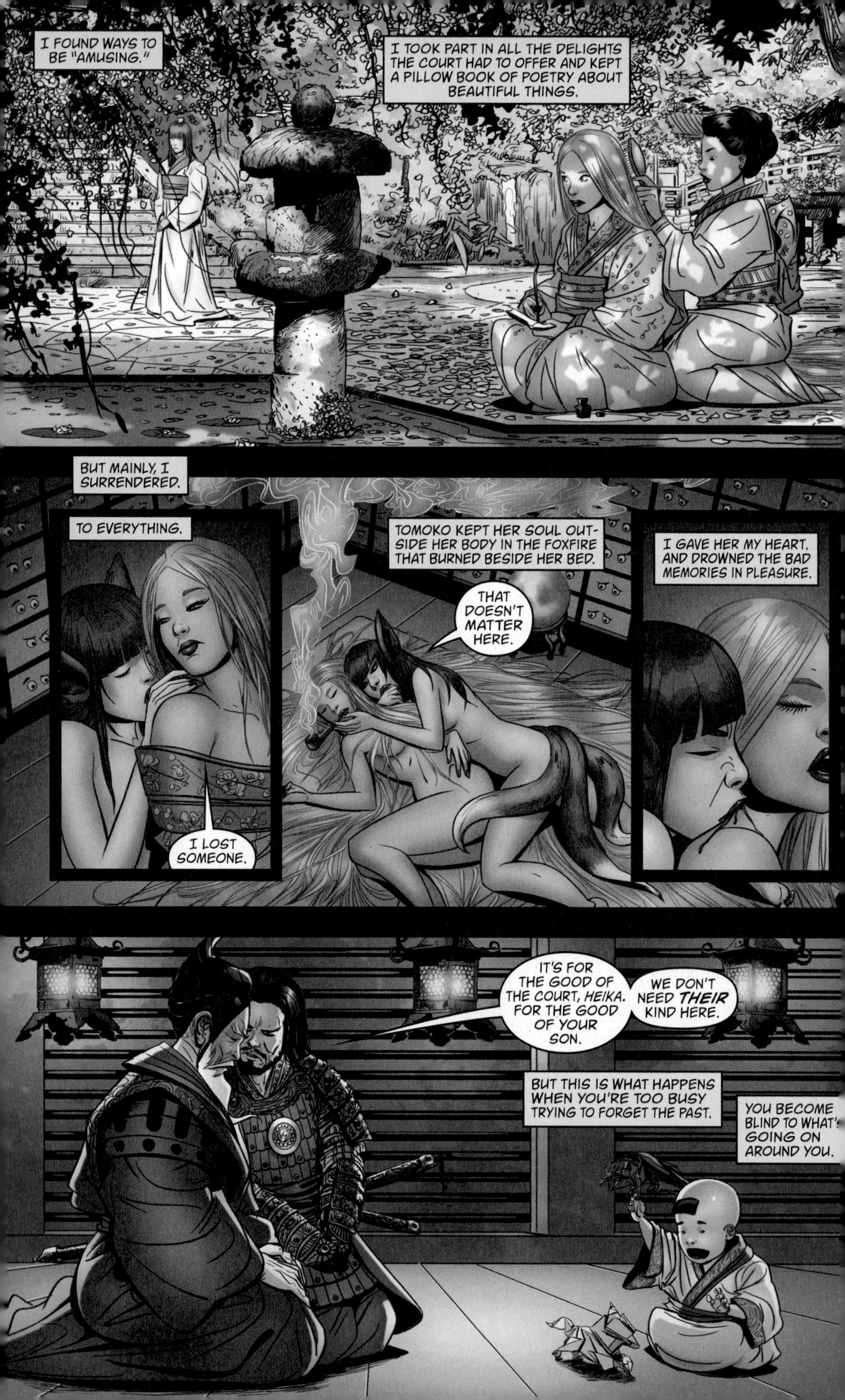
I FOUND WAYS TO BE "AMUSING."
I TOOK PART IN ALL THE DELIGHTS THE COURT HAD TO OFFER AND KEPT A PILLOW BOOK OF POETRY ABOUT BEAUTIFUL THINGS.
BUT MAINLY, I SURRENDERED.
TO EVERYTHING.
I LOST SOMEONE.
TOMOKO KEPT HER SOUL OUTSIDE HER BODY IN THE FOXFIRE THAT BURNED BESIDE HER BED.
THAT DOESN'T MATTER HERE.
I GAVE HER MY HEART. AND DROWNED THE BAD MEMORIES IN PLEASURE.
IT'S FOR THE GOOD OF THE COURT, *HEIKA*. FOR THE GOOD OF YOUR SON.
WE DON'T NEED ***THEIR*** KIND HERE.
BUT THIS IS WHAT HAPPENS WHEN YOU'RE TOO BUSY TRYING TO FORGET THE PAST.
YOU BECOME BLIND TO WHAT'S GOING ON AROUND YOU.

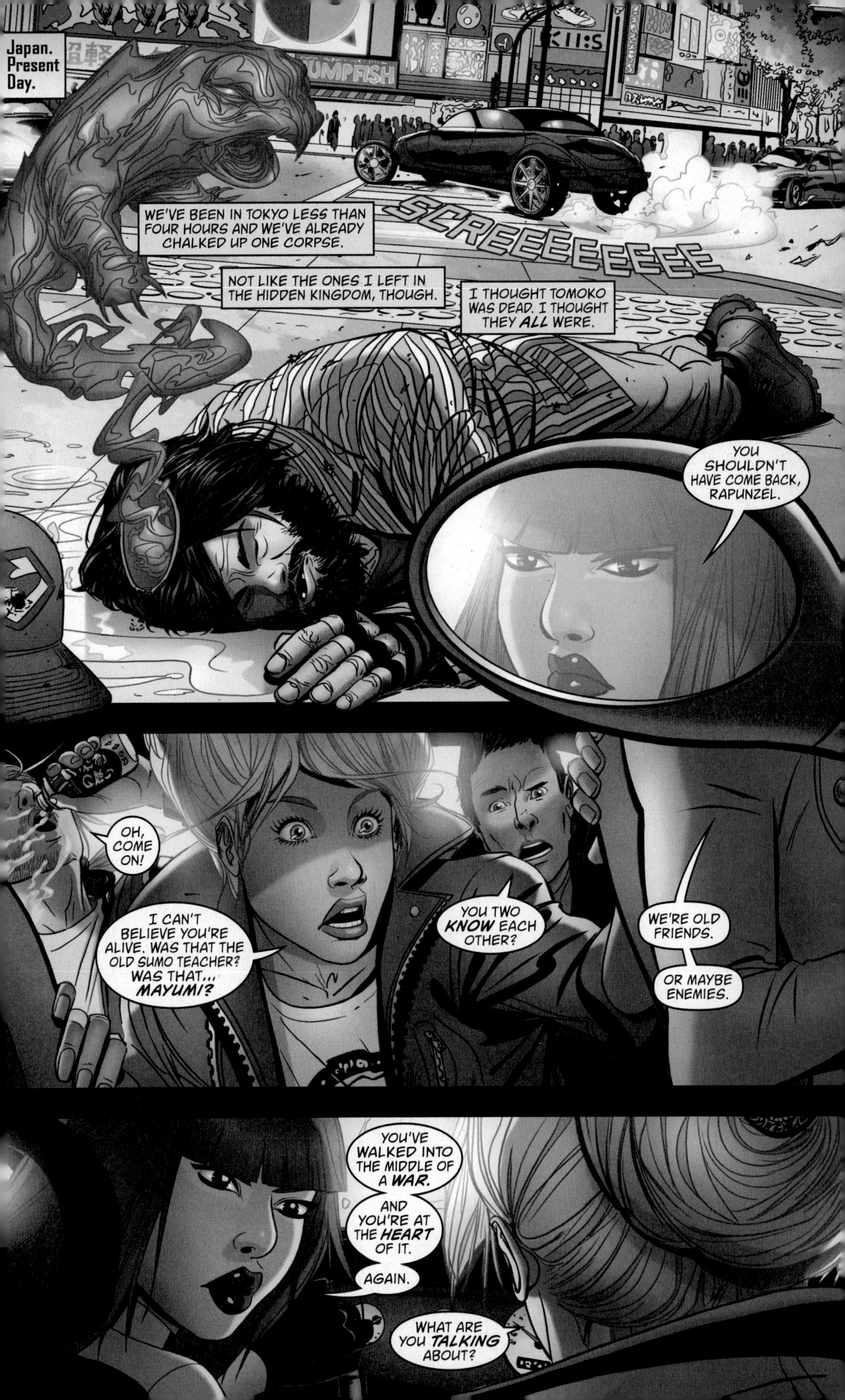
Japan. Present Day.
WE'VE BEEN IN TOKYO LESS THAN FOUR HOURS AND WE'VE ALREADY CHALKED UP ONE CORPSE.
SCREEEEEEEEE
NOT LIKE THE ONES I LEFT IN THE HIDDEN KINGDOM, THOUGH.
I THOUGHT TOMOKO WAS DEAD. I THOUGHT THEY ALL WERE.
YOU SHOULDN'T HAVE COME BACK, RAPUNZEL.
OH, COME ON!
I CAN'T BELIEVE YOU'RE ALIVE. WAS THAT THE OLD SUMO TEACHER? WAS THAT... MAYUMI?
YOU TWO KNOW EACH OTHER?
WE'RE OLD FRIENDS.
OR MAYBE ENEMIES.
YOU'VE WALKED INTO THE MIDDLE OF A WAR.
AND YOU'RE AT THE HEART OF IT.
AGAIN.
WHAT ARE YOU TALKING ABOUT?

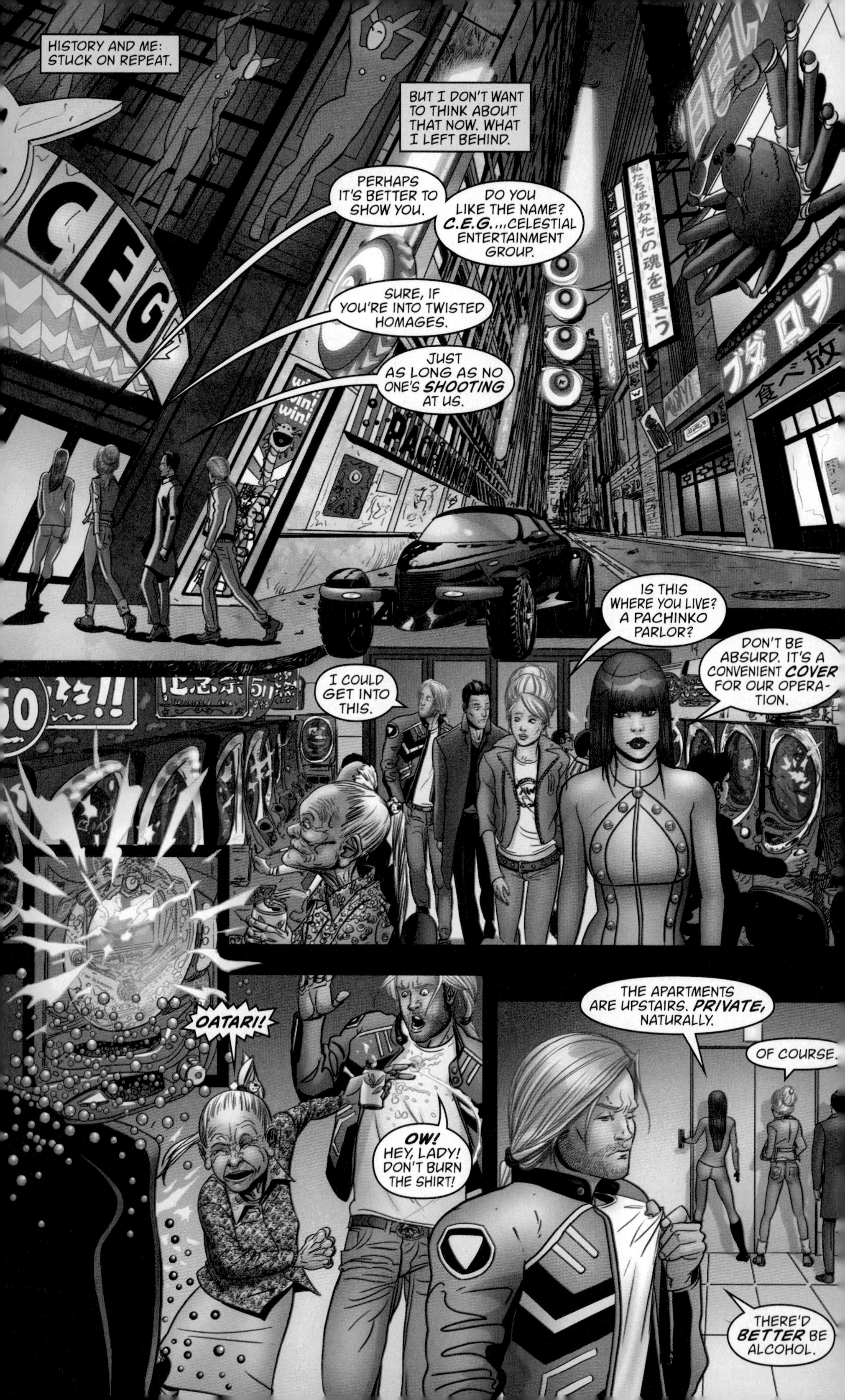
HISTORY AND ME: STUCK ON REPEAT.
BUT I DON'T WANT TO THINK ABOUT THAT NOW. WHAT I LEFT BEHIND.
PERHAPS IT'S BETTER TO SHOW YOU.
DO YOU LIKE THE NAME? C.E.G....CELESTIAL ENTERTAINMENT GROUP.
SURE, IF YOU'RE INTO TWISTED HOMAGES.
JUST AS LONG AS NO ONE'S SHOOTING AT US.
CEG
PACHINKO
私たちはあなたの魂を買う
IS THIS WHERE YOU LIVE? A PACHINKO PARLOR?
DON'T BE ABSURD. IT'S A CONVENIENT COVER FOR OUR OPERATION.
I COULD GET INTO THIS.
OATARI!
OW! HEY, LADY! DON'T BURN THE SHIRT!
THE APARTMENTS ARE UPSTAIRS. PRIVATE, NATURALLY.
OF COURSE.
THERE'D BETTER BE ALCOHOL.

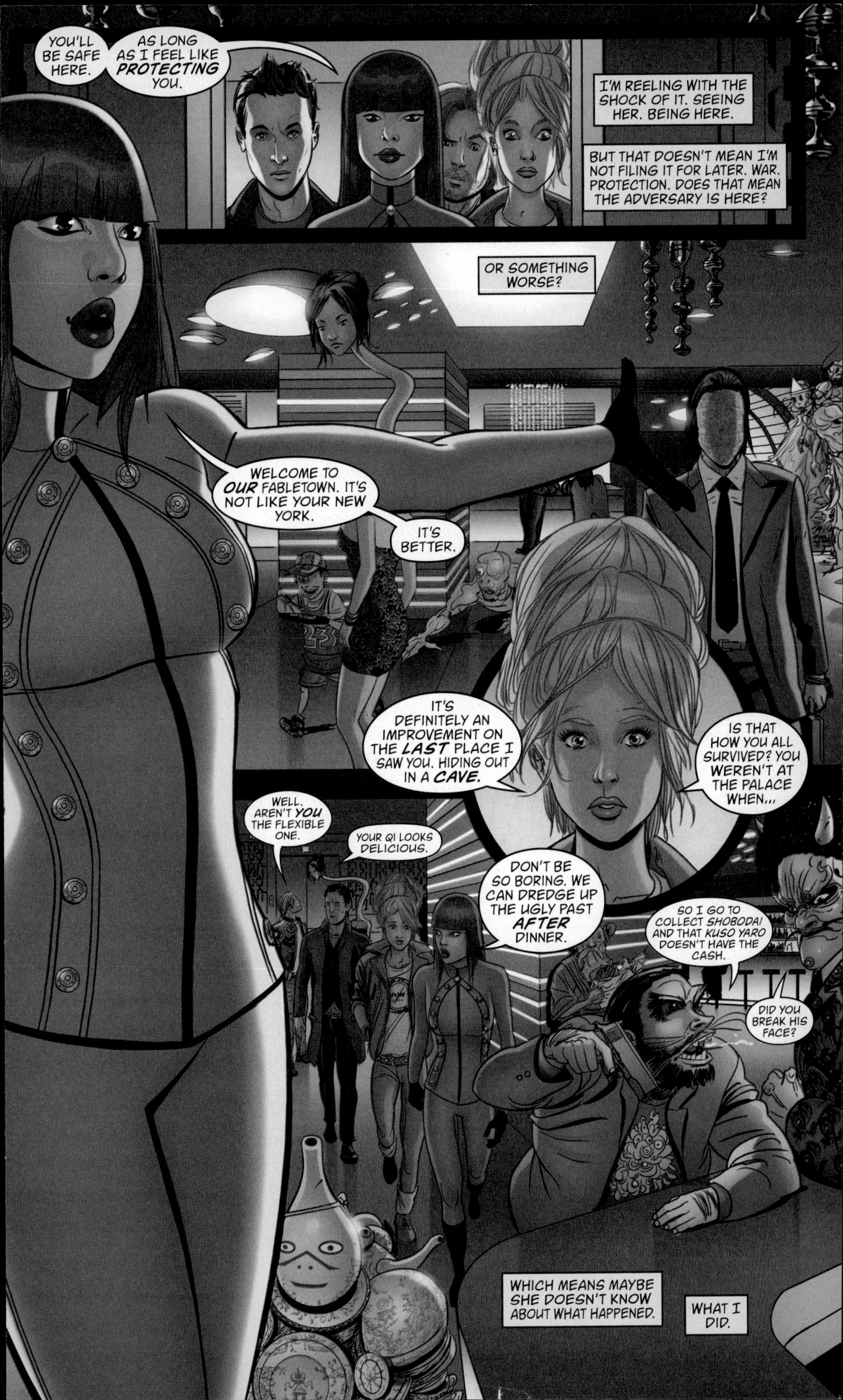
YOU'LL BE SAFE HERE.
AS LONG AS I FEEL LIKE ***PROTECTING*** YOU.
I'M REELING WITH THE SHOCK OF IT. SEEING HER. BEING HERE.
BUT THAT DOESN'T MEAN I'M NOT FILING IT FOR LATER. WAR. PROTECTION. DOES THAT MEAN THE ADVERSARY IS HERE?
OR SOMETHING WORSE?
WELCOME TO ***OUR*** FABLETOWN. IT'S NOT LIKE YOUR NEW YORK.
IT'S BETTER.
IT'S DEFINITELY AN IMPROVEMENT ON THE ***LAST*** PLACE I SAW YOU. HIDING OUT IN A ***CAVE.***
IS THAT HOW YOU ALL SURVIVED? YOU WEREN'T AT THE PALACE WHEN...
WELL, AREN'T ***YOU*** THE FLEXIBLE ONE.
YOUR QI LOOKS DELICIOUS.
DON'T BE SO BORING. WE CAN DREDGE UP THE UGLY PAST ***AFTER*** DINNER.
SO I GO TO COLLECT *SHOBODAI* AND THAT *KUSO YARO* DOESN'T HAVE THE CASH.
DID YOU BREAK HIS FACE?
WHICH MEANS MAYBE SHE DOESN'T KNOW ABOUT WHAT HAPPENED.
WHAT I DID.

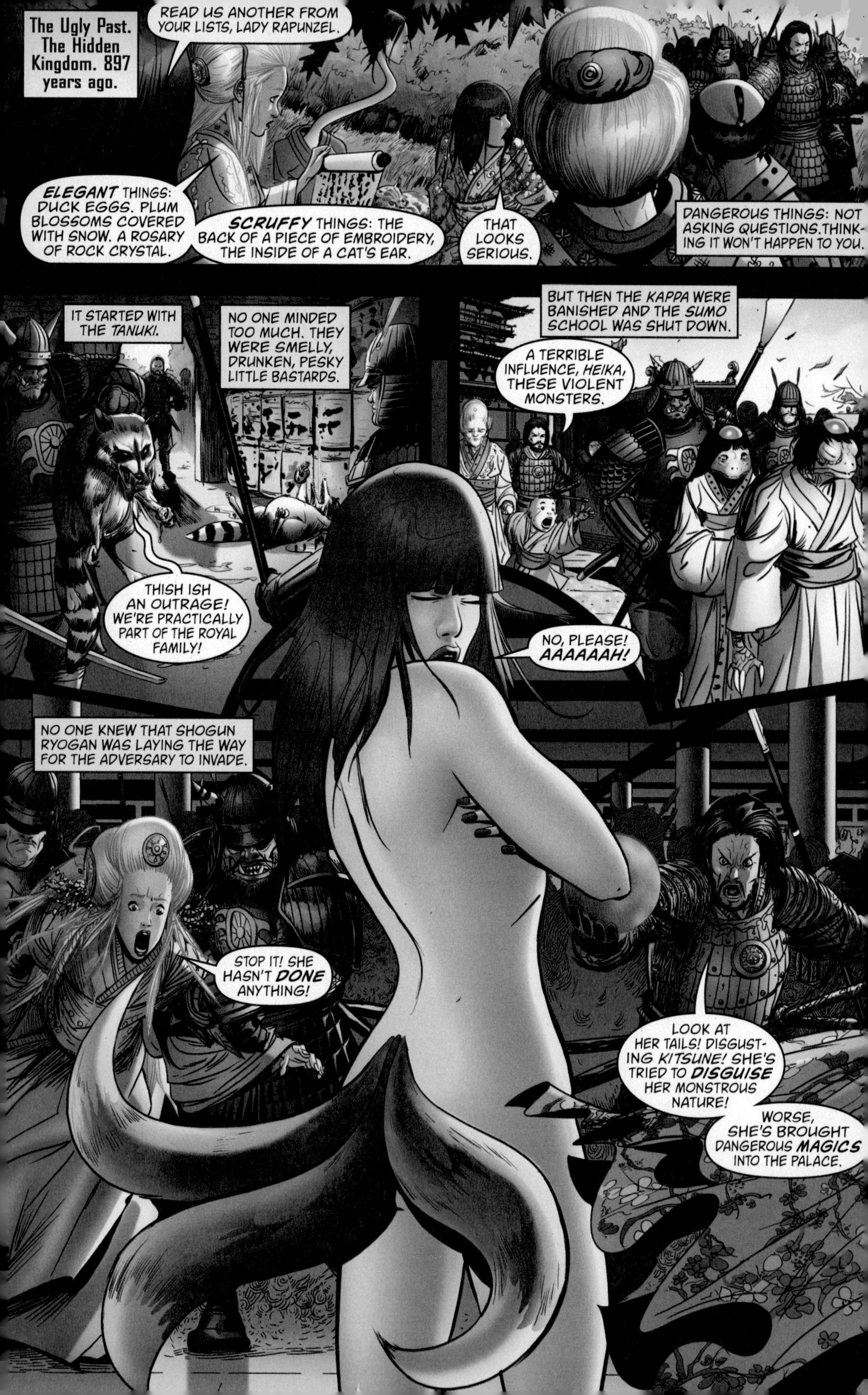
The Ugly Past. The Hidden Kingdom. 897 years ago.
READ US ANOTHER FROM YOUR LISTS, LADY RAPUNZEL.
ELEGANT THINGS: DUCK EGGS. PLUM BLOSSOMS COVERED WITH SNOW. A ROSARY OF ROCK CRYSTAL.
SCRUFFY THINGS: THE BACK OF A PIECE OF EMBROIDERY, THE INSIDE OF A CAT'S EAR.
THAT LOOKS SERIOUS.
DANGEROUS THINGS: NOT ASKING QUESTIONS. THINKING IT WON'T HAPPEN TO YOU.
IT STARTED WITH THE TANUKI.
NO ONE MINDED TOO MUCH. THEY WERE SMELLY, DRUNKEN, PESKY LITTLE BASTARDS.
THISH ISH AN OUTRAGE! WE'RE PRACTICALLY PART OF THE ROYAL FAMILY!
BUT THEN THE KAPPA WERE BANISHED AND THE SUMO SCHOOL WAS SHUT DOWN.
A TERRIBLE INFLUENCE, HEIKA, THESE VIOLENT MONSTERS.
NO, PLEASE! AAAAAAH!
NO ONE KNEW THAT SHOGUN RYOGAN WAS LAYING THE WAY FOR THE ADVERSARY TO INVADE.
STOP IT! SHE HASN'T DONE ANYTHING!
LOOK AT HER TAILS! DISGUSTING KITSUNE! SHE'S TRIED TO DISGUISE HER MONSTROUS NATURE!
WORSE, SHE'S BROUGHT DANGEROUS MAGICS INTO THE PALACE.

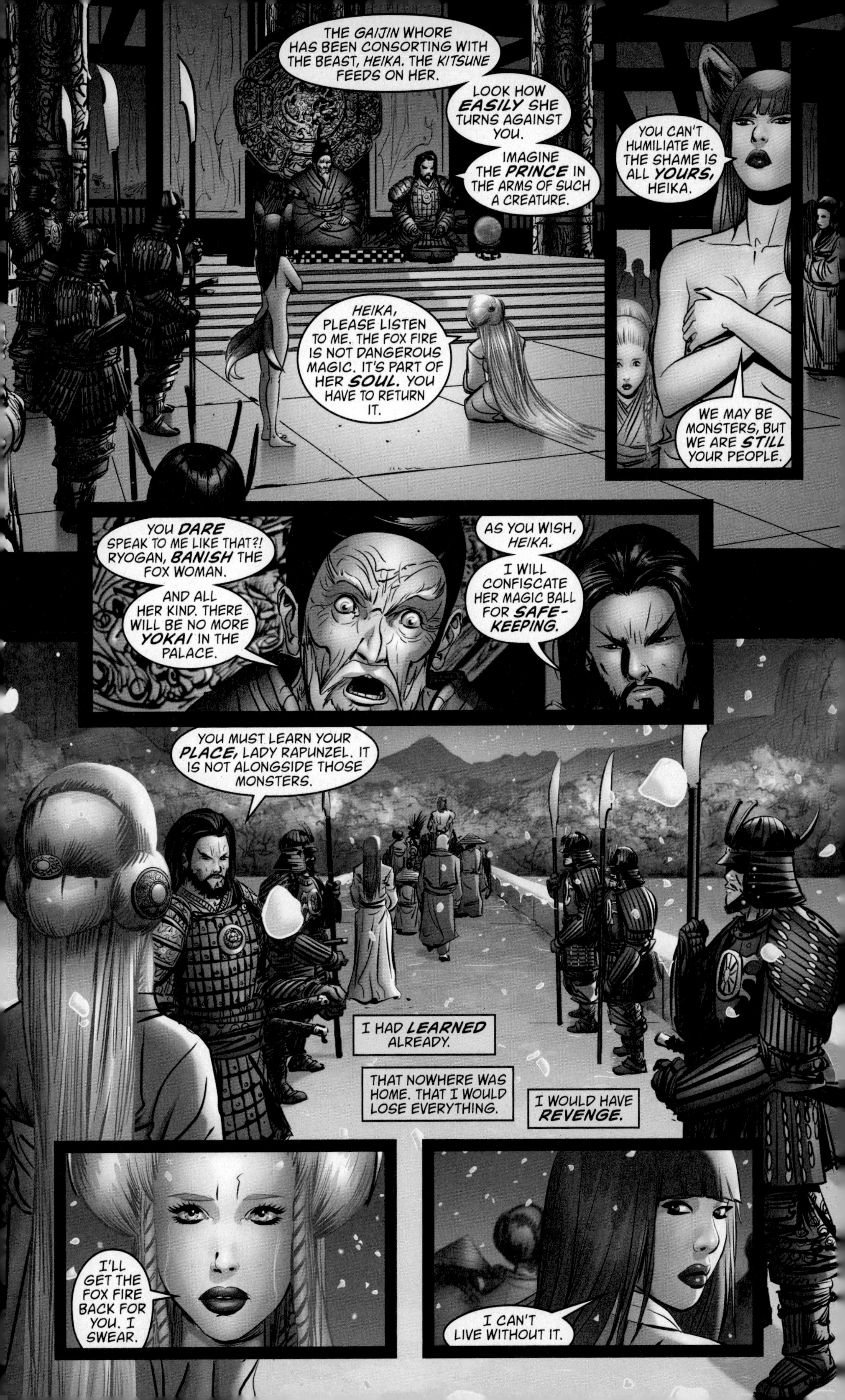

THE GAIJIN WHORE HAS BEEN CONSORTING WITH THE BEAST, HEIKA. THE KITSUNE FEEDS ON HER.
LOOK HOW EASILY SHE TURNS AGAINST YOU.
IMAGINE THE PRINCE IN THE ARMS OF SUCH A CREATURE.
HEIKA, PLEASE LISTEN TO ME. THE FOX FIRE IS NOT DANGEROUS MAGIC. IT'S PART OF HER SOUL. YOU HAVE TO RETURN IT.
YOU CAN'T HUMILIATE ME. THE SHAME IS ALL YOURS, HEIKA.
WE MAY BE MONSTERS, BUT WE ARE STILL YOUR PEOPLE.
YOU DARE SPEAK TO ME LIKE THAT?! RYOGAN, BANISH THE FOX WOMAN.
AND ALL HER KIND. THERE WILL BE NO MORE YOKAI IN THE PALACE.
AS YOU WISH, HEIKA.
I WILL CONFISCATE HER MAGIC BALL FOR SAFE-KEEPING.
YOU MUST LEARN YOUR PLACE, LADY RAPUNZEL. IT IS NOT ALONGSIDE THOSE MONSTERS.
I HAD LEARNED ALREADY.
THAT NOWHERE WAS HOME. THAT I WOULD LOSE EVERYTHING.
I WOULD HAVE REVENGE.
I'LL GET THE FOX FIRE BACK FOR YOU. I SWEAR.
I CAN'T LIVE WITHOUT IT.

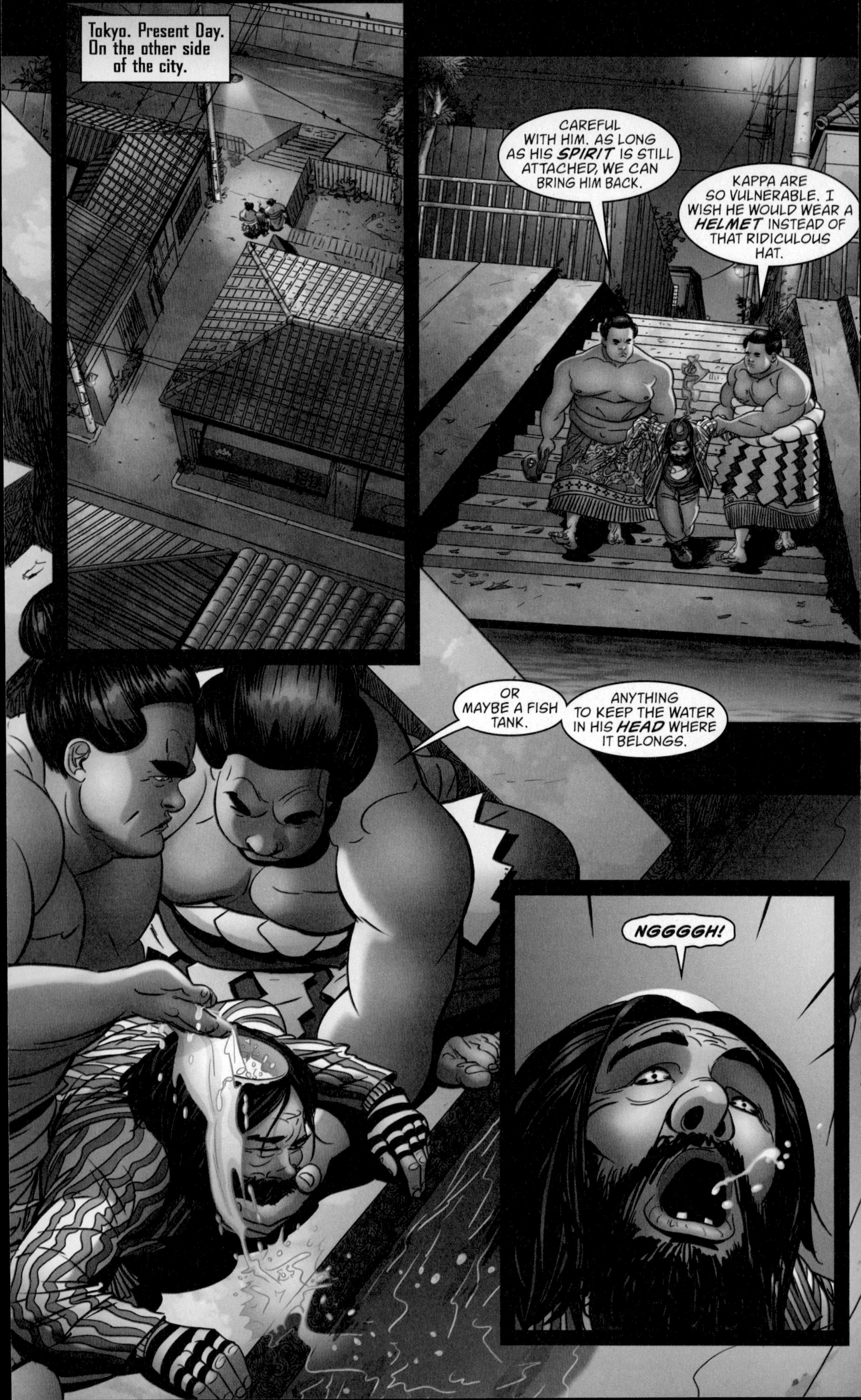
Tokyo. Present Day. On the other side of the city.
CAREFUL WITH HIM. AS LONG AS HIS SPIRIT IS STILL ATTACHED, WE CAN BRING HIM BACK.
KAPPA ARE SO VULNERABLE. I WISH HE WOULD WEAR A HELMET INSTEAD OF THAT RIDICULOUS HAT.
OR MAYBE A FISH TANK.
ANYTHING TO KEEP THE WATER IN HIS HEAD WHERE IT BELONGS.
NGGGGH!

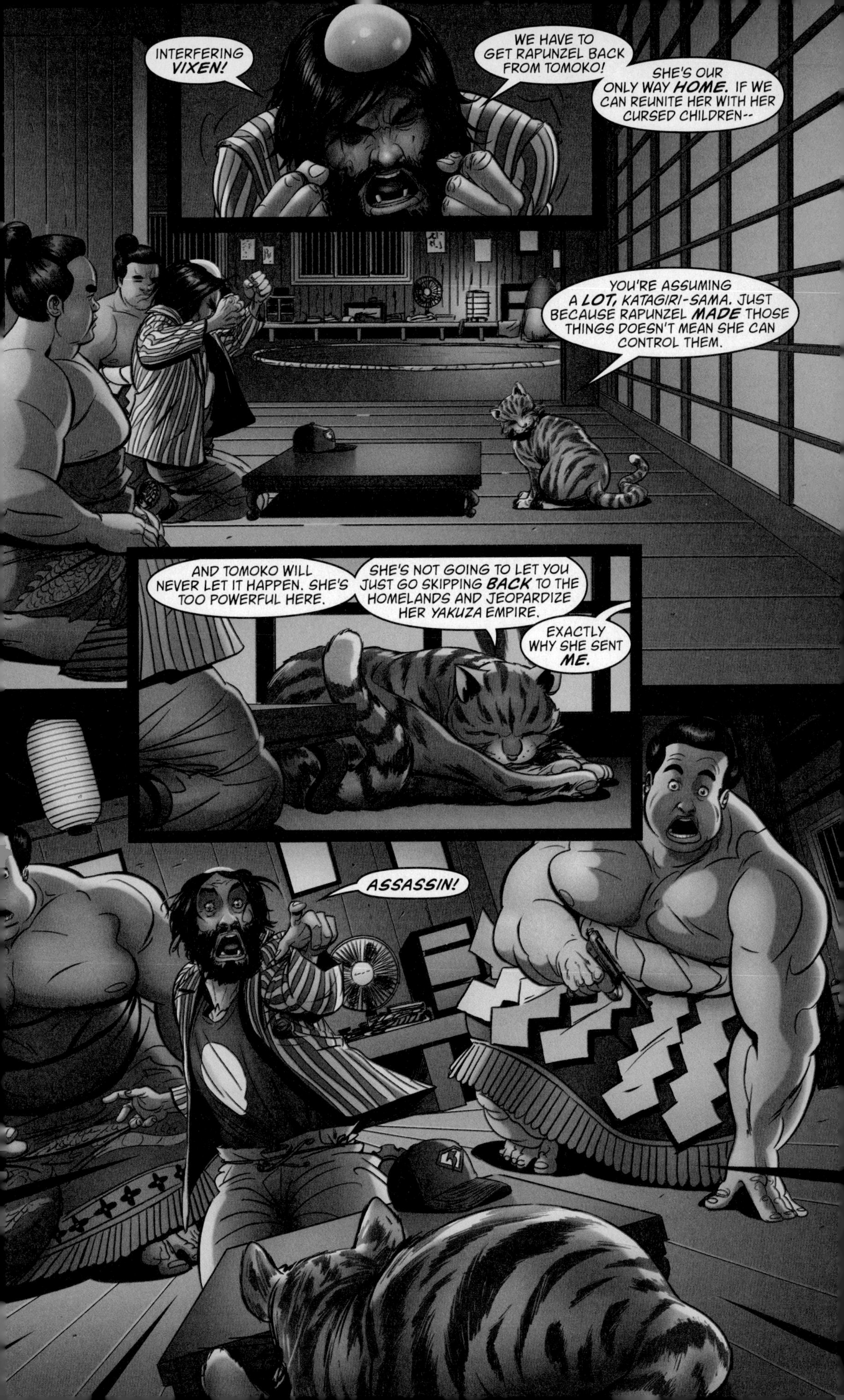

INTERFERING VIXEN!
WE HAVE TO GET RAPUNZEL BACK FROM TOMOKO!
SHE'S OUR ONLY WAY HOME. IF WE CAN REUNITE HER WITH HER CURSED CHILDREN--
YOU'RE ASSUMING A LOT, KATAGIRI-SAMA. JUST BECAUSE RAPUNZEL MADE THOSE THINGS DOESN'T MEAN SHE CAN CONTROL THEM.
AND TOMOKO WILL NEVER LET IT HAPPEN. SHE'S TOO POWERFUL HERE.
SHE'S NOT GOING TO LET YOU JUST GO SKIPPING BACK TO THE HOMELANDS AND JEOPARDIZE HER YAKUZA EMPIRE.
EXACTLY WHY SHE SENT ME.
ASSASSIN!

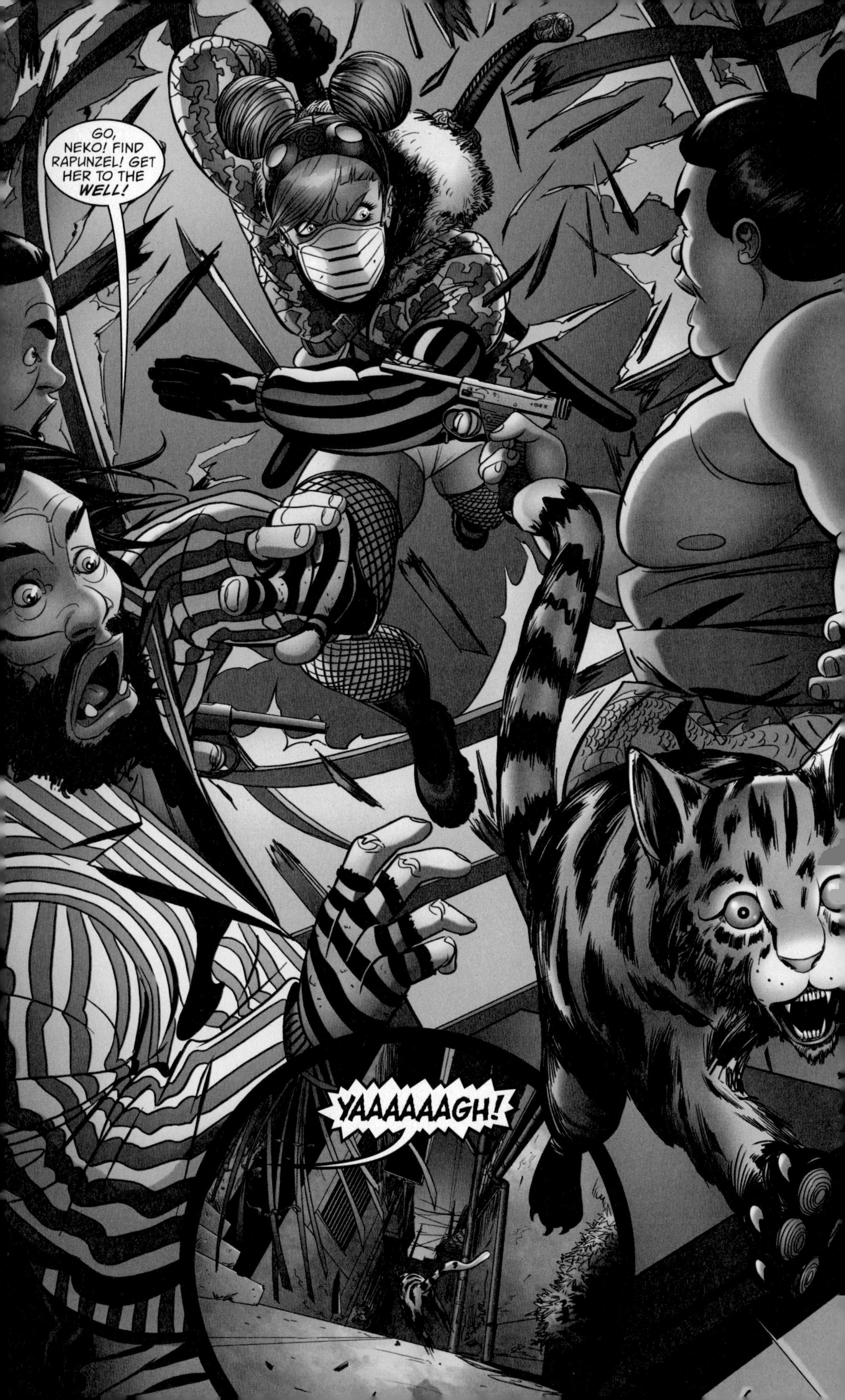
GO, NEKO! FIND RAPUNZEL! GET HER TO THE WELL!
YAAAAAAGH!

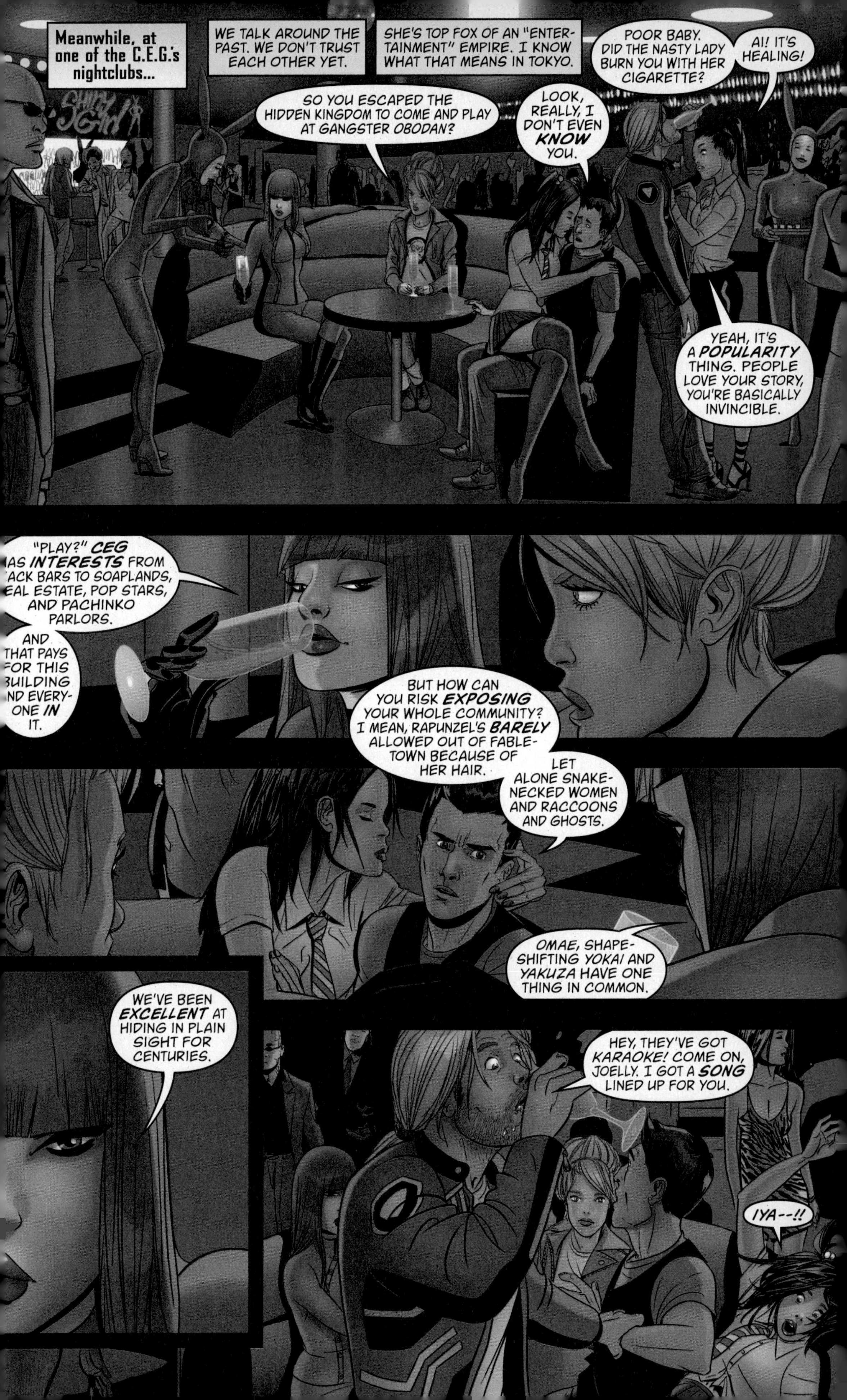
Meanwhile, at one of the C.E.G.'s nightclubs...
WE TALK AROUND THE PAST. WE DON'T TRUST EACH OTHER YET.
SHE'S TOP FOX OF AN "ENTERTAINMENT" EMPIRE. I KNOW WHAT THAT MEANS IN TOKYO.
SO YOU ESCAPED THE HIDDEN KINGDOM TO COME AND PLAY AT GANGSTER OBODAN?
LOOK, REALLY, I DON'T EVEN KNOW YOU.
POOR BABY. DID THE NASTY LADY BURN YOU WITH HER CIGARETTE?
AI! IT'S HEALING!
YEAH, IT'S A POPULARITY THING. PEOPLE LOVE YOUR STORY, YOU'RE BASICALLY INVINCIBLE.
"PLAY?" CEG
AS INTERESTS FROM
ACK BARS TO SOAPLANDS,
EAL ESTATE, POP STARS,
AND PACHINKO PARLORS.
AND THAT PAYS FOR THIS BUILDING
ND EVERY-ONE IN IT.
BUT HOW CAN YOU RISK EXPOSING YOUR WHOLE COMMUNITY? I MEAN, RAPUNZEL'S BARELY ALLOWED OUT OF FABLE-TOWN BECAUSE OF HER HAIR.
LET ALONE SNAKE-NECKED WOMEN AND RACCOONS AND GHOSTS.
OMAE, SHAPE-SHIFTING YOKAI AND YAKUZA HAVE ONE THING IN COMMON.
WE'VE BEEN EXCELLENT AT HIDING IN PLAIN SIGHT FOR CENTURIES.
HEY, THEY'VE GOT KARAOKE! COME ON, JOELLY. I GOT A SONG LINED UP FOR YOU.
IYA--!!

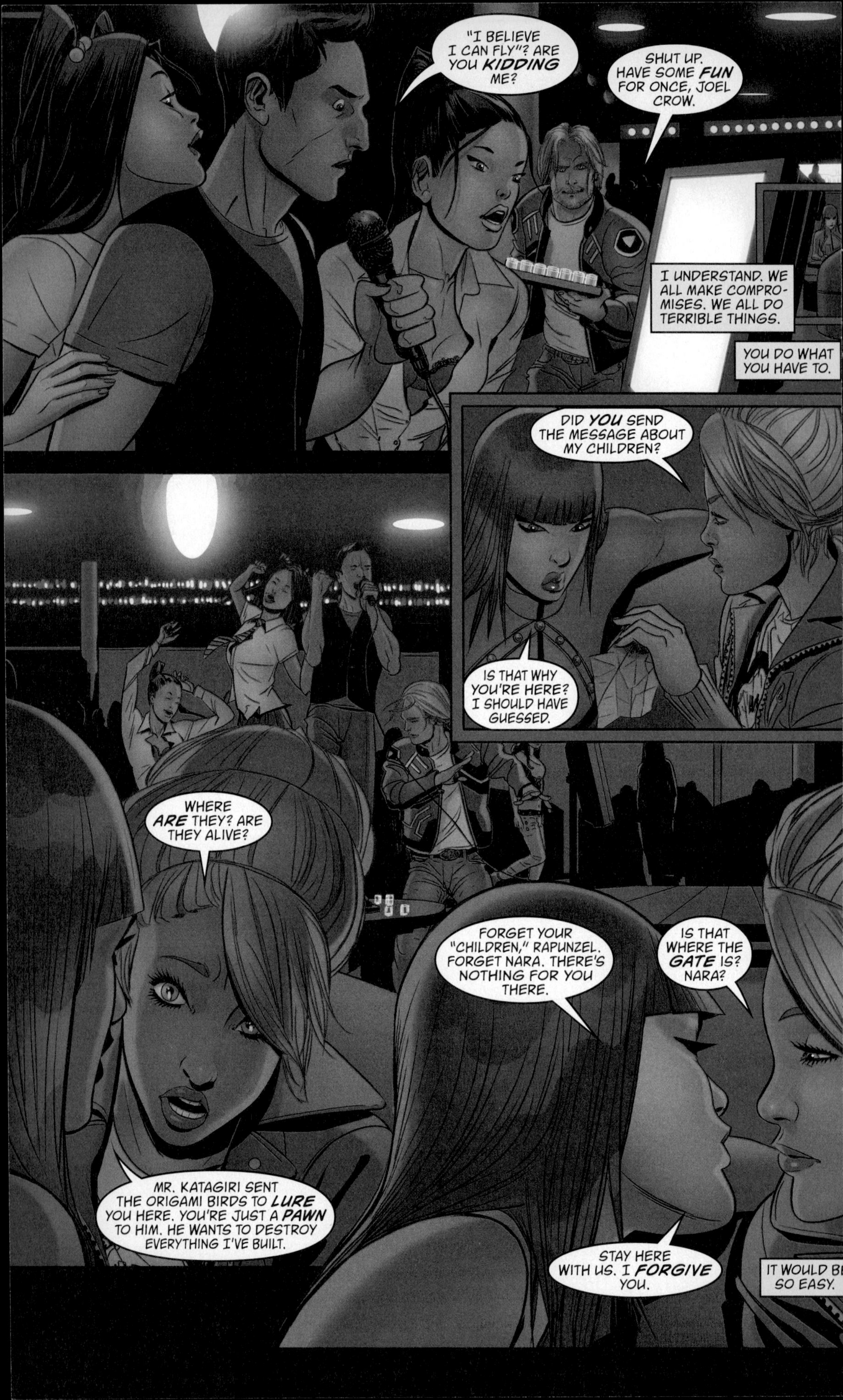
"I BELIEVE I CAN FLY"? ARE YOU KIDDING ME?
SHUT UP. HAVE SOME FUN FOR ONCE, JOEL CROW.
I UNDERSTAND. WE ALL MAKE COMPROMISES. WE ALL DO TERRIBLE THINGS.
YOU DO WHAT YOU HAVE TO.
DID YOU SEND THE MESSAGE ABOUT MY CHILDREN?
IS THAT WHY YOU'RE HERE? I SHOULD HAVE GUESSED.
WHERE ARE THEY? ARE THEY ALIVE?
MR. KATAGIRI SENT THE ORIGAMI BIRDS TO LURE YOU HERE. YOU'RE JUST A PAWN TO HIM. HE WANTS TO DESTROY EVERYTHING I'VE BUILT.
FORGET YOUR "CHILDREN," RAPUNZEL. FORGET NARA. THERE'S NOTHING FOR YOU THERE.
IS THAT WHERE THE GATE IS? NARA?
STAY HERE WITH US. I FORGIVE YOU.
IT WOULD BE SO EASY.

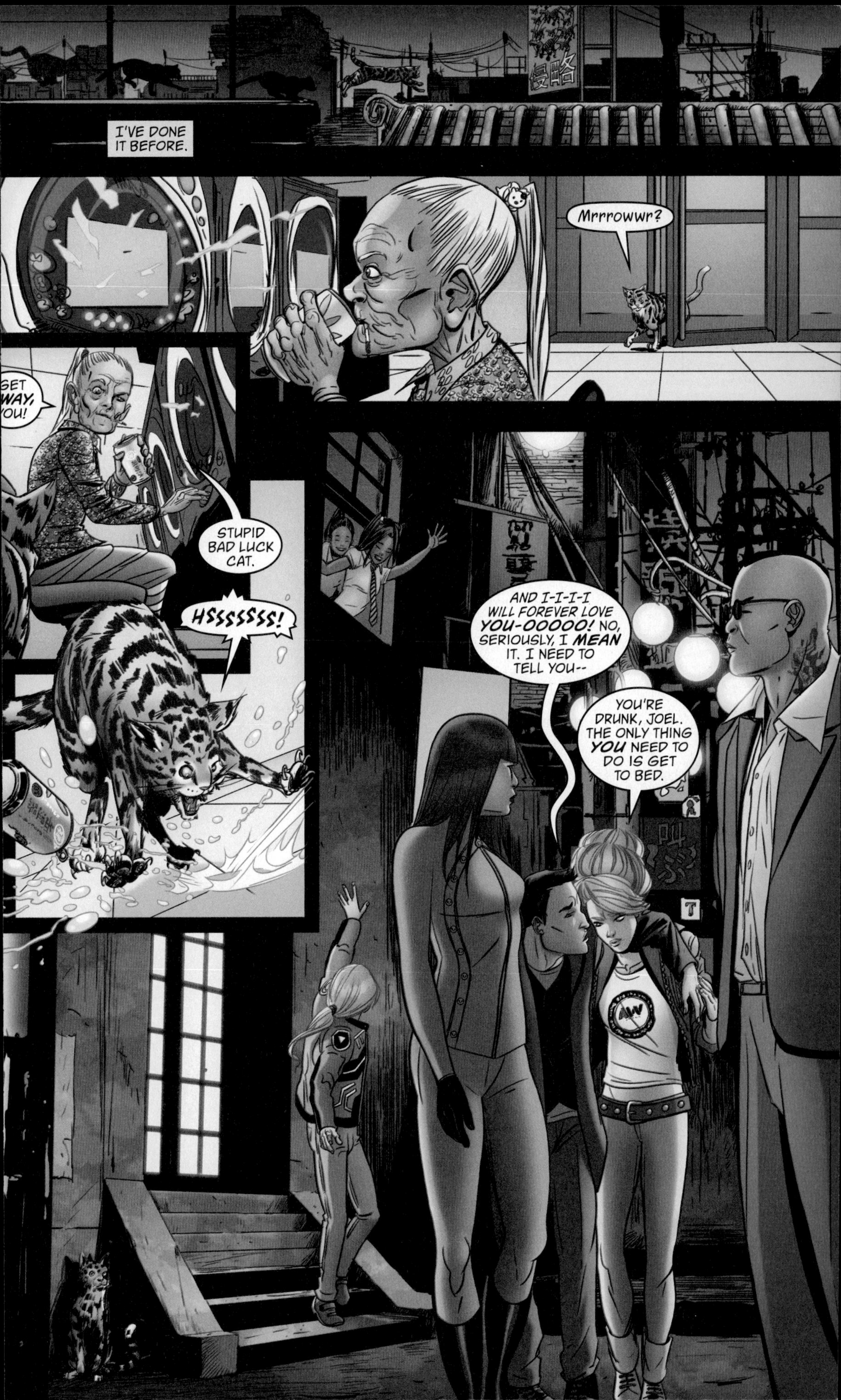
I'VE DONE IT BEFORE.
Mrrrowwr?
GET AWAY, YOU!
STUPID BAD LUCK CAT.
HSSSSSSS!
AND I-I-I-I WILL FOREVER LOVE YOU-OOOOO! NO, SERIOUSLY, I MEAN IT. I NEED TO TELL YOU--
YOU'RE DRUNK, JOEL. THE ONLY THING YOU NEED TO DO IS GET TO BED.

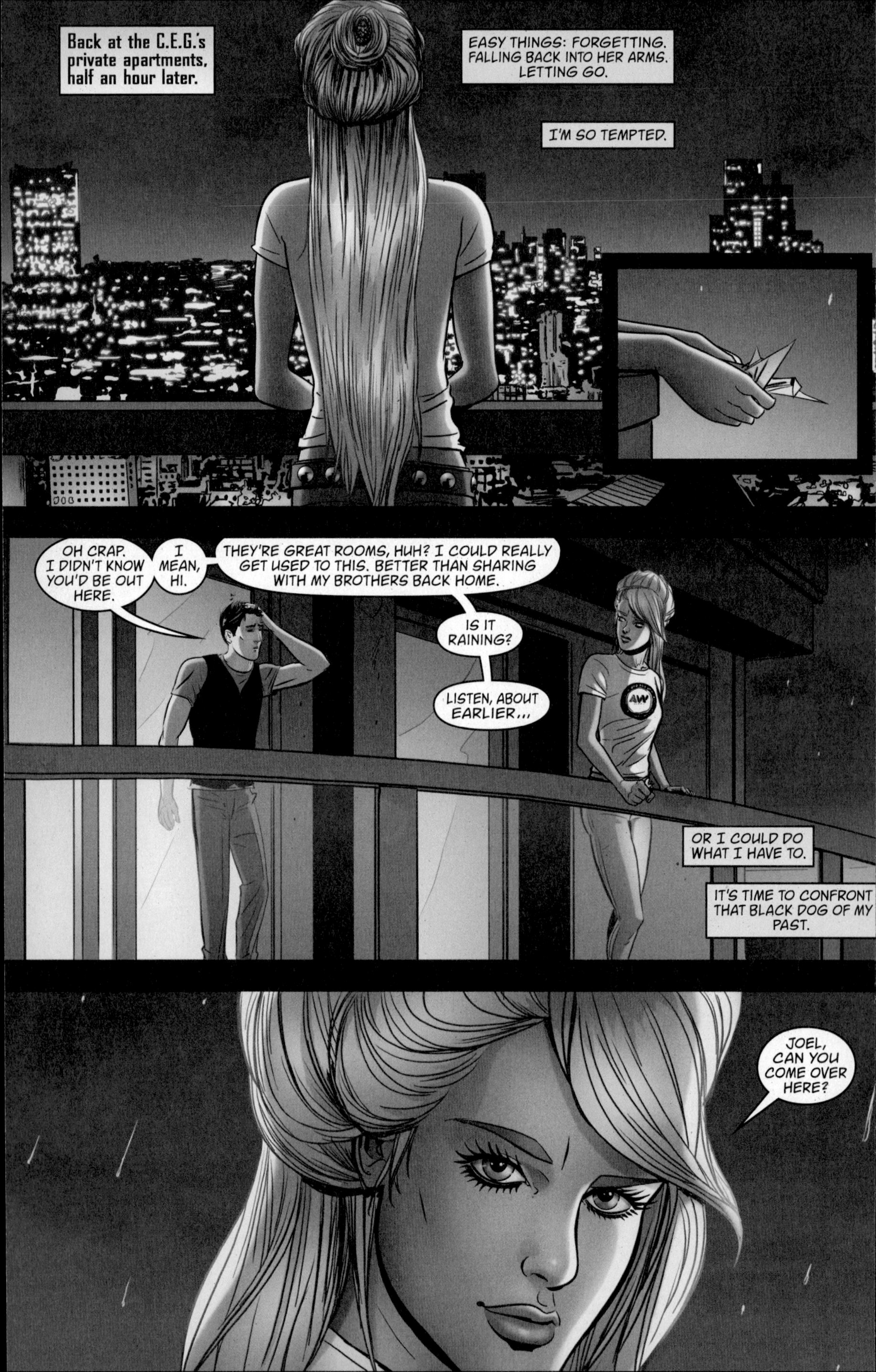

Back at the C.E.G.'s private apartments, half an hour later.
EASY THINGS: FORGETTING. FALLING BACK INTO HER ARMS. LETTING GO.
I'M SO TEMPTED.
OH CRAP. I DIDN'T KNOW YOU'D BE OUT HERE.
I MEAN, HI.
THEY'RE GREAT ROOMS, HUH? I COULD REALLY GET USED TO THIS. BETTER THAN SHARING WITH MY BROTHERS BACK HOME.
IS IT RAINING?
LISTEN, ABOUT EARLIER...
OR I COULD DO WHAT I HAVE TO.
IT'S TIME TO CONFRONT THAT BLACK DOG OF MY PAST.
JOEL, CAN YOU COME OVER HERE?

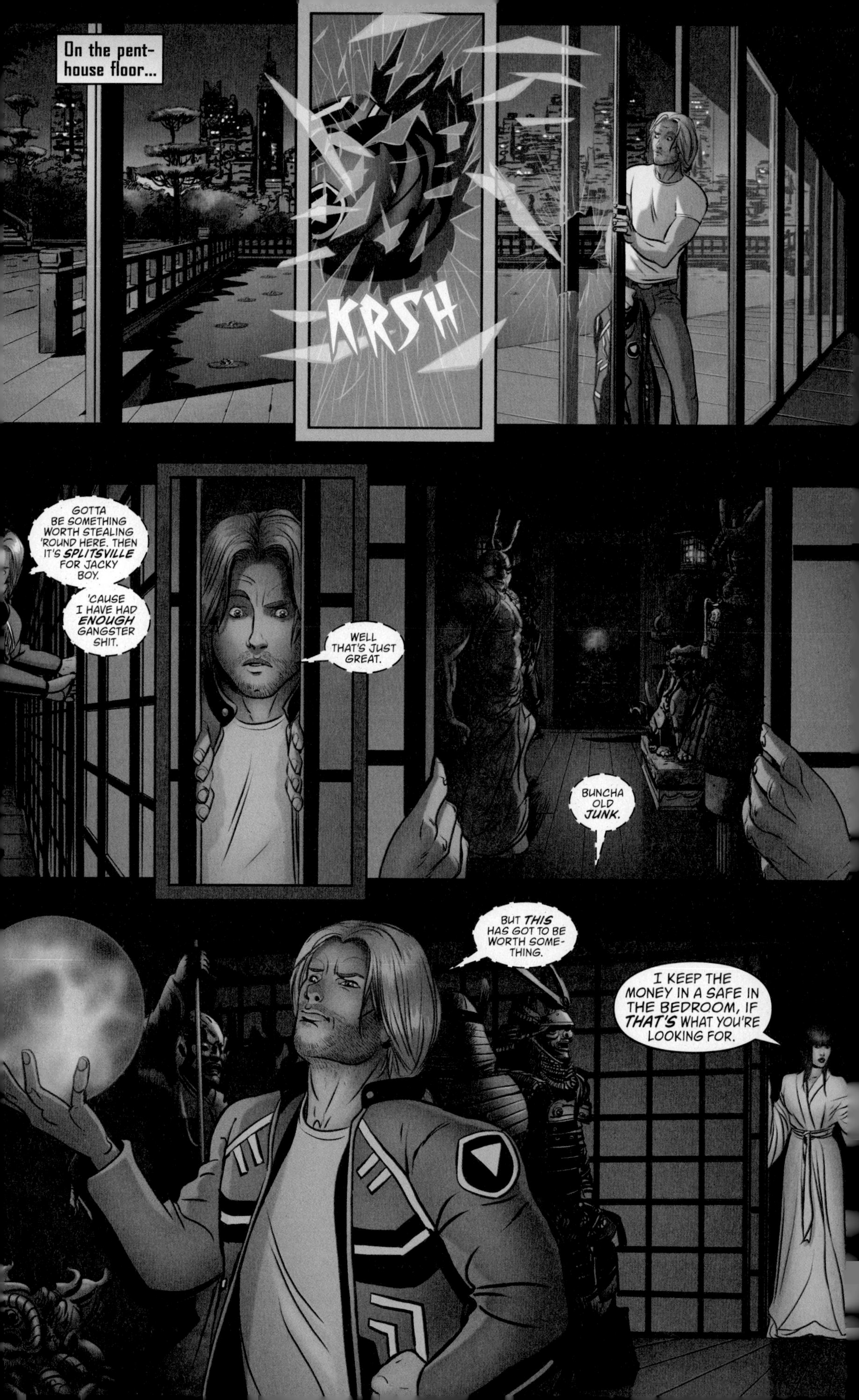
On the pent-house floor...
KRSH
GOTTA BE SOMETHING WORTH STEALING 'ROUND HERE. THEN IT'S SPLITSVILLE FOR JACKY BOY.
'CAUSE I HAVE HAD ENOUGH GANGSTER SHIT.
WELL THAT'S JUST GREAT.
BUNCHA OLD JUNK.
BUT THIS HAS GOT TO BE WORTH SOME-THING.
I KEEP THE MONEY IN A SAFE IN THE BEDROOM, IF THAT'S WHAT YOU'RE LOOKING FOR.

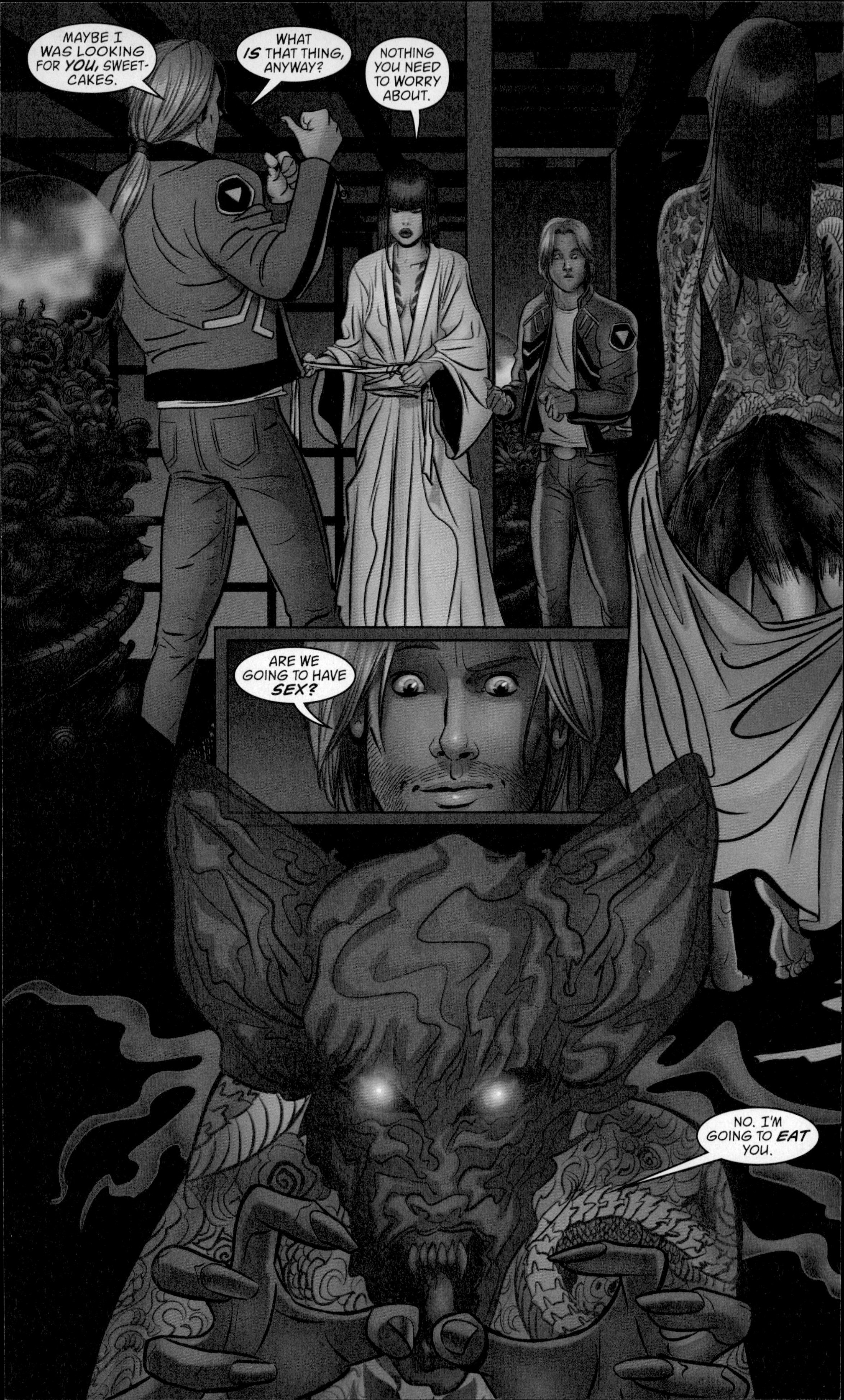
MAYBE I WAS LOOKING FOR YOU, SWEET-CAKES.
WHAT IS THAT THING, ANYWAY?
NOTHING YOU NEED TO WORRY ABOUT.
ARE WE GOING TO HAVE SEX?
NO. I'M GOING TO EAT YOU.

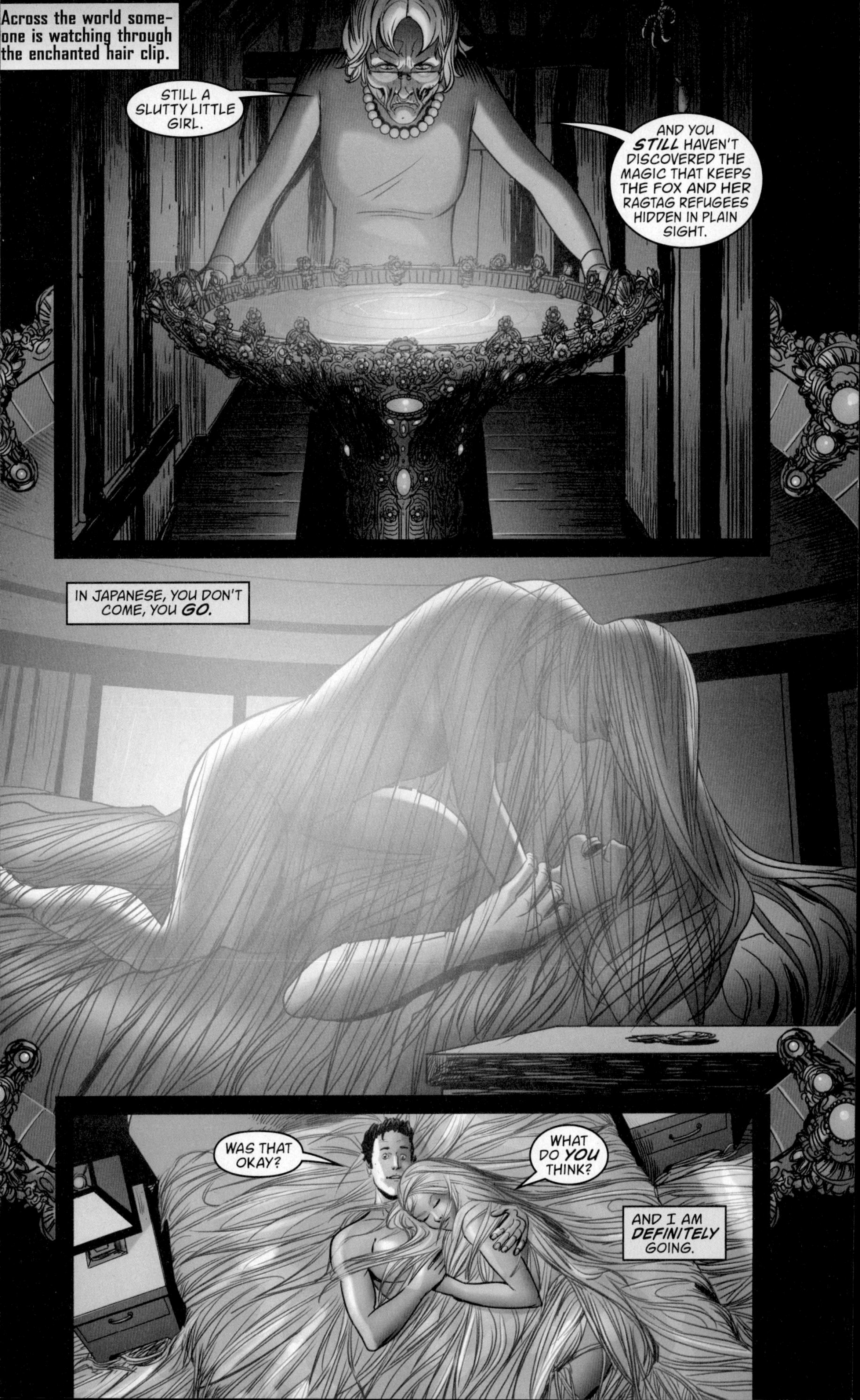
Across the world someone is watching through the enchanted hair clip.
STILL A SLUTTY LITTLE GIRL.
AND YOU STILL HAVEN'T DISCOVERED THE MAGIC THAT KEEPS THE FOX AND HER RAGTAG REFUGEES HIDDEN IN PLAIN SIGHT.
IN JAPANESE, YOU DON'T COME, YOU GO.
WAS THAT OKAY?
WHAT DO YOU THINK?
AND I AM DEFINITELY GOING.

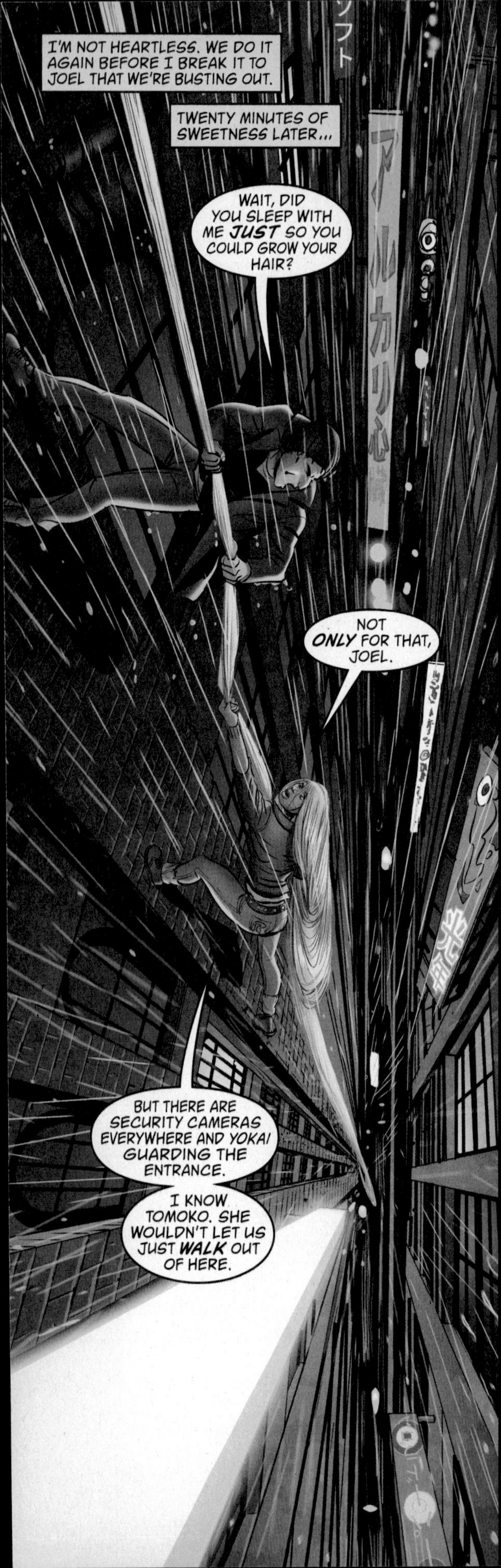
I'M NOT HEARTLESS. WE DO IT AGAIN BEFORE I BREAK IT TO JOEL THAT WE'RE BUSTING OUT.
TWENTY MINUTES OF SWEETNESS LATER...
WAIT, DID YOU SLEEP WITH ME JUST SO YOU COULD GROW YOUR HAIR?
NOT ONLY FOR THAT, JOEL.
BUT THERE ARE SECURITY CAMERAS EVERYWHERE AND YOKAI GUARDING THE ENTRANCE.
I KNOW TOMOKO. SHE WOULDN'T LET US JUST WALK OUT OF HERE.

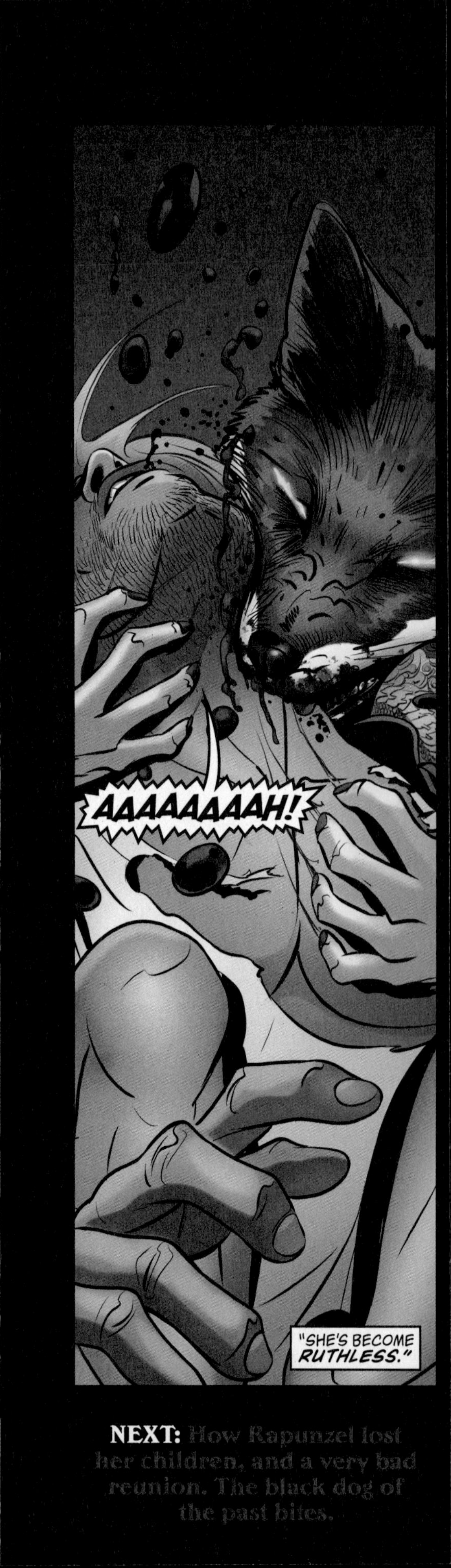
AAAAAAAAH!
"SHE'S BECOME RUTHLESS."

NEXT: How Rapunzel lost her children, and a very bad reunion. The black dog of the past bites.

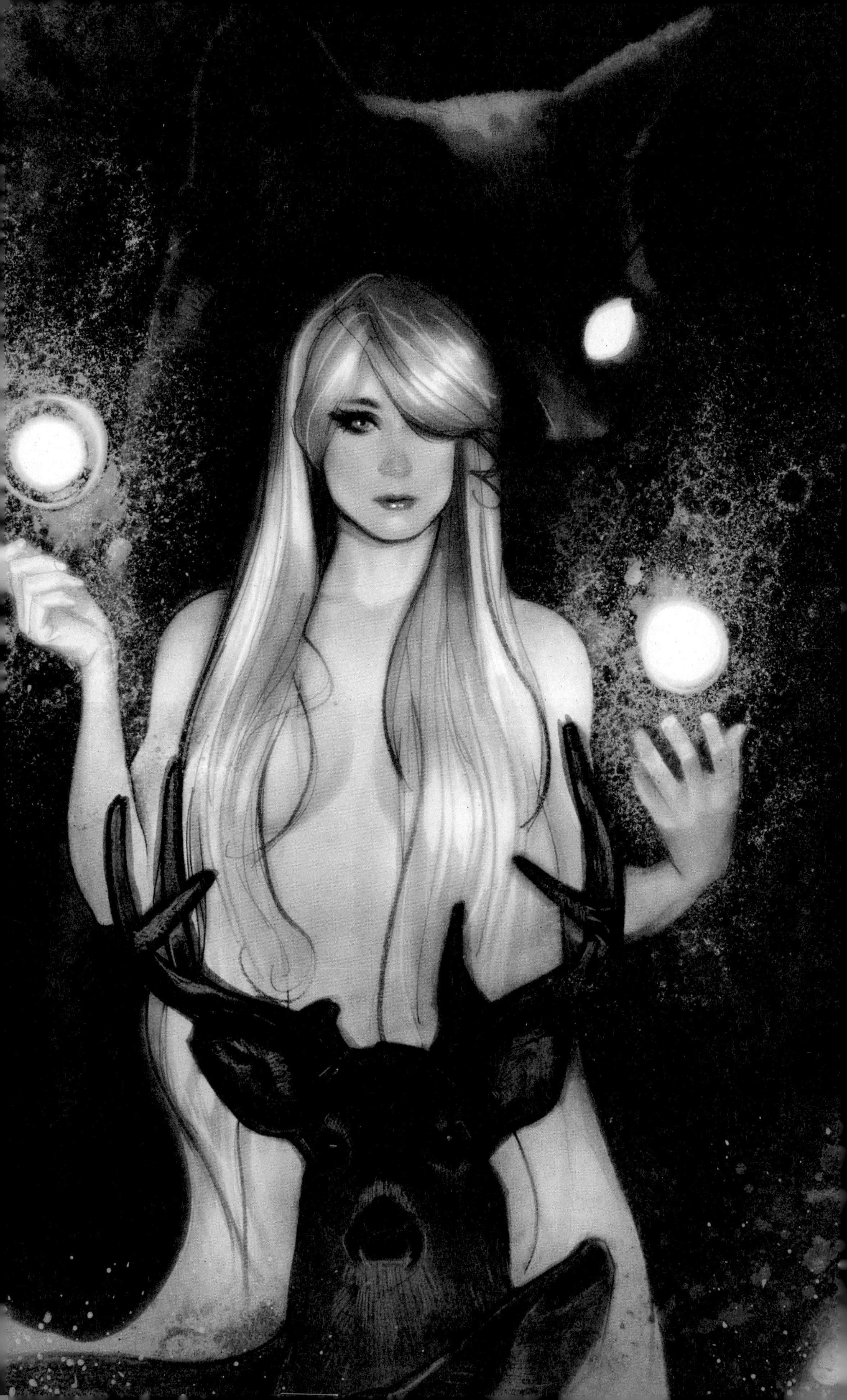

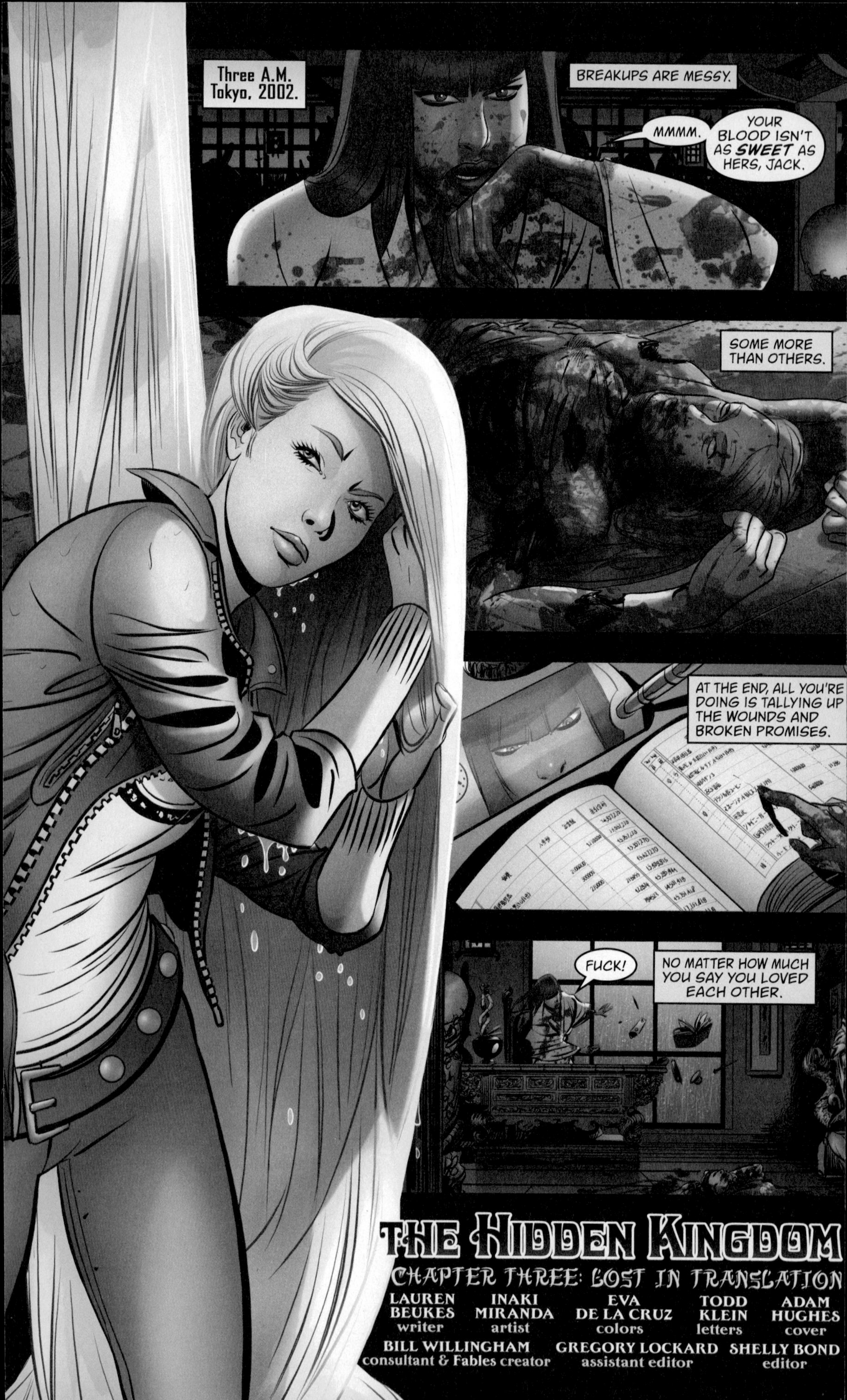
Three A.M. Tokyo, 2002.
BREAKUPS ARE MESSY.
MMMM.
YOUR BLOOD ISN'T AS SWEET AS HERS, JACK.
SOME MORE THAN OTHERS.
AT THE END, ALL YOU'RE DOING IS TALLYING UP THE WOUNDS AND BROKEN PROMISES.
FUCK!
NO MATTER HOW MUCH YOU SAY YOU LOVED EACH OTHER.
THE HIDDEN KINGDOM
CHAPTER THREE: LOST IN TRANSLATION
LAUREN BEUKES writer
INAKI MIRANDA artist
EVA DE LA CRUZ colors
TODD KLEIN letters
ADAM HUGHES cover
BILL WILLINGHAM consultant & Fables creator
GREGORY LOCKARD assistant editor
SHELLY BOND editor

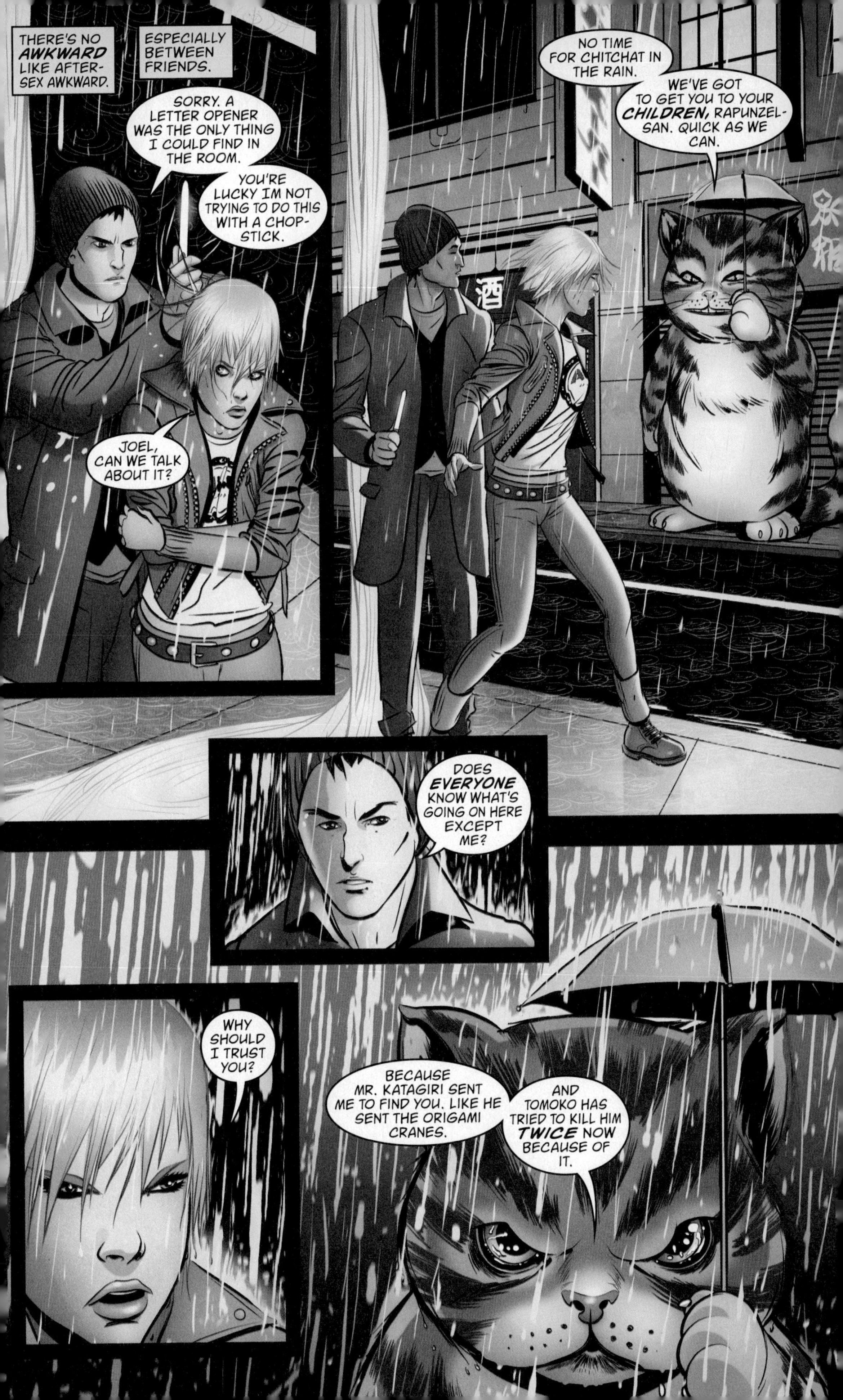

THERE'S NO AWKWARD LIKE AFTER-SEX AWKWARD.
ESPECIALLY BETWEEN FRIENDS.
SORRY. A LETTER OPENER WAS THE ONLY THING I COULD FIND IN THE ROOM.
YOU'RE LUCKY I'M NOT TRYING TO DO THIS WITH A CHOP-STICK.
JOEL, CAN WE TALK ABOUT IT?
NO TIME FOR CHITCHAT IN THE RAIN.
WE'VE GOT TO GET YOU TO YOUR CHILDREN, RAPUNZEL-SAN. QUICK AS WE CAN.
酒
DOES EVERYONE KNOW WHAT'S GOING ON HERE EXCEPT ME?
WHY SHOULD I TRUST YOU?
BECAUSE MR. KATAGIRI SENT ME TO FIND YOU. LIKE HE SENT THE ORIGAMI CRANES.
AND TOMOKO HAS TRIED TO KILL HIM TWICE NOW BECAUSE OF IT.

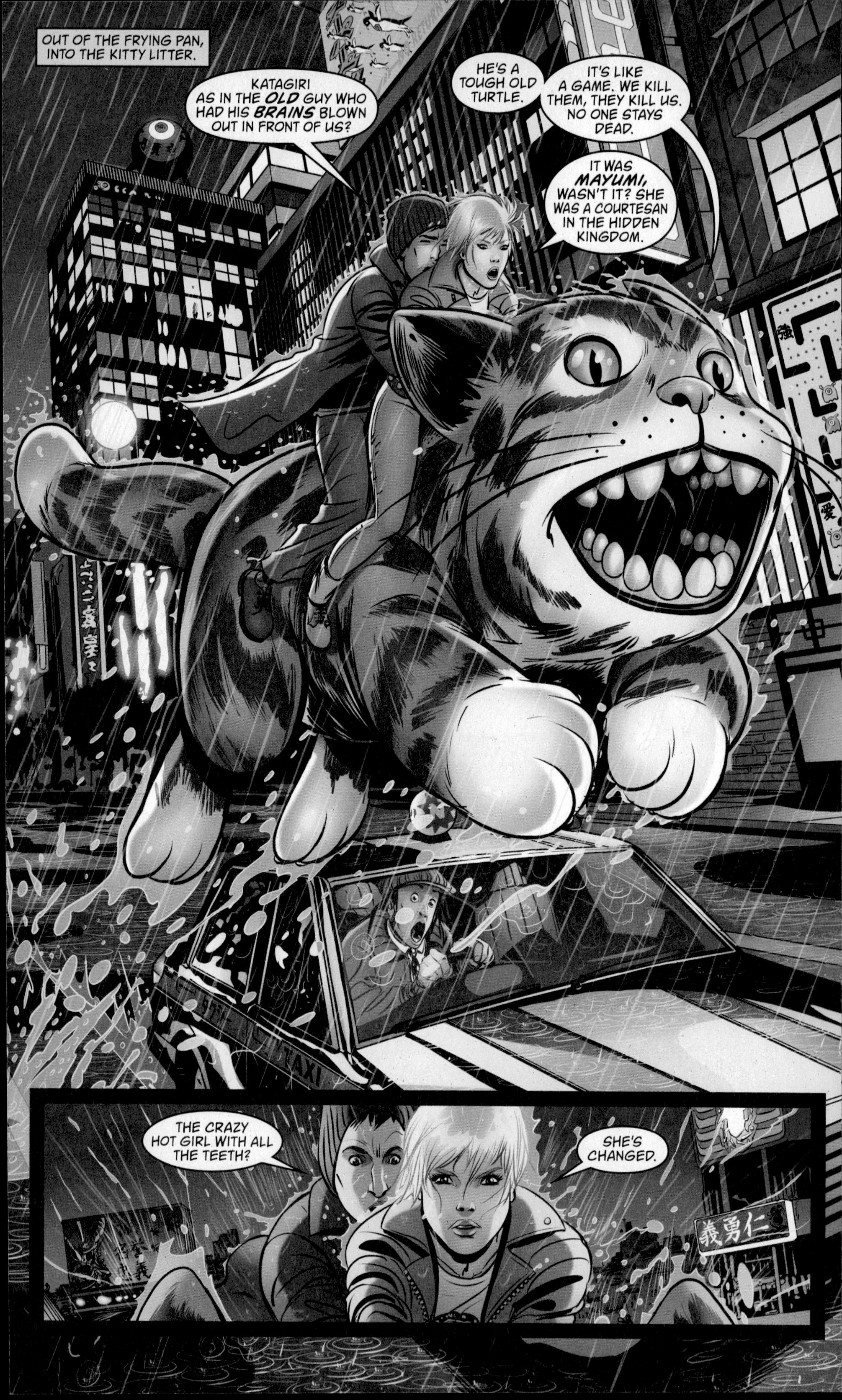

OUT OF THE FRYING PAN, INTO THE KITTY LITTER.
KATAGIRI! AS IN THE OLD GUY WHO HAD HIS BRAINS BLOWN OUT IN FRONT OF US?
HE'S A TOUGH OLD TURTLE.
IT'S LIKE A GAME. WE KILL THEM, THEY KILL US. NO ONE STAYS DEAD.
IT WAS MAYUMI, WASN'T IT? SHE WAS A COURTESAN IN THE HIDDEN KINGDOM.
TAXI
THE CRAZY HOT GIRL WITH ALL THE TEETH?
SHE'S CHANGED.
義勇仁

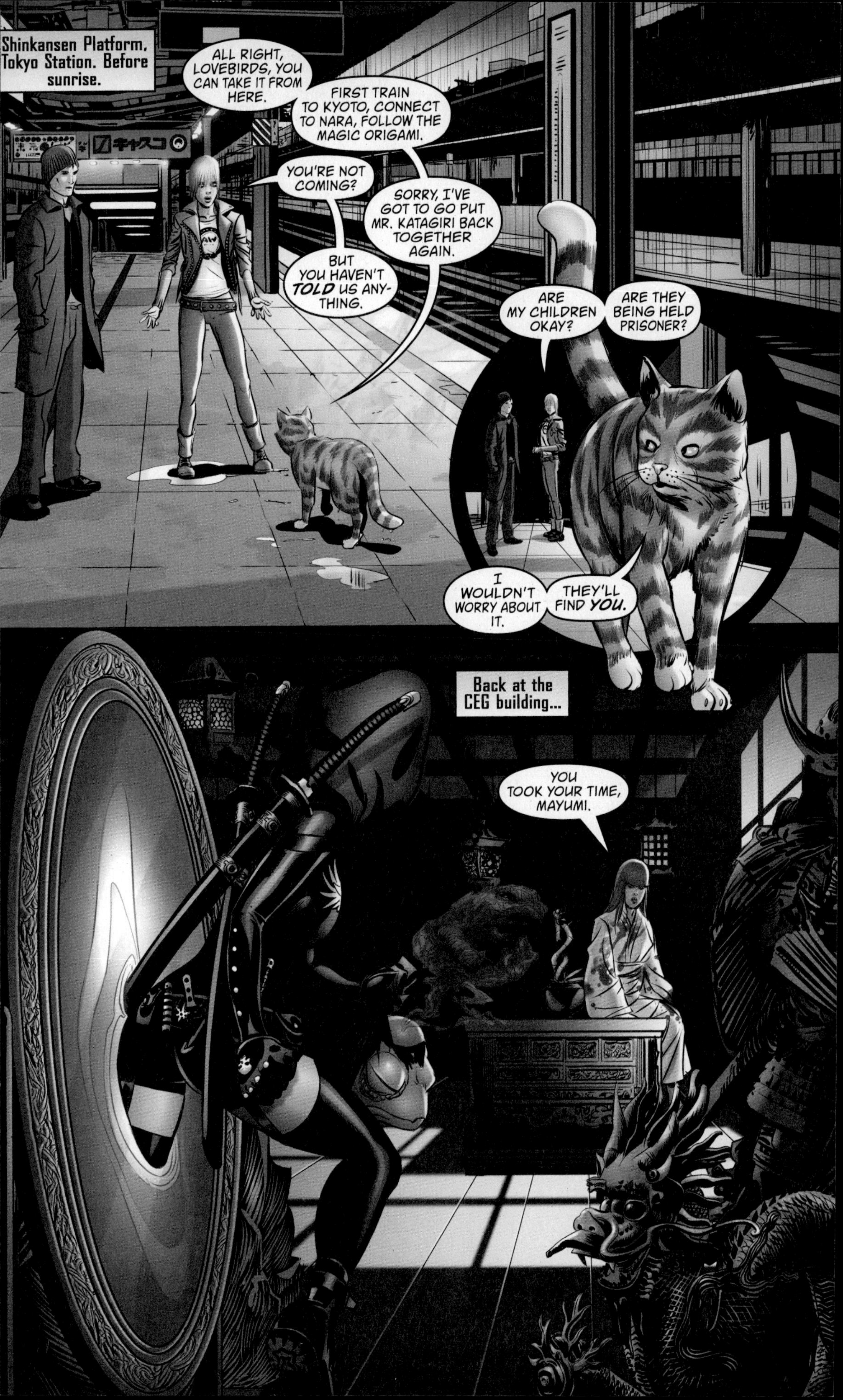
Shinkansen Platform, Tokyo Station. Before sunrise.
ALL RIGHT, LOVEBIRDS, YOU CAN TAKE IT FROM HERE.
FIRST TRAIN TO KYOTO, CONNECT TO NARA, FOLLOW THE MAGIC ORIGAMI.
YOU'RE NOT COMING?
SORRY, I'VE GOT TO GO PUT MR. KATAGIRI BACK TOGETHER AGAIN.
BUT YOU HAVEN'T TOLD US ANYTHING.
ARE MY CHILDREN OKAY?
ARE THEY BEING HELD PRISONER?
I WOULDN'T WORRY ABOUT IT.
THEY'LL FIND YOU.
Back at the CEG building...
YOU TOOK YOUR TIME, MAYUMI.

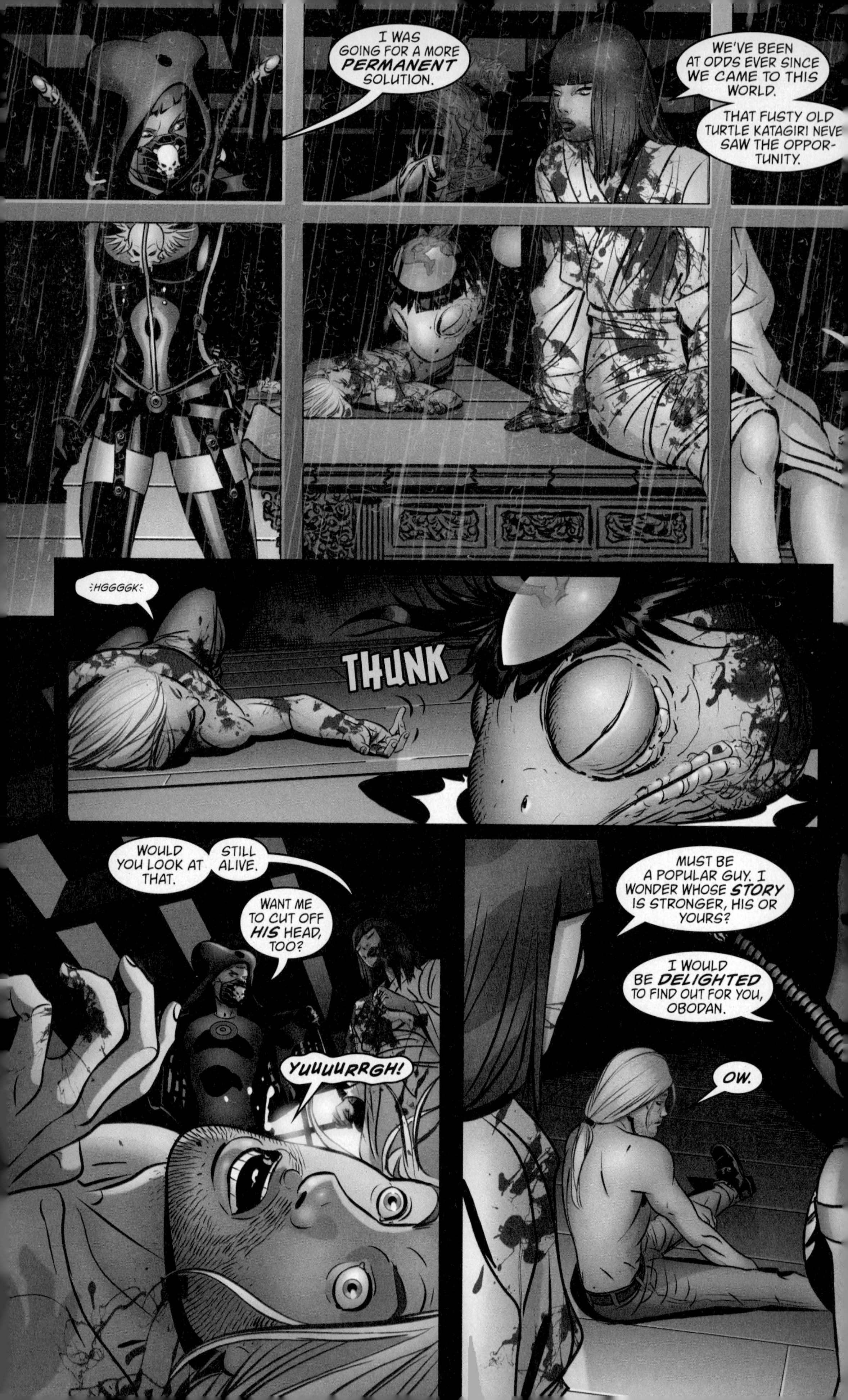
I WAS GOING FOR A MORE PERMANENT SOLUTION.
WE'VE BEEN AT ODDS EVER SINCE WE CAME TO THIS WORLD.
THAT FUSTY OLD TURTLE KATAGIRI NEVE SAW THE OPPORTUNITY.
HGGGGK
THUNK
WOULD YOU LOOK AT THAT.
STILL ALIVE.
WANT ME TO CUT OFF HIS HEAD, TOO?
YUUUURRGH!
MUST BE A POPULAR GUY. I WONDER WHOSE STORY IS STRONGER, HIS OR YOURS?
I WOULD BE DELIGHTED TO FIND OUT FOR YOU, OBODAN.
OW.

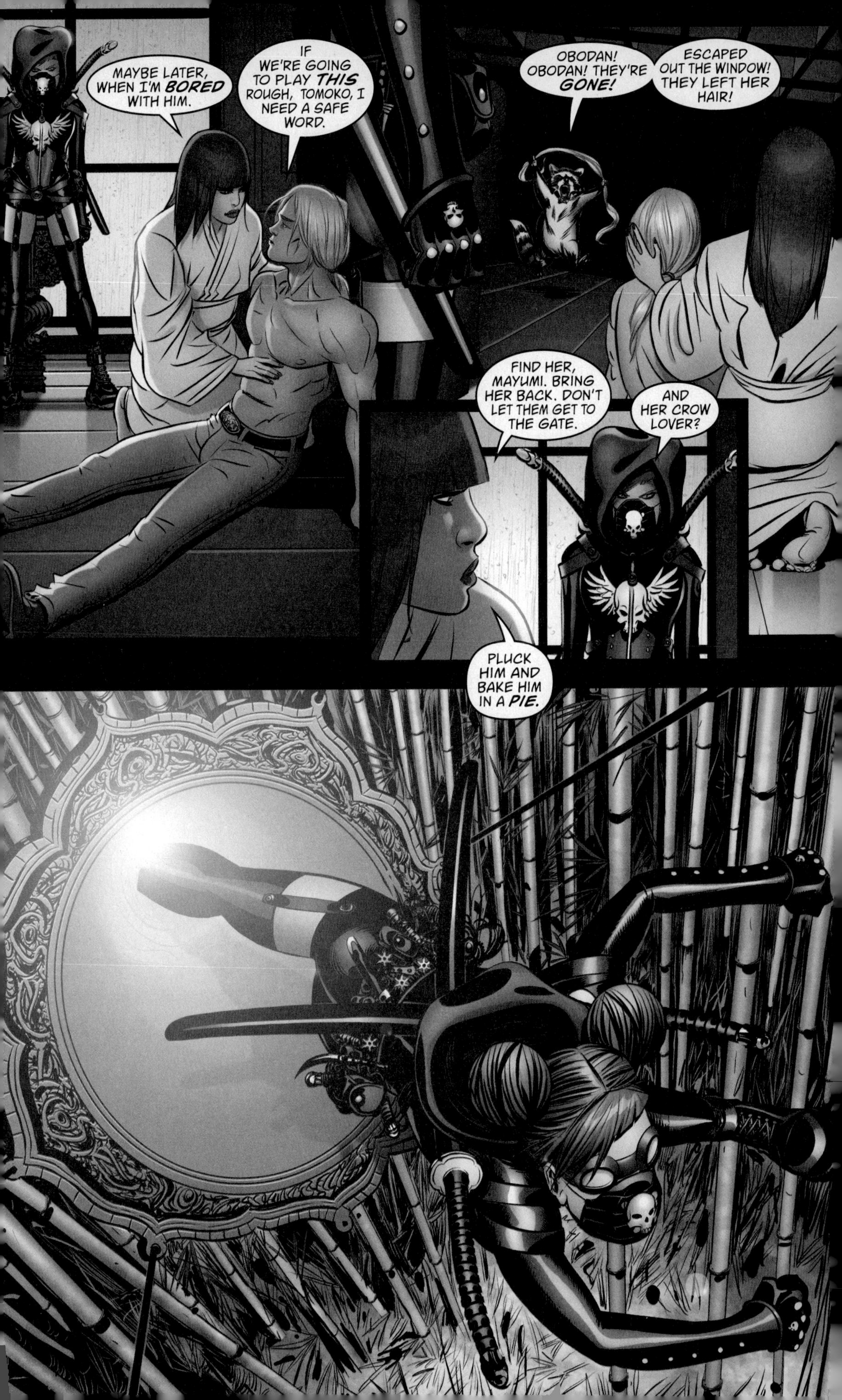
MAYBE LATER, WHEN I'M BORED WITH HIM.
IF WE'RE GOING TO PLAY THIS ROUGH, TOMOKO, I NEED A SAFE WORD.
OBODAN! OBODAN! THEY'RE GONE!
ESCAPED OUT THE WINDOW! THEY LEFT HER HAIR!
FIND HER, MAYUMI. BRING HER BACK. DON'T LET THEM GET TO THE GATE.
AND HER CROW LOVER?
PLUCK HIM AND BAKE HIM IN A PIE.

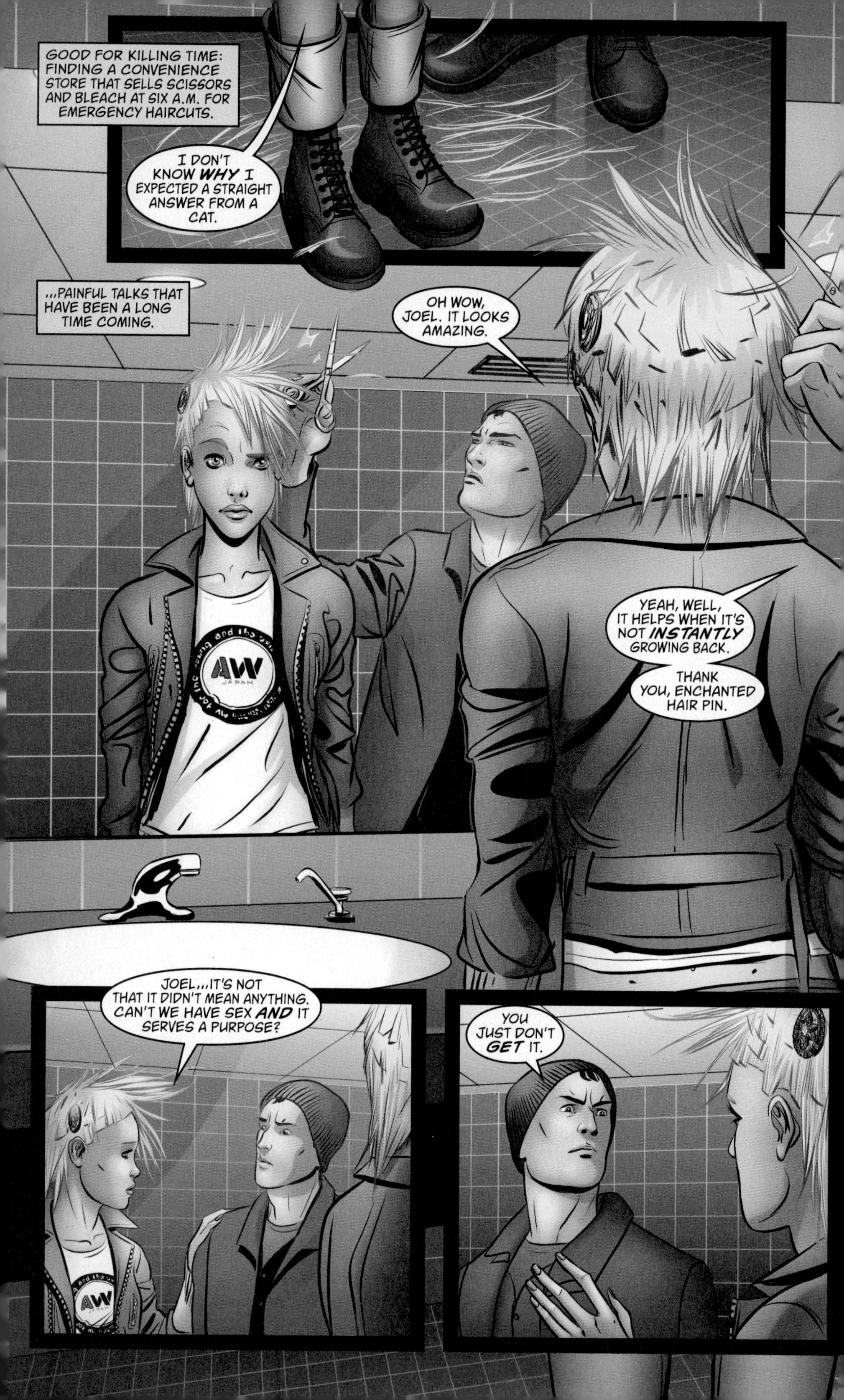
GOOD FOR KILLING TIME: FINDING A CONVENIENCE STORE THAT SELLS SCISSORS AND BLEACH AT SIX A.M. FOR EMERGENCY HAIRCUTS.
I DON'T KNOW **WHY** I EXPECTED A STRAIGHT ANSWER FROM A CAT.
...PAINFUL TALKS THAT HAVE BEEN A LONG TIME COMING.
OH WOW, JOEL. IT LOOKS AMAZING.
YEAH, WELL, IT HELPS WHEN IT'S NOT ***INSTANTLY*** GROWING BACK.
THANK YOU, ENCHANTED HAIR PIN.
JOEL...IT'S NOT THAT IT DIDN'T MEAN ANYTHING. CAN'T WE HAVE SEX **AND** IT SERVES A PURPOSE?
YOU JUST DON'T **GET** IT.

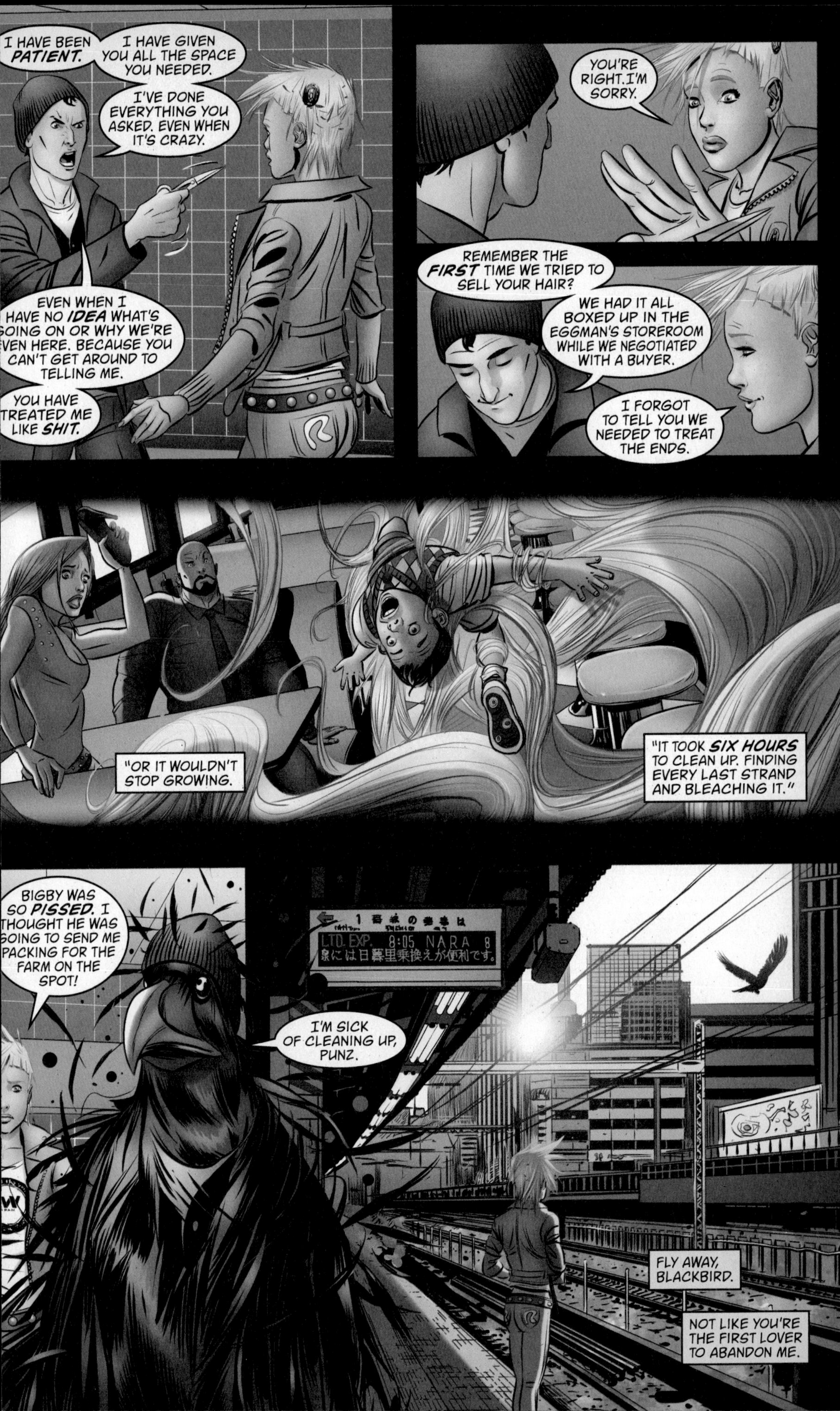
I HAVE BEEN *PATIENT.*
I HAVE GIVEN YOU ALL THE SPACE YOU NEEDED.
I'VE DONE EVERYTHING YOU ASKED. EVEN WHEN IT'S CRAZY.
EVEN WHEN I HAVE NO *IDEA* WHAT'S GOING ON OR WHY WE'RE EVEN HERE. BECAUSE YOU CAN'T GET AROUND TO TELLING ME.
YOU HAVE TREATED ME LIKE *SHIT.*
YOU'RE RIGHT. I'M SORRY.
REMEMBER THE *FIRST* TIME WE TRIED TO SELL YOUR HAIR?
WE HAD IT ALL BOXED UP IN THE EGGMAN'S STOREROOM WHILE WE NEGOTIATED WITH A BUYER.
I FORGOT TO TELL YOU WE NEEDED TO TREAT THE ENDS.
"OR IT WOULDN'T STOP GROWING.
"IT TOOK *SIX HOURS* TO CLEAN UP. FINDING EVERY LAST STRAND AND BLEACHING IT."
BIGBY WAS SO *PISSED.* I THOUGHT HE WAS GOING TO SEND ME PACKING FOR THE FARM ON THE SPOT!
LTD. EXP. 8:05 NARA 8
泉には日暮里乗換えが便利です。
I'M SICK OF CLEANING UP, PUNZ.
FLY AWAY, BLACKBIRD.
NOT LIKE YOU'RE THE FIRST LOVER TO ABANDON ME.

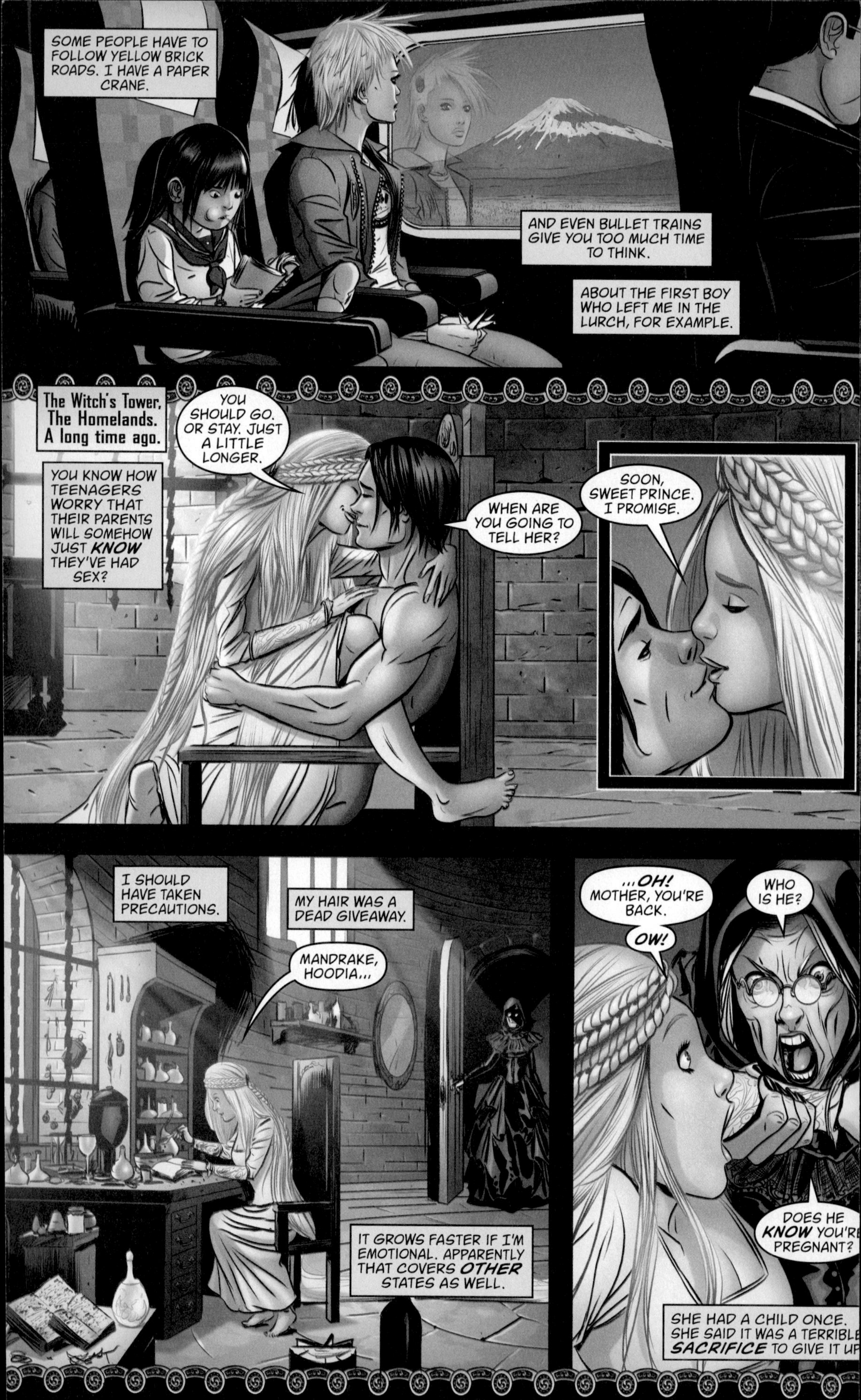
SOME PEOPLE HAVE TO FOLLOW YELLOW BRICK ROADS. I HAVE A PAPER CRANE.
AND EVEN BULLET TRAINS GIVE YOU TOO MUCH TIME TO THINK.
ABOUT THE FIRST BOY WHO LEFT ME IN THE LURCH, FOR EXAMPLE.
The Witch's Tower, The Homelands. A long time ago.
YOU KNOW HOW TEENAGERS WORRY THAT THEIR PARENTS WILL SOMEHOW JUST KNOW THEY'VE HAD SEX?
YOU SHOULD GO. OR STAY. JUST A LITTLE LONGER.
WHEN ARE YOU GOING TO TELL HER?
SOON, SWEET PRINCE. I PROMISE.
I SHOULD HAVE TAKEN PRECAUTIONS.
MY HAIR WAS A DEAD GIVEAWAY.
MANDRAKE, HOODIA...
IT GROWS FASTER IF I'M EMOTIONAL. APPARENTLY THAT COVERS OTHER STATES AS WELL.
...OH! MOTHER, YOU'RE BACK.
OW!
WHO IS HE?
DOES HE KNOW YOU'RE PREGNANT?
SHE HAD A CHILD ONCE. SHE SAID IT WAS A TERRIBLE SACRIFICE TO GIVE IT UP.

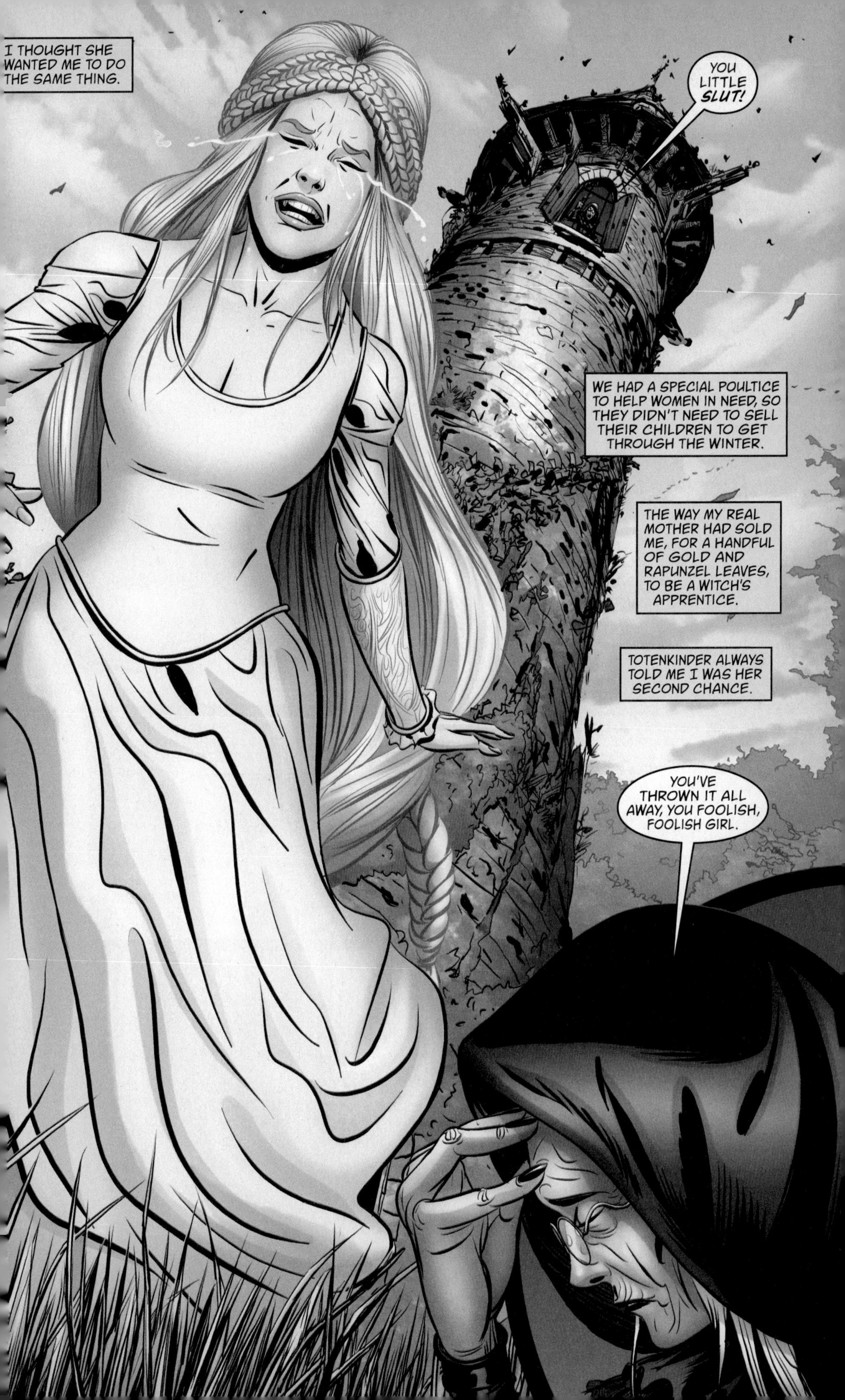
I THOUGHT SHE WANTED ME TO DO THE SAME THING.
YOU LITTLE SLUT!
WE HAD A SPECIAL POULTICE TO HELP WOMEN IN NEED, SO THEY DIDN'T NEED TO SELL THEIR CHILDREN TO GET THROUGH THE WINTER.
THE WAY MY REAL MOTHER HAD SOLD ME, FOR A HANDFUL OF GOLD AND RAPUNZEL LEAVES, TO BE A WITCH'S APPRENTICE.
TOTENKINDER ALWAYS TOLD ME I WAS HER SECOND CHANCE.
YOU'VE THROWN IT ALL AWAY, YOU FOOLISH, FOOLISH GIRL.

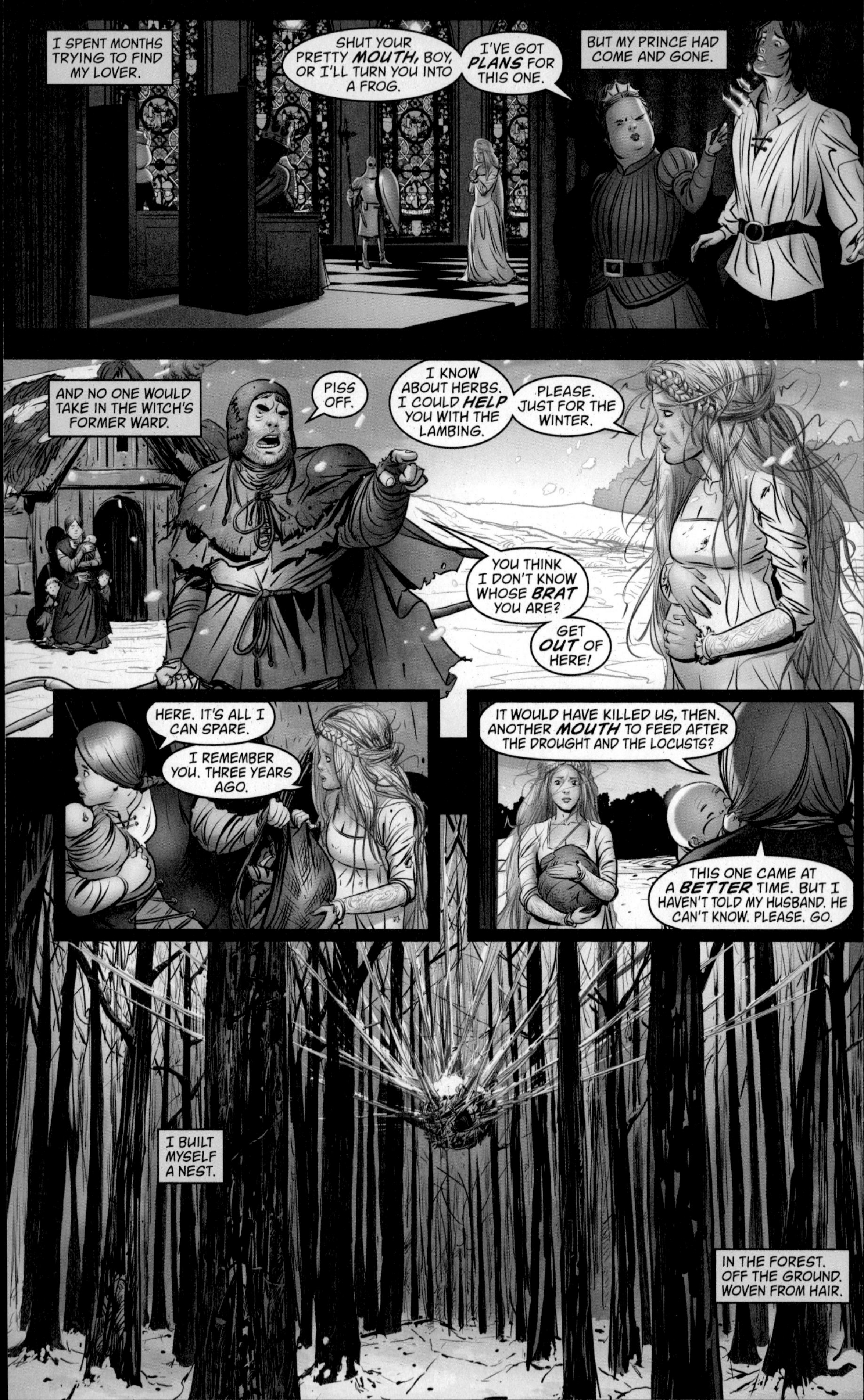
I SPENT MONTHS TRYING TO FIND MY LOVER.
SHUT YOUR PRETTY MOUTH, BOY, OR I'LL TURN YOU INTO A FROG.
I'VE GOT PLANS FOR THIS ONE.
BUT MY PRINCE HAD COME AND GONE.
AND NO ONE WOULD TAKE IN THE WITCH'S FORMER WARD.
PISS OFF.
I KNOW ABOUT HERBS. I COULD HELP YOU WITH THE LAMBING.
PLEASE. JUST FOR THE WINTER.
YOU THINK I DON'T KNOW WHOSE BRAT YOU ARE?
GET OUT OF HERE!
HERE. IT'S ALL I CAN SPARE.
I REMEMBER YOU. THREE YEARS AGO.
IT WOULD HAVE KILLED US, THEN. ANOTHER MOUTH TO FEED AFTER THE DROUGHT AND THE LOCUSTS?
THIS ONE CAME AT A BETTER TIME. BUT I HAVEN'T TOLD MY HUSBAND. HE CAN'T KNOW. PLEASE. GO.
I BUILT MYSELF A NEST.
IN THE FOREST. OFF THE GROUND. WOVEN FROM HAIR.

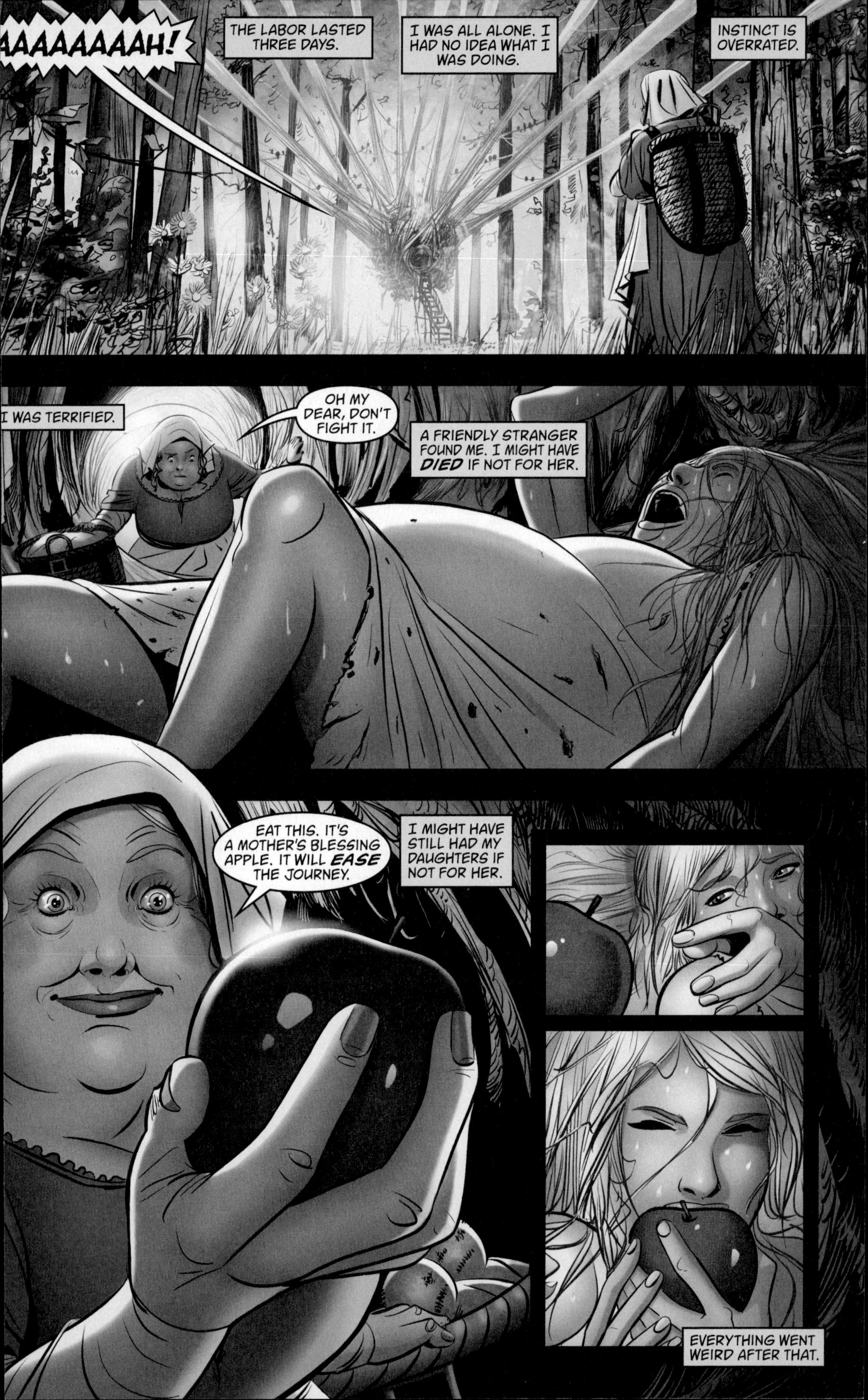
AAAAAAAAH!
THE LABOR LASTED THREE DAYS.
I WAS ALL ALONE. I HAD NO IDEA WHAT I WAS DOING.
INSTINCT IS OVERRATED.
I WAS TERRIFIED.
OH MY DEAR, DON'T FIGHT IT.
A FRIENDLY STRANGER FOUND ME. I MIGHT HAVE *DIED* IF NOT FOR HER.
EAT THIS. IT'S A MOTHER'S BLESSING APPLE. IT WILL *EASE* THE JOURNEY.
I MIGHT HAVE STILL HAD MY DAUGHTERS IF NOT FOR HER.
EVERYTHING WENT WEIRD AFTER THAT.

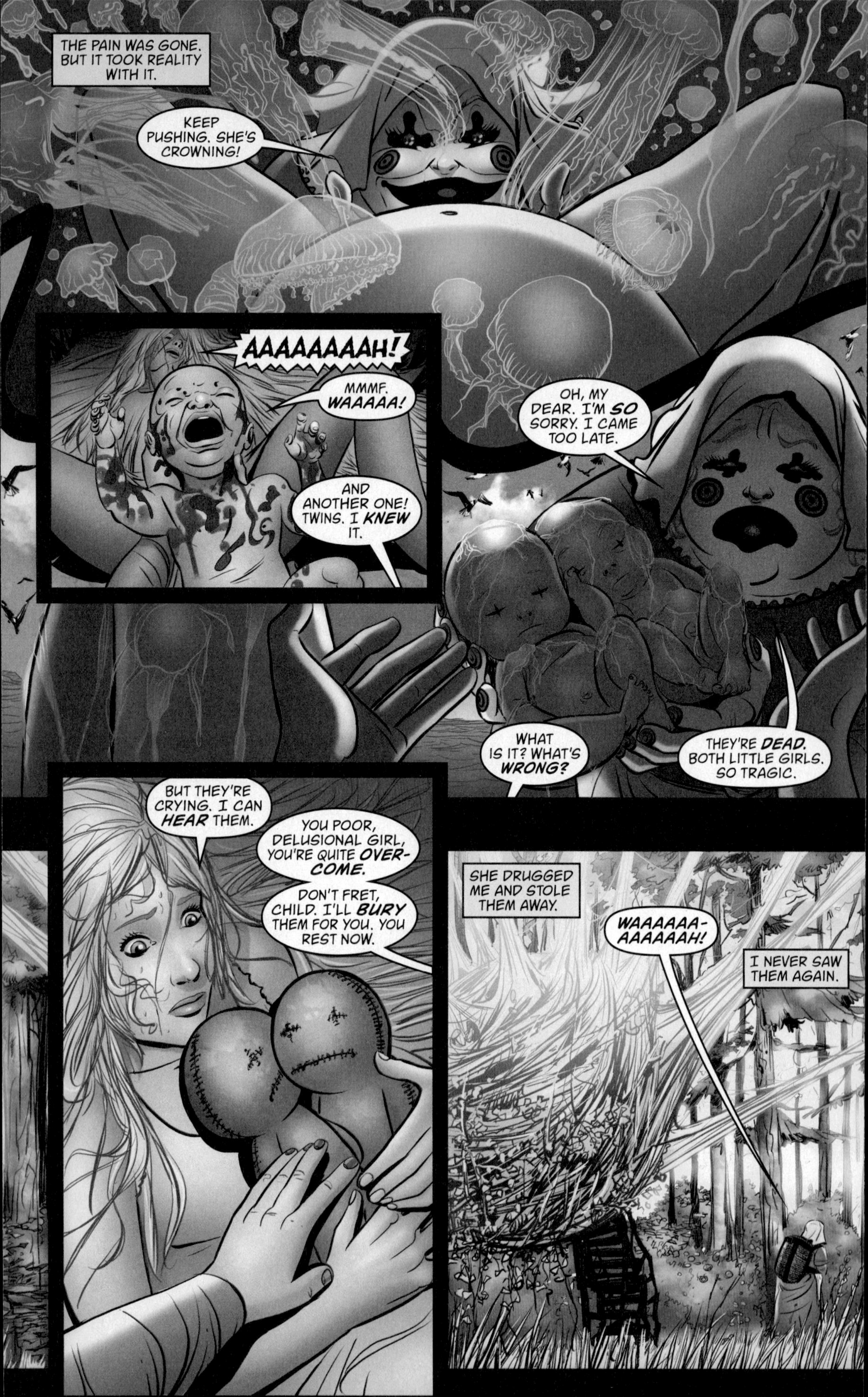
THE PAIN WAS GONE. BUT IT TOOK REALITY WITH IT.
KEEP PUSHING. SHE'S CROWNING!
AAAAAAAAH!
MMMF. WAAAAA!
AND ANOTHER ONE! TWINS. I KNEW IT.
OH, MY DEAR. I'M SO SORRY. I CAME TOO LATE.
WHAT IS IT? WHAT'S WRONG?
THEY'RE DEAD. BOTH LITTLE GIRLS. SO TRAGIC.
BUT THEY'RE CRYING. I CAN HEAR THEM.
YOU POOR, DELUSIONAL GIRL, YOU'RE QUITE OVER-COME.
DON'T FRET, CHILD. I'LL BURY THEM FOR YOU. YOU REST NOW.
SHE DRUGGED ME AND STOLE THEM AWAY.
WAAAAAA-AAAAAAH!
I NEVER SAW THEM AGAIN.

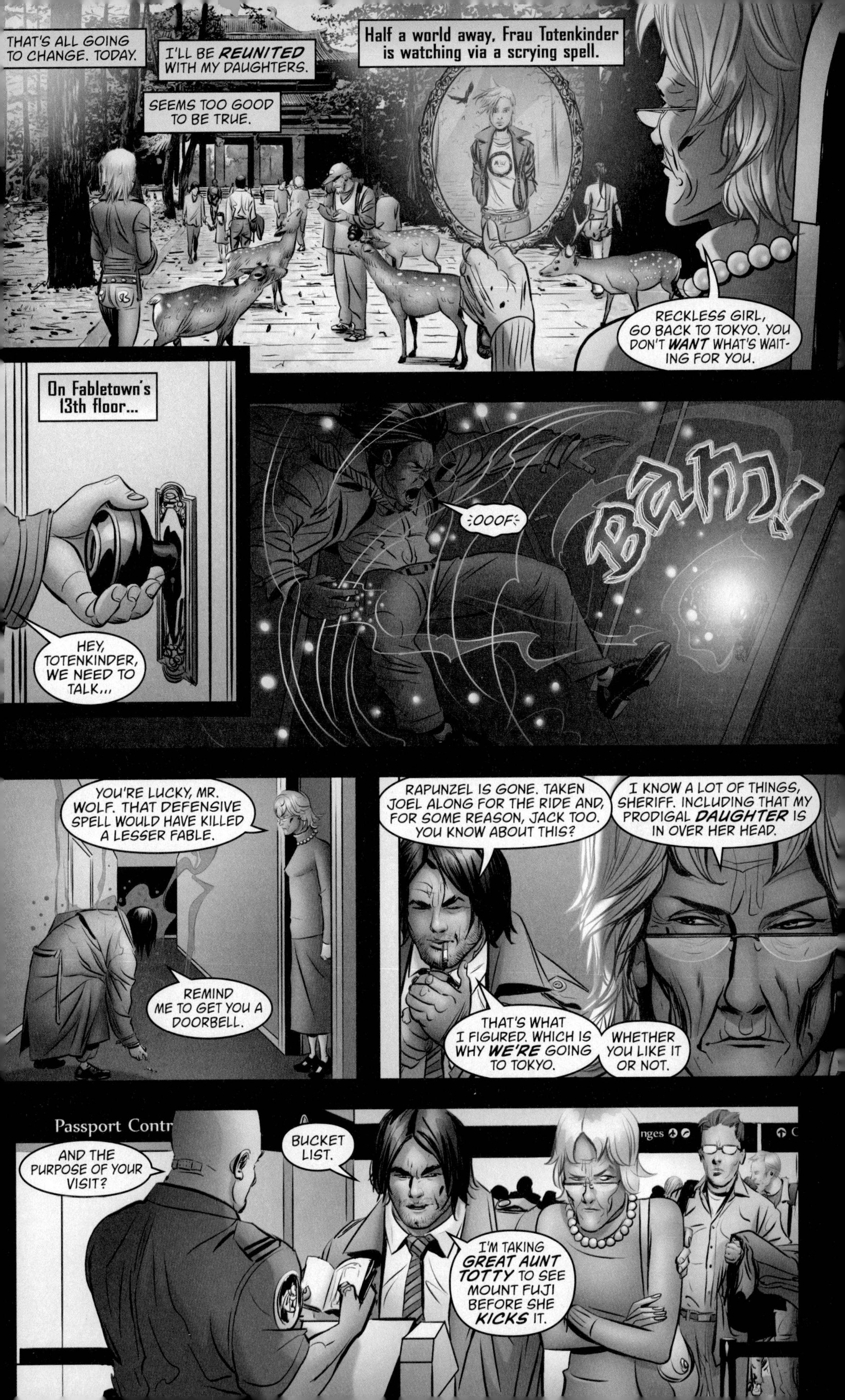
THAT'S ALL GOING TO CHANGE. TODAY.
I'LL BE REUNITED WITH MY DAUGHTERS.
SEEMS TOO GOOD TO BE TRUE.
Half a world away, Frau Totenkinder is watching via a scrying spell.
RECKLESS GIRL, GO BACK TO TOKYO. YOU DON'T WANT WHAT'S WAITING FOR YOU.
On Fabletown's 13th floor...
HEY, TOTENKINDER, WE NEED TO TALK...
OOOF
BAM!
YOU'RE LUCKY, MR. WOLF. THAT DEFENSIVE SPELL WOULD HAVE KILLED A LESSER FABLE.
REMIND ME TO GET YOU A DOORBELL.
RAPUNZEL IS GONE. TAKEN JOEL ALONG FOR THE RIDE AND, FOR SOME REASON, JACK TOO. YOU KNOW ABOUT THIS?
I KNOW A LOT OF THINGS, SHERIFF. INCLUDING THAT MY PRODIGAL DAUGHTER IS IN OVER HER HEAD.
THAT'S WHAT I FIGURED. WHICH IS WHY WE'RE GOING TO TOKYO.
WHETHER YOU LIKE IT OR NOT.
Passport Contr
AND THE PURPOSE OF YOUR VISIT?
BUCKET LIST.
I'M TAKING GREAT AUNT TOTTY TO SEE MOUNT FUJI BEFORE SHE KICKS IT.

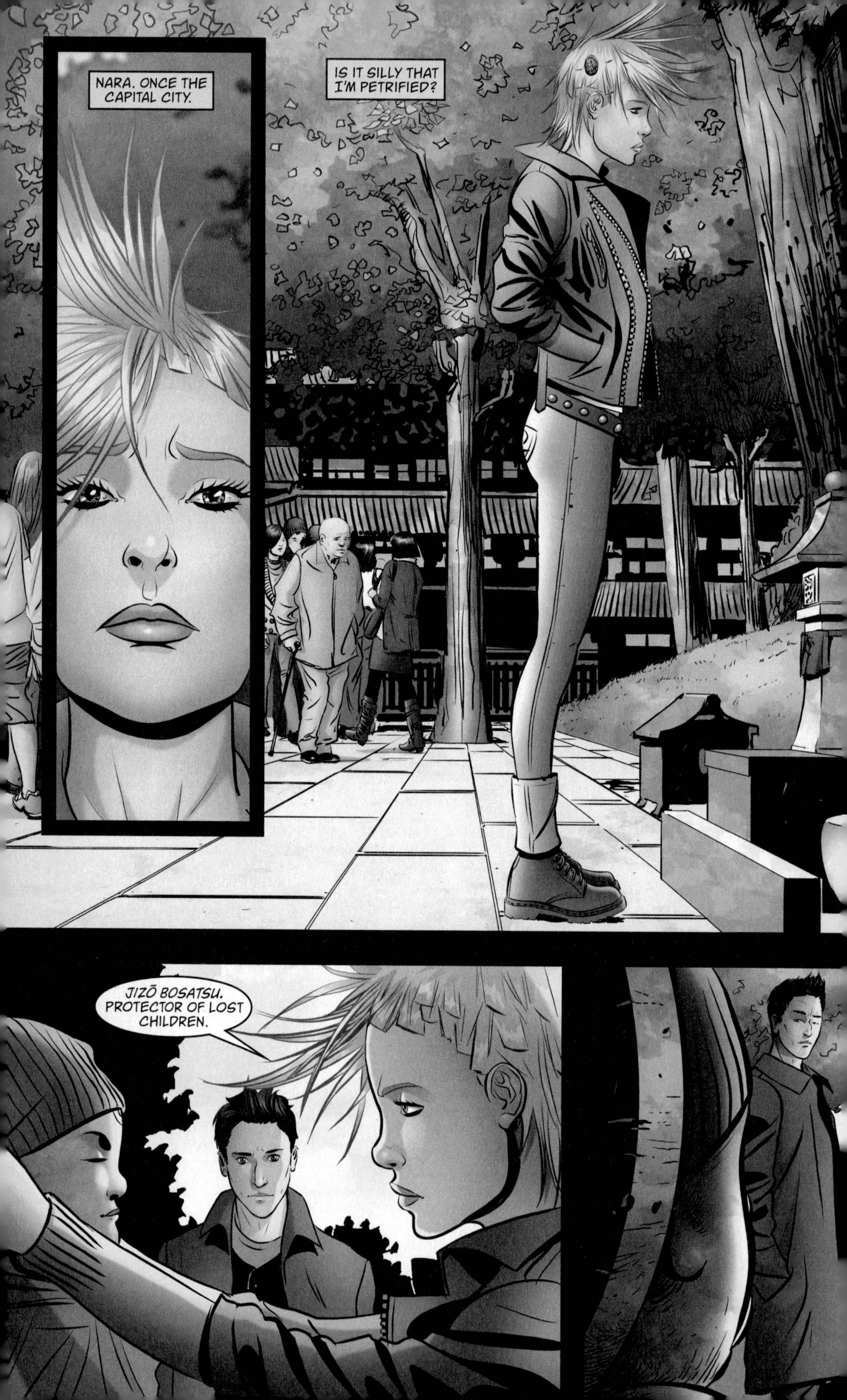
NARA. ONCE THE CAPITAL CITY.
IS IT SILLY THAT I'M PETRIFIED?
JIZŌ BOSATSU. PROTECTOR OF LOST CHILDREN.

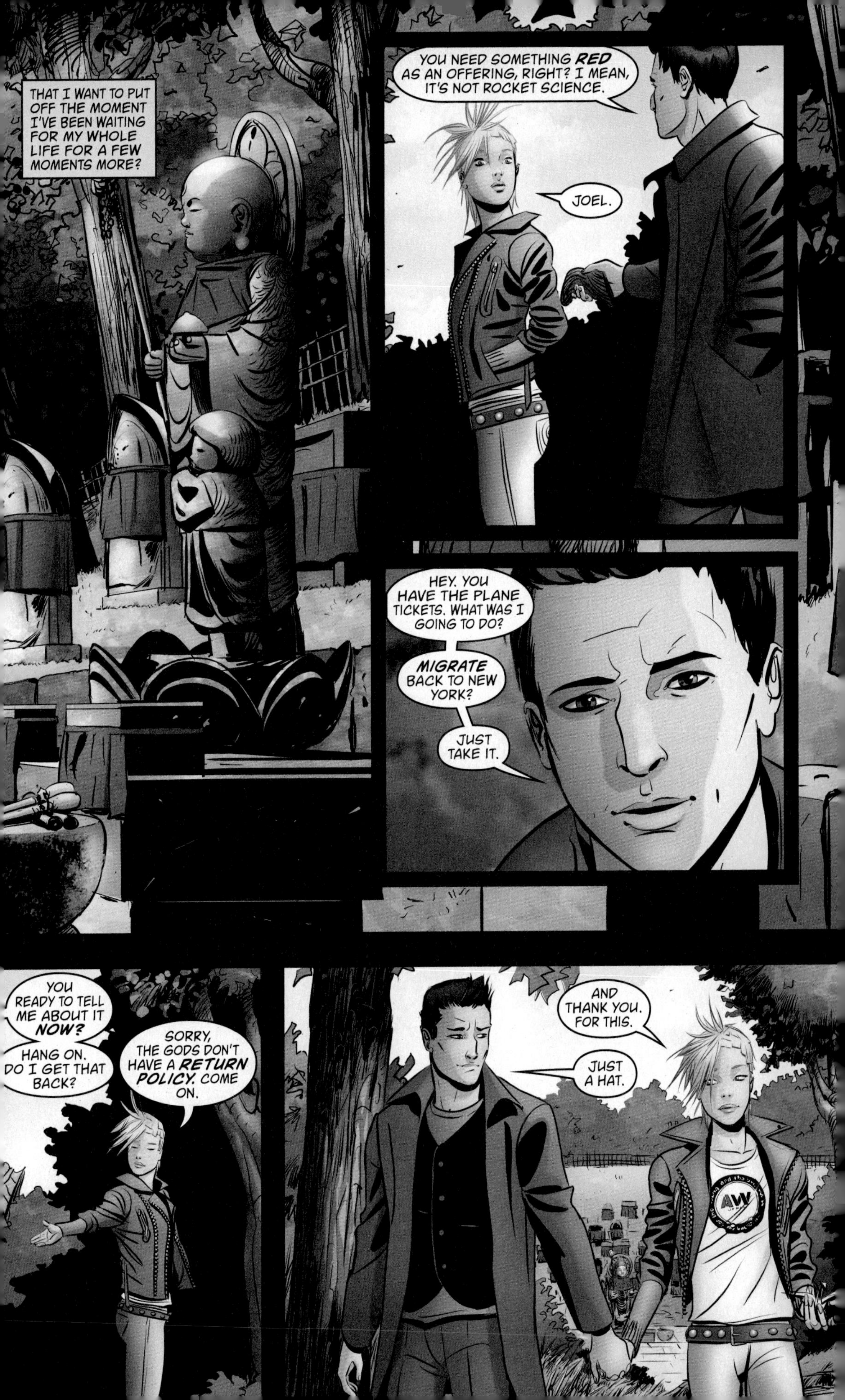
THAT I WANT TO PUT OFF THE MOMENT I'VE BEEN WAITING FOR MY WHOLE LIFE FOR A FEW MOMENTS MORE?
YOU NEED SOMETHING RED AS AN OFFERING, RIGHT? I MEAN, IT'S NOT ROCKET SCIENCE.
JOEL.
HEY. YOU HAVE THE PLANE TICKETS. WHAT WAS I GOING TO DO?
MIGRATE BACK TO NEW YORK?
JUST TAKE IT.
YOU READY TO TELL ME ABOUT IT NOW?
HANG ON. DO I GET THAT BACK?
SORRY, THE GODS DON'T HAVE A RETURN POLICY. COME ON.
AND THANK YOU. FOR THIS.
JUST A HAT.

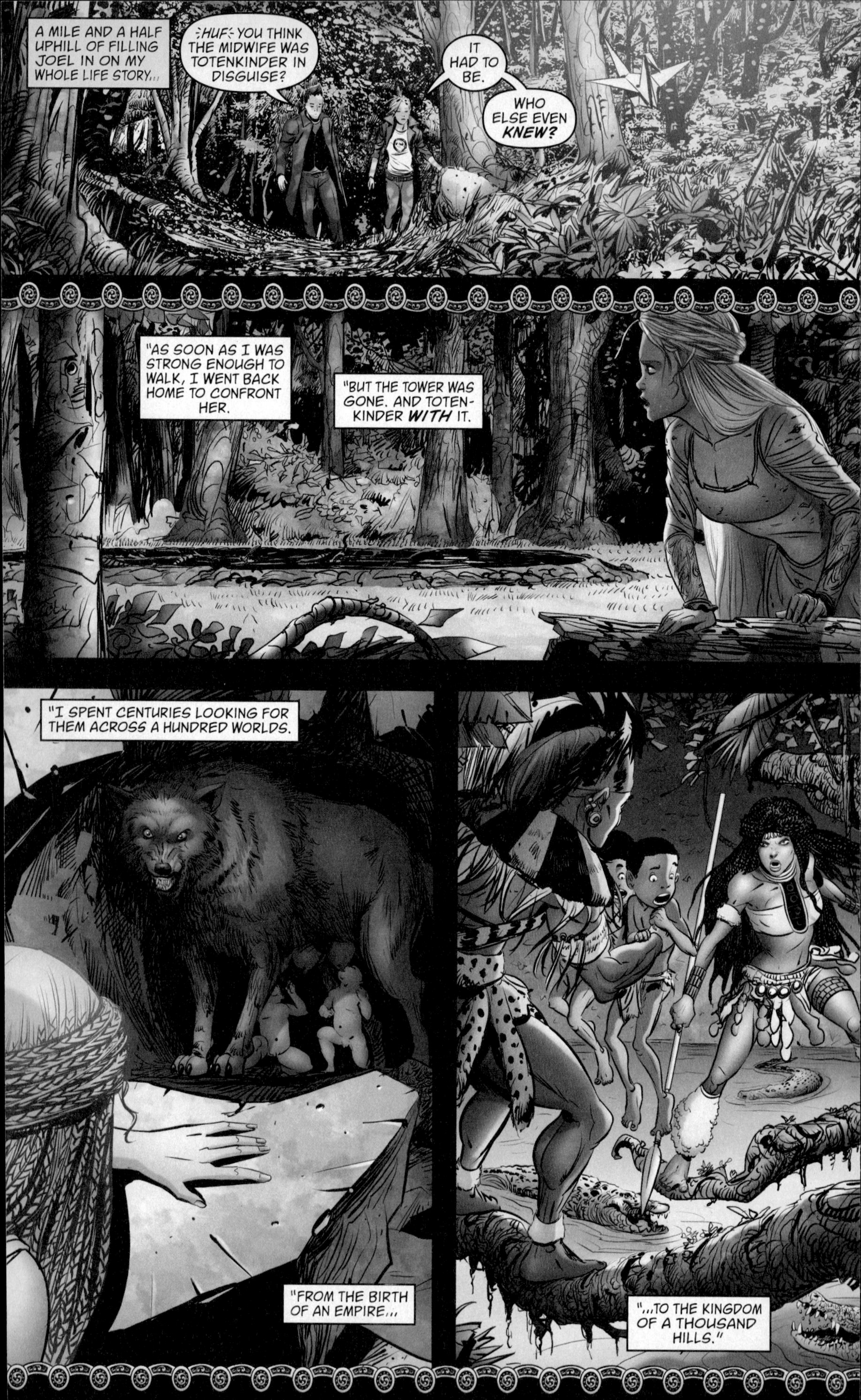
A MILE AND A HALF UPHILL OF FILLING JOEL IN ON MY WHOLE LIFE STORY...
HUF YOU THINK THE MIDWIFE WAS TOTENKINDER IN DISGUISE?
IT HAD TO BE.
WHO ELSE EVEN KNEW?
"AS SOON AS I WAS STRONG ENOUGH TO WALK, I WENT BACK HOME TO CONFRONT HER.
"BUT THE TOWER WAS GONE. AND TOTEN-KINDER WITH IT.
"I SPENT CENTURIES LOOKING FOR THEM ACROSS A HUNDRED WORLDS.
"FROM THE BIRTH OF AN EMPIRE...
"...TO THE KINGDOM OF A THOUSAND HILLS."

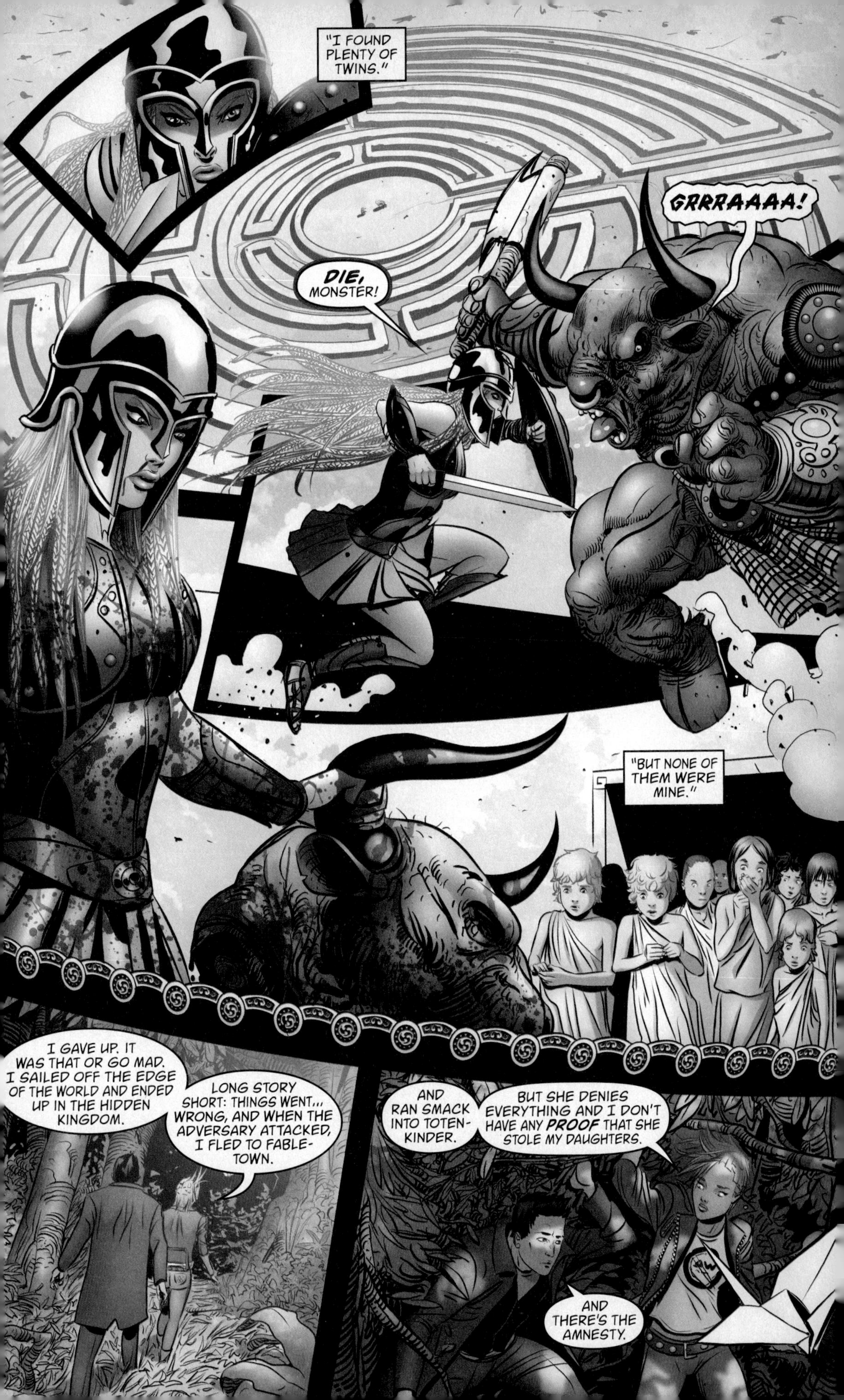
"I FOUND PLENTY OF TWINS."
DIE, MONSTER!
GRRRAAAA!
"BUT NONE OF THEM WERE MINE."
I GAVE UP. IT WAS THAT OR GO MAD. I SAILED OFF THE EDGE OF THE WORLD AND ENDED UP IN THE HIDDEN KINGDOM.
LONG STORY SHORT: THINGS WENT... WRONG, AND WHEN THE ADVERSARY ATTACKED, I FLED TO FABLE-TOWN.
AND RAN SMACK INTO TOTEN-KINDER.
BUT SHE DENIES EVERYTHING AND I DON'T HAVE ANY PROOF THAT SHE STOLE MY DAUGHTERS.
AND THERE'S THE AMNESTY.

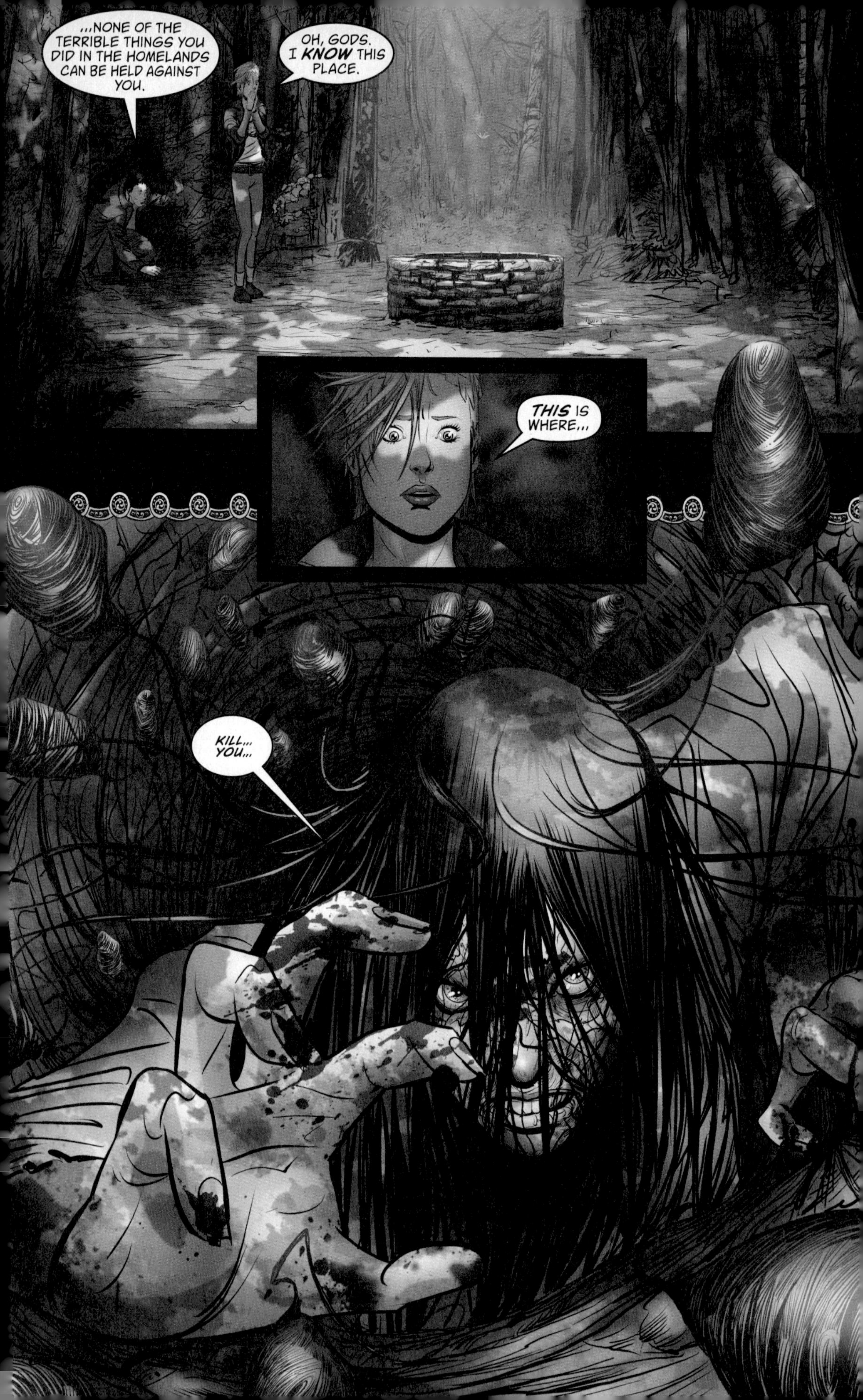
...NONE OF THE TERRIBLE THINGS YOU DID IN THE HOMELANDS CAN BE HELD AGAINST YOU.
OH, GODS. I KNOW THIS PLACE.
THIS IS WHERE...
KILL... YOU...

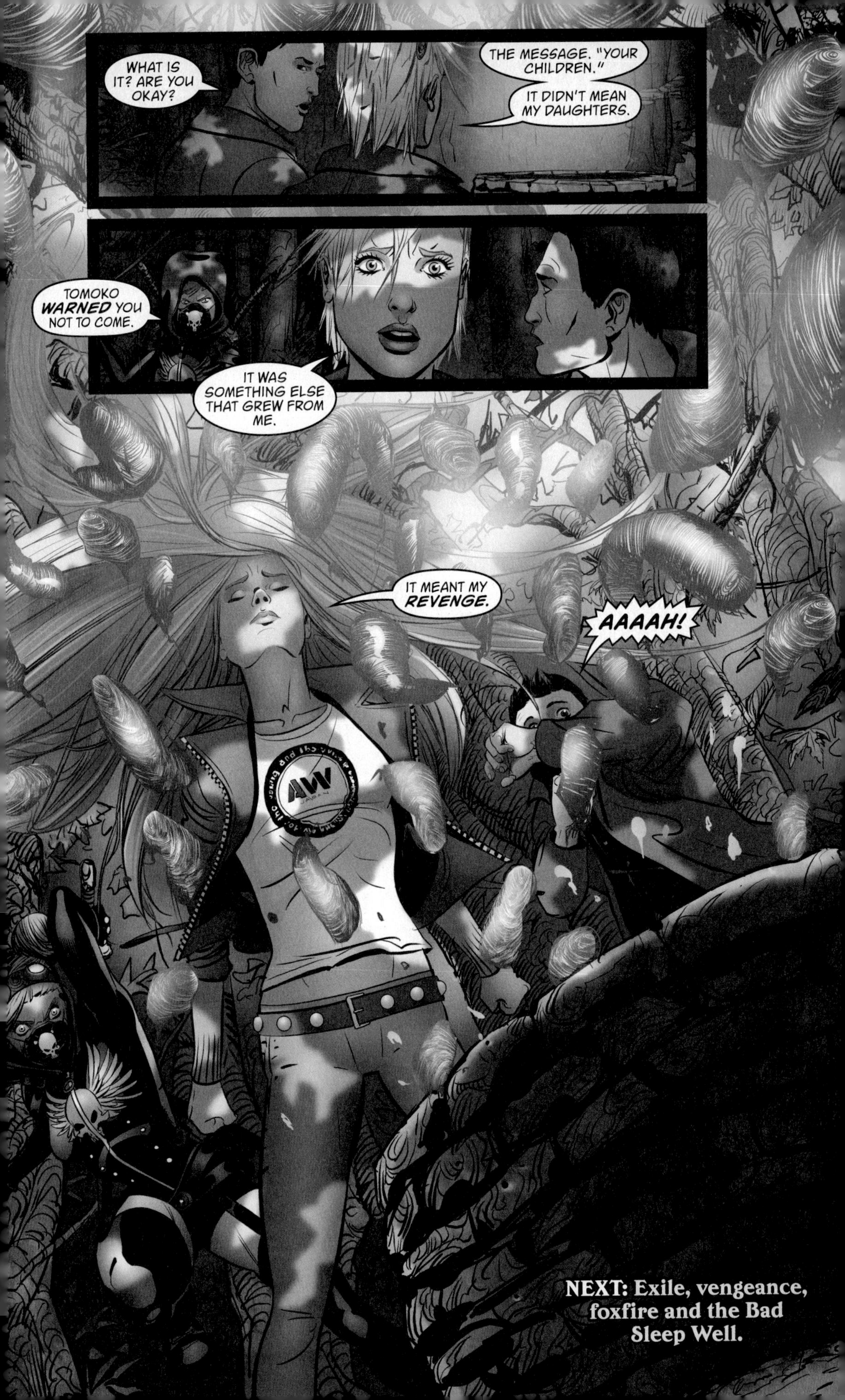
WHAT IS IT? ARE YOU OKAY?
THE MESSAGE. "YOUR CHILDREN."
IT DIDN'T MEAN MY DAUGHTERS.
TOMOKO WARNED YOU NOT TO COME.
IT WAS SOMETHING ELSE THAT GREW FROM ME.
IT MEANT MY REVENGE.
AAAAH!
NEXT: Exile, vengeance, foxfire and the Bad Sleep Well.

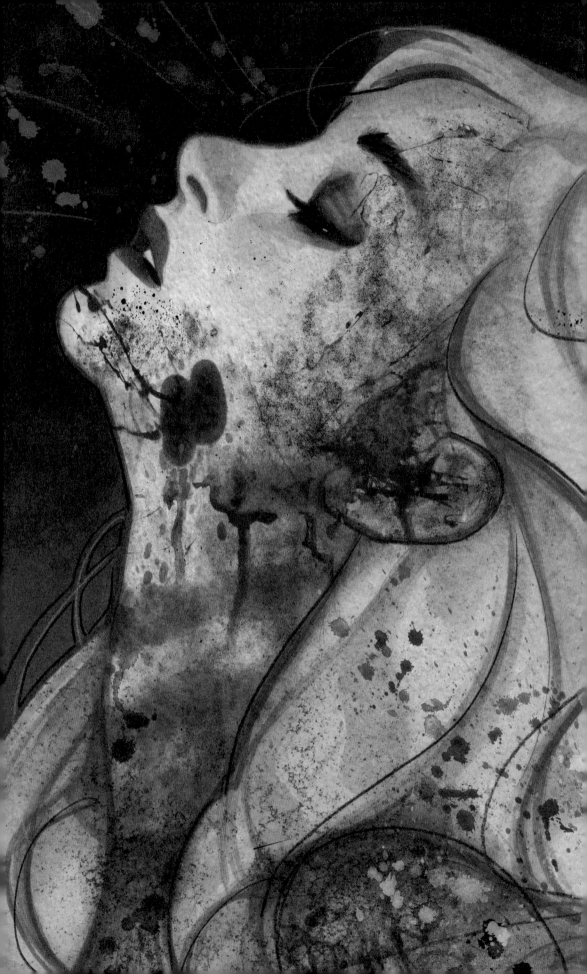

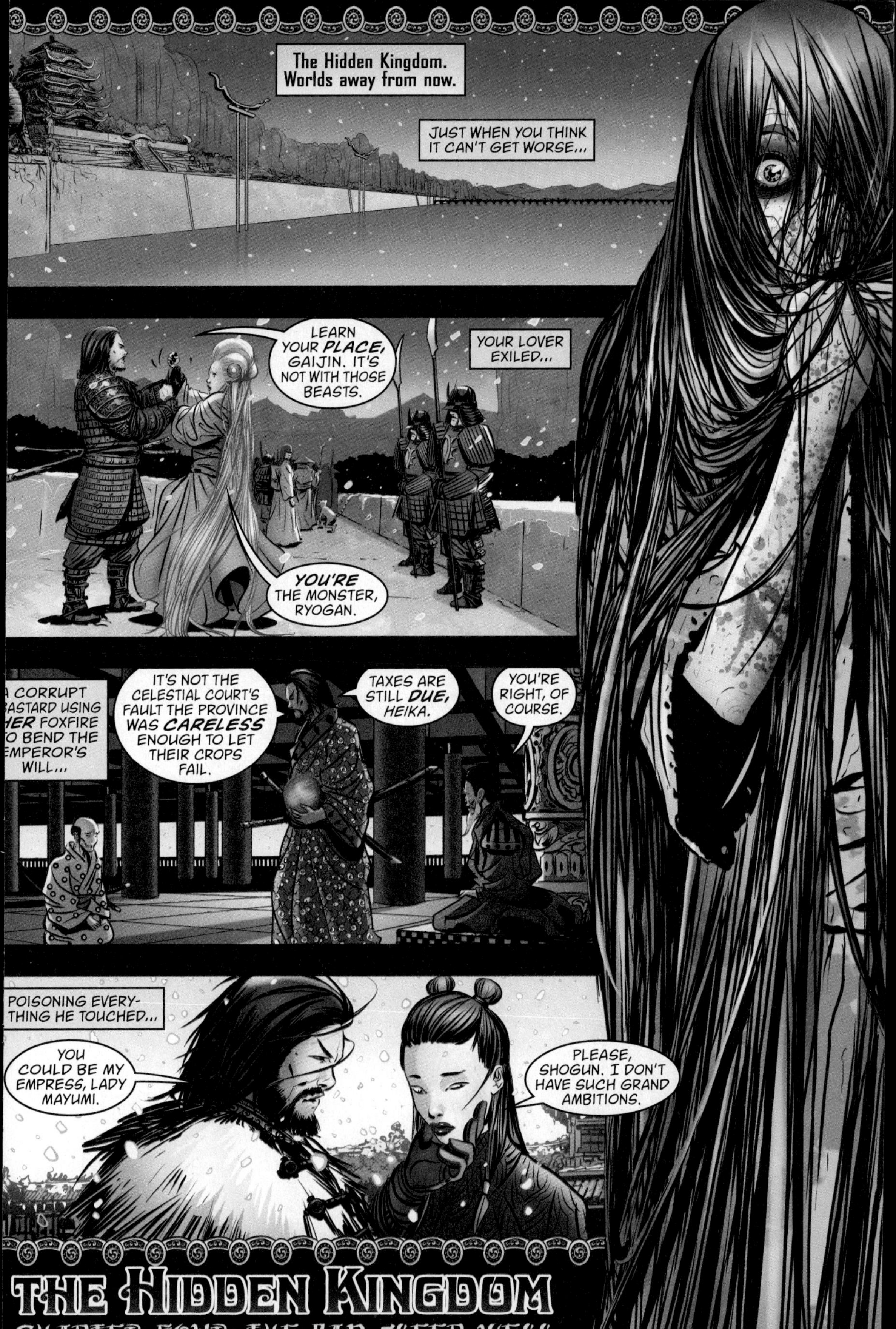

The Hidden Kingdom. Worlds away from now.
JUST WHEN YOU THINK IT CAN'T GET WORSE...
LEARN YOUR *PLACE,* GAIJIN. IT'S NOT WITH THOSE BEASTS.
YOUR LOVER EXILED...
YOU'RE THE MONSTER, RYOGAN.
A CORRUPT BASTARD USING *HER* FOXFIRE TO BEND THE EMPEROR'S WILL...
IT'S NOT THE CELESTIAL COURT'S FAULT THE PROVINCE WAS *CARELESS* ENOUGH TO LET THEIR CROPS FAIL.
TAXES ARE STILL *DUE,* HEIKA.
YOU'RE RIGHT, OF COURSE.
POISONING EVERYTHING HE TOUCHED...
YOU COULD BE MY EMPRESS, LADY MAYUMI.
PLEASE, SHOGUN. I DON'T HAVE SUCH GRAND AMBITIONS.

THE HIDDEN KINGDOM

CHAPTER FOUR: THE BAD SLEEP WELL

LAUREN BEUKES writer · **INAKI MIRANDA** artist · **EVA DE LA CRUZ** colors · **TODD KLEIN** letters · **ADAM HUGHES** cover

BILL WILLINGHAM consultant & Fables creator · **GREGORY LOCKARD** assistant editor · **SHELLY BOND** editor

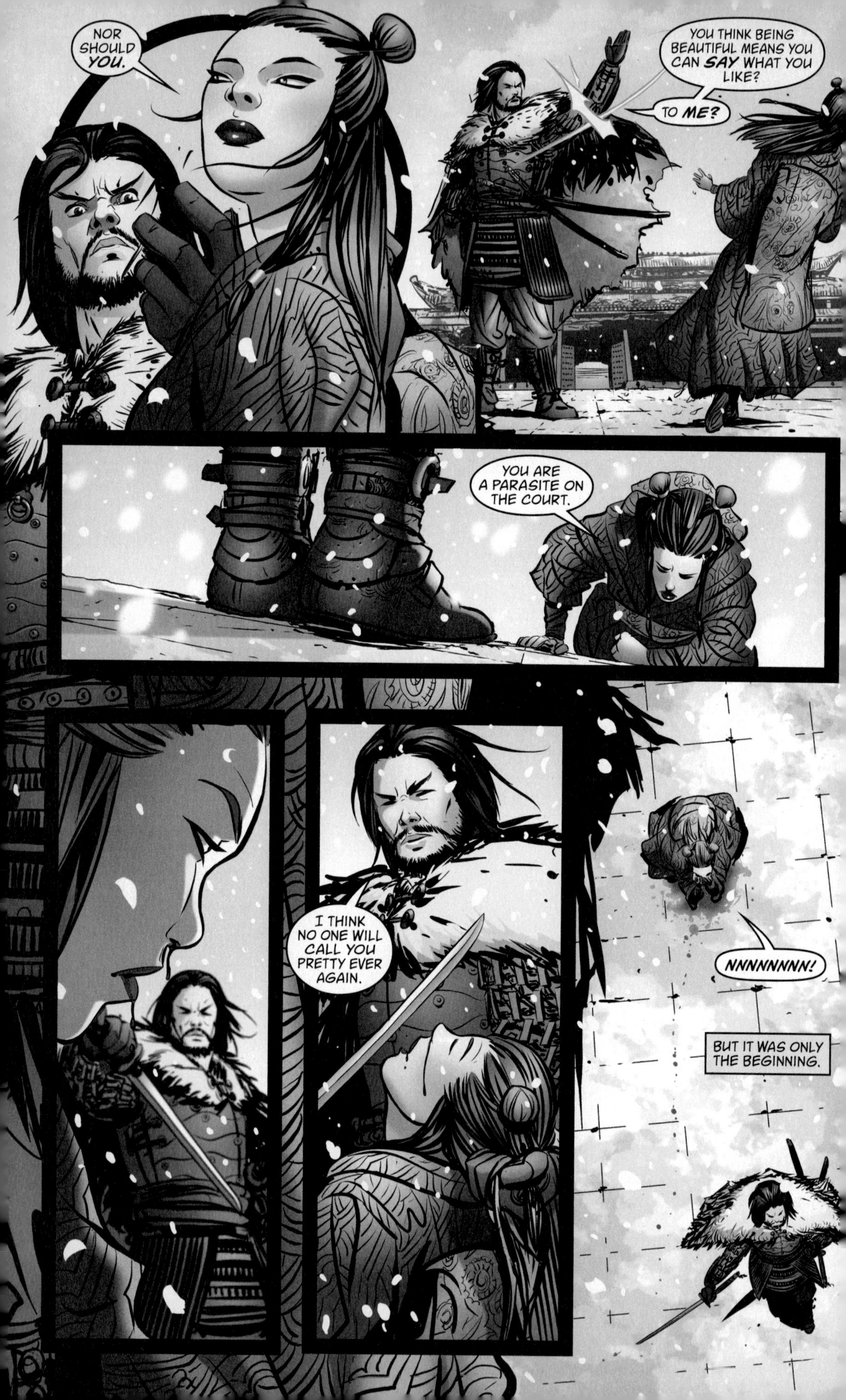
NOR SHOULD YOU.
YOU THINK BEING BEAUTIFUL MEANS YOU CAN SAY WHAT YOU LIKE?
TO ME?
YOU ARE A PARASITE ON THE COURT.
I THINK NO ONE WILL CALL YOU PRETTY EVER AGAIN.
NNNNNNN!
BUT IT WAS ONLY THE BEGINNING.

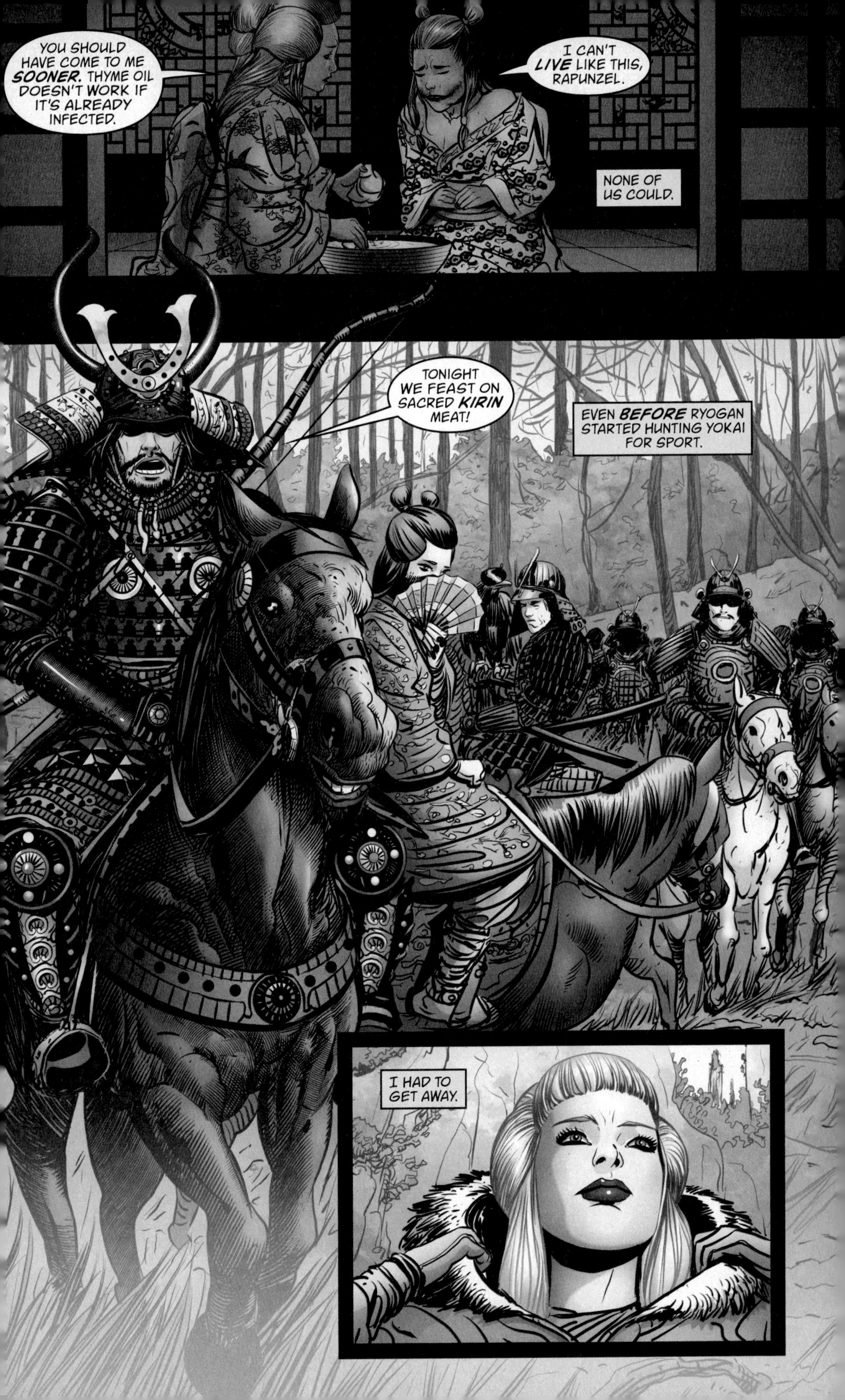
YOU SHOULD HAVE COME TO ME SOONER. THYME OIL DOESN'T WORK IF IT'S ALREADY INFECTED.
I CAN'T LIVE LIKE THIS, RAPUNZEL.
NONE OF US COULD.
TONIGHT WE FEAST ON SACRED KIRIN MEAT!
EVEN BEFORE RYOGAN STARTED HUNTING YOKAI FOR SPORT.
I HAD TO GET AWAY.

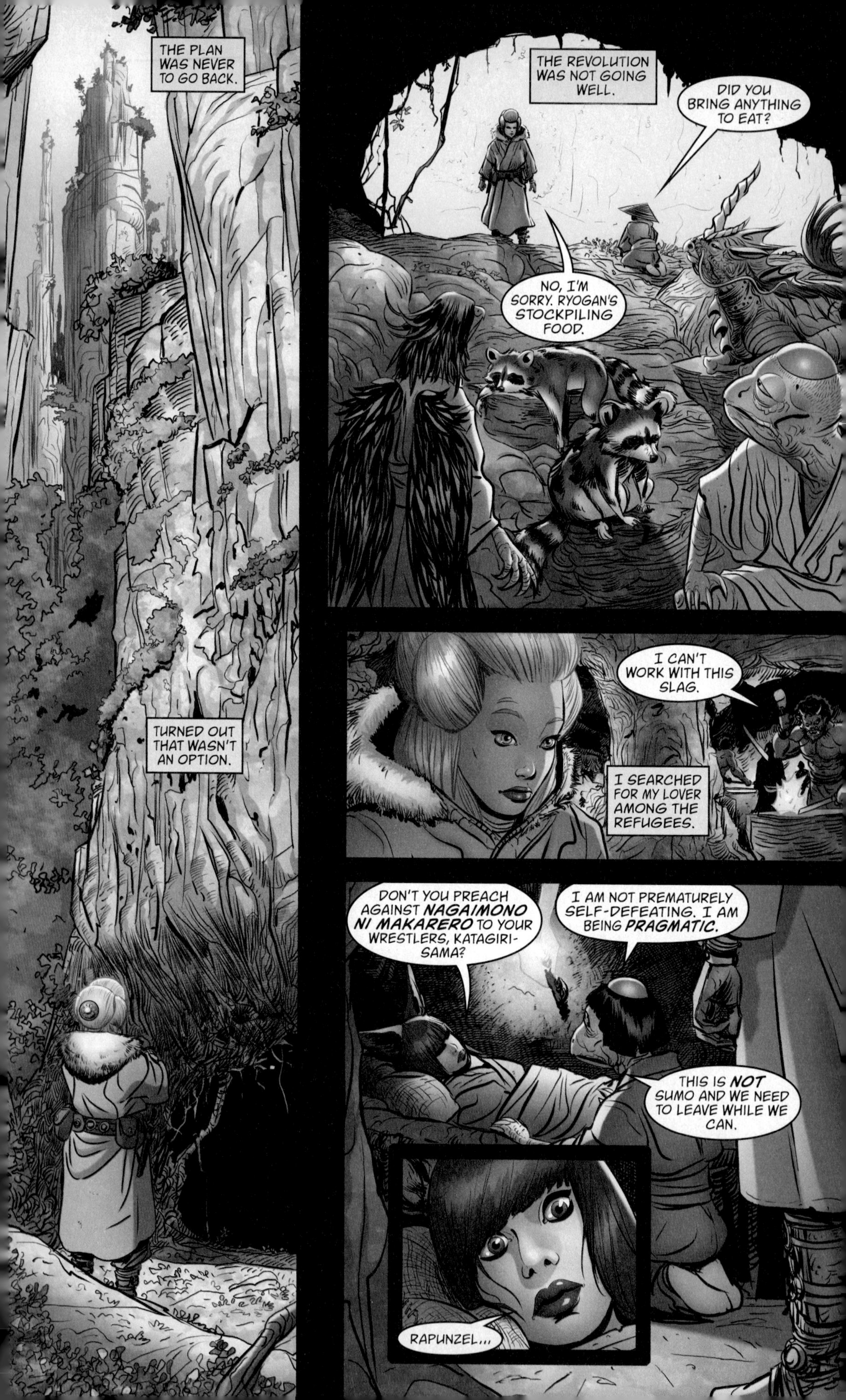
THE PLAN WAS NEVER TO GO BACK.
TURNED OUT THAT WASN'T AN OPTION.
THE REVOLUTION WAS NOT GOING WELL.
DID YOU BRING ANYTHING TO EAT?
NO, I'M SORRY. RYOGAN'S STOCKPILING FOOD.
I CAN'T WORK WITH THIS SLAG.
I SEARCHED FOR MY LOVER AMONG THE REFUGEES.
DON'T YOU PREACH AGAINST NAGAIMONO NI MAKARERO TO YOUR WRESTLERS, KATAGIRI-SAMA?
I AM NOT PREMATURELY SELF-DEFEATING. I AM BEING PRAGMATIC.
THIS IS NOT SUMO AND WE NEED TO LEAVE WHILE WE CAN.
RAPUNZEL...

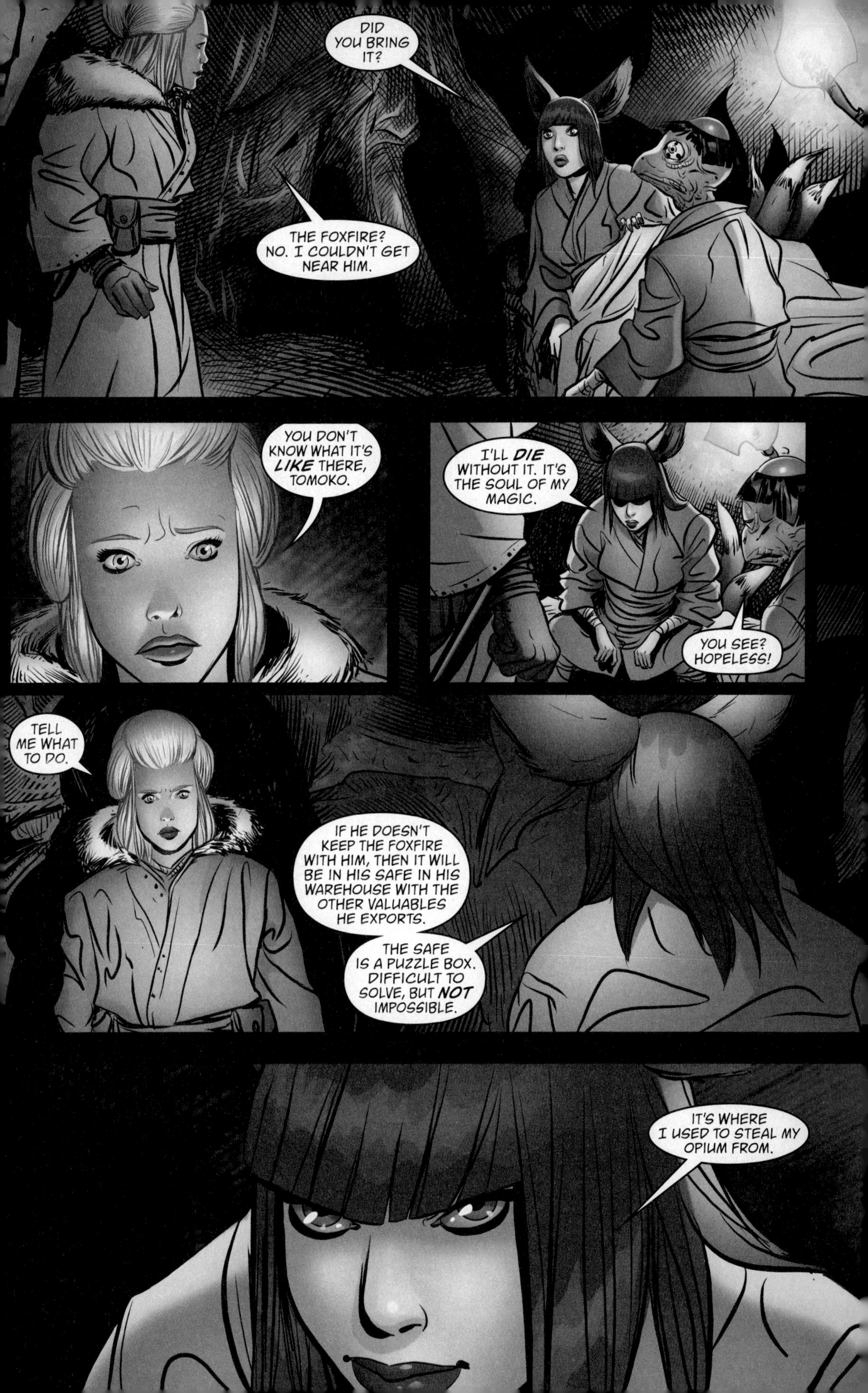
DID YOU BRING IT?
THE FOXFIRE? NO. I COULDN'T GET NEAR HIM.
YOU DON'T KNOW WHAT IT'S LIKE THERE, TOMOKO.
I'LL DIE WITHOUT IT. IT'S THE SOUL OF MY MAGIC.
YOU SEE? HOPELESS!
TELL ME WHAT TO DO.
IF HE DOESN'T KEEP THE FOXFIRE WITH HIM, THEN IT WILL BE IN HIS SAFE IN HIS WAREHOUSE WITH THE OTHER VALUABLES HE EXPORTS.
THE SAFE IS A PUZZLE BOX. DIFFICULT TO SOLVE, BUT NOT IMPOSSIBLE.
IT'S WHERE I USED TO STEAL MY OPIUM FROM.

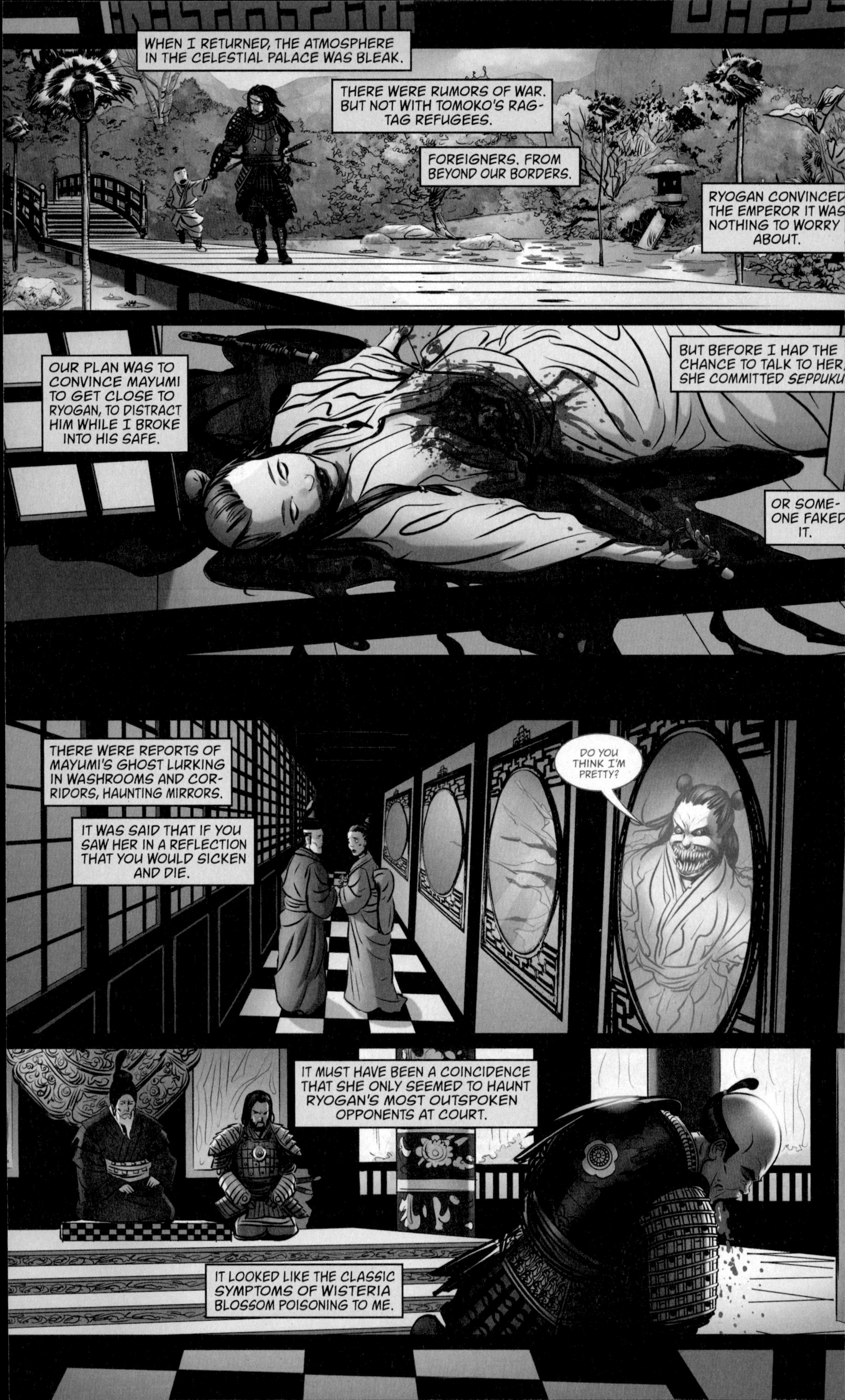
WHEN I RETURNED, THE ATMOSPHERE IN THE CELESTIAL PALACE WAS BLEAK.
THERE WERE RUMORS OF WAR. BUT NOT WITH TOMOKO'S RAG-TAG REFUGEES.
FOREIGNERS. FROM BEYOND OUR BORDERS.
RYOGAN CONVINCED THE EMPEROR IT WAS NOTHING TO WORRY ABOUT.
OUR PLAN WAS TO CONVINCE MAYUMI TO GET CLOSE TO RYOGAN, TO DISTRACT HIM WHILE I BROKE INTO HIS SAFE.
BUT BEFORE I HAD THE CHANCE TO TALK TO HER, SHE COMMITTED *SEPPUKU*
OR SOME-ONE FAKED IT.
THERE WERE REPORTS OF MAYUMI'S GHOST LURKING IN WASHROOMS AND COR-RIDORS, HAUNTING MIRRORS.
IT WAS SAID THAT IF YOU SAW HER IN A REFLECTION THAT YOU WOULD SICKEN AND DIE.
DO YOU THINK I'M PRETTY?
IT MUST HAVE BEEN A COINCIDENCE THAT SHE ONLY SEEMED TO HAUNT RYOGAN'S MOST OUTSPOKEN OPPONENTS AT COURT.
IT LOOKED LIKE THE CLASSIC SYMPTOMS OF WISTERIA BLOSSOM POISONING TO ME.

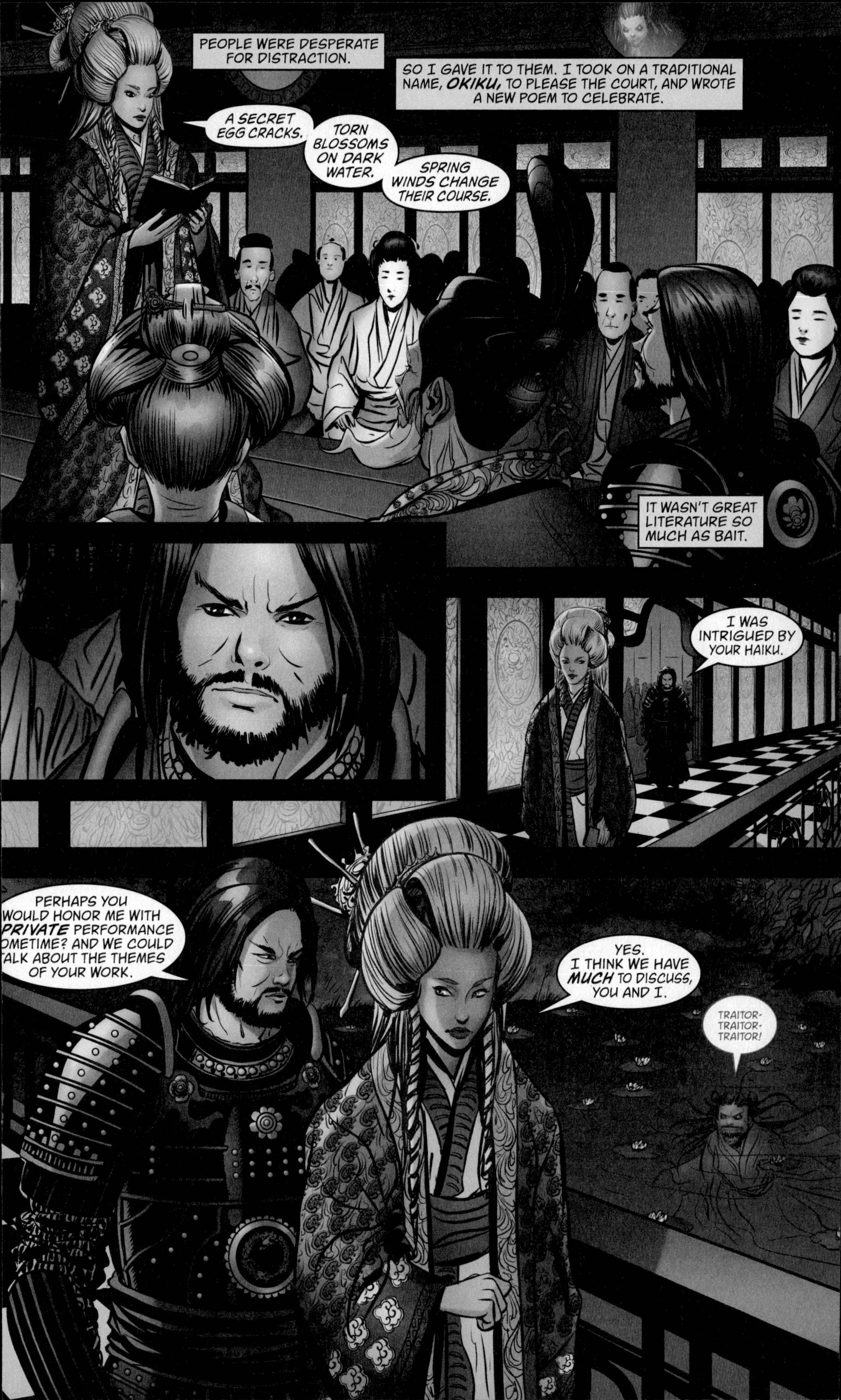
PEOPLE WERE DESPERATE FOR DISTRACTION.
SO I GAVE IT TO THEM. I TOOK ON A TRADITIONAL NAME, OKIKU, TO PLEASE THE COURT, AND WROTE A NEW POEM TO CELEBRATE.
A SECRET EGG CRACKS.
TORN BLOSSOMS ON DARK WATER.
SPRING WINDS CHANGE THEIR COURSE.
IT WASN'T GREAT LITERATURE SO MUCH AS BAIT.
I WAS INTRIGUED BY YOUR HAIKU.
PERHAPS YOU WOULD HONOR ME WITH PRIVATE PERFORMANCE OMETIME? AND WE COULD TALK ABOUT THE THEMES OF YOUR WORK.
YES. I THINK WE HAVE MUCH TO DISCUSS, YOU AND I.
TRAITOR-TRAITOR-TRAITOR!

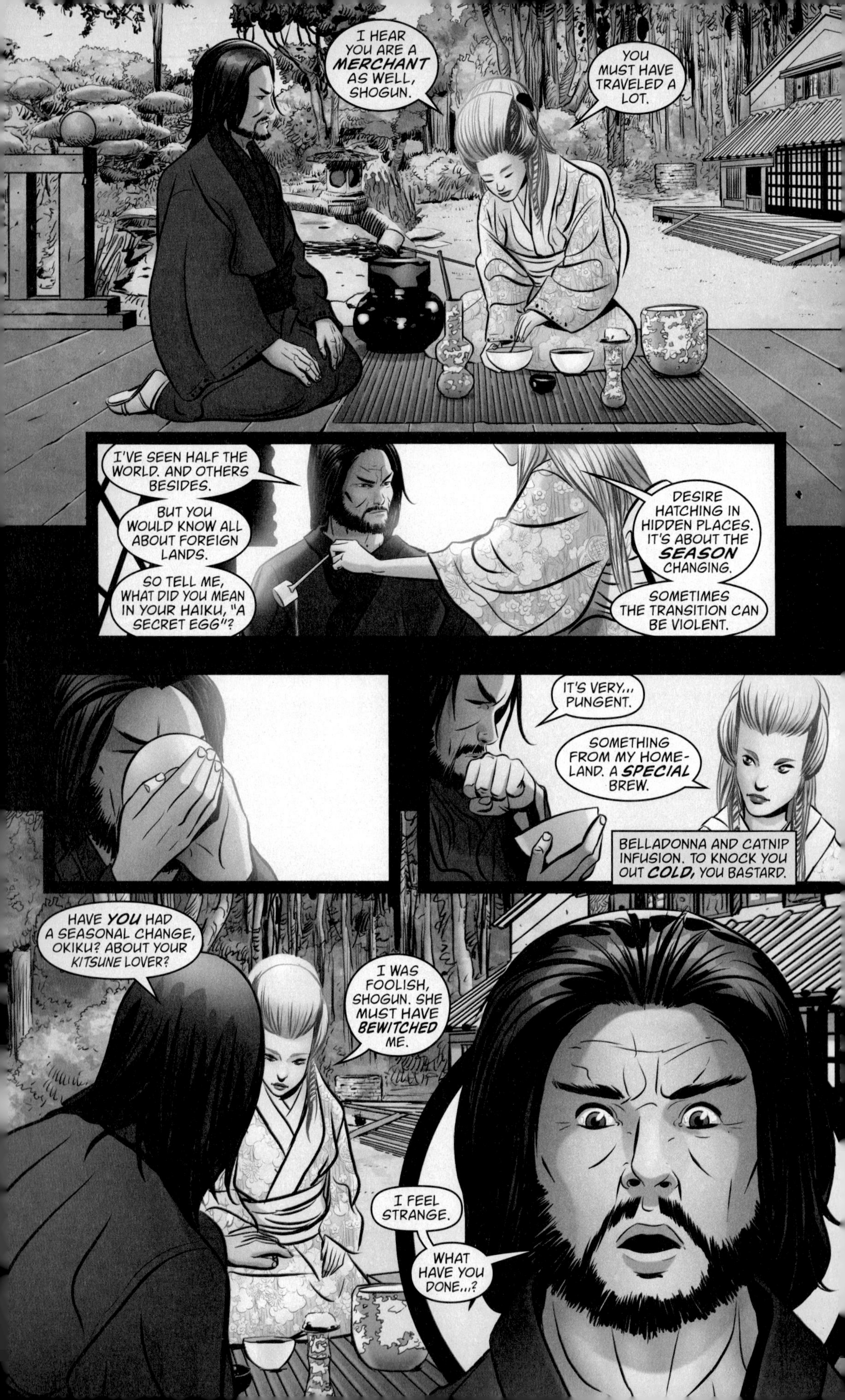
I HEAR YOU ARE A MERCHANT AS WELL, SHOGUN.
YOU MUST HAVE TRAVELED A LOT.
I'VE SEEN HALF THE WORLD. AND OTHERS BESIDES.
BUT YOU WOULD KNOW ALL ABOUT FOREIGN LANDS.
SO TELL ME, WHAT DID YOU MEAN IN YOUR HAIKU, "A SECRET EGG"?
DESIRE HATCHING IN HIDDEN PLACES. IT'S ABOUT THE SEASON CHANGING.
SOMETIMES THE TRANSITION CAN BE VIOLENT.
IT'S VERY... PUNGENT.
SOMETHING FROM MY HOME-LAND. A SPECIAL BREW.
BELLADONNA AND CATNIP INFUSION. TO KNOCK YOU OUT COLD, YOU BASTARD.
HAVE YOU HAD A SEASONAL CHANGE, OKIKU? ABOUT YOUR KITSUNE LOVER?
I WAS FOOLISH, SHOGUN. SHE MUST HAVE BEWITCHED ME.
I FEEL STRANGE.
WHAT HAVE YOU DONE...?

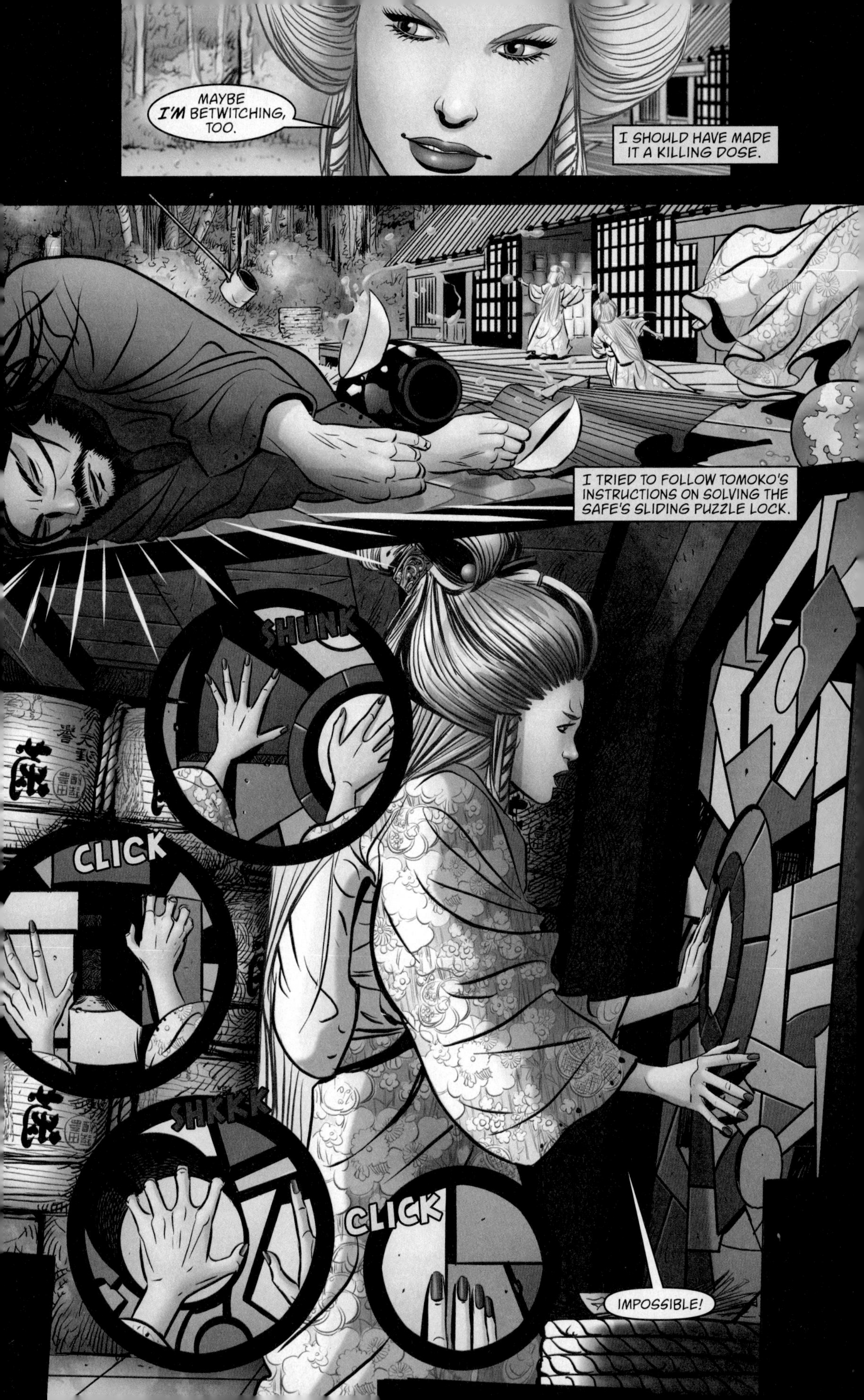
MAYBE I'M BETWITCHING, TOO.
I SHOULD HAVE MADE IT A KILLING DOSE.
I TRIED TO FOLLOW TOMOKO'S INSTRUCTIONS ON SOLVING THE SAFE'S SLIDING PUZZLE LOCK.
SHUNK
CLICK
SHKKK
CLICK
IMPOSSIBLE!

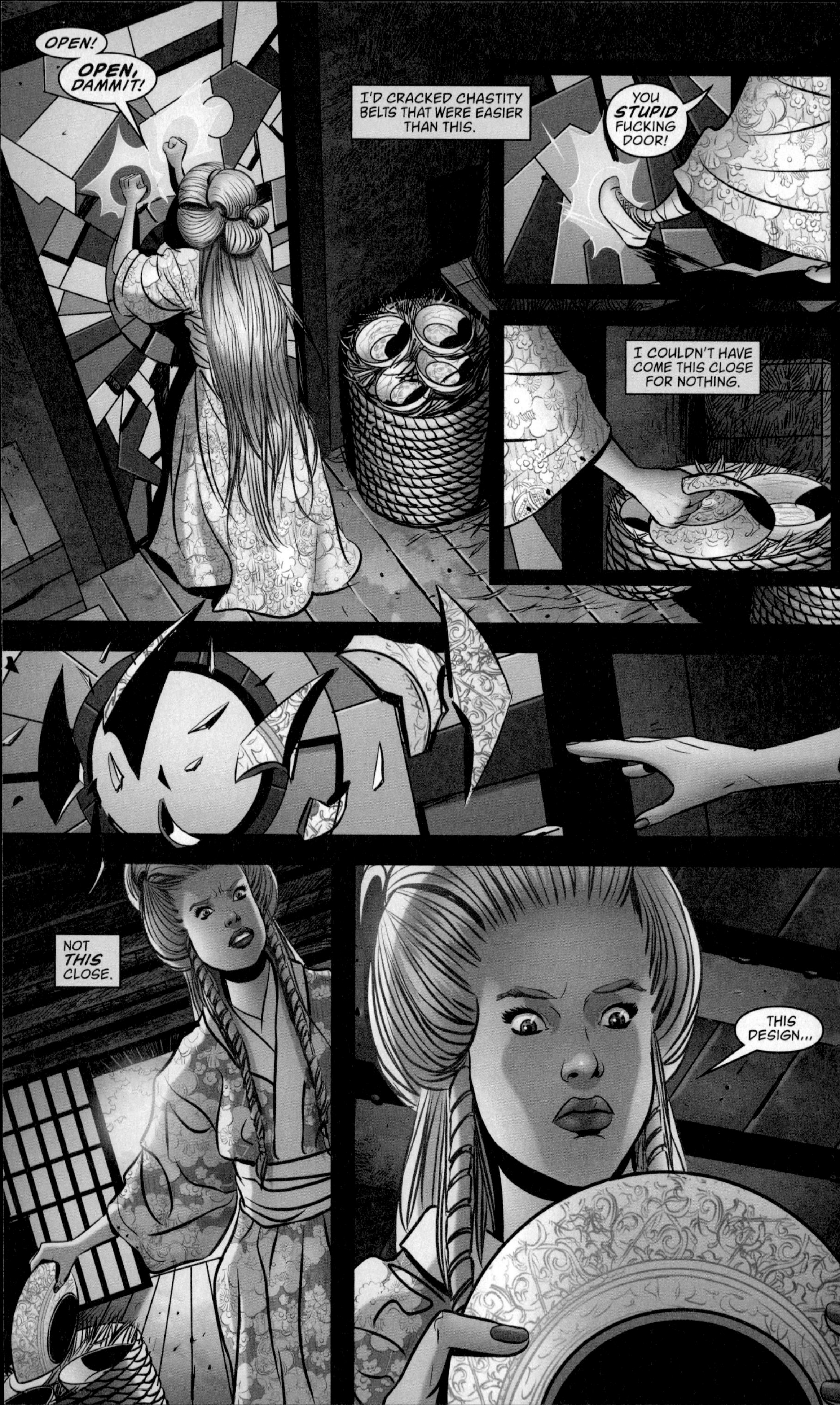
OPEN!
OPEN, DAMMIT!
I'D CRACKED CHASTITY BELTS THAT WERE EASIER THAN THIS.
YOU STUPID FUCKING DOOR!
I COULDN'T HAVE COME THIS CLOSE FOR NOTHING.
NOT THIS CLOSE.
THIS DESIGN...

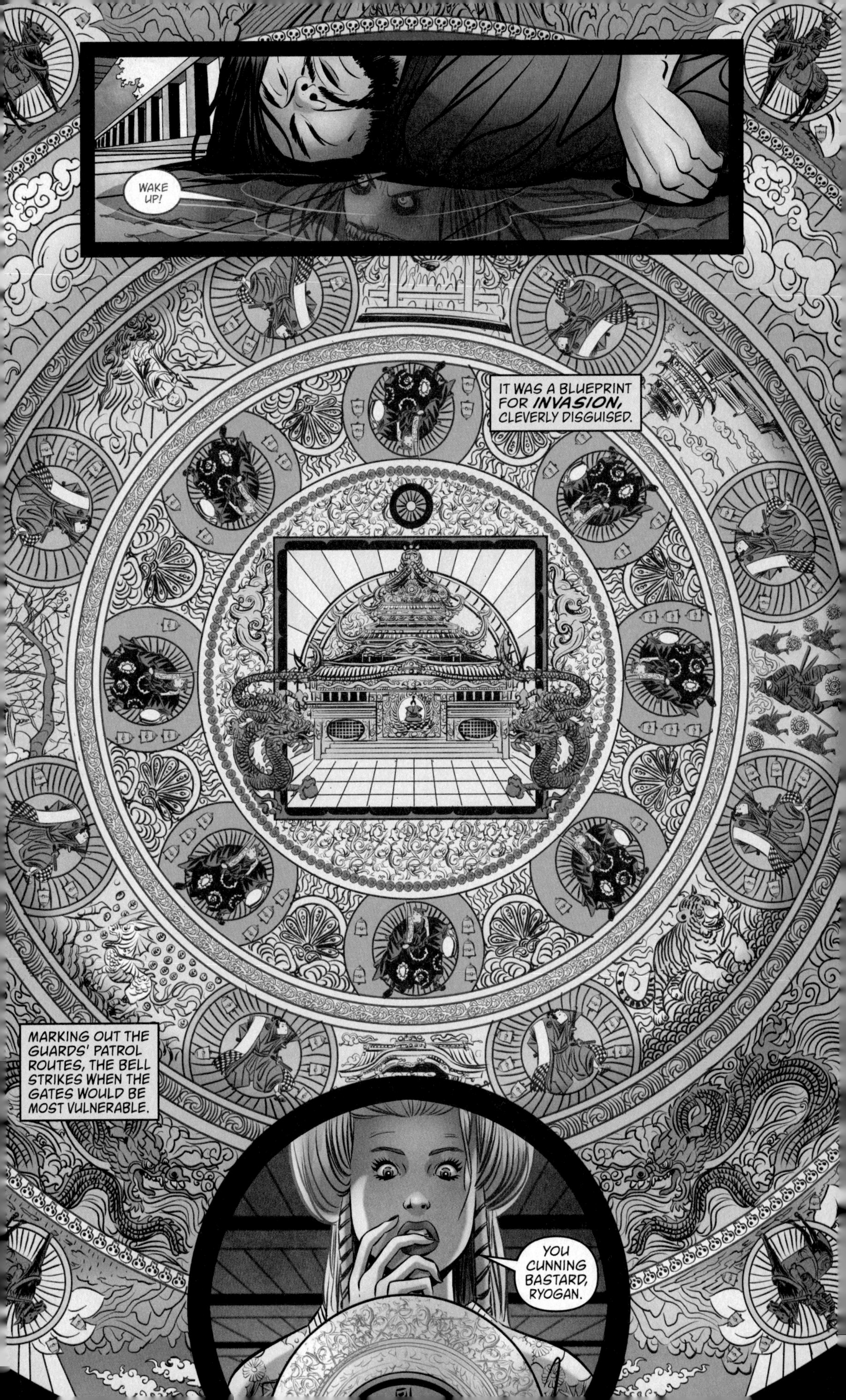
WAKE UP!
IT WAS A BLUEPRINT FOR INVASION, CLEVERLY DISGUISED.
MARKING OUT THE GUARDS' PATROL ROUTES, THE BELL STRIKES WHEN THE GATES WOULD BE MOST VULNERABLE.
YOU CUNNING BASTARD, RYOGAN.

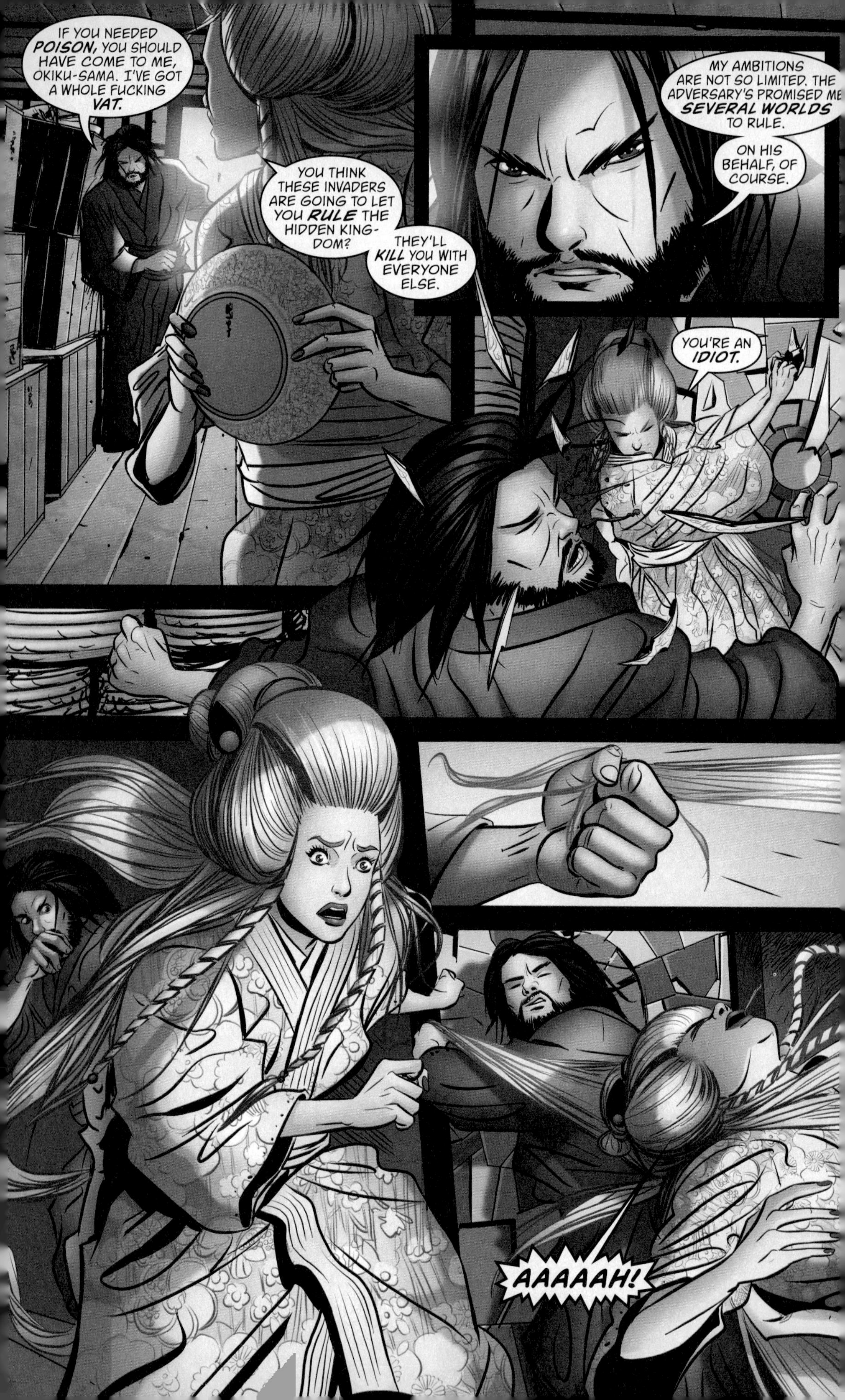
IF YOU NEEDED POISON, YOU SHOULD HAVE COME TO ME, OKIKU-SAMA. I'VE GOT A WHOLE FUCKING VAT.
YOU THINK THESE INVADERS ARE GOING TO LET YOU RULE THE HIDDEN KING-DOM?
THEY'LL KILL YOU WITH EVERYONE ELSE.
MY AMBITIONS ARE NOT SO LIMITED. THE ADVERSARY'S PROMISED ME SEVERAL WORLDS TO RULE.
ON HIS BEHALF, OF COURSE.
YOU'RE AN IDIOT.
AAAAAH!

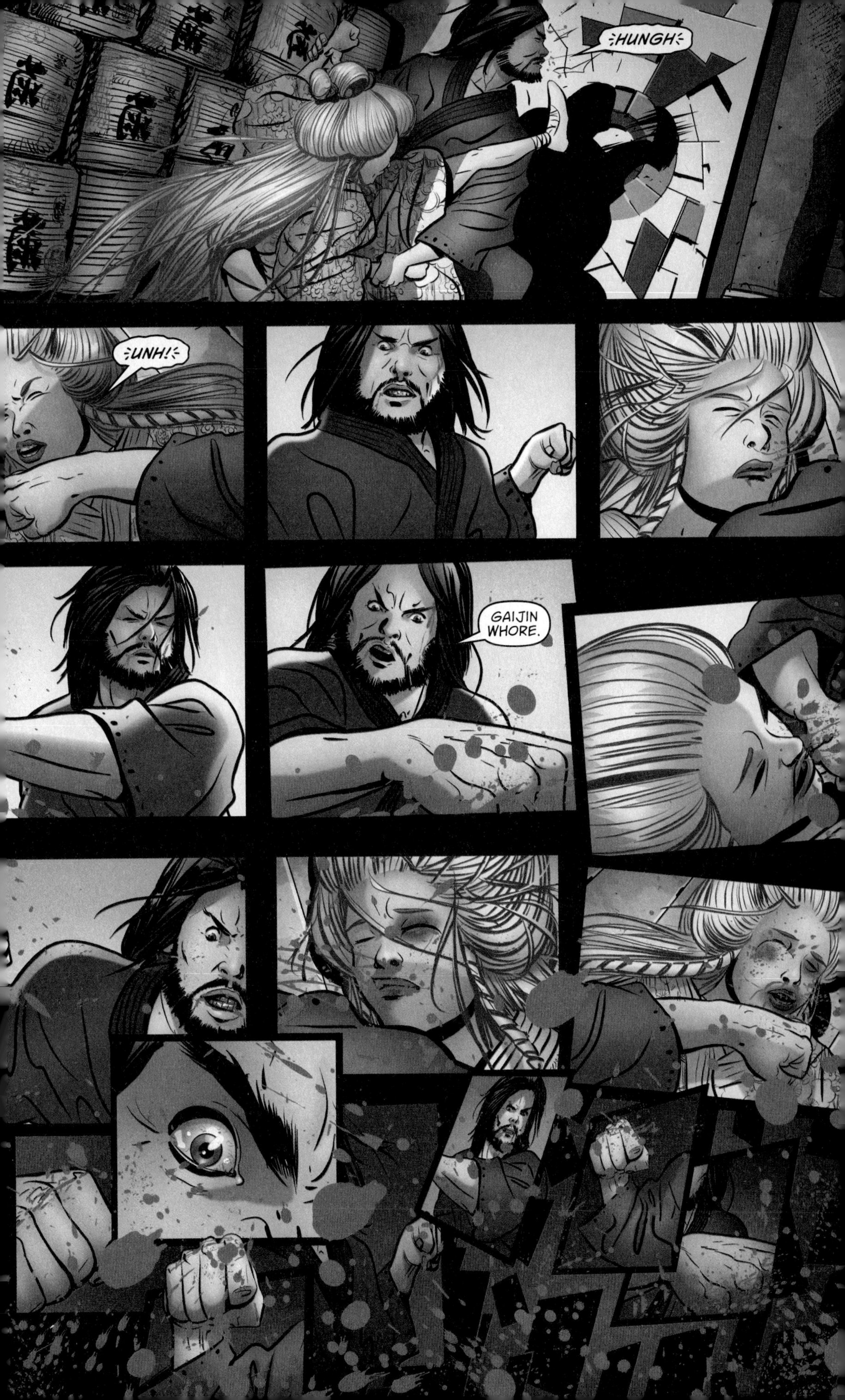
HUNGH
UNH!
GAIJIN WHORE.

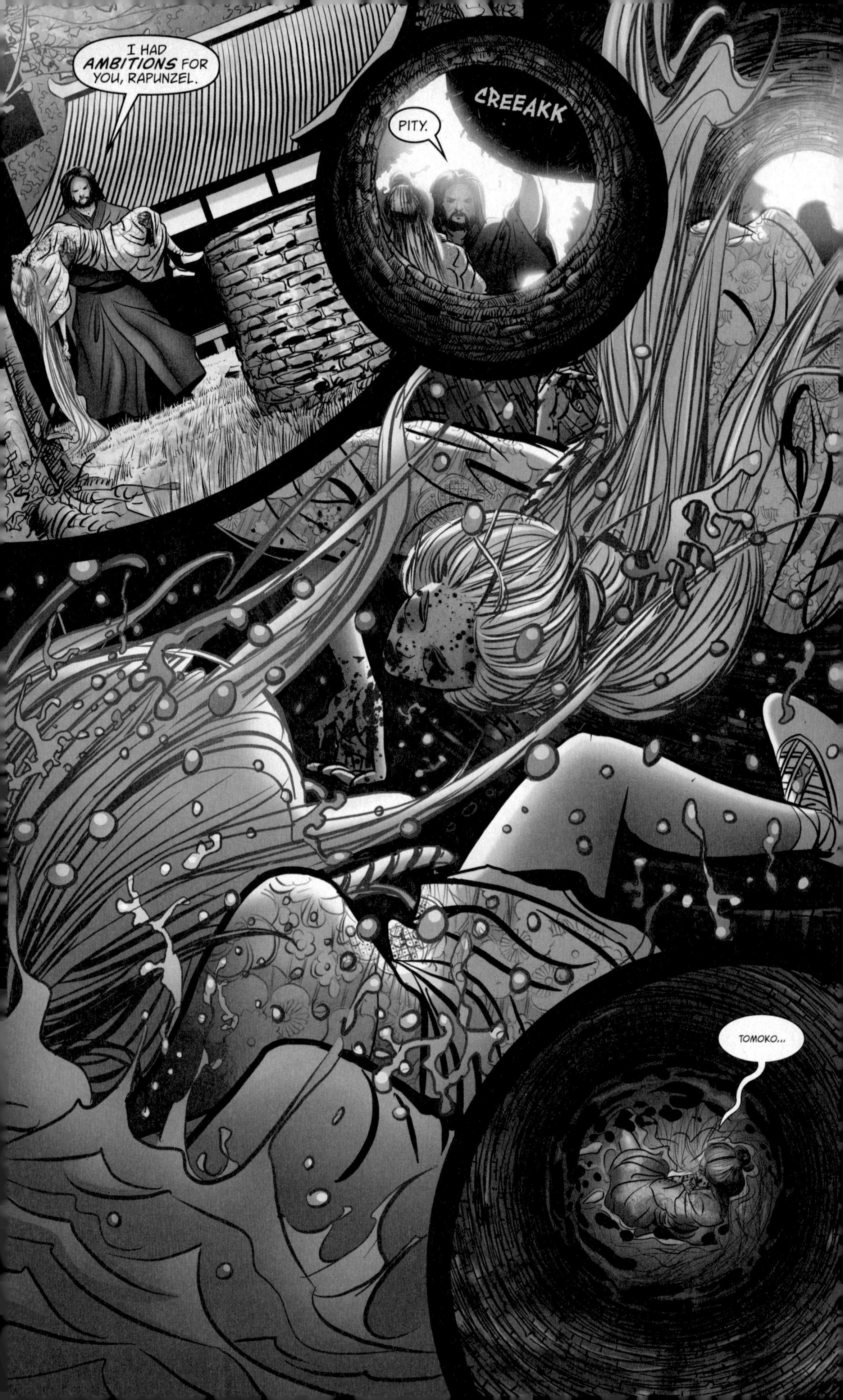
I HAD AMBITIONS FOR YOU, RAPUNZEL.
PITY.
CREEAKK
TOMOKO...

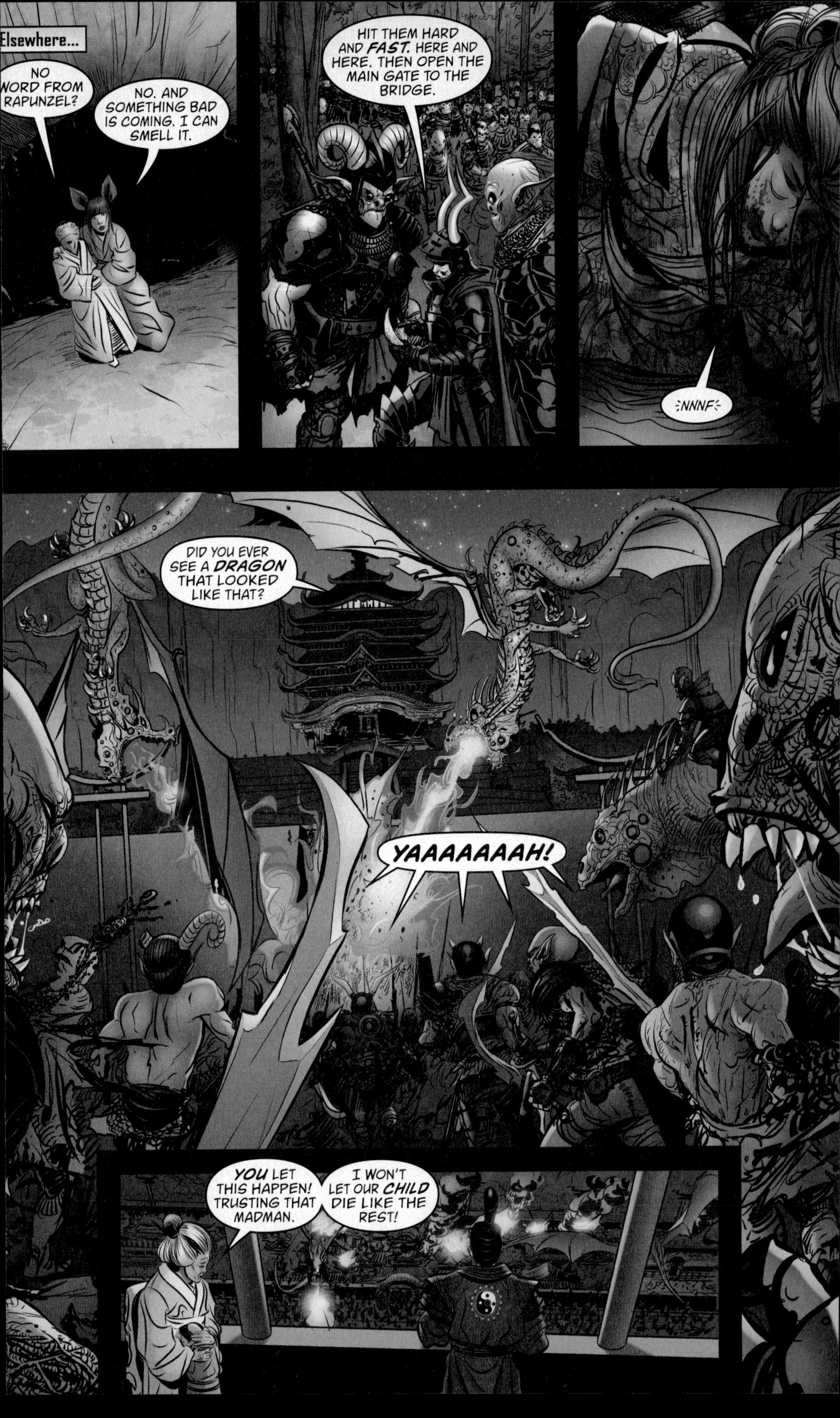
Elsewhere...
NO WORD FROM RAPUNZEL?
NO. AND SOMETHING BAD IS COMING. I CAN SMELL IT.
HIT THEM HARD AND FAST. HERE AND HERE. THEN OPEN THE MAIN GATE TO THE BRIDGE.
NNNF
DID YOU EVER SEE A DRAGON THAT LOOKED LIKE THAT?
YAAAAAAAH!
YOU LET THIS HAPPEN! TRUSTING THAT MADMAN.
I WON'T LET OUR CHILD DIE LIKE THE REST!

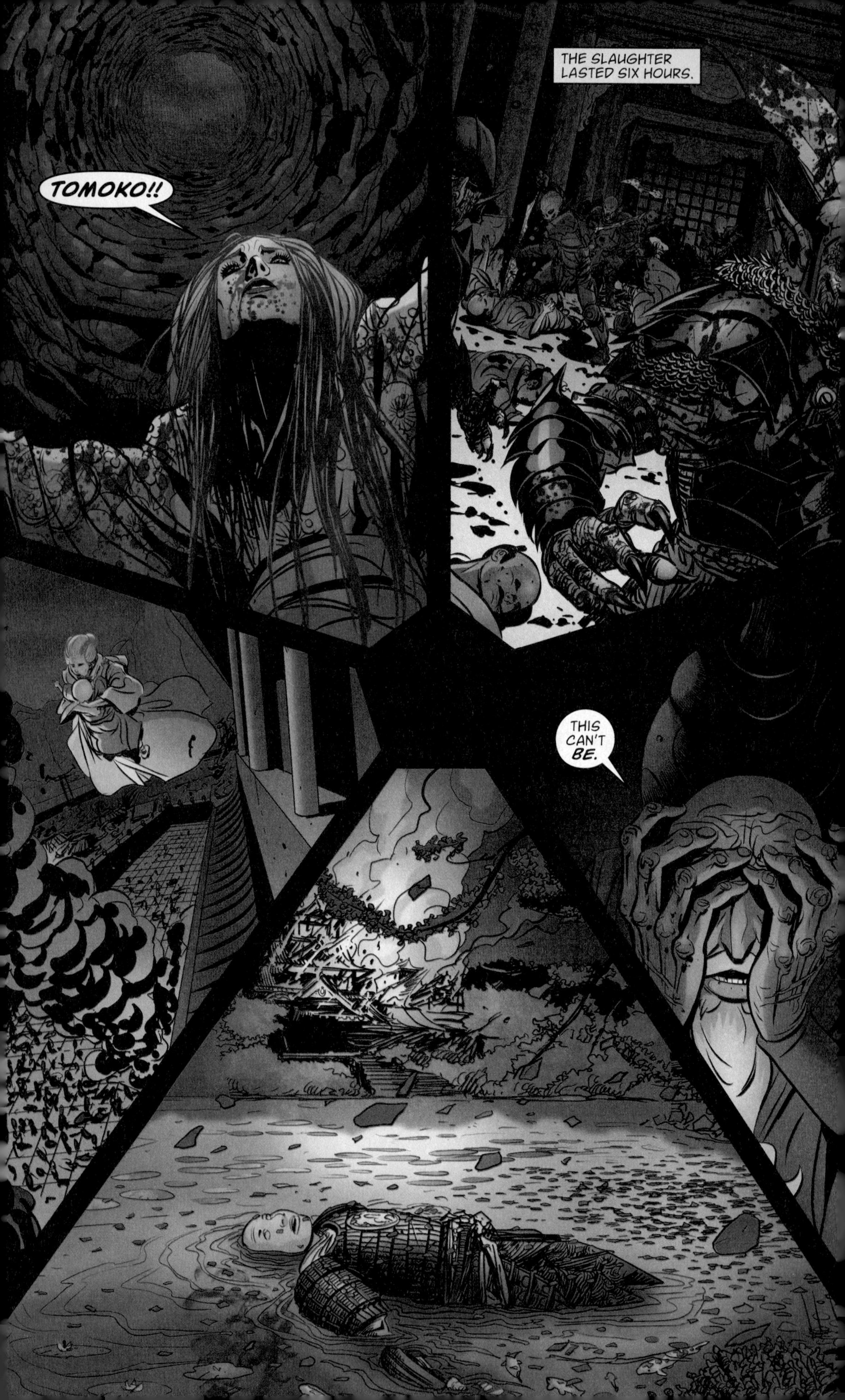
TOMOKO!!
THE SLAUGHTER LASTED SIX HOURS.
THIS CAN'T BE.

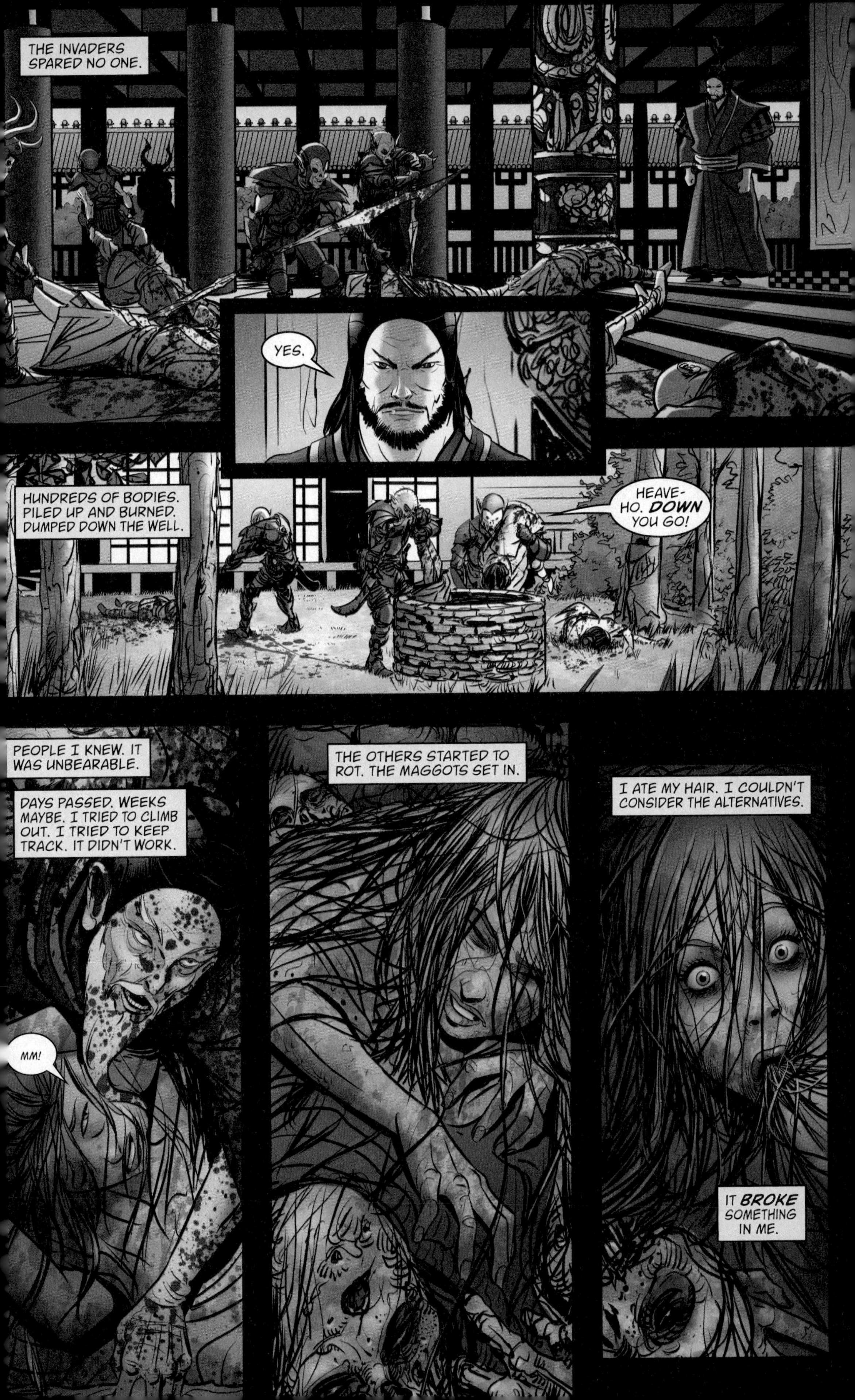
THE INVADERS SPARED NO ONE.
YES.
HUNDREDS OF BODIES. PILED UP AND BURNED. DUMPED DOWN THE WELL.
HEAVE-HO. DOWN YOU GO!
PEOPLE I KNEW. IT WAS UNBEARABLE.
DAYS PASSED. WEEKS MAYBE. I TRIED TO CLIMB OUT. I TRIED TO KEEP TRACK. IT DIDN'T WORK.
MM!
THE OTHERS STARTED TO ROT. THE MAGGOTS SET IN.
I ATE MY HAIR. I COULDN'T CONSIDER THE ALTERNATIVES.
IT BROKE SOMETHING IN ME.

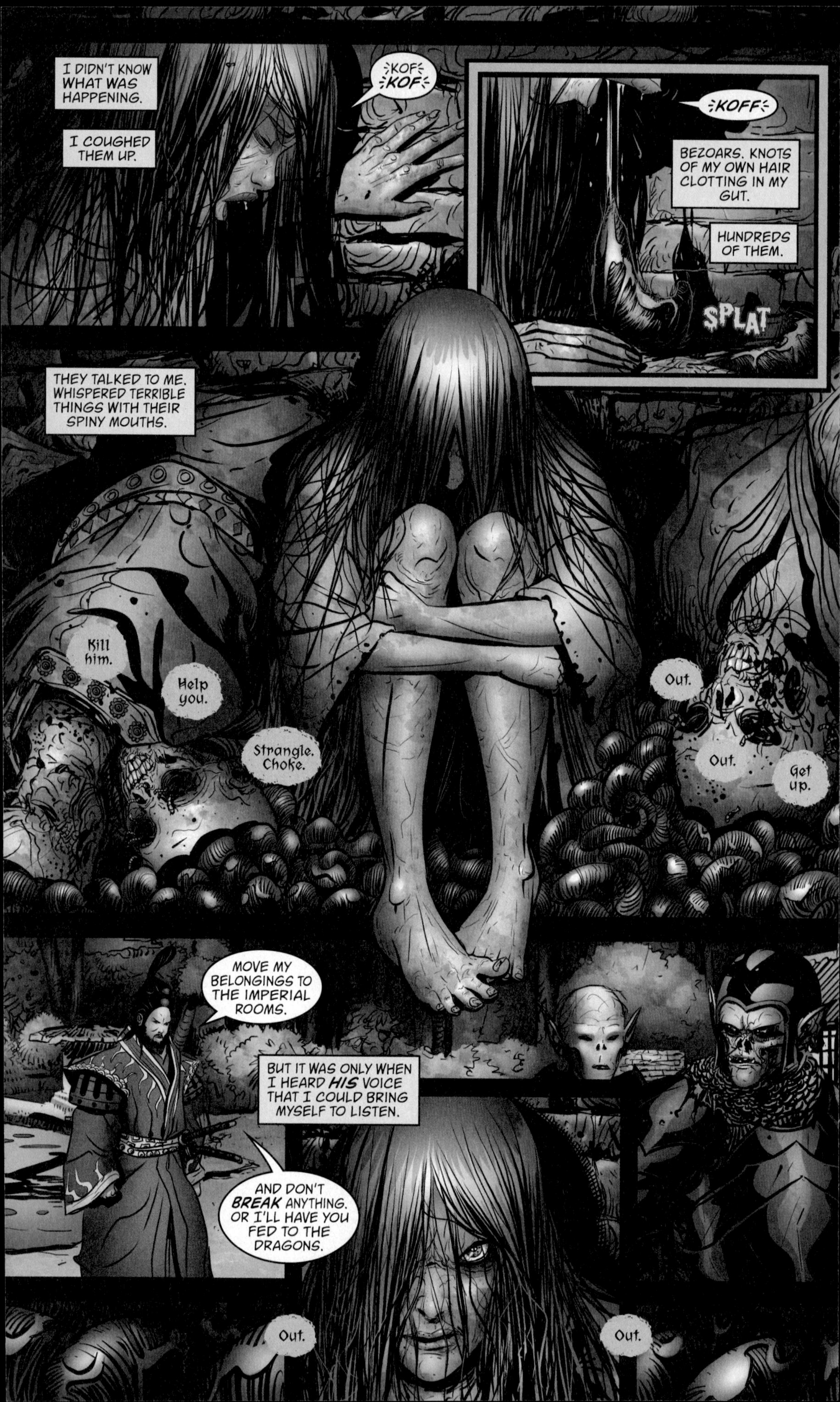

I DIDN'T KNOW WHAT WAS HAPPENING.
I COUGHED THEM UP.
KOF KOF
KOFF
BEZOARS. KNOTS OF MY OWN HAIR CLOTTING IN MY GUT.
HUNDREDS OF THEM.
SPLAT
THEY TALKED TO ME. WHISPERED TERRIBLE THINGS WITH THEIR SPINY MOUTHS.
Kill him.
Help you.
Strangle. Choke.
Out.
Out.
Get up.
MOVE MY BELONGINGS TO THE IMPERIAL ROOMS.
BUT IT WAS ONLY WHEN I HEARD HIS VOICE THAT I COULD BRING MYSELF TO LISTEN.
AND DON'T BREAK ANYTHING. OR I'LL HAVE YOU FED TO THE DRAGONS.
Out.
Out.

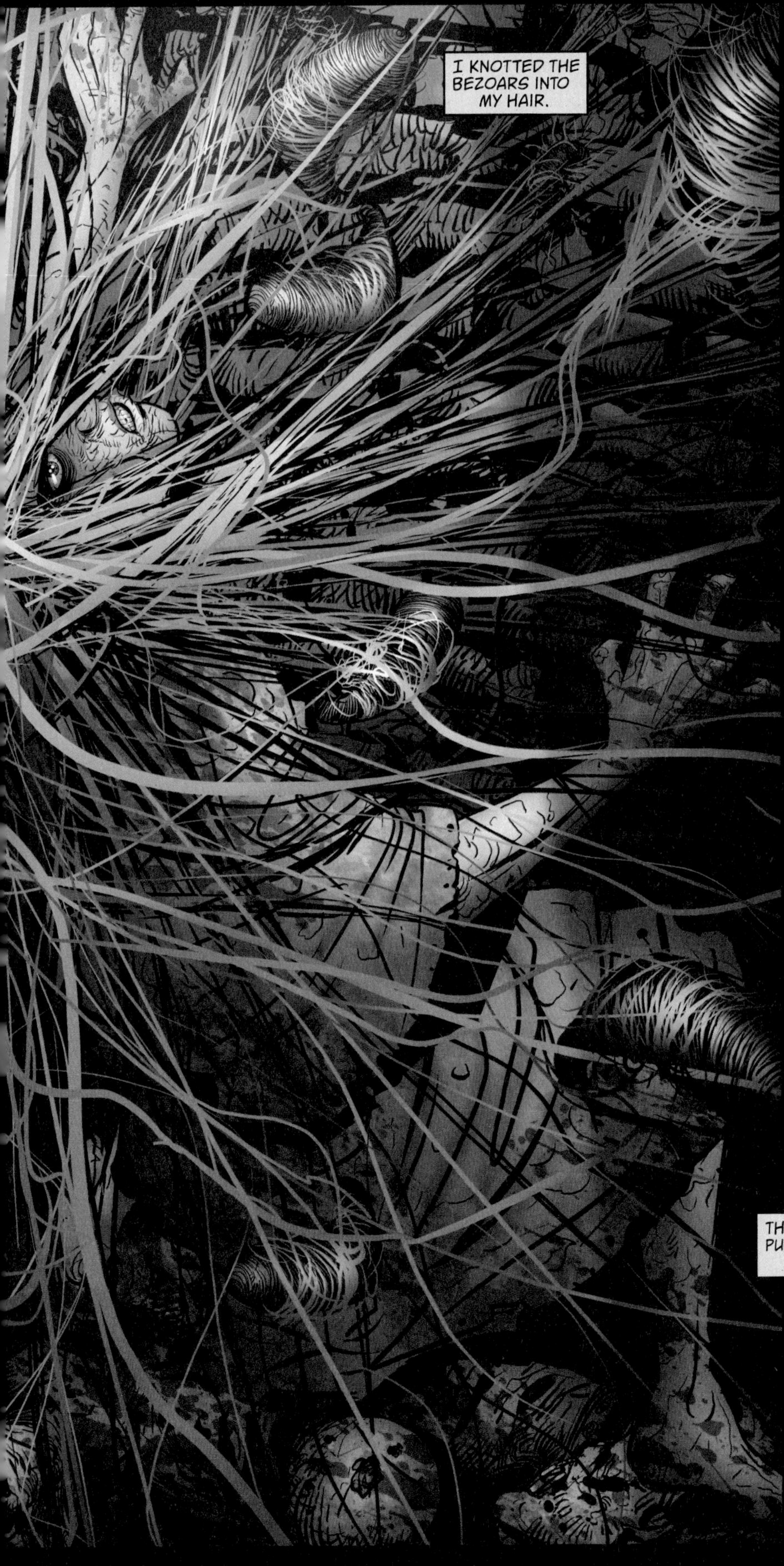
I KNOTTED THE BEZOARS INTO MY HAIR.
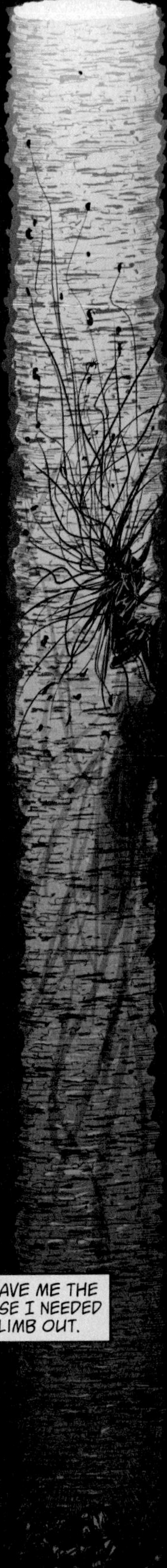
THEY GAVE ME THE PURCHASE I NEEDED TO CLIMB OUT.

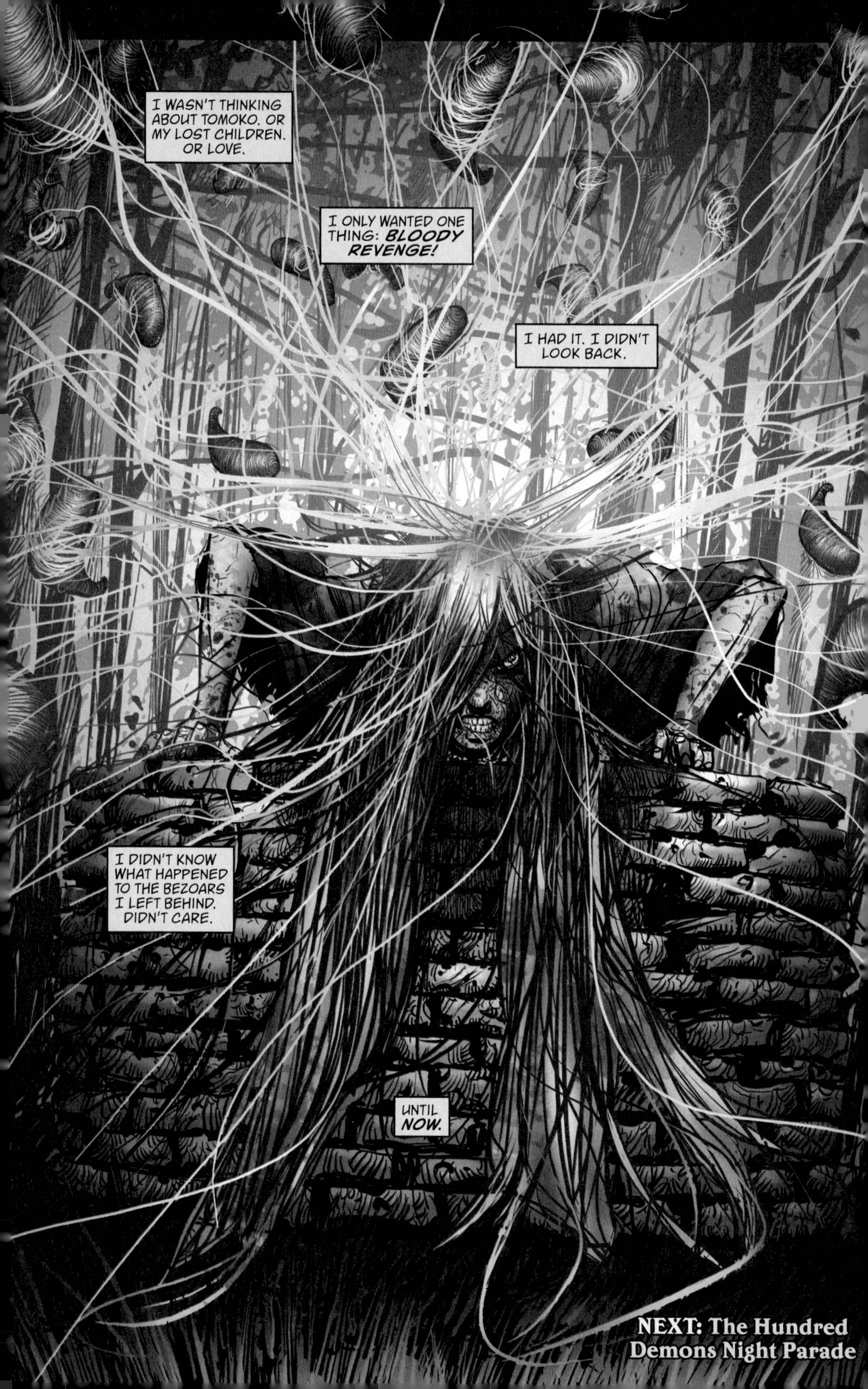
I WASN'T THINKING ABOUT TOMOKO. OR MY LOST CHILDREN. OR LOVE.
I ONLY WANTED ONE THING: BLOODY REVENGE!
I HAD IT. I DIDN'T LOOK BACK.
I DIDN'T KNOW WHAT HAPPENED TO THE BEZOARS I LEFT BEHIND. DIDN'T CARE.
UNTIL NOW.
NEXT: The Hundred Demons Night Parade

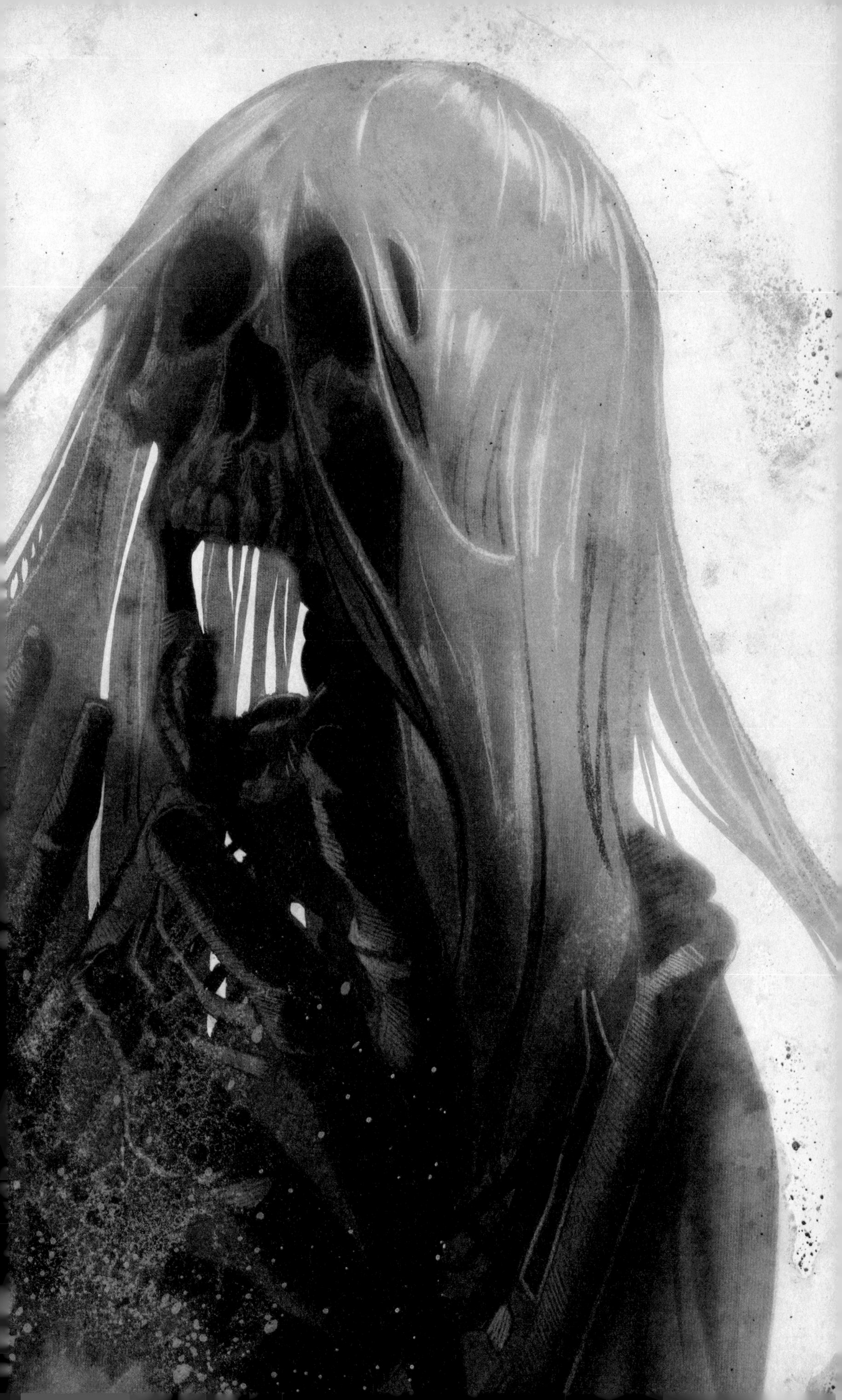

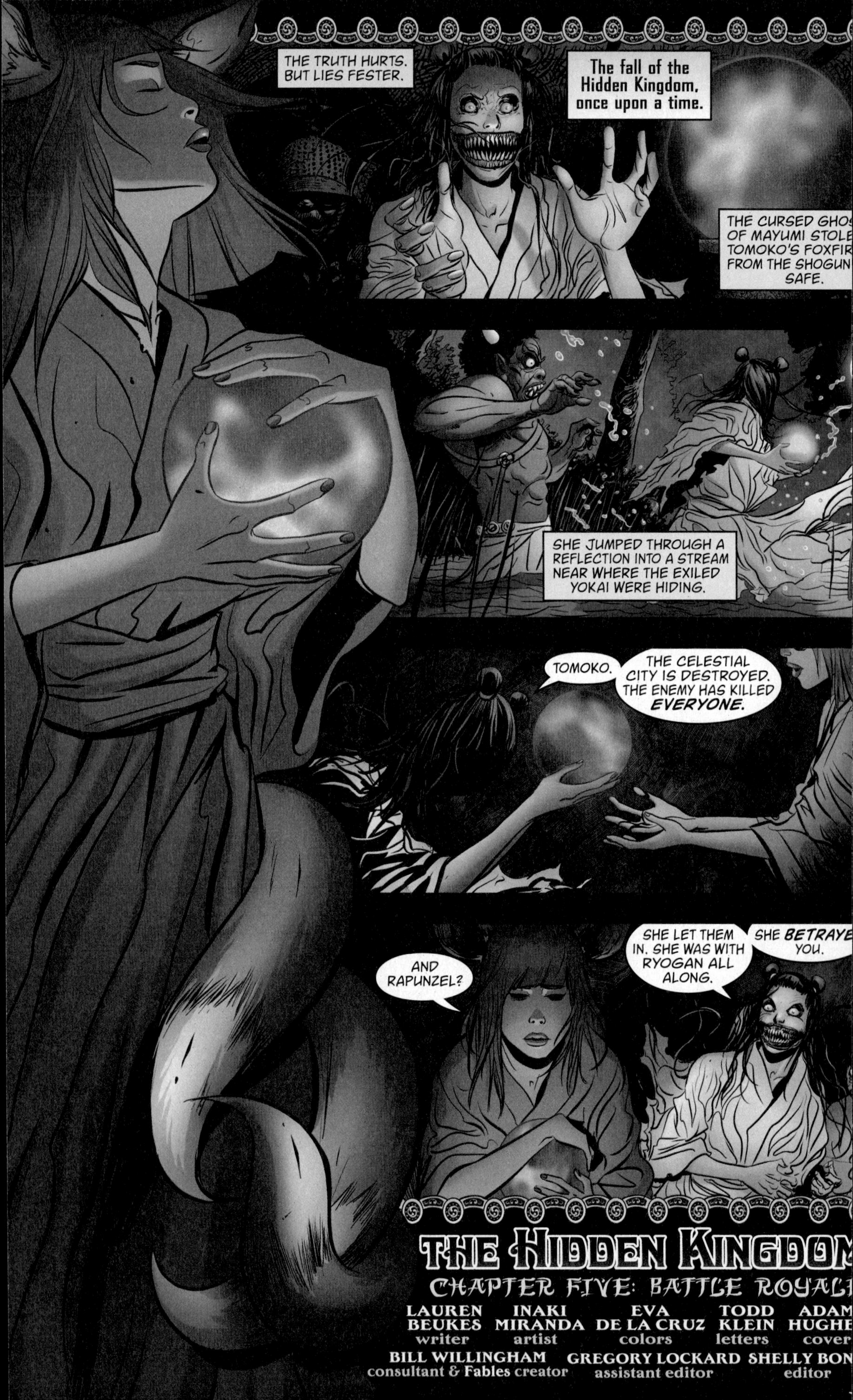

THE TRUTH HURTS. BUT LIES FESTER.
The fall of the Hidden Kingdom, once upon a time.
THE CURSED GHOS OF MAYUMI STOLE TOMOKO'S FOXFIR FROM THE SHOGUN SAFE.
SHE JUMPED THROUGH A REFLECTION INTO A STREAM NEAR WHERE THE EXILED YOKAI WERE HIDING.
TOMOKO.
THE CELESTIAL CITY IS DESTROYED. THE ENEMY HAS KILLED EVERYONE.
AND RAPUNZEL?
SHE LET THEM IN. SHE WAS WITH RYOGAN ALL ALONG.
SHE BETRAYE YOU.
THE HIDDEN KINGDOM
CHAPTER FIVE: BATTLE ROYAL
LAUREN BEUKES writer
INAKI MIRANDA artist
EVA DE LA CRUZ colors
TODD KLEIN letters
ADAM HUGHE cover
BILL WILLINGHAM consultant & Fables creator
GREGORY LOCKARD assistant editor
SHELLY BON editor

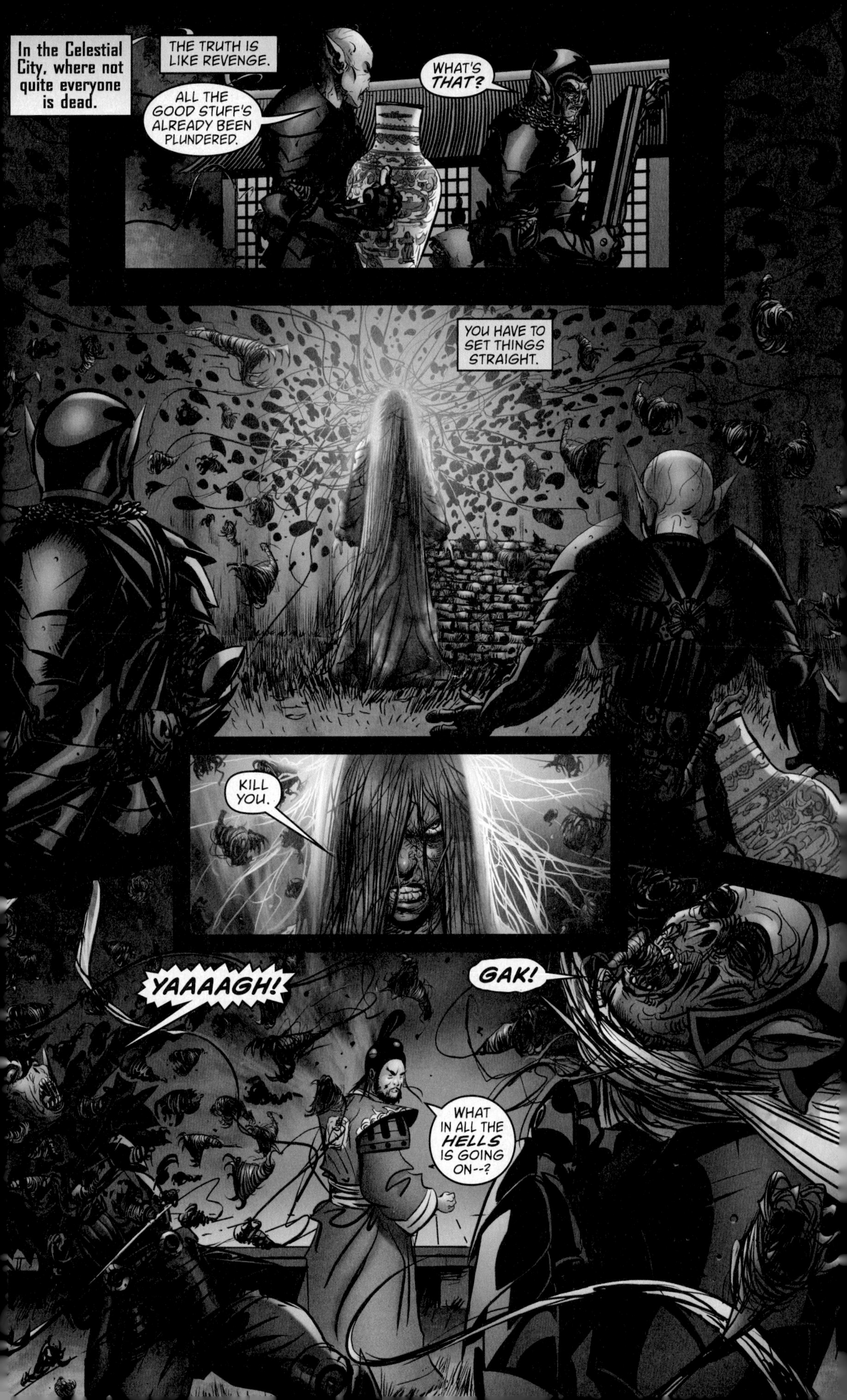
In the Celestial City, where not quite everyone is dead.
THE TRUTH IS LIKE REVENGE.
ALL THE GOOD STUFF'S ALREADY BEEN PLUNDERED.
WHAT'S THAT?
YOU HAVE TO SET THINGS STRAIGHT.
KILL YOU.
YAAAAGH!
GAK!
WHAT IN ALL THE HELLS IS GOING ON--?

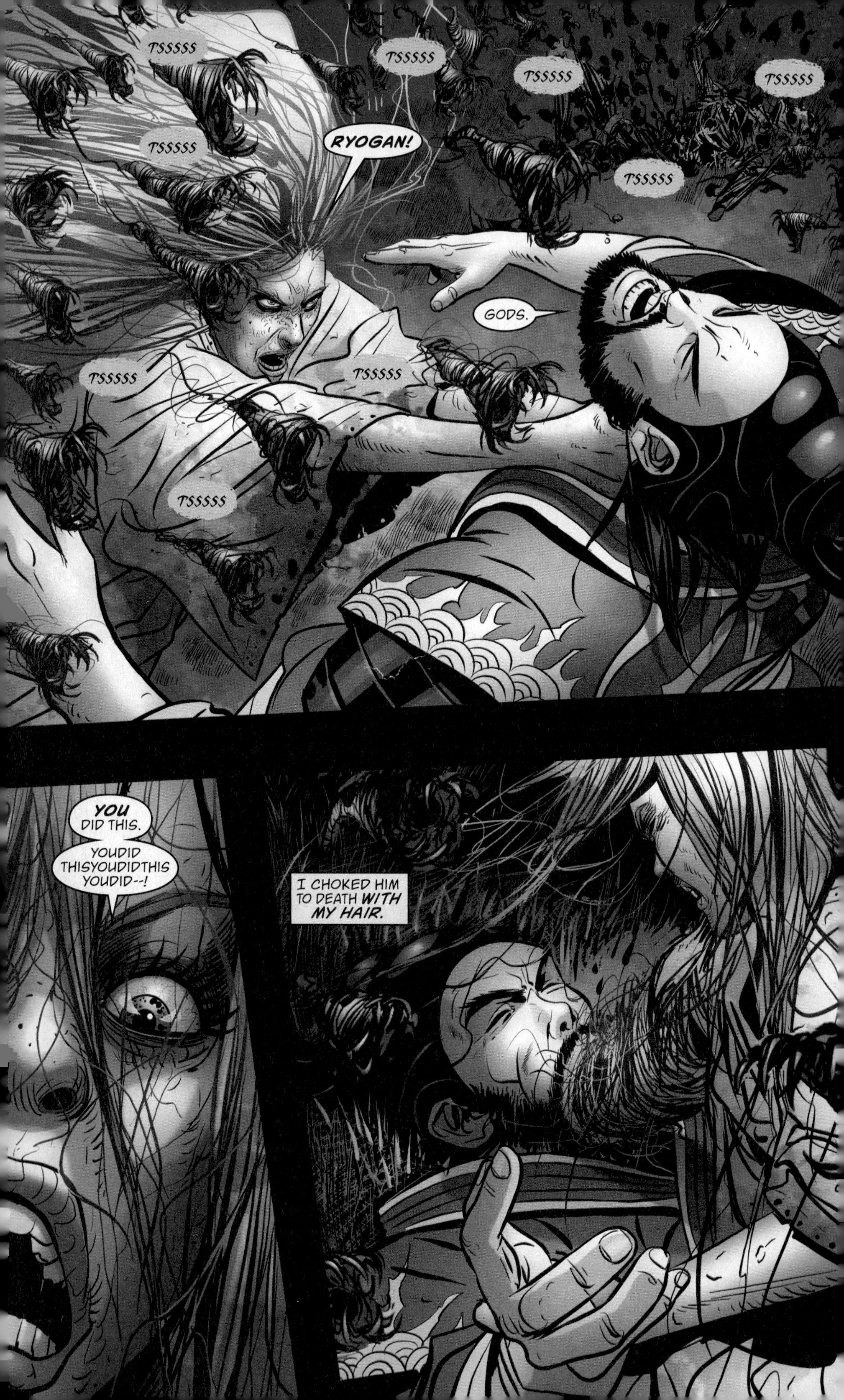
TSSSSS
TSSSSS
TSSSSS
TSSSSS
TSSSSS
RYOGAN!
TSSSSS
GODS.
TSSSSS
TSSSSS
TSSSSS
YOU DID THIS.
YOUDID THISYOUDIDTHIS YOUDID--!
I CHOKED HIM TO DEATH WITH MY HAIR.

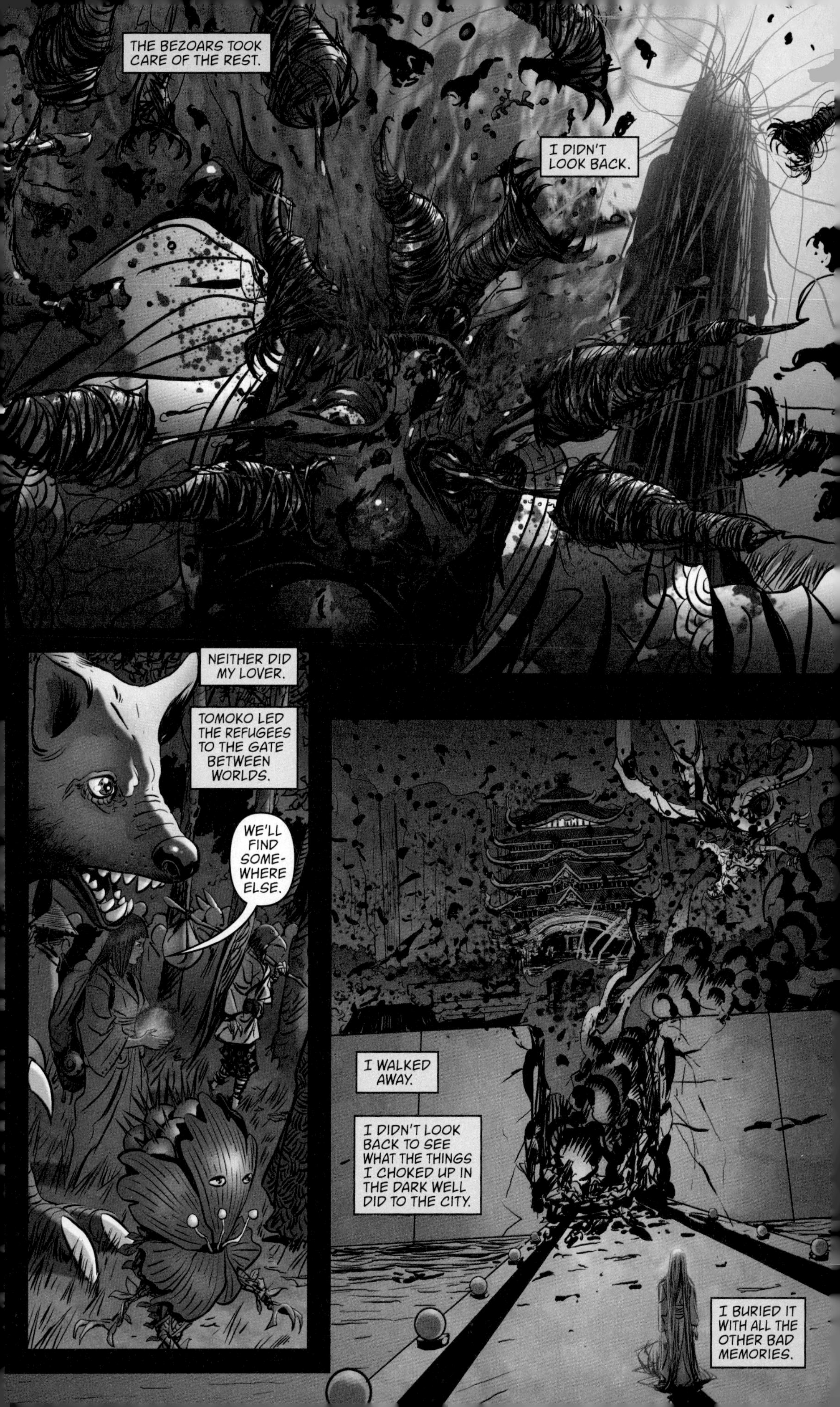

THE BEZOARS TOOK CARE OF THE REST.
I DIDN'T LOOK BACK.
NEITHER DID MY LOVER.
TOMOKO LED THE REFUGEES TO THE GATE BETWEEN WORLDS.
WE'LL FIND SOME-WHERE ELSE.
I WALKED AWAY.
I DIDN'T LOOK BACK TO SEE WHAT THE THINGS I CHOKED UP IN THE DARK WELL DID TO THE CITY.
I BURIED IT WITH ALL THE OTHER BAD MEMORIES.

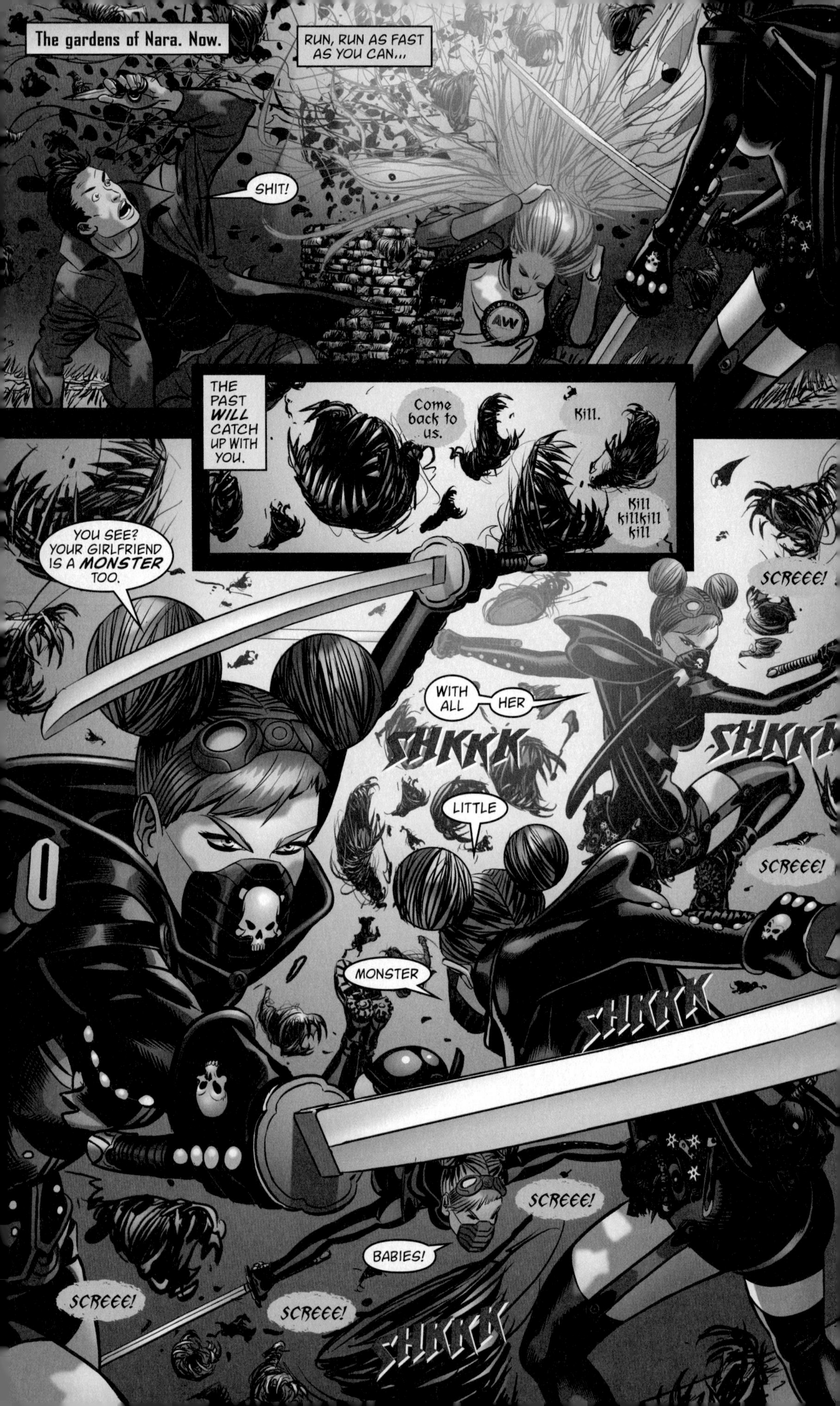

The gardens of Nara. Now.
RUN, RUN AS FAST AS YOU CAN...
SHIT!
THE PAST WILL CATCH UP WITH YOU.
Come back to us.
Kill.
Kill killkill kill
YOU SEE? YOUR GIRLFRIEND IS A MONSTER TOO.
SCREEE!
WITH ALL
HER
SHKKK
SHKKK
LITTLE
SCREEE!
MONSTER
SHKKK
SCREEE!
BABIES!
SCREEE!
SCREEE!
SHKKK

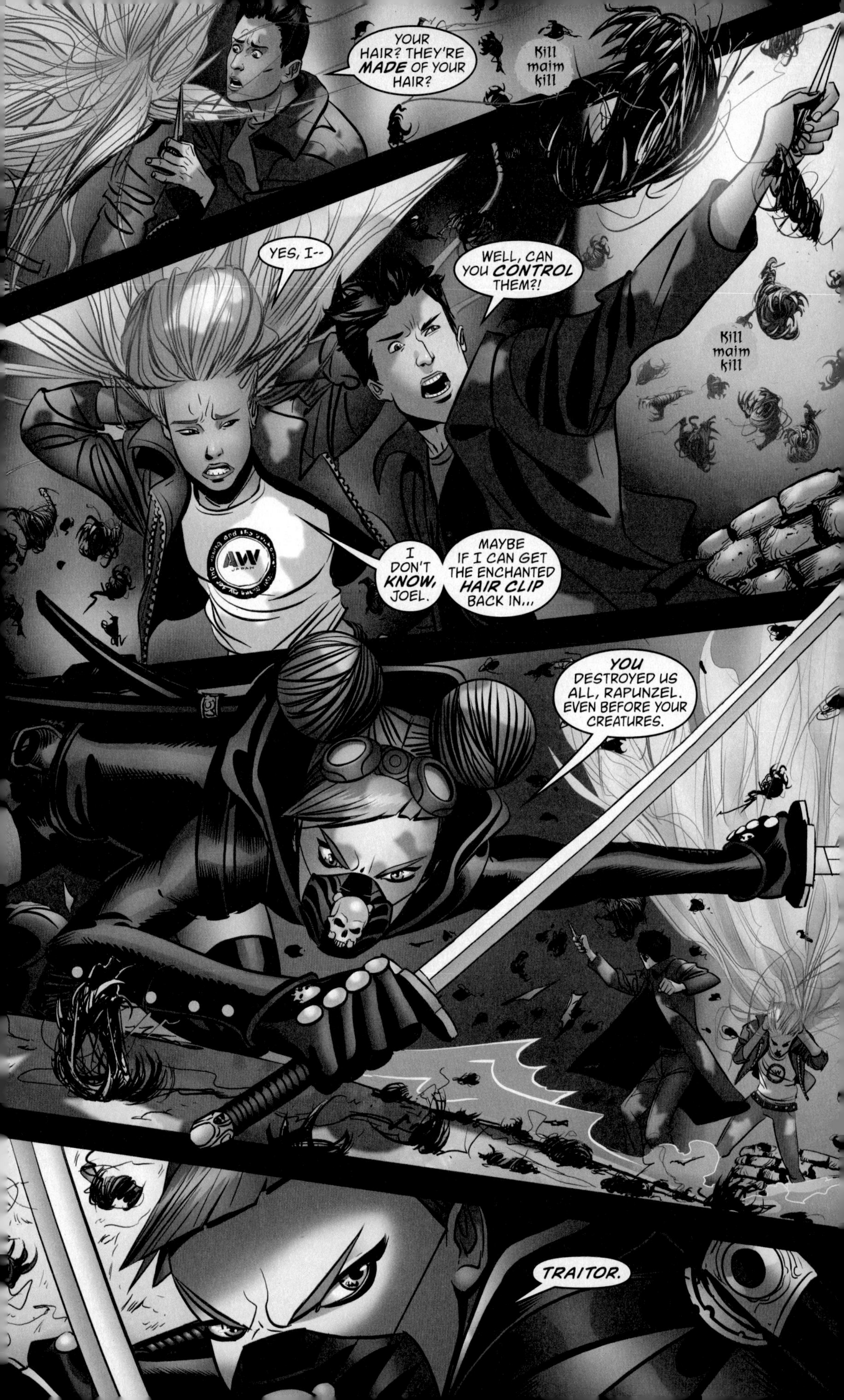

YOUR HAIR? THEY'RE MADE OF YOUR HAIR?
Kill maim kill
YES, I--
WELL, CAN YOU CONTROL THEM?!
Kill maim kill
I DON'T KNOW, JOEL.
MAYBE IF I CAN GET THE ENCHANTED HAIR CLIP BACK IN...
YOU DESTROYED US ALL, RAPUNZEL. EVEN BEFORE YOUR CREATURES.
TRAITOR.

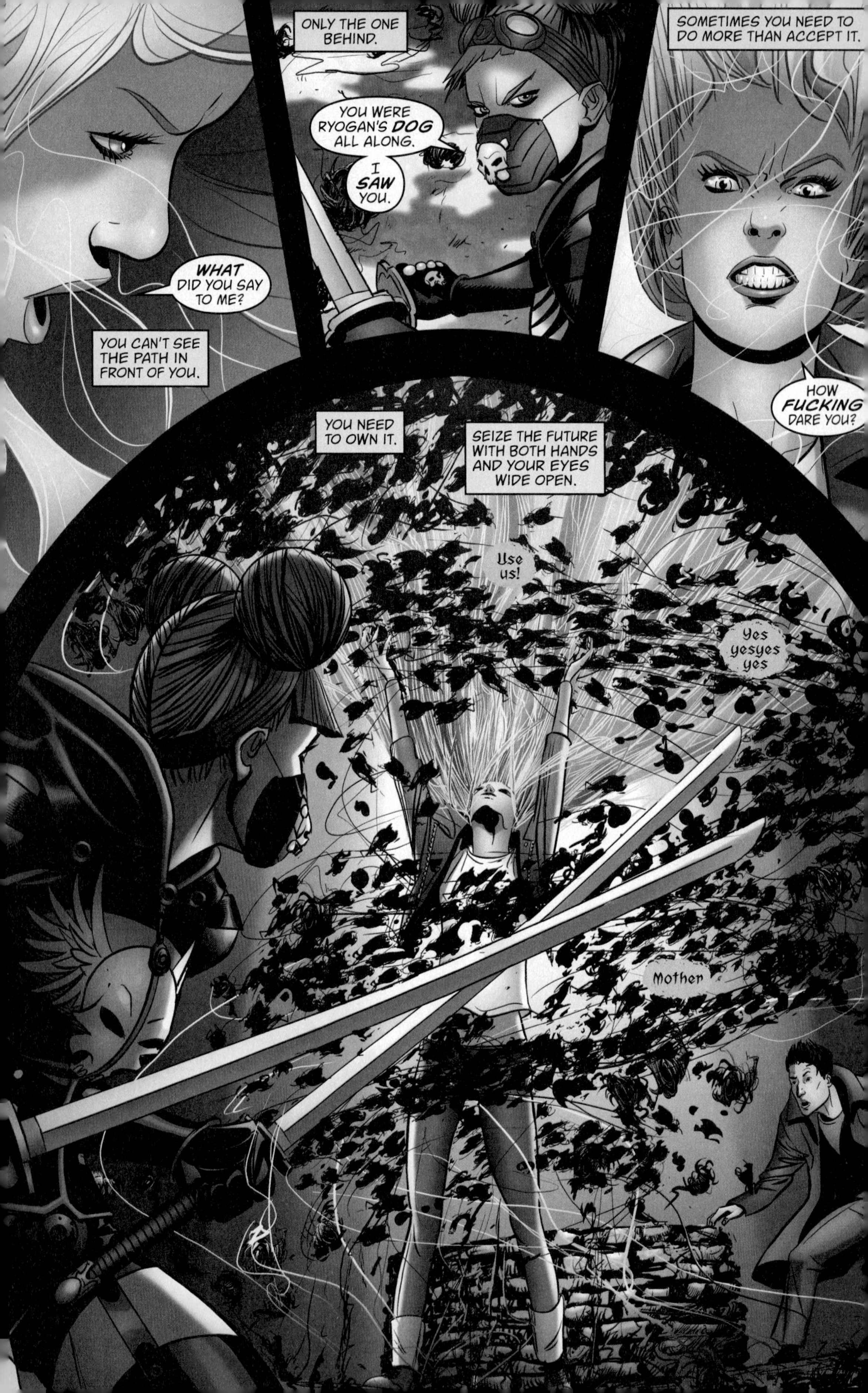
ONLY THE ONE BEHIND.
YOU WERE RYOGAN'S DOG ALL ALONG.
I SAW YOU.
SOMETIMES YOU NEED TO DO MORE THAN ACCEPT IT.
WHAT DID YOU SAY TO ME?
YOU CAN'T SEE THE PATH IN FRONT OF YOU.
HOW FUCKING DARE YOU?
YOU NEED TO OWN IT.
SEIZE THE FUTURE WITH BOTH HANDS AND YOUR EYES WIDE OPEN.
Use us!
Yes yesyes yes
Mother

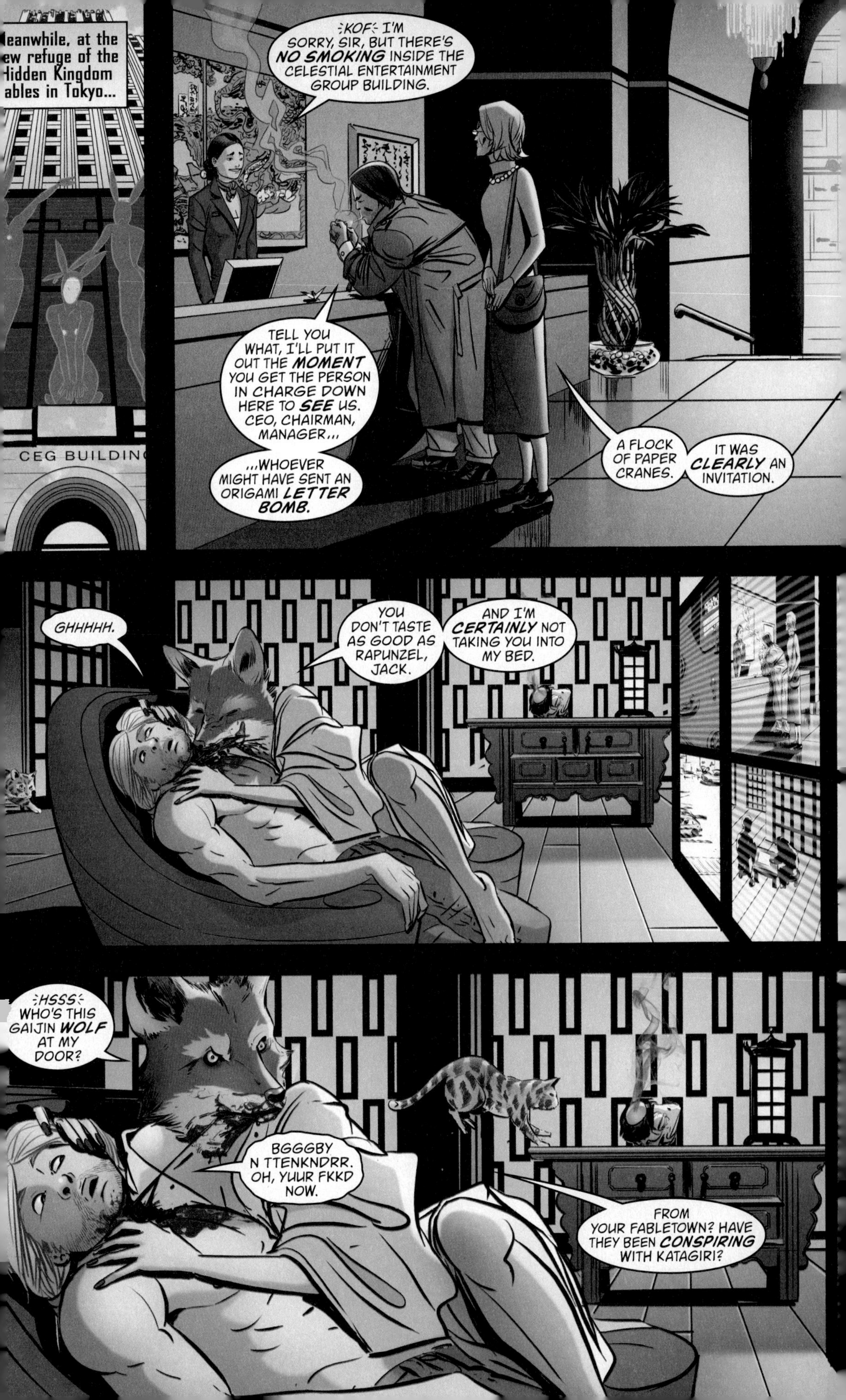

eanwhile, at the ew refuge of the Hidden Kingdom ables in Tokyo...
CEG BUILDING
:KOF: I'M SORRY, SIR, BUT THERE'S NO SMOKING INSIDE THE CELESTIAL ENTERTAINMENT GROUP BUILDING.
TELL YOU WHAT, I'LL PUT IT OUT THE MOMENT YOU GET THE PERSON IN CHARGE DOWN HERE TO SEE US. CEO, CHAIRMAN, MANAGER...
...WHOEVER MIGHT HAVE SENT AN ORIGAMI LETTER BOMB.
A FLOCK OF PAPER CRANES.
IT WAS CLEARLY AN INVITATION.
GHHHHH.
YOU DON'T TASTE AS GOOD AS RAPUNZEL, JACK.
AND I'M CERTAINLY NOT TAKING YOU INTO MY BED.
:HSSS: WHO'S THIS GAIJIN WOLF AT MY DOOR?
BGGGBY N TTENKNDRR. OH, YUUR FKKD NOW.
FROM YOUR FABLETOWN? HAVE THEY BEEN CONSPIRING WITH KATAGIRI?

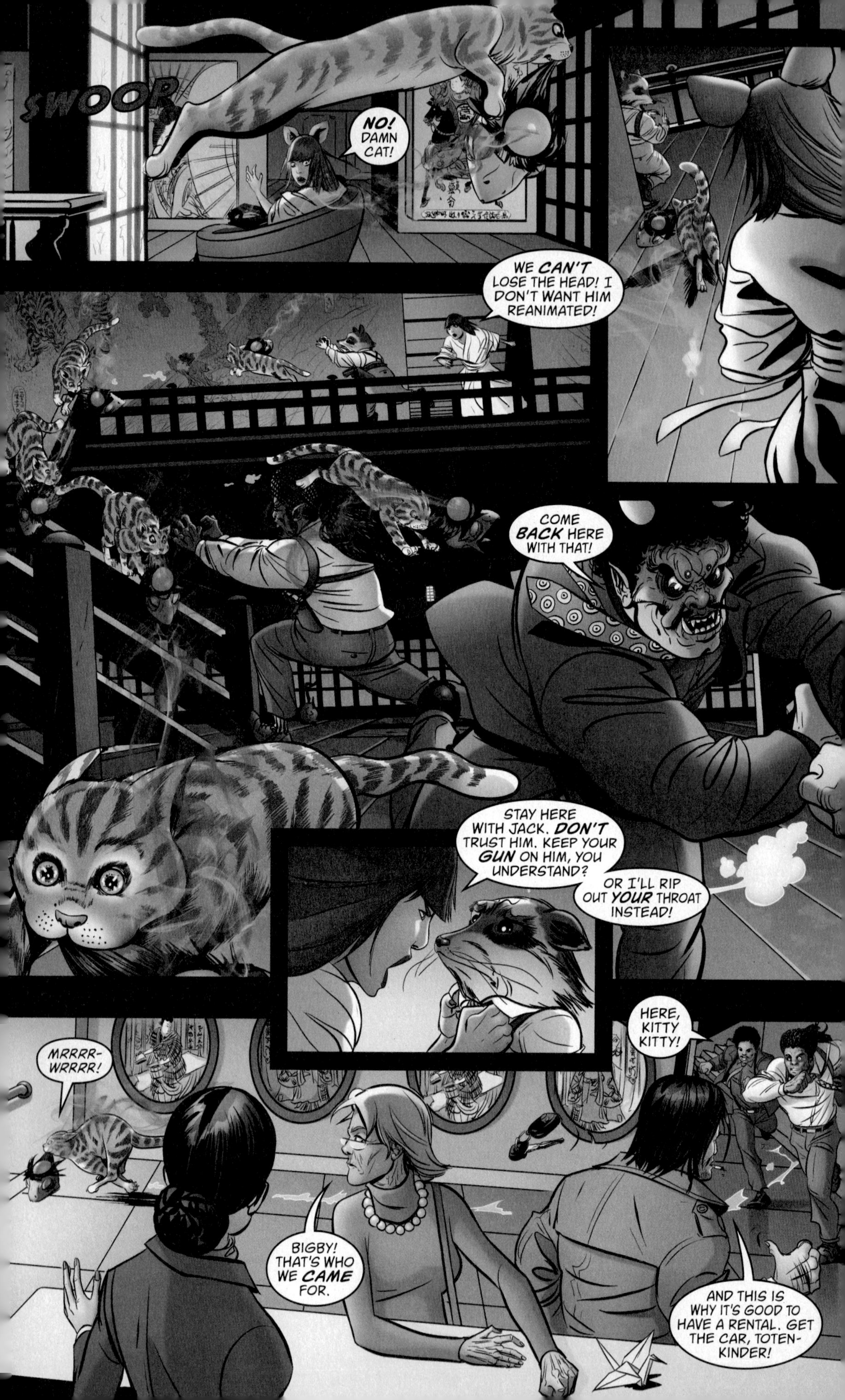
SWOOP
NO! DAMN CAT!
WE CAN'T LOSE THE HEAD! I DON'T WANT HIM REANIMATED!
COME BACK HERE WITH THAT!
STAY HERE WITH JACK. DON'T TRUST HIM. KEEP YOUR GUN ON HIM, YOU UNDERSTAND?
OR I'LL RIP OUT YOUR THROAT INSTEAD!
MRRRR-WRRRR!
HERE, KITTY KITTY!
BIGBY! THAT'S WHO WE CAME FOR.
AND THIS IS WHY IT'S GOOD TO HAVE A RENTAL. GET THE CAR, TOTEN-KINDER!

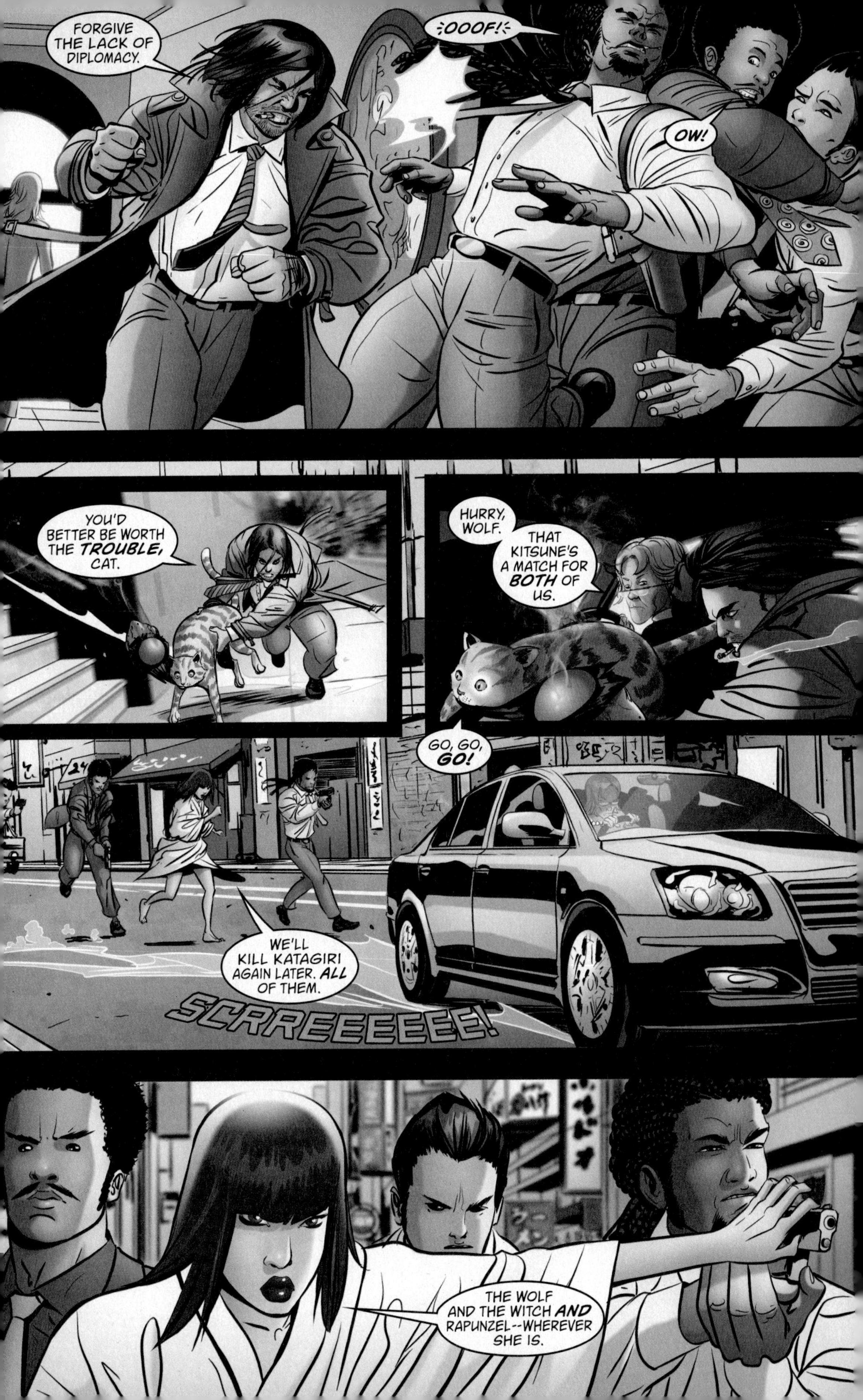
FORGIVE THE LACK OF DIPLOMACY.
OOOF!
OW!
YOU'D BETTER BE WORTH THE TROUBLE, CAT.
HURRY, WOLF.
THAT KITSUNE'S A MATCH FOR BOTH OF US.
GO, GO, GO!
WE'LL KILL KATAGIRI AGAIN LATER. ALL OF THEM.
SCRREEEEEEE!
THE WOLF AND THE WITCH AND RAPUNZEL--WHEREVER SHE IS.

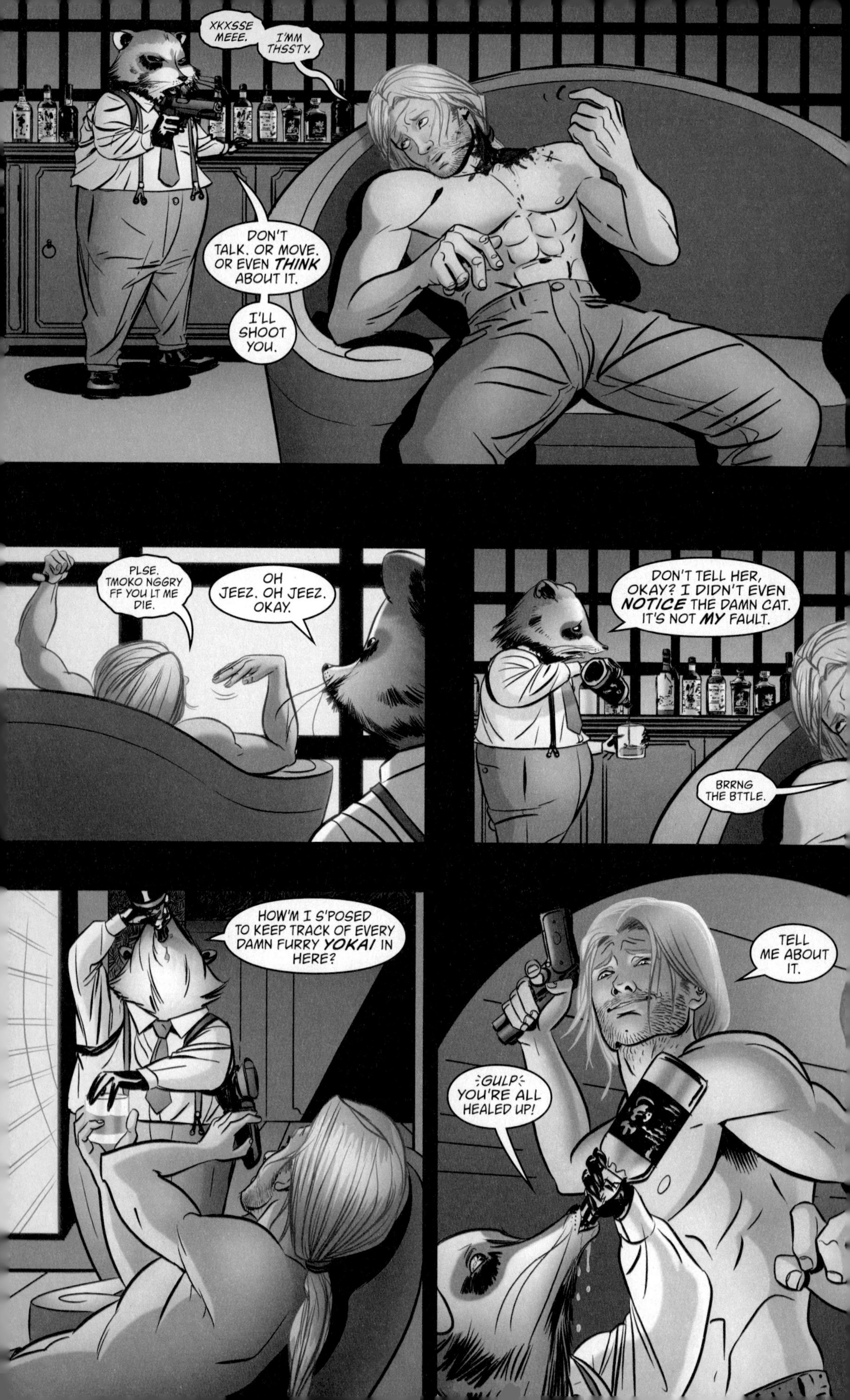
XKXSSE MEEE.
I'MM THSSTY.
DON'T TALK. OR MOVE. OR EVEN THINK ABOUT IT.
I'LL SHOOT YOU.
PLSE. TMOKO NGGRY FF YOU LT ME DIE.
OH JEEZ. OH JEEZ. OKAY.
DON'T TELL HER, OKAY? I DIDN'T EVEN NOTICE THE DAMN CAT. IT'S NOT MY FAULT.
BRRNG THE BTTLE.
HOW'M I S'POSED TO KEEP TRACK OF EVERY DAMN FURRY YOKAI IN HERE?
TELL ME ABOUT IT.
GULP YOU'RE ALL HEALED UP!

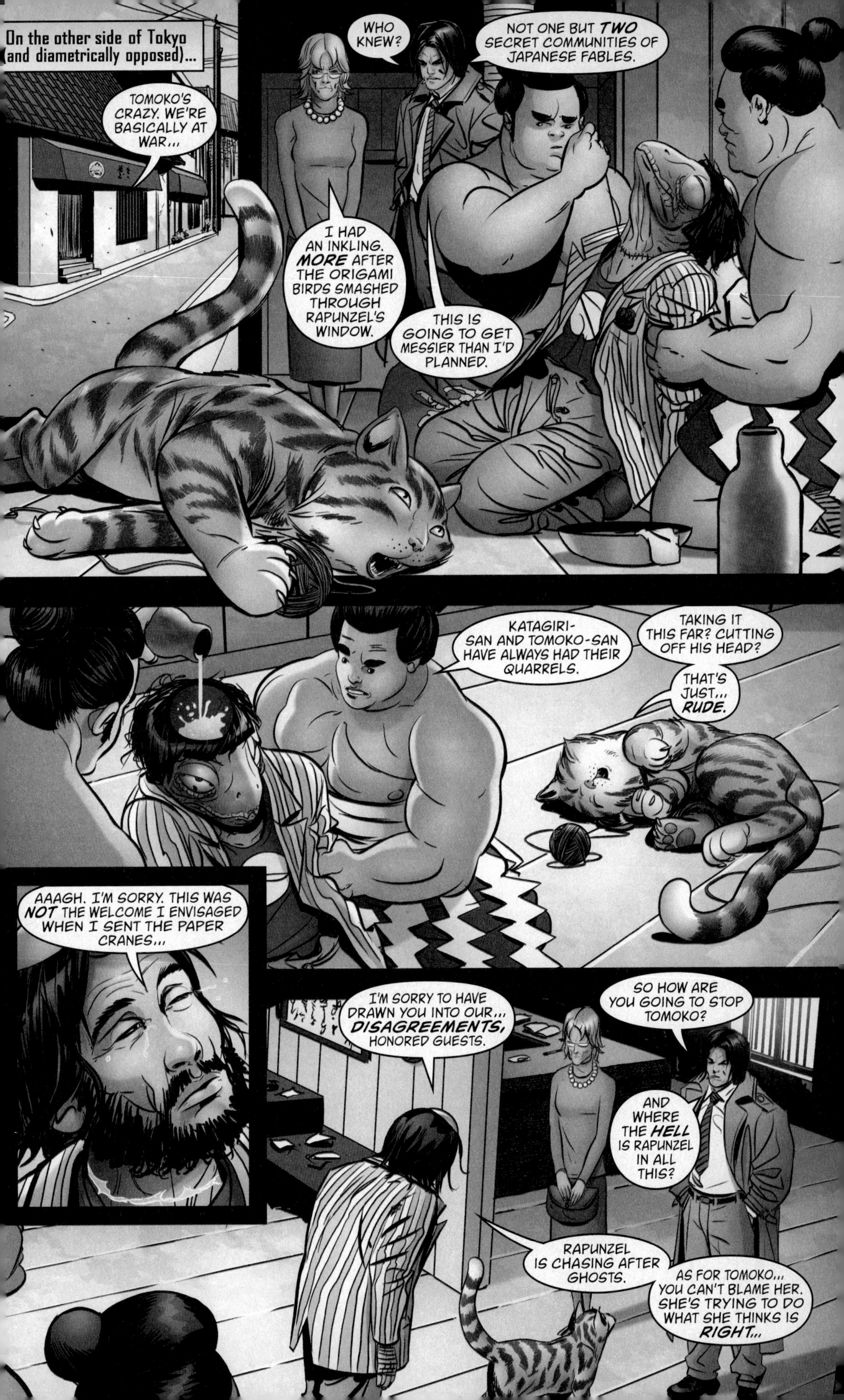
On the other side of Tokyo (and diametrically opposed)...
TOMOKO'S CRAZY. WE'RE BASICALLY AT WAR...
WHO KNEW?
NOT ONE BUT TWO SECRET COMMUNITIES OF JAPANESE FABLES.
I HAD AN INKLING. MORE AFTER THE ORIGAMI BIRDS SMASHED THROUGH RAPUNZEL'S WINDOW.
THIS IS GOING TO GET MESSIER THAN I'D PLANNED.
KATAGIRI-SAN AND TOMOKO-SAN HAVE ALWAYS HAD THEIR QUARRELS.
TAKING IT THIS FAR? CUTTING OFF HIS HEAD?
THAT'S JUST... RUDE.
AAAGH. I'M SORRY. THIS WAS NOT THE WELCOME I ENVISAGED WHEN I SENT THE PAPER CRANES...
I'M SORRY TO HAVE DRAWN YOU INTO OUR... DISAGREEMENTS, HONORED GUESTS.
SO HOW ARE YOU GOING TO STOP TOMOKO?
AND WHERE THE HELL IS RAPUNZEL IN ALL THIS?
RAPUNZEL IS CHASING AFTER GHOSTS.
AS FOR TOMOKO... YOU CAN'T BLAME HER. SHE'S TRYING TO DO WHAT SHE THINKS IS RIGHT...

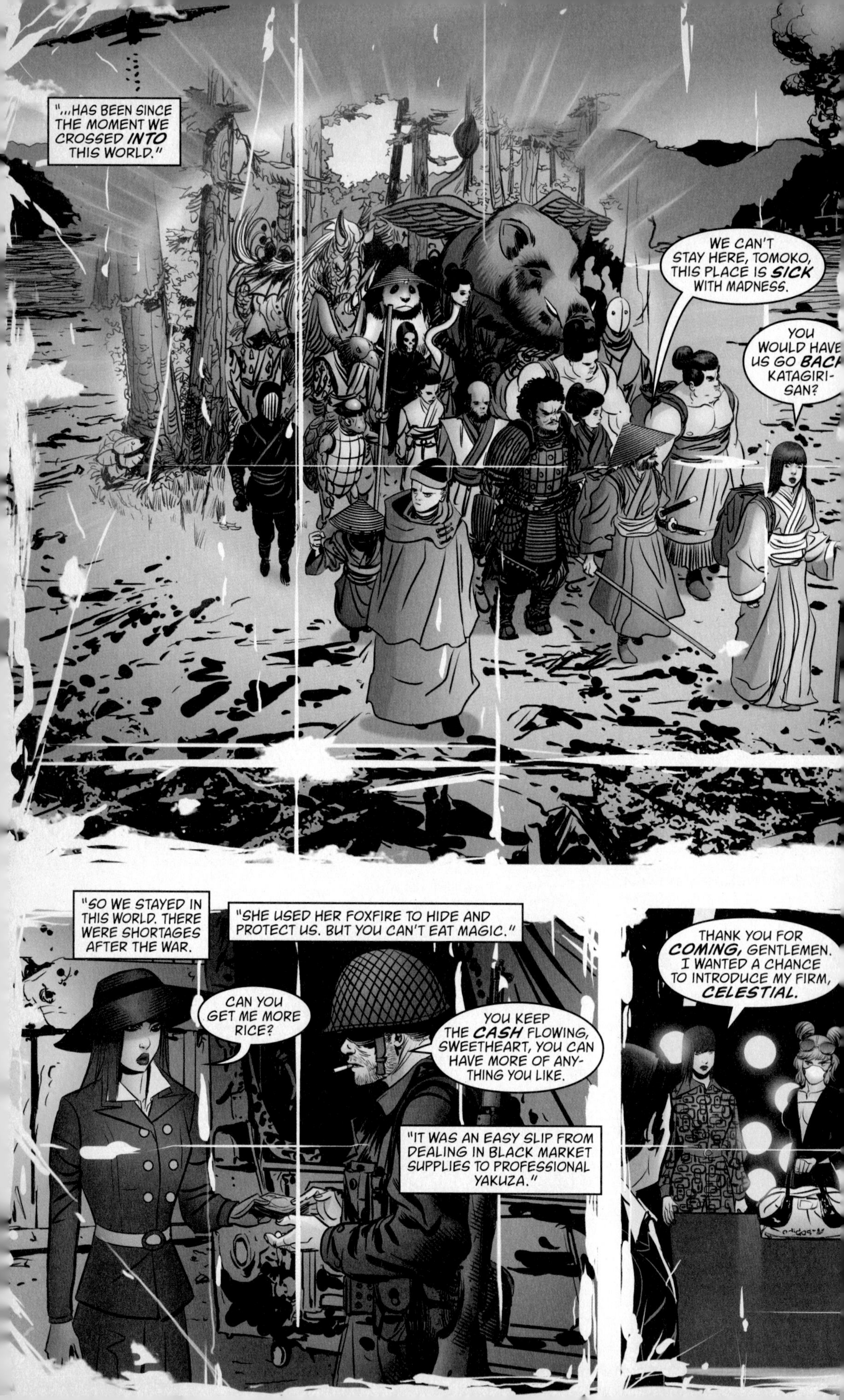
"...HAS BEEN SINCE THE MOMENT WE CROSSED INTO THIS WORLD."
WE CAN'T STAY HERE, TOMOKO, THIS PLACE IS SICK WITH MADNESS.
YOU WOULD HAVE US GO BAC KATAGIRI-SAN?
"SO WE STAYED IN THIS WORLD. THERE WERE SHORTAGES AFTER THE WAR.
"SHE USED HER FOXFIRE TO HIDE AND PROTECT US. BUT YOU CAN'T EAT MAGIC."
CAN YOU GET ME MORE RICE?
YOU KEEP THE CASH FLOWING, SWEETHEART, YOU CAN HAVE MORE OF ANY-THING YOU LIKE.
"IT WAS AN EASY SLIP FROM DEALING IN BLACK MARKET SUPPLIES TO PROFESSIONAL YAKUZA."
THANK YOU FOR COMING, GENTLEMEN. I WANTED A CHANCE TO INTRODUCE MY FIRM, CELESTIAL.

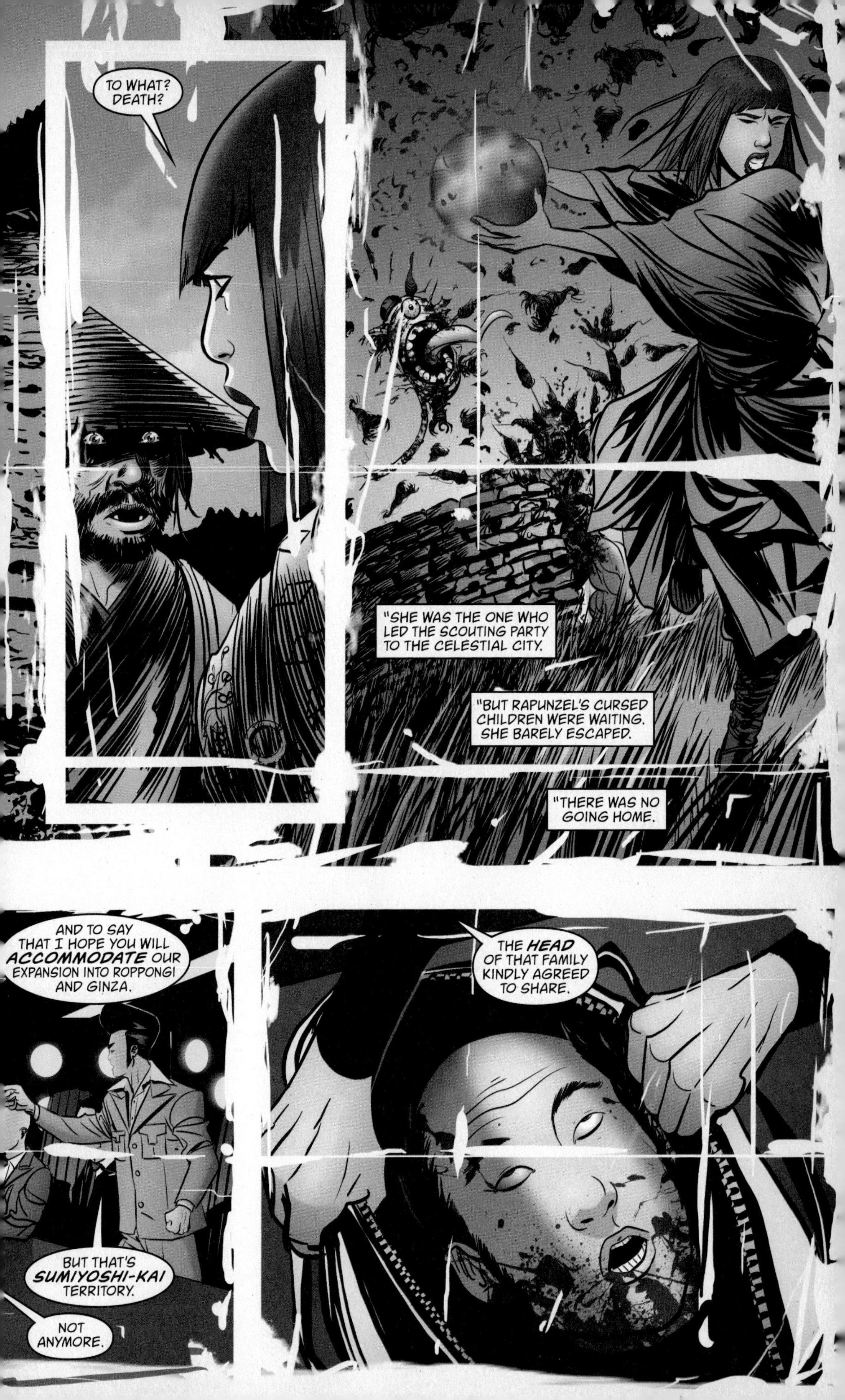
TO WHAT? DEATH?
"SHE WAS THE ONE WHO LED THE SCOUTING PARTY TO THE CELESTIAL CITY.
"BUT RAPUNZEL'S CURSED CHILDREN WERE WAITING. SHE BARELY ESCAPED.
"THERE WAS NO GOING HOME.
AND TO SAY THAT I HOPE YOU WILL ACCOMMODATE OUR EXPANSION INTO ROPPONGI AND GINZA.
BUT THAT'S SUMIYOSHI-KAI TERRITORY.
NOT ANYMORE.
THE HEAD OF THAT FAMILY KINDLY AGREED TO SHARE.

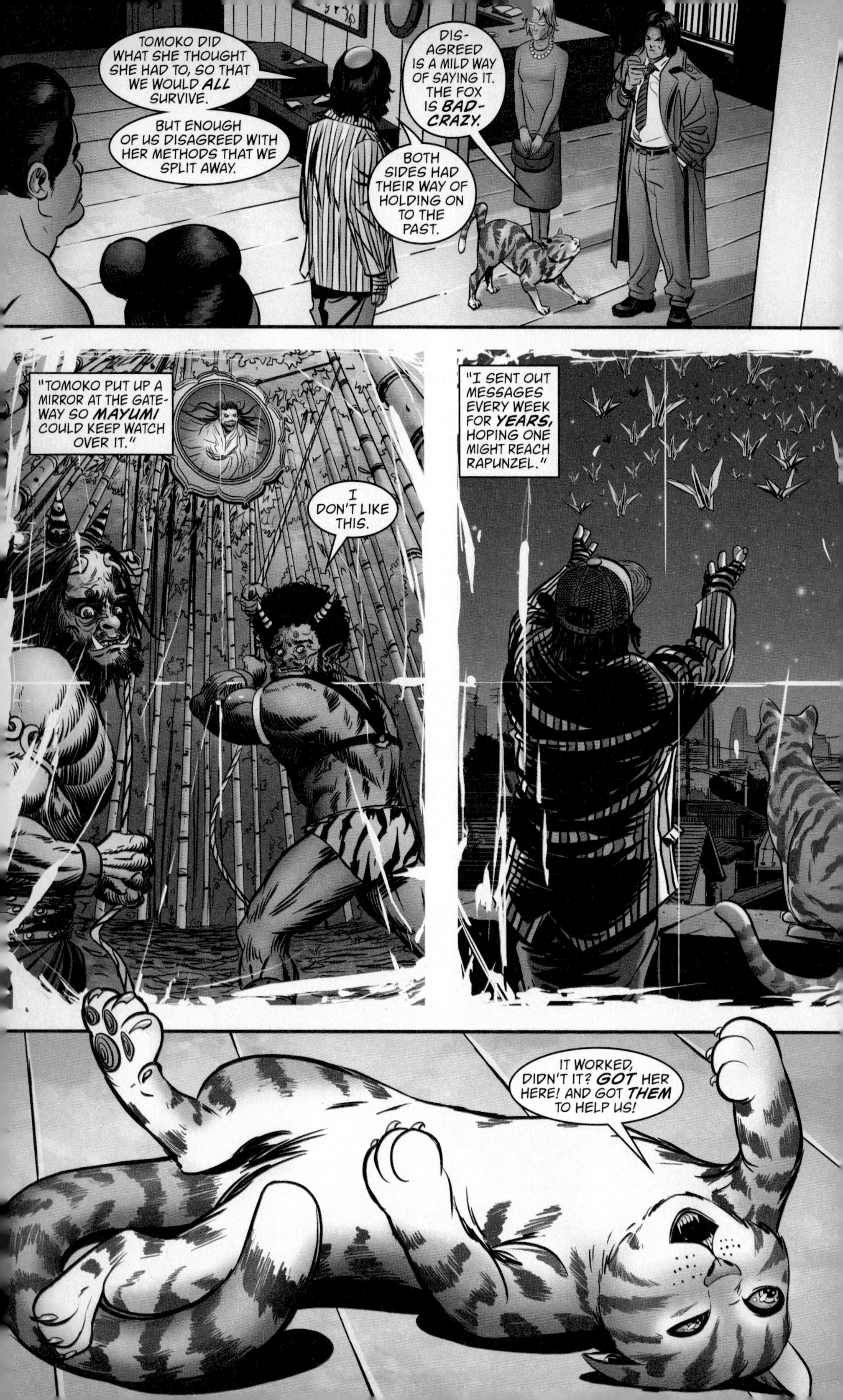
TOMOKO DID WHAT SHE THOUGHT SHE HAD TO, SO THAT WE WOULD ALL SURVIVE.
BUT ENOUGH OF US DISAGREED WITH HER METHODS THAT WE SPLIT AWAY.
DIS-AGREED IS A MILD WAY OF SAYING IT. THE FOX IS BAD-CRAZY.
BOTH SIDES HAD THEIR WAY OF HOLDING ON TO THE PAST.
"TOMOKO PUT UP A MIRROR AT THE GATE-WAY SO MAYUMI COULD KEEP WATCH OVER IT."
I DON'T LIKE THIS.
"I SENT OUT MESSAGES EVERY WEEK FOR YEARS, HOPING ONE MIGHT REACH RAPUNZEL."
IT WORKED, DIDN'T IT? GOT HER HERE! AND GOT THEM TO HELP US!

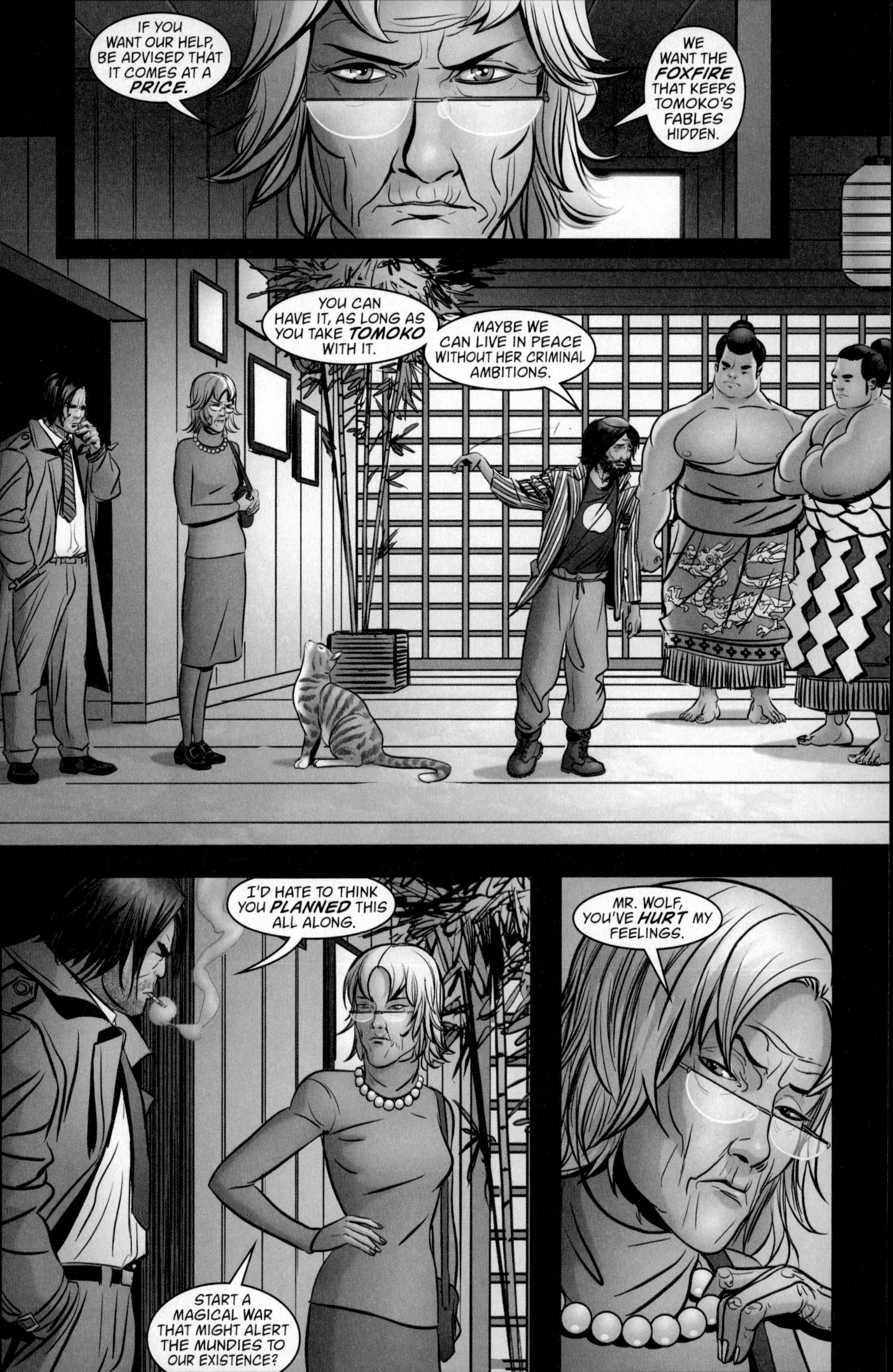
IF YOU WANT OUR HELP, BE ADVISED THAT IT COMES AT A PRICE.
WE WANT THE FOXFIRE THAT KEEPS TOMOKO'S FABLES HIDDEN.
YOU CAN HAVE IT, AS LONG AS YOU TAKE TOMOKO WITH IT.
MAYBE WE CAN LIVE IN PEACE WITHOUT HER CRIMINAL AMBITIONS.
I'D HATE TO THINK YOU PLANNED THIS ALL ALONG.
START A MAGICAL WAR THAT MIGHT ALERT THE MUNDIES TO OUR EXISTENCE?
MR. WOLF, YOU'VE HURT MY FEELINGS.

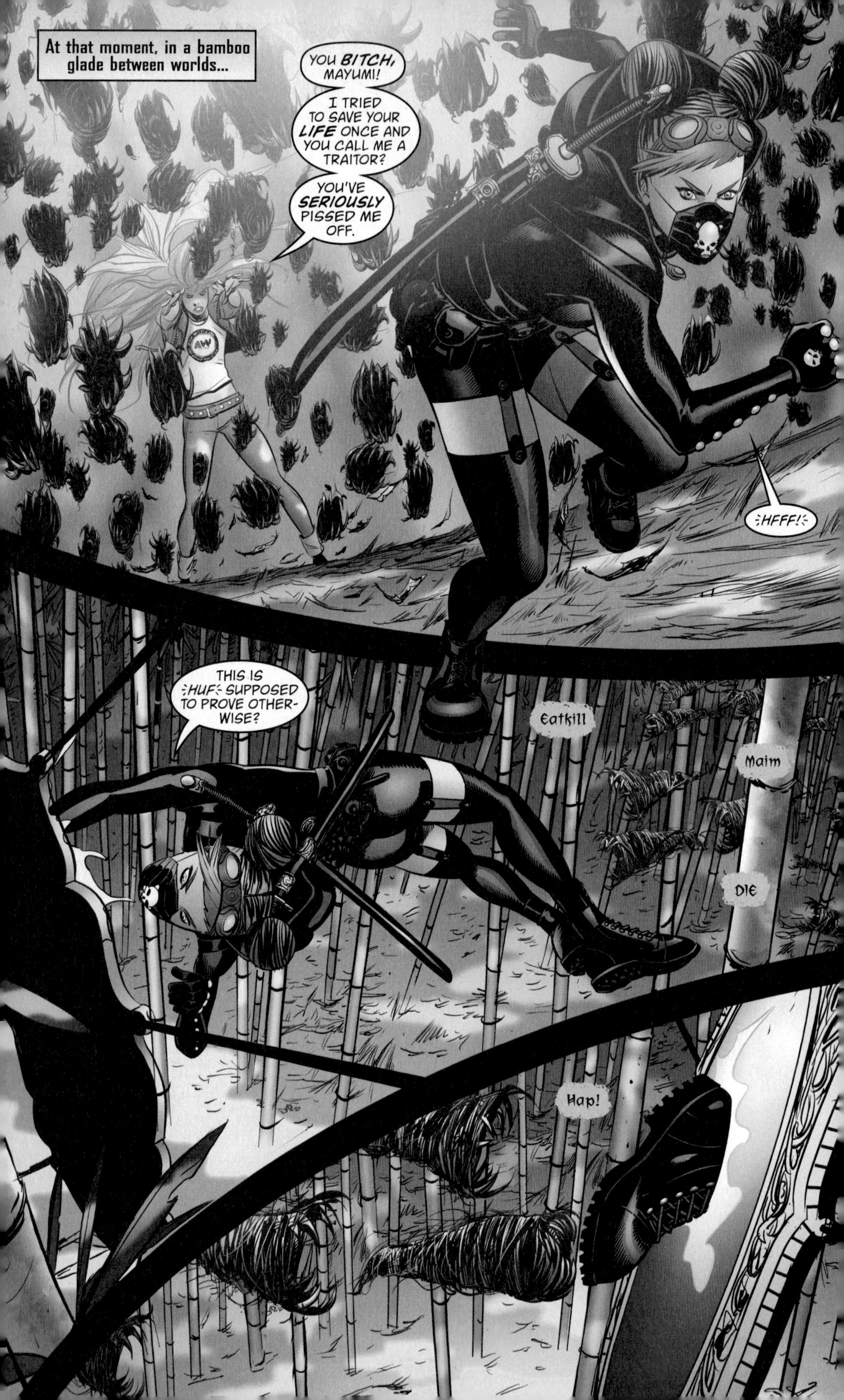
At that moment, in a bamboo glade between worlds...
YOU BITCH, MAYUMI!
I TRIED TO SAVE YOUR LIFE ONCE AND YOU CALL ME A TRAITOR?
YOU'VE SERIOUSLY PISSED ME OFF.
HFFF!
THIS IS HUF SUPPOSED TO PROVE OTHER-WISE?
Eatkill
Maim
DIE
Hap!

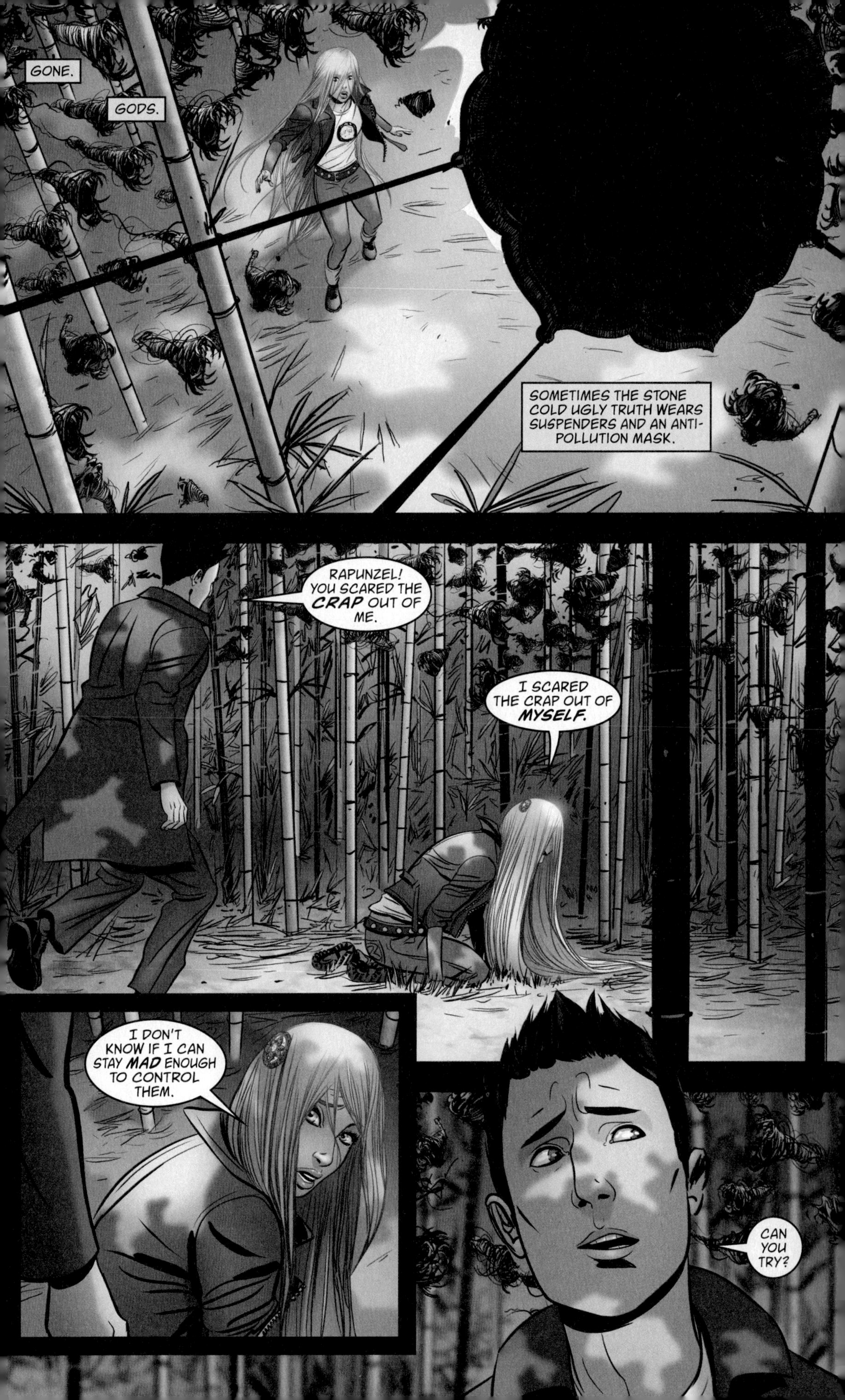

GONE.
GODS.
SOMETIMES THE STONE COLD UGLY TRUTH WEARS SUSPENDERS AND AN ANTI-POLLUTION MASK.
RAPUNZEL! YOU SCARED THE CRAP OUT OF ME.
I SCARED THE CRAP OUT OF MYSELF.
I DON'T KNOW IF I CAN STAY MAD ENOUGH TO CONTROL THEM.
CAN YOU TRY?

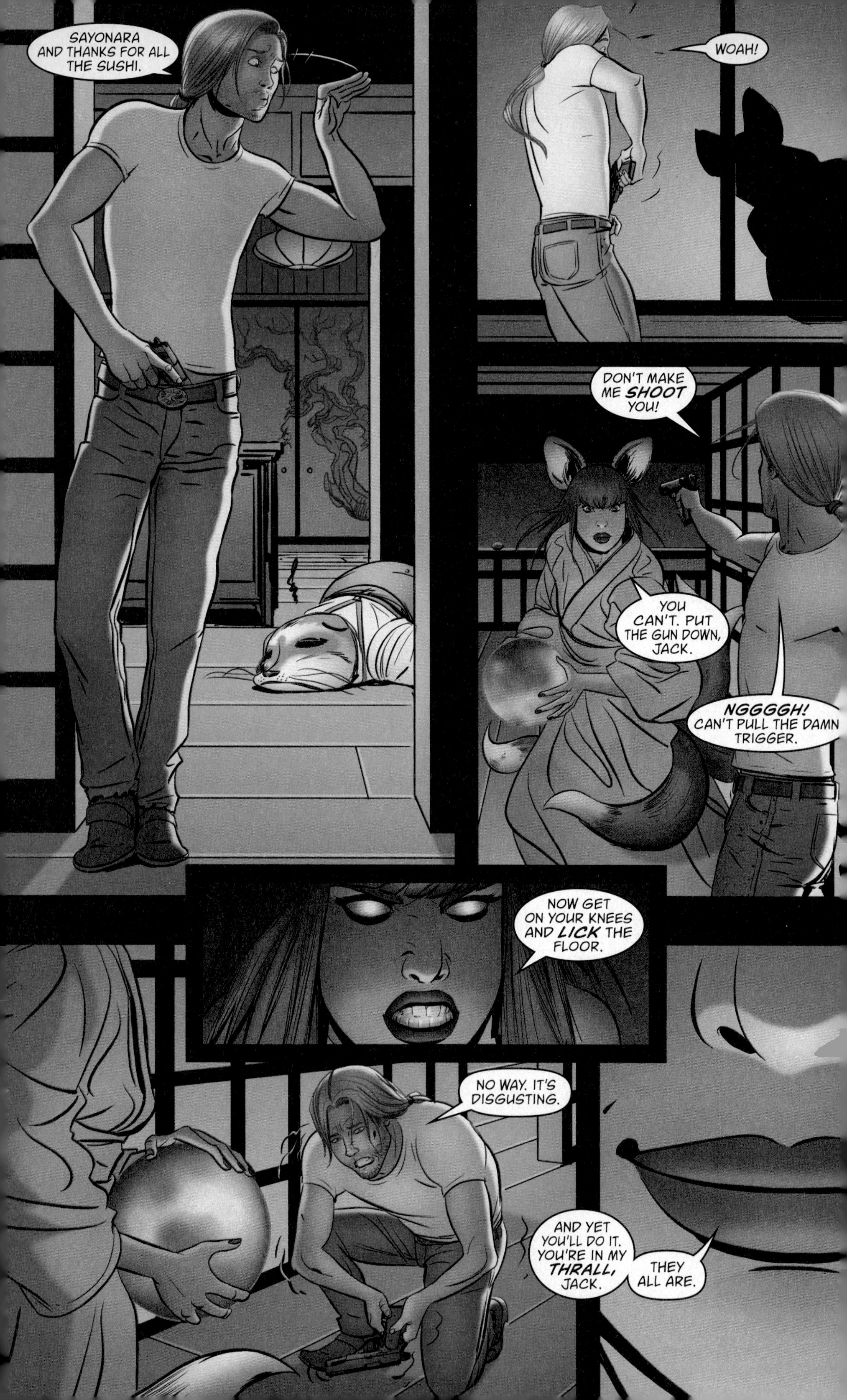
SAYONARA AND THANKS FOR ALL THE SUSHI.
WOAH!
DON'T MAKE ME SHOOT YOU!
YOU CAN'T. PUT THE GUN DOWN, JACK.
NGGGGH! CAN'T PULL THE DAMN TRIGGER.
NOW GET ON YOUR KNEES AND LICK THE FLOOR.
NO WAY. IT'S DISGUSTING.
AND YET YOU'LL DO IT. YOU'RE IN MY THRALL, JACK.
THEY ALL ARE.

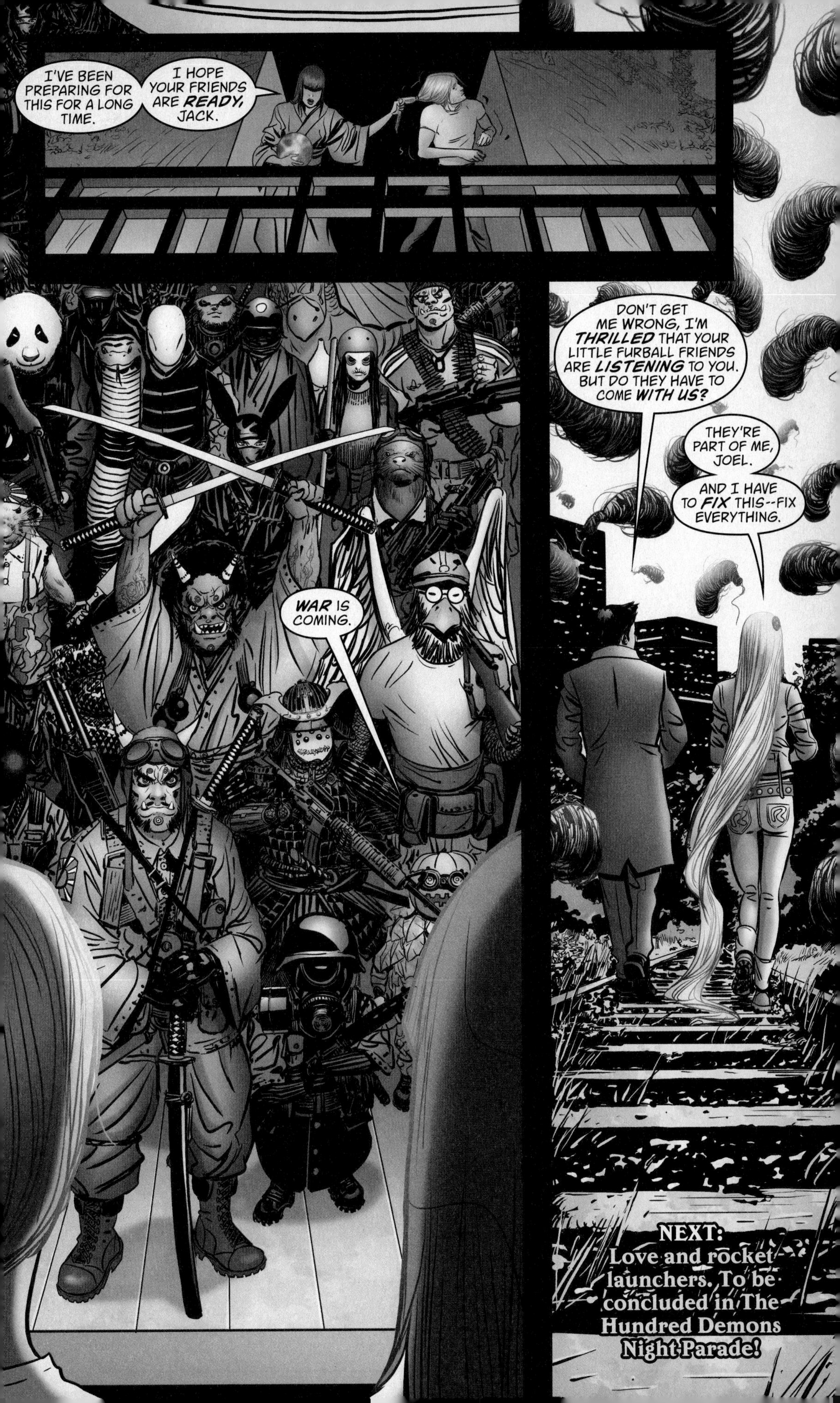

I'VE BEEN PREPARING FOR THIS FOR A LONG TIME.
I HOPE YOUR FRIENDS ARE *READY,* JACK.
WAR IS COMING.
DON'T GET ME WRONG, I'M *THRILLED* THAT YOUR LITTLE FURBALL FRIENDS ARE *LISTENING* TO YOU. BUT DO THEY HAVE TO COME *WITH US?*
THEY'RE PART OF ME, JOEL.
AND I HAVE TO *FIX* THIS--FIX EVERYTHING.
NEXT: Love and rocket launchers. To be concluded in The Hundred Demons Night Parade!

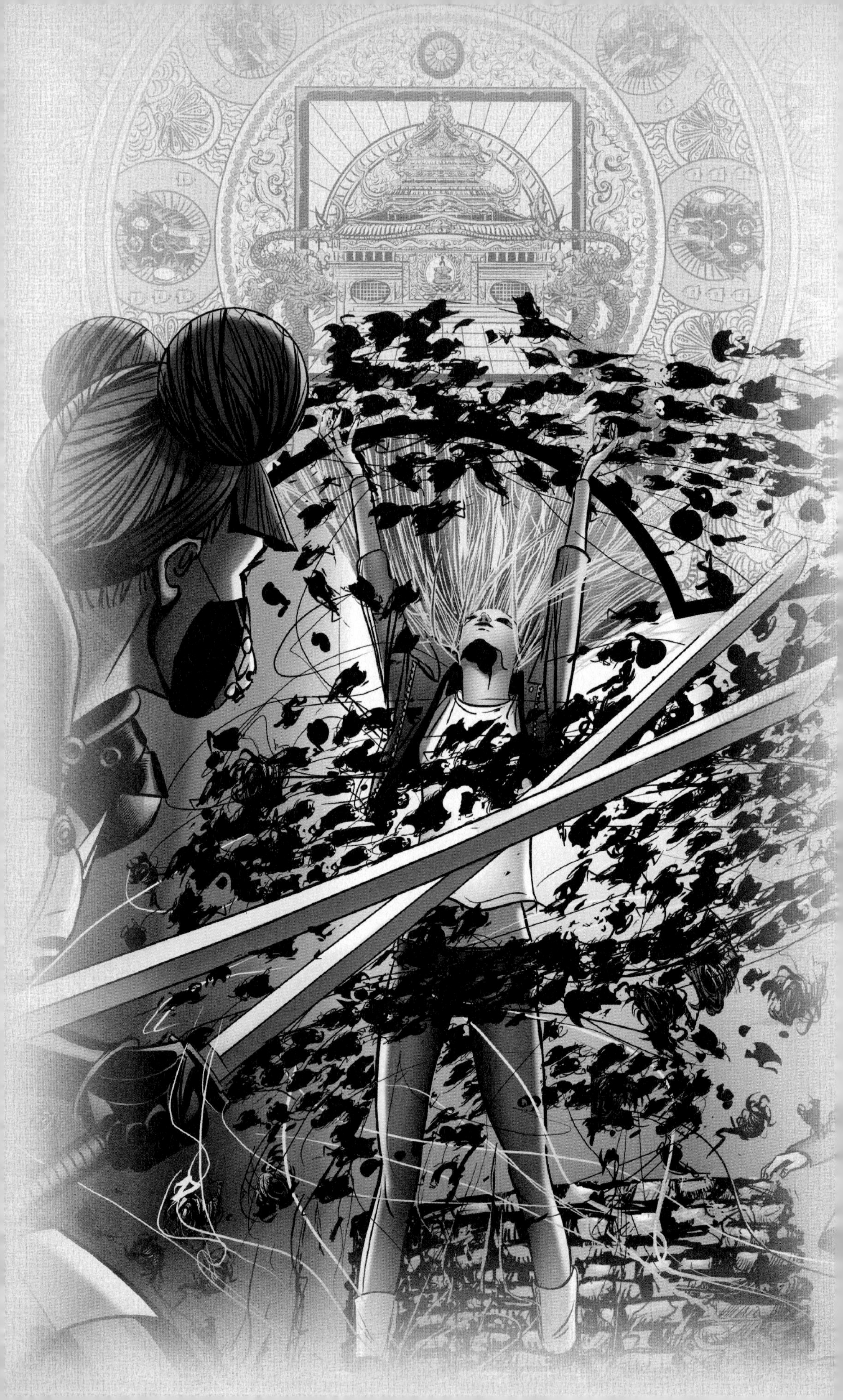

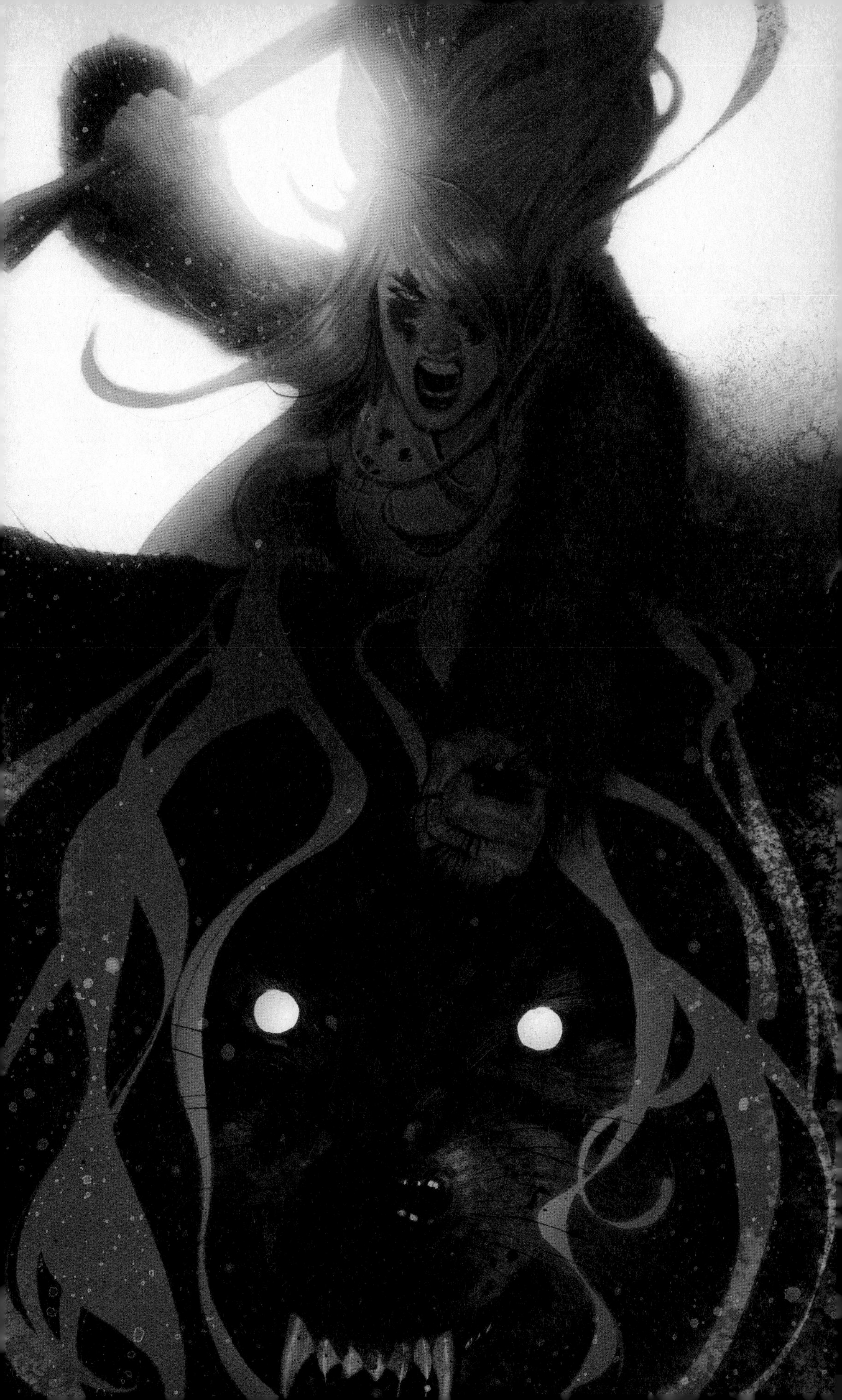

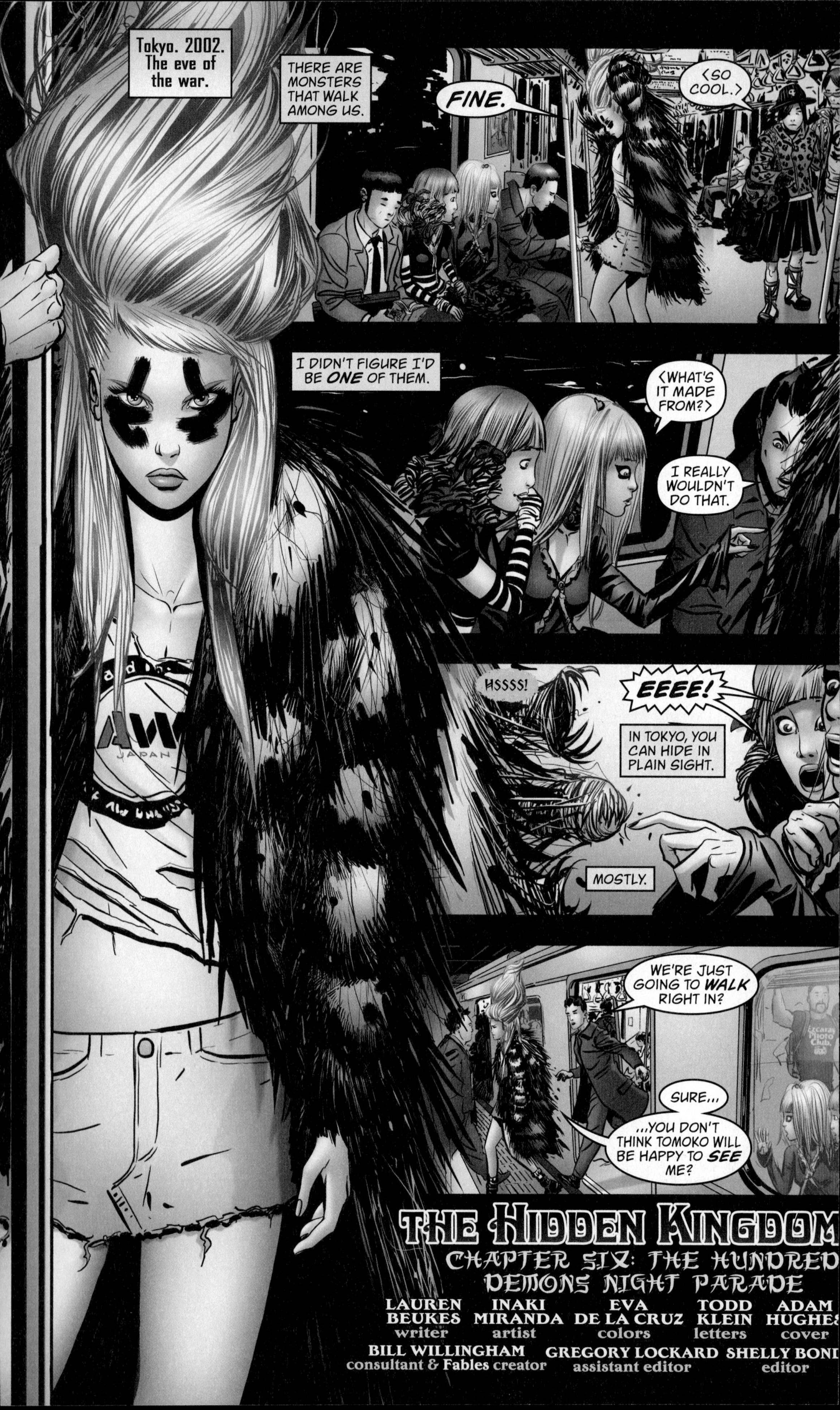
Tokyo. 2002. The eve of the war.
THERE ARE MONSTERS THAT WALK AMONG US.
FINE.
<SO COOL.>
I DIDN'T FIGURE I'D BE ONE OF THEM.
<WHAT'S IT MADE FROM?>
I REALLY WOULDN'T DO THAT.
HSSSS!
EEEE!
IN TOKYO, YOU CAN HIDE IN PLAIN SIGHT.
MOSTLY.
WE'RE JUST GOING TO WALK RIGHT IN?
SURE...
...YOU DON'T THINK TOMOKO WILL BE HAPPY TO SEE ME?
THE HIDDEN KINGDOM
CHAPTER SIX: THE HUNDRED DEMONS NIGHT PARADE
LAUREN BEUKES writer
INAKI MIRANDA artist
EVA DE LA CRUZ colors
TODD KLEIN letters
ADAM HUGHES cover
BILL WILLINGHAM consultant & Fables creator
GREGORY LOCKARD assistant editor
SHELLY BOND editor

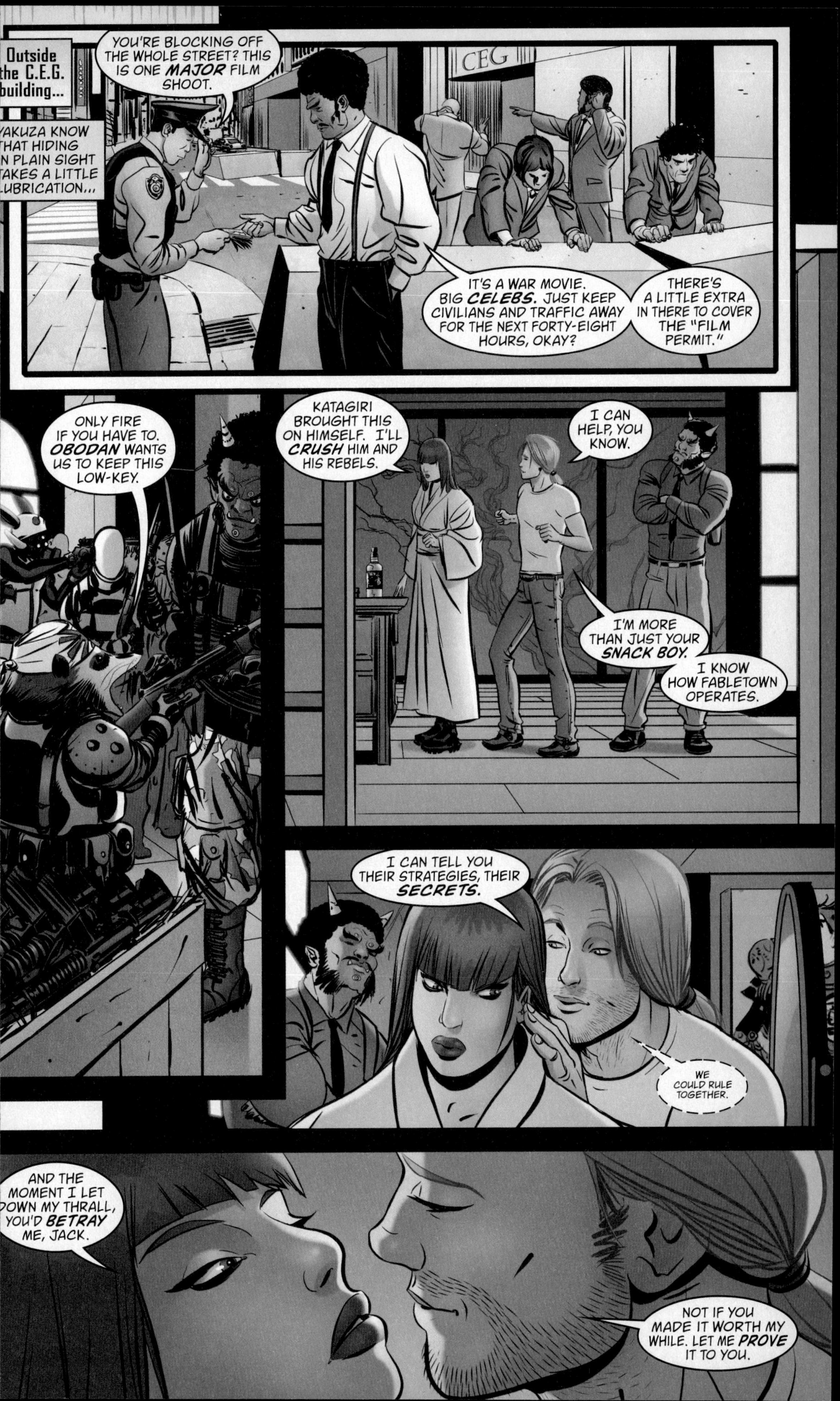
Outside the C.E.G. building...
YAKUZA KNOW THAT HIDING IN PLAIN SIGHT TAKES A LITTLE LUBRICATION...
YOU'RE BLOCKING OFF THE WHOLE STREET? THIS IS ONE MAJOR FILM SHOOT.
CEG
IT'S A WAR MOVIE. BIG CELEBS. JUST KEEP CIVILIANS AND TRAFFIC AWAY FOR THE NEXT FORTY-EIGHT HOURS, OKAY?
THERE'S A LITTLE EXTRA IN THERE TO COVER THE "FILM PERMIT."
ONLY FIRE IF YOU HAVE TO. OBODAN WANTS US TO KEEP THIS LOW-KEY.
KATAGIRI BROUGHT THIS ON HIMSELF. I'LL CRUSH HIM AND HIS REBELS.
I CAN HELP, YOU KNOW.
I'M MORE THAN JUST YOUR SNACK BOY.
I KNOW HOW FABLETOWN OPERATES.
I CAN TELL YOU THEIR STRATEGIES, THEIR SECRETS.
WE COULD RULE TOGETHER.
AND THE MOMENT I LET DOWN MY THRALL, YOU'D BETRAY ME, JACK.
NOT IF YOU MADE IT WORTH MY WHILE. LET ME PROVE IT TO YOU.

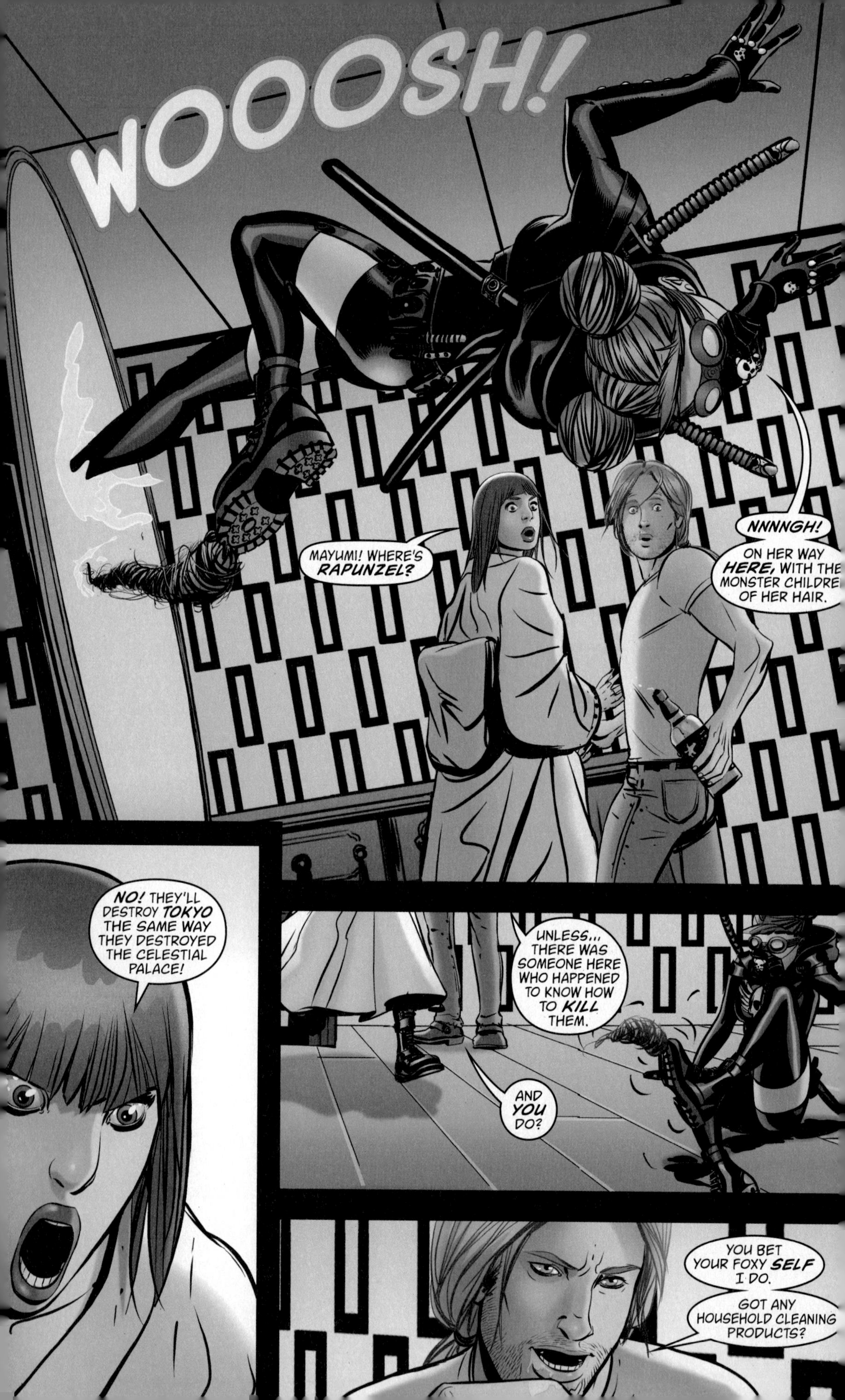
WOOOSH!
MAYUMI! WHERE'S RAPUNZEL?
NNNNGH!
ON HER WAY HERE, WITH THE MONSTER CHILDRE OF HER HAIR.
NO! THEY'LL DESTROY TOKYO THE SAME WAY THEY DESTROYED THE CELESTIAL PALACE!
UNLESS... THERE WAS SOMEONE HERE WHO HAPPENED TO KNOW HOW TO KILL THEM.
AND YOU DO?
YOU BET YOUR FOXY SELF I DO.
GOT ANY HOUSEHOLD CLEANING PRODUCTS?

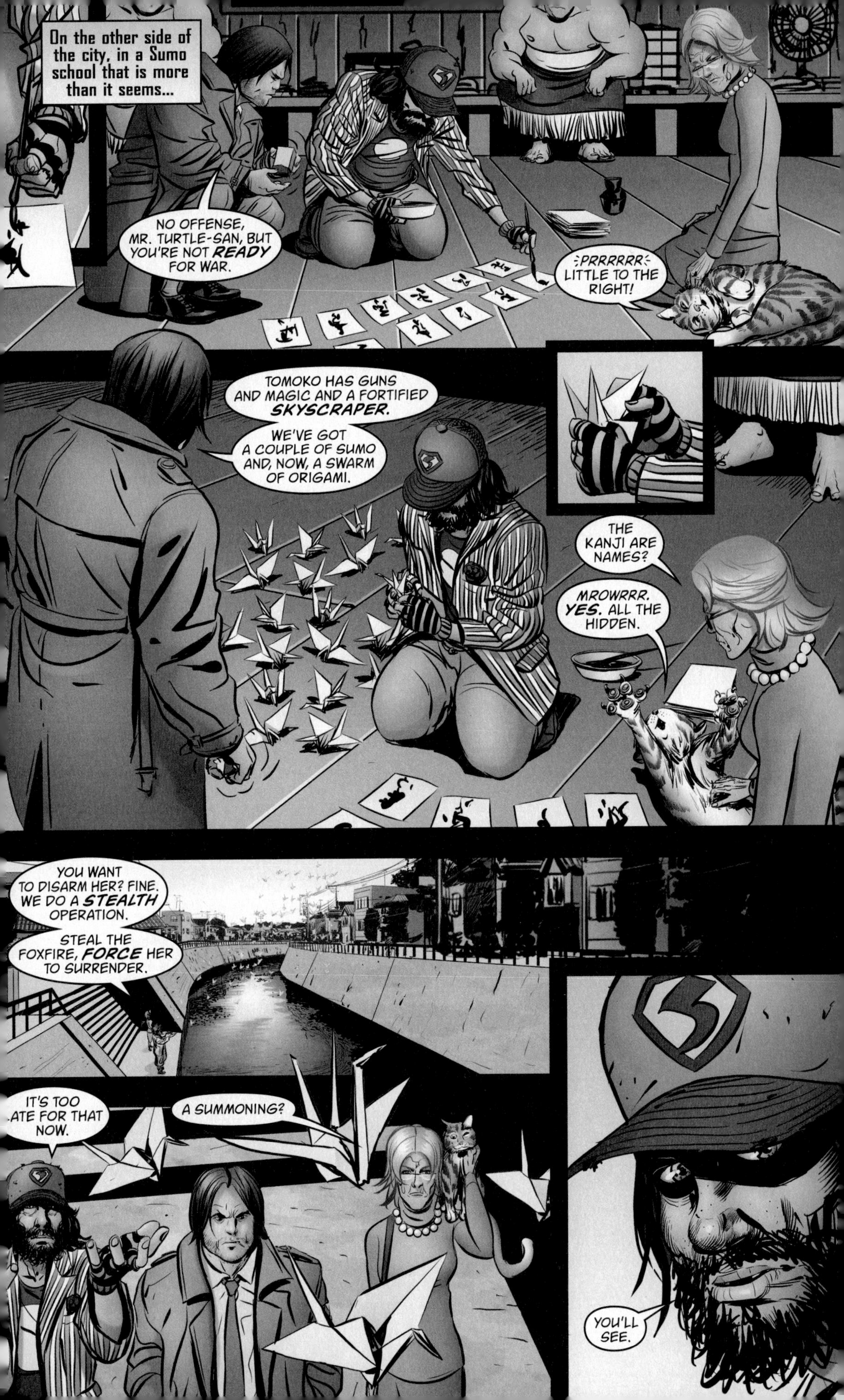
On the other side of the city, in a Sumo school that is more than it seems...
NO OFFENSE, MR. TURTLE-SAN, BUT YOU'RE NOT READY FOR WAR.
PRRRRRR LITTLE TO THE RIGHT!
TOMOKO HAS GUNS AND MAGIC AND A FORTIFIED SKYSCRAPER.
WE'VE GOT A COUPLE OF SUMO AND, NOW, A SWARM OF ORIGAMI.
THE KANJI ARE NAMES?
MROWRRR. YES. ALL THE HIDDEN.
YOU WANT TO DISARM HER? FINE. WE DO A STEALTH OPERATION.
STEAL THE FOXFIRE, FORCE HER TO SURRENDER.
IT'S TOO LATE FOR THAT NOW.
A SUMMONING?
YOU'LL SEE.

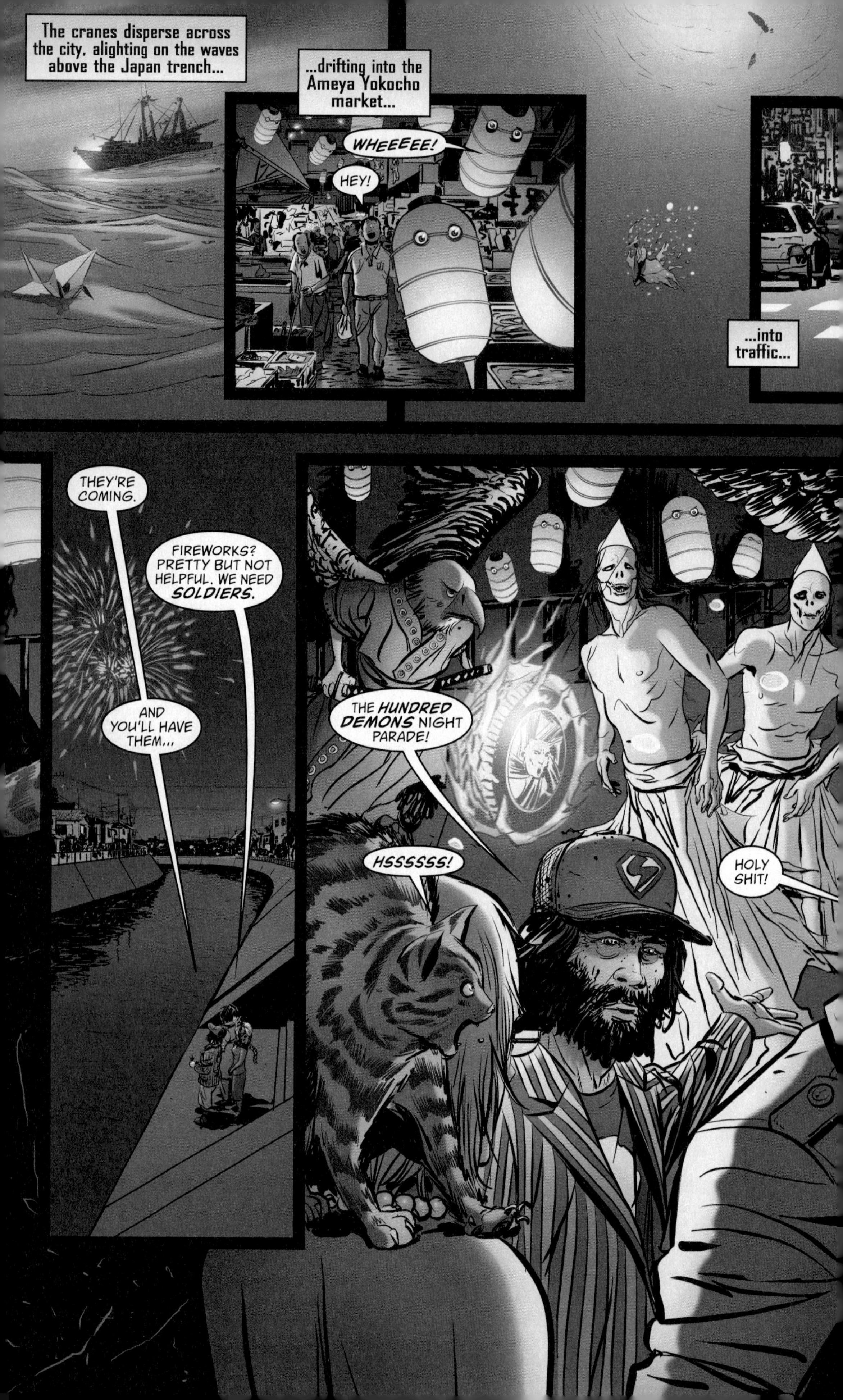

The cranes disperse across the city, alighting on the waves above the Japan trench...
...drifting into the Ameya Yokocho market...
WHEEEEE!
HEY!
...into traffic...
THEY'RE COMING.
FIREWORKS? PRETTY BUT NOT HELPFUL. WE NEED SOLDIERS.
AND YOU'LL HAVE THEM...
THE HUNDRED DEMONS NIGHT PARADE!
HSSSSSS!
HOLY SHIT!

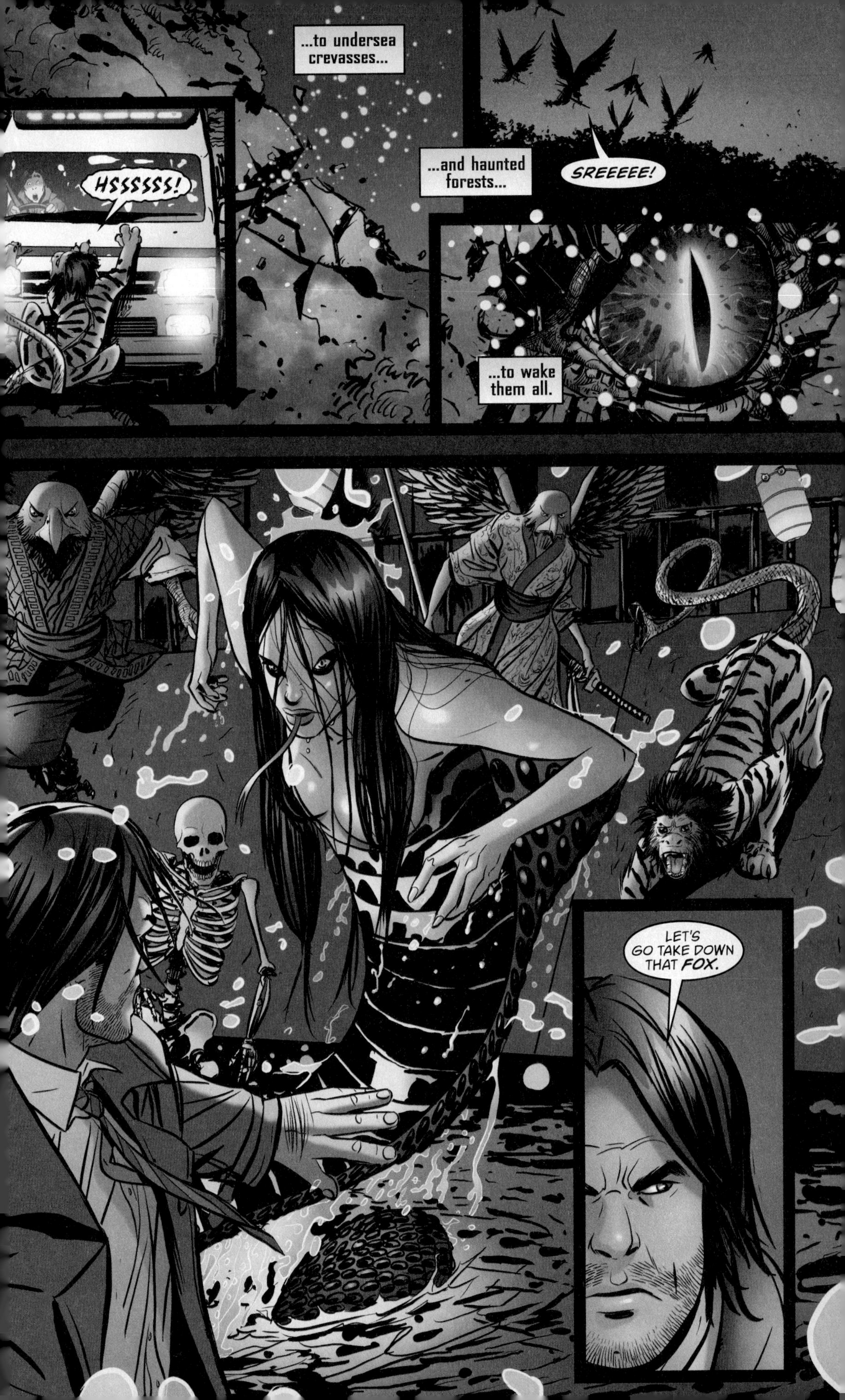
HSSSSSS!
...to undersea crevasses...
...and haunted forests...
SREEEEE!
...to wake them all.
LET'S GO TAKE DOWN THAT FOX.

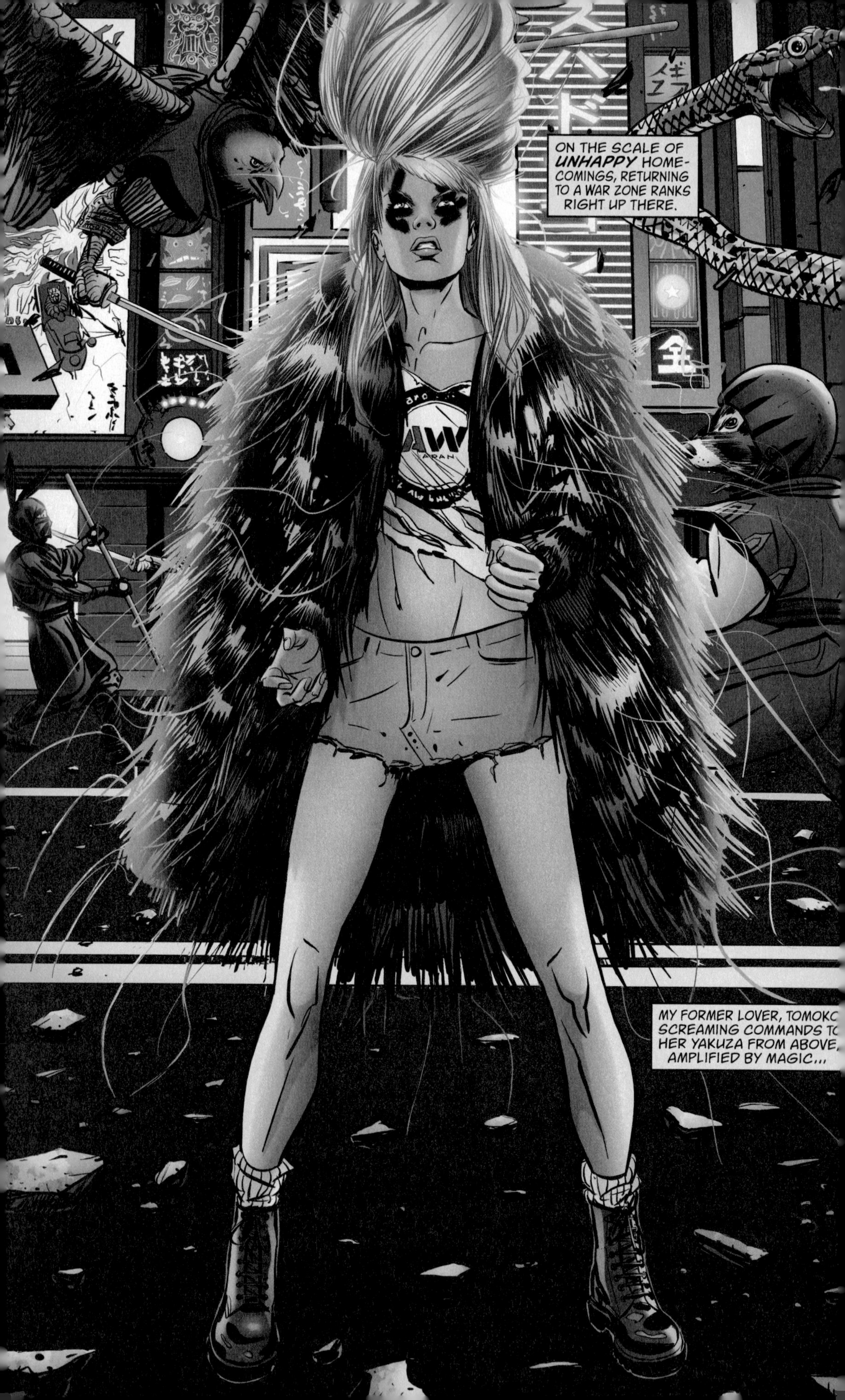

ON THE SCALE OF UNHAPPY HOME-COMINGS, RETURNING TO A WAR ZONE RANKS RIGHT UP THERE.
MY FORMER LOVER, TOMOKO SCREAMING COMMANDS TO HER YAKUZA FROM ABOVE, AMPLIFIED BY MAGIC...

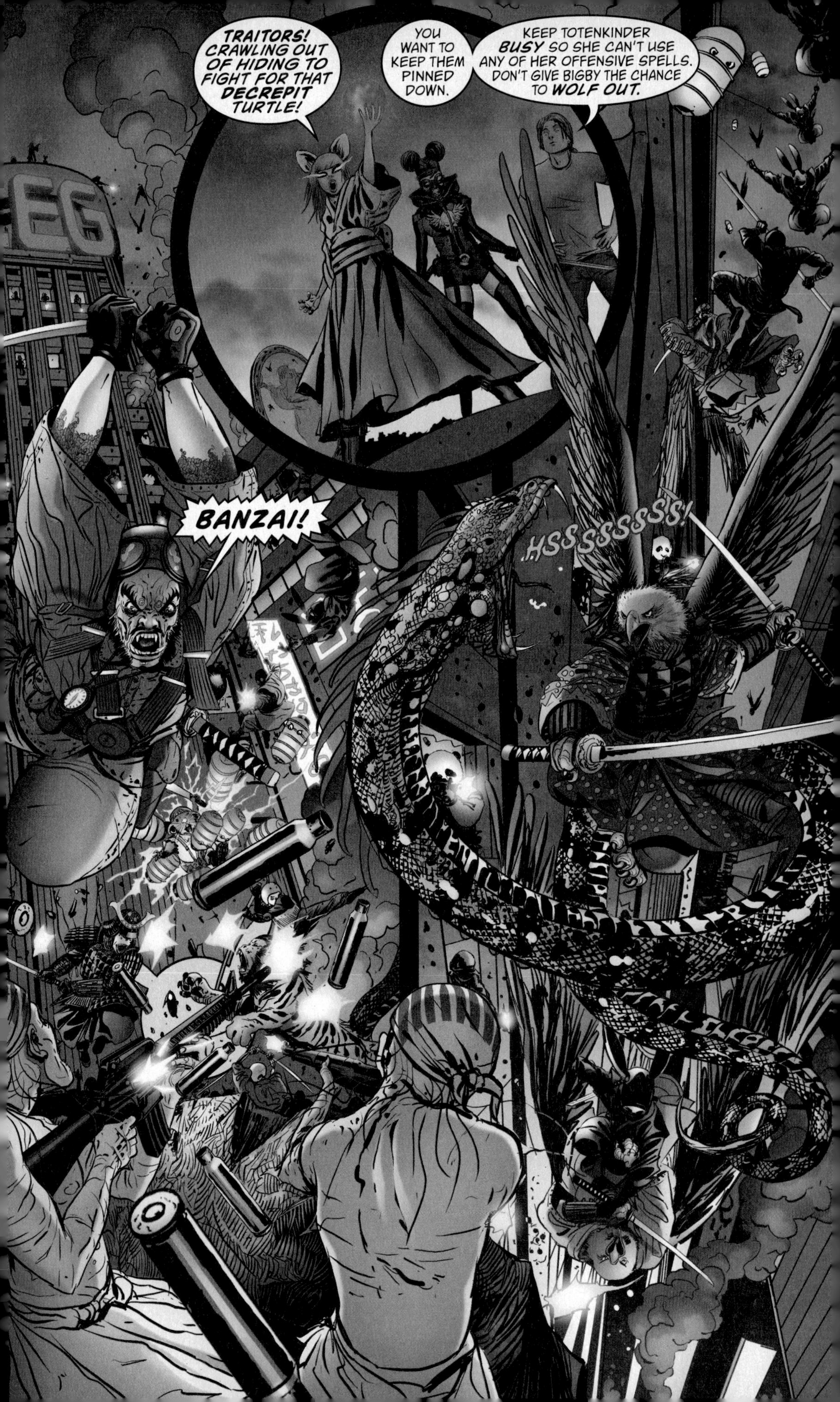
TRAITORS! CRAWLING OUT OF HIDING TO FIGHT FOR THAT DECREPIT TURTLE!
YOU WANT TO KEEP THEM PINNED DOWN.
KEEP TOTENKINDER BUSY SO SHE CAN'T USE ANY OF HER OFFENSIVE SPELLS. DON'T GIVE BIGBY THE CHANCE TO WOLF OUT.
BANZAI!
HSSSSSSSSS!

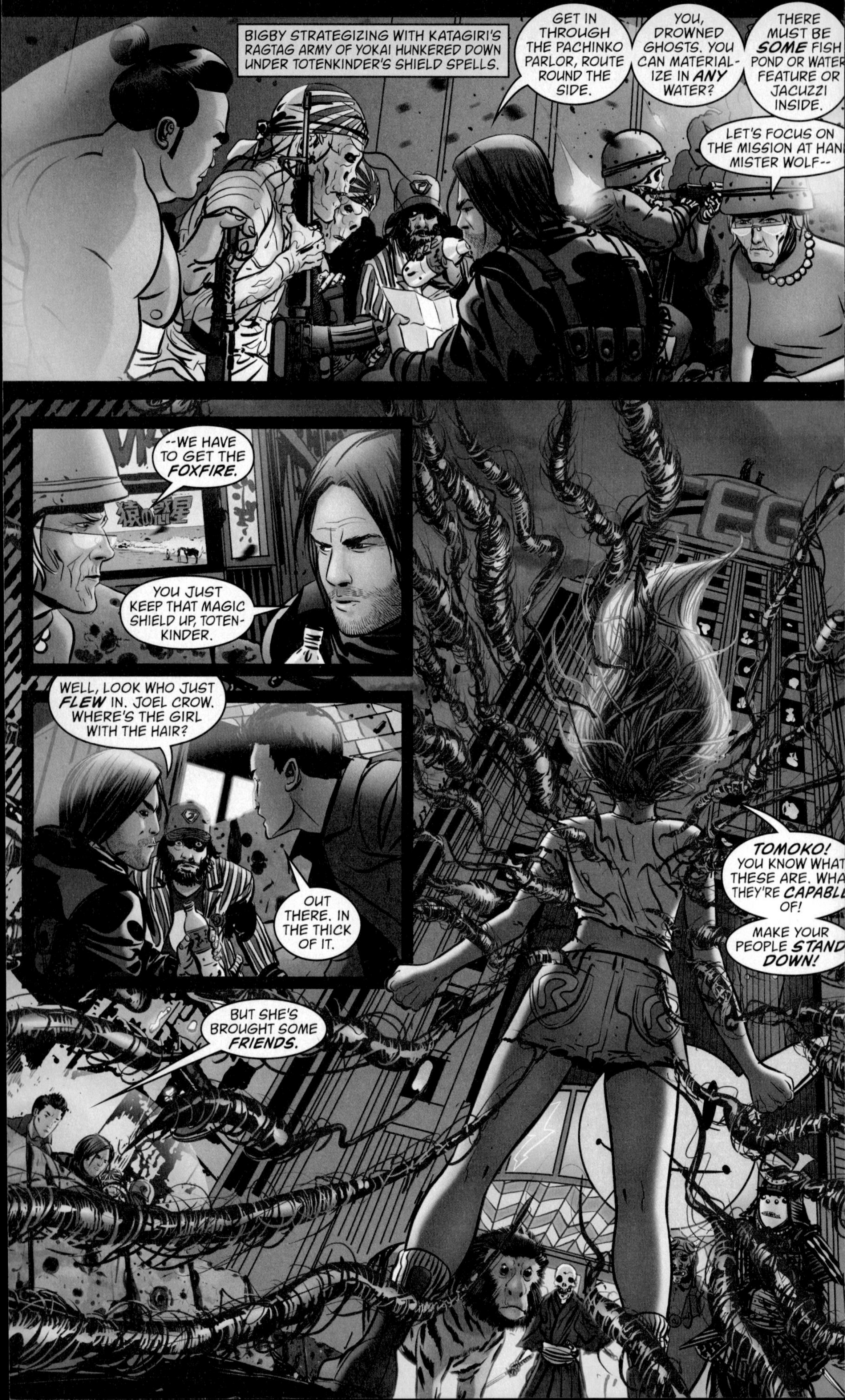
BIGBY STRATEGIZING WITH KATAGIRI'S RAGTAG ARMY OF YOKAI HUNKERED DOWN UNDER TOTENKINDER'S SHIELD SPELLS.
GET IN THROUGH THE PACHINKO PARLOR, ROUTE ROUND THE SIDE.
YOU, DROWNED GHOSTS. YOU CAN MATERIAL-IZE IN ANY WATER?
THERE MUST BE SOME FISH POND OR WATER FEATURE OR JACUZZI INSIDE.
LET'S FOCUS ON THE MISSION AT HAND MISTER WOLF--
--WE HAVE TO GET THE FOXFIRE.
YOU JUST KEEP THAT MAGIC SHIELD UP, TOTEN-KINDER.
WELL, LOOK WHO JUST FLEW IN. JOEL CROW. WHERE'S THE GIRL WITH THE HAIR?
OUT THERE. IN THE THICK OF IT.
BUT SHE'S BROUGHT SOME FRIENDS.
TOMOKO! YOU KNOW WHAT THESE ARE. WHAT THEY'RE CAPABLE OF!
MAKE YOUR PEOPLE STAND DOWN!

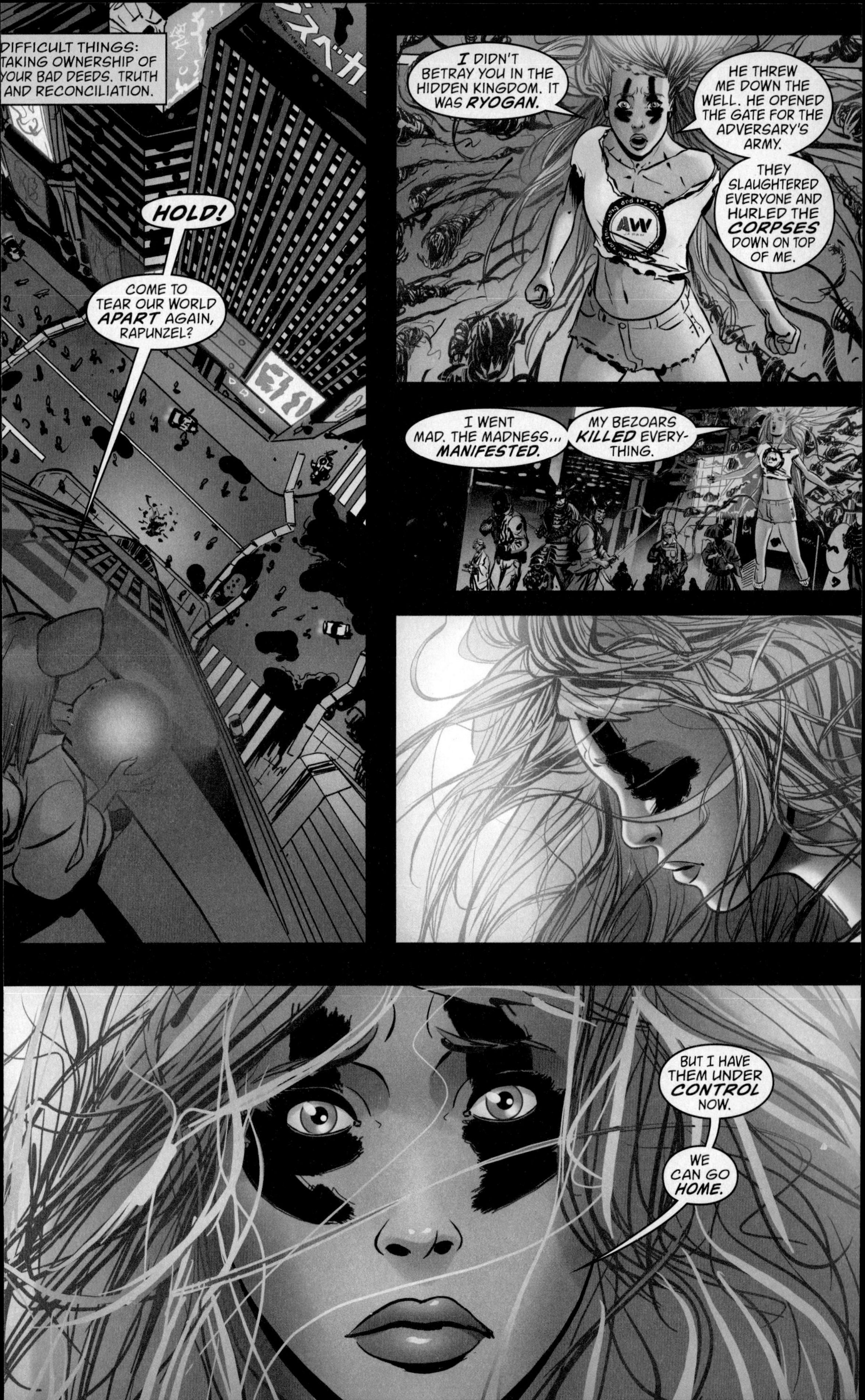
DIFFICULT THINGS: TAKING OWNERSHIP OF YOUR BAD DEEDS. TRUTH AND RECONCILIATION.
HOLD!
COME TO TEAR OUR WORLD APART AGAIN, RAPUNZEL?
I DIDN'T BETRAY YOU IN THE HIDDEN KINGDOM. IT WAS RYOGAN.
HE THREW ME DOWN THE WELL. HE OPENED THE GATE FOR THE ADVERSARY'S ARMY.
THEY SLAUGHTERED EVERYONE AND HURLED THE CORPSES DOWN ON TOP OF ME.
I WENT MAD. THE MADNESS... MANIFESTED.
MY BEZOARS KILLED EVERY-THING.
BUT I HAVE THEM UNDER CONTROL NOW.
WE CAN GO HOME.

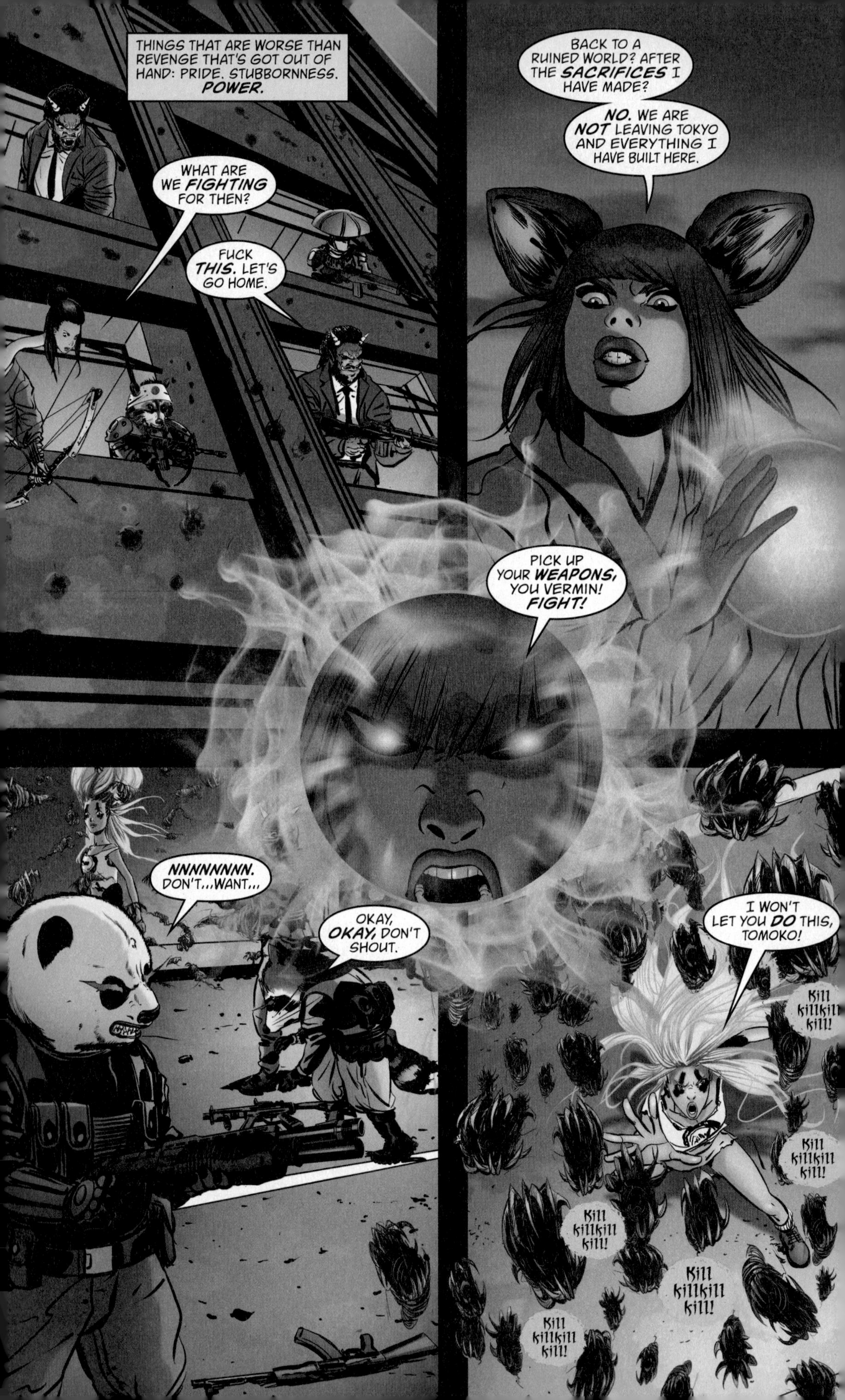
THINGS THAT ARE WORSE THAN REVENGE THAT'S GOT OUT OF HAND: PRIDE. STUBBORNNESS. POWER.
WHAT ARE WE FIGHTING FOR THEN?
FUCK THIS. LET'S GO HOME.
BACK TO A RUINED WORLD? AFTER THE SACRIFICES I HAVE MADE?
NO. WE ARE NOT LEAVING TOKYO AND EVERYTHING I HAVE BUILT HERE.
PICK UP YOUR WEAPONS, YOU VERMIN! FIGHT!
NNNNNNNN. DON'T...WANT...
OKAY, OKAY, DON'T SHOUT.
I WON'T LET YOU DO THIS, TOMOKO!
Kill killkill kill!
Kill killkill kill!
Kill killkill kill!
Kill killkill kill!
Kill killkill kill!

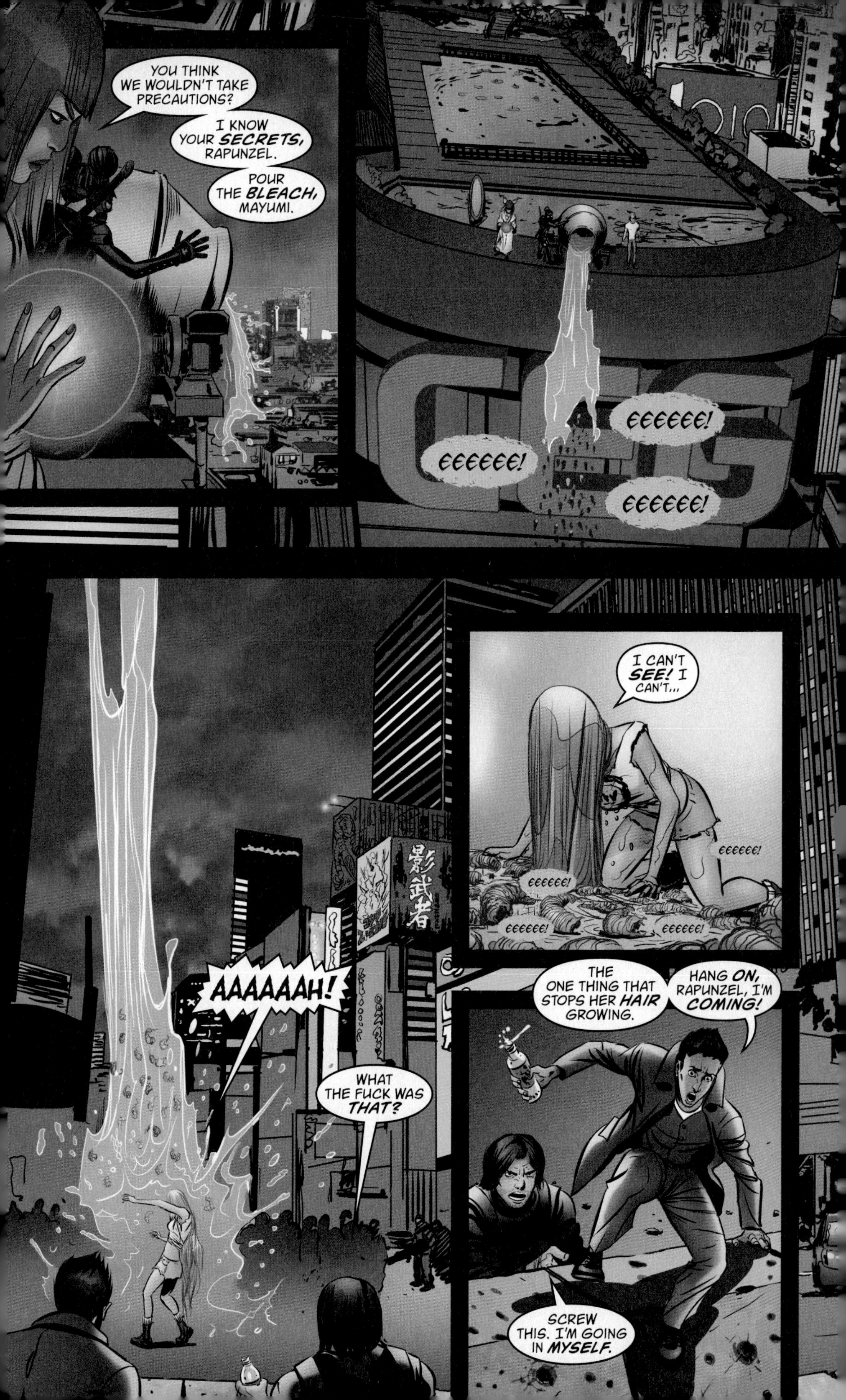
YOU THINK WE WOULDN'T TAKE PRECAUTIONS?
I KNOW YOUR SECRETS, RAPUNZEL.
POUR THE BLEACH, MAYUMI.
EEEEEE!
EEEEEE!
EEEEEE!
AAAAAAH!
WHAT THE FUCK WAS THAT?
影武者
I CAN'T SEE! I CAN'T...
EEEEEE!
EEEEEE!
EEEEEE!
EEEEEE!
THE ONE THING THAT STOPS HER HAIR GROWING.
HANG ON, RAPUNZEL, I'M COMING!
SCREW THIS. I'M GOING IN MYSELF.

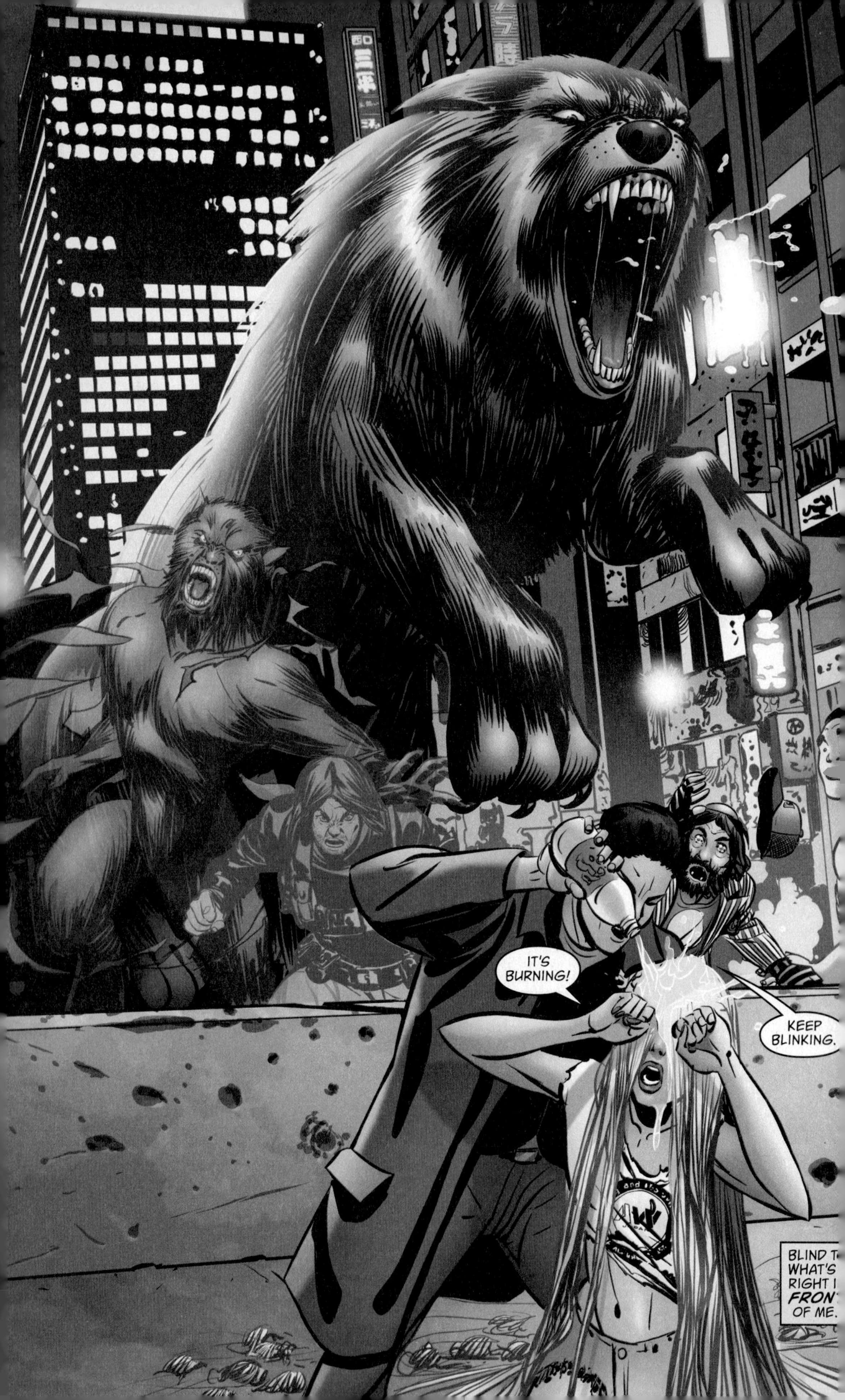
IT'S BURNING!
KEEP BLINKING.
BLIND T
WHAT'S
RIGHT I
FRONT
OF ME.

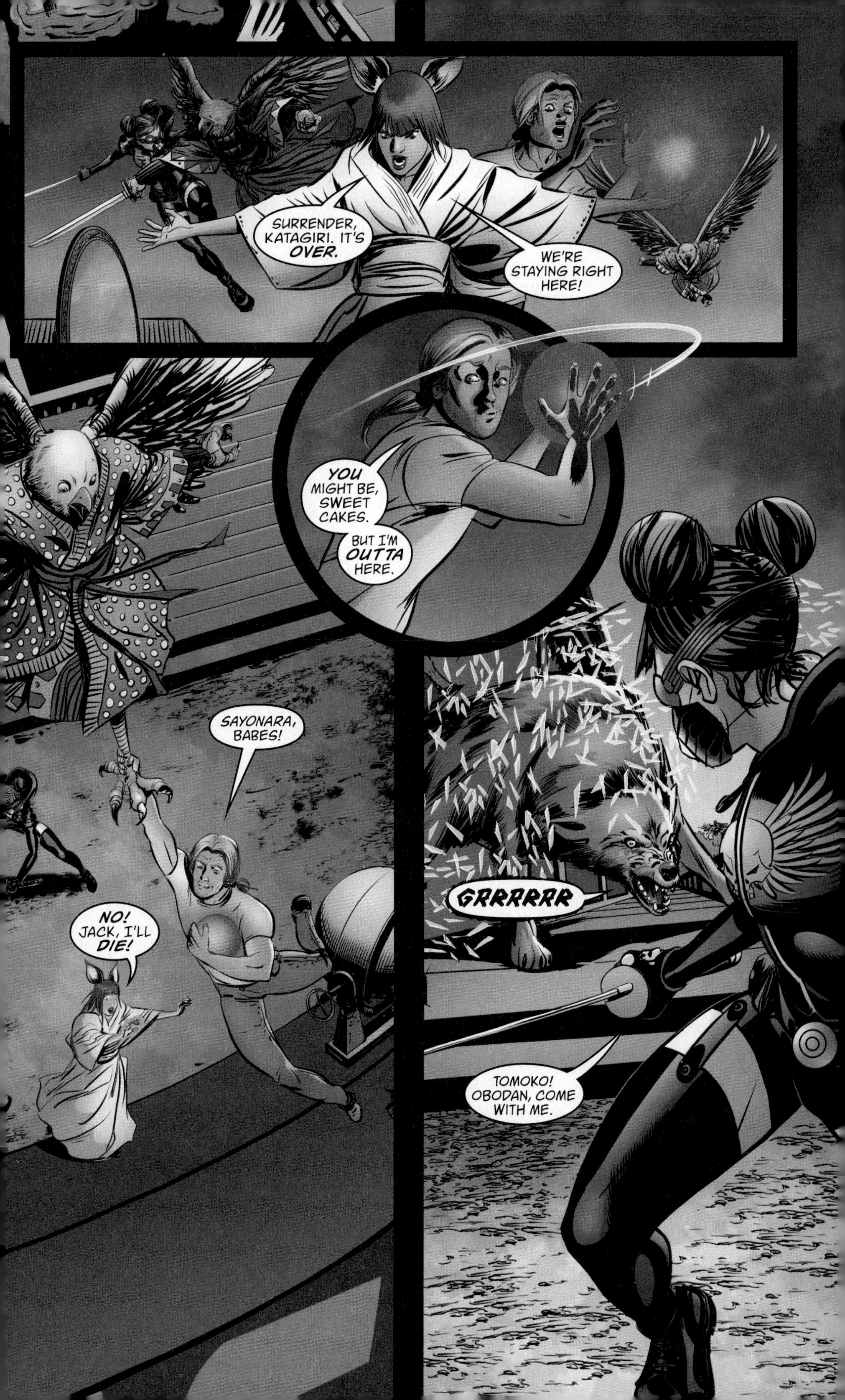
SURRENDER, KATAGIRI. IT'S OVER.
WE'RE STAYING RIGHT HERE!
YOU MIGHT BE, SWEET CAKES.
BUT I'M OUTTA HERE.
SAYONARA, BABES!
NO! JACK, I'LL DIE!
GRRRRRR
TOMOKO! OBODAN, COME WITH ME.

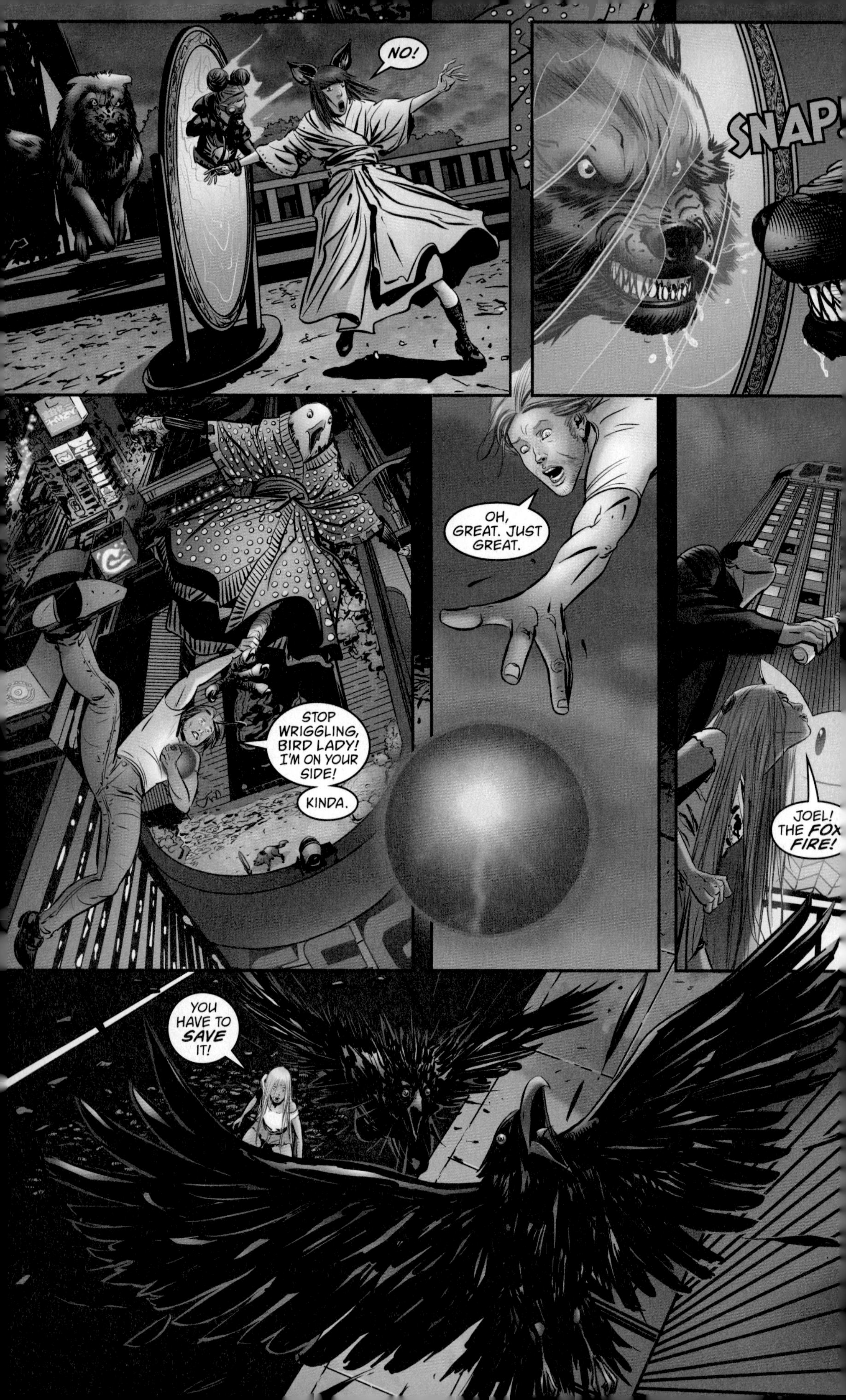
NO!
SNAP!
STOP WRIGGLING, BIRD LADY! I'M ON YOUR SIDE!
KINDA.
OH, GREAT. JUST GREAT.
JOEL! THE FOX FIRE!
YOU HAVE TO SAVE IT!

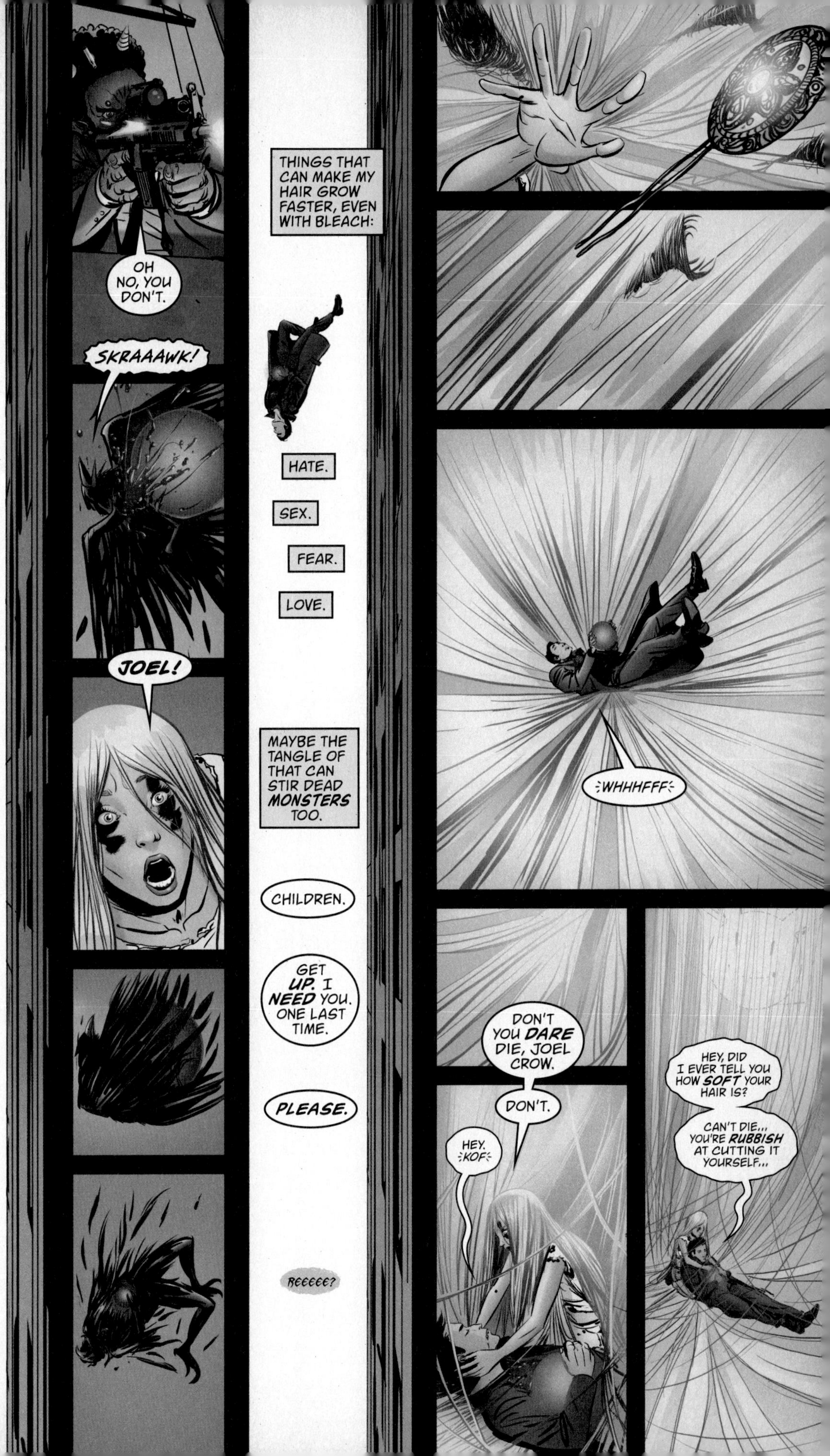
THINGS THAT CAN MAKE MY HAIR GROW FASTER, EVEN WITH BLEACH:
OH NO, YOU DON'T.
SKRAAAWK!
HATE.
SEX.
FEAR.
LOVE.
JOEL!
MAYBE THE TANGLE OF THAT CAN STIR DEAD MONSTERS TOO.
CHILDREN.
GET UP. I NEED YOU. ONE LAST TIME.
PLEASE.
REEEEE?
WHHHFFF
DON'T YOU DARE DIE, JOEL CROW.
DON'T.
HEY. KOF
HEY, DID I EVER TELL YOU HOW SOFT YOUR HAIR IS?
CAN'T DIE... YOU'RE RUBBISH AT CUTTING IT YOURSELF...

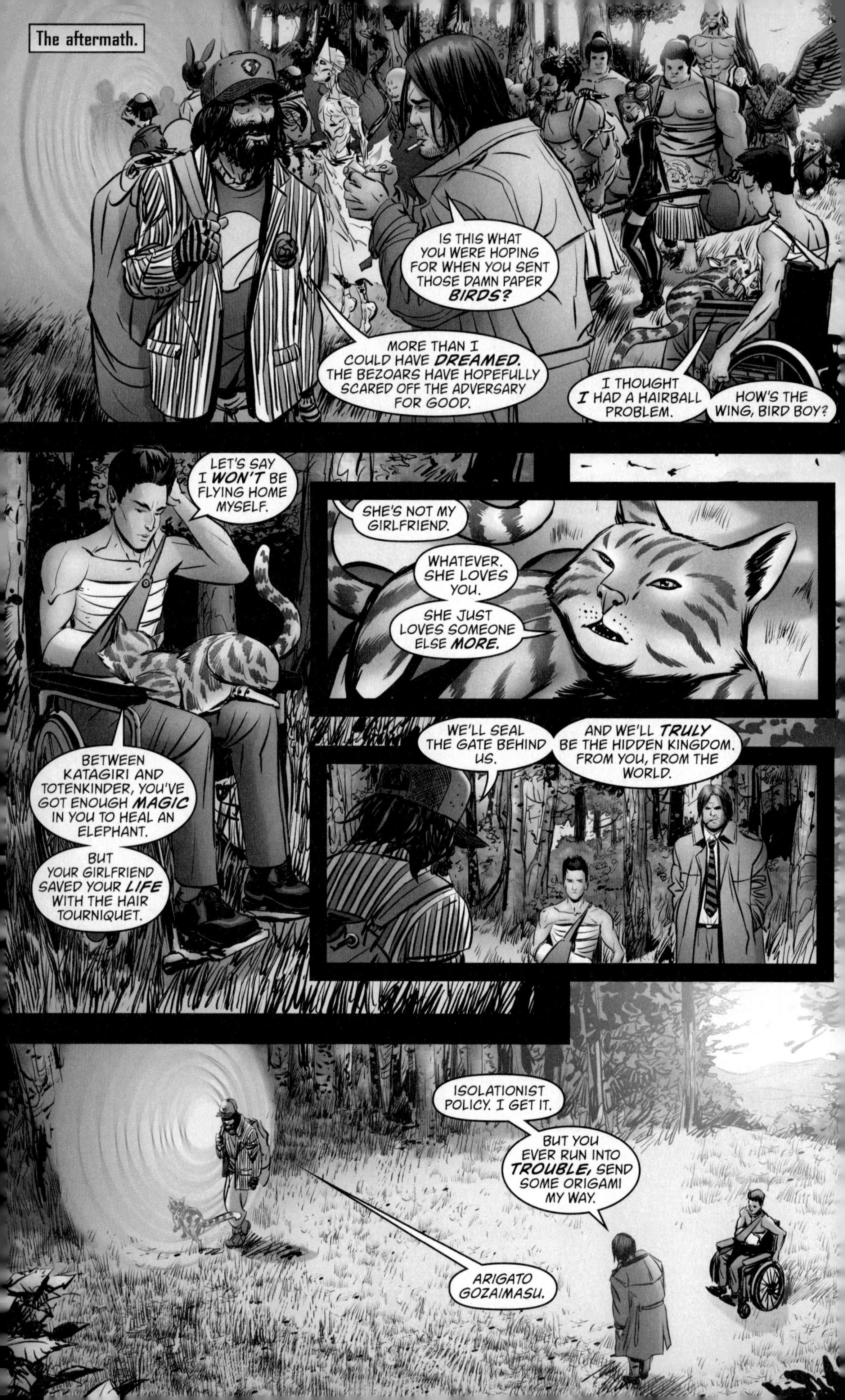

The aftermath.
IS THIS WHAT YOU WERE HOPING FOR WHEN YOU SENT THOSE DAMN PAPER BIRDS?
MORE THAN I COULD HAVE DREAMED. THE BEZOARS HAVE HOPEFULLY SCARED OFF THE ADVERSARY FOR GOOD.
I THOUGHT I HAD A HAIRBALL PROBLEM.
HOW'S THE WING, BIRD BOY?
LET'S SAY I WON'T BE FLYING HOME MYSELF.
BETWEEN KATAGIRI AND TOTENKINDER, YOU'VE GOT ENOUGH MAGIC IN YOU TO HEAL AN ELEPHANT.
BUT YOUR GIRLFRIEND SAVED YOUR LIFE WITH THE HAIR TOURNIQUET.
SHE'S NOT MY GIRLFRIEND.
WHATEVER. SHE LOVES YOU.
SHE JUST LOVES SOMEONE ELSE MORE.
WE'LL SEAL THE GATE BEHIND US.
AND WE'LL TRULY BE THE HIDDEN KINGDOM. FROM YOU, FROM THE WORLD.
ISOLATIONIST POLICY. I GET IT.
BUT YOU EVER RUN INTO TROUBLE, SEND SOME ORIGAMI MY WAY.
ARIGATO GOZAIMASU.

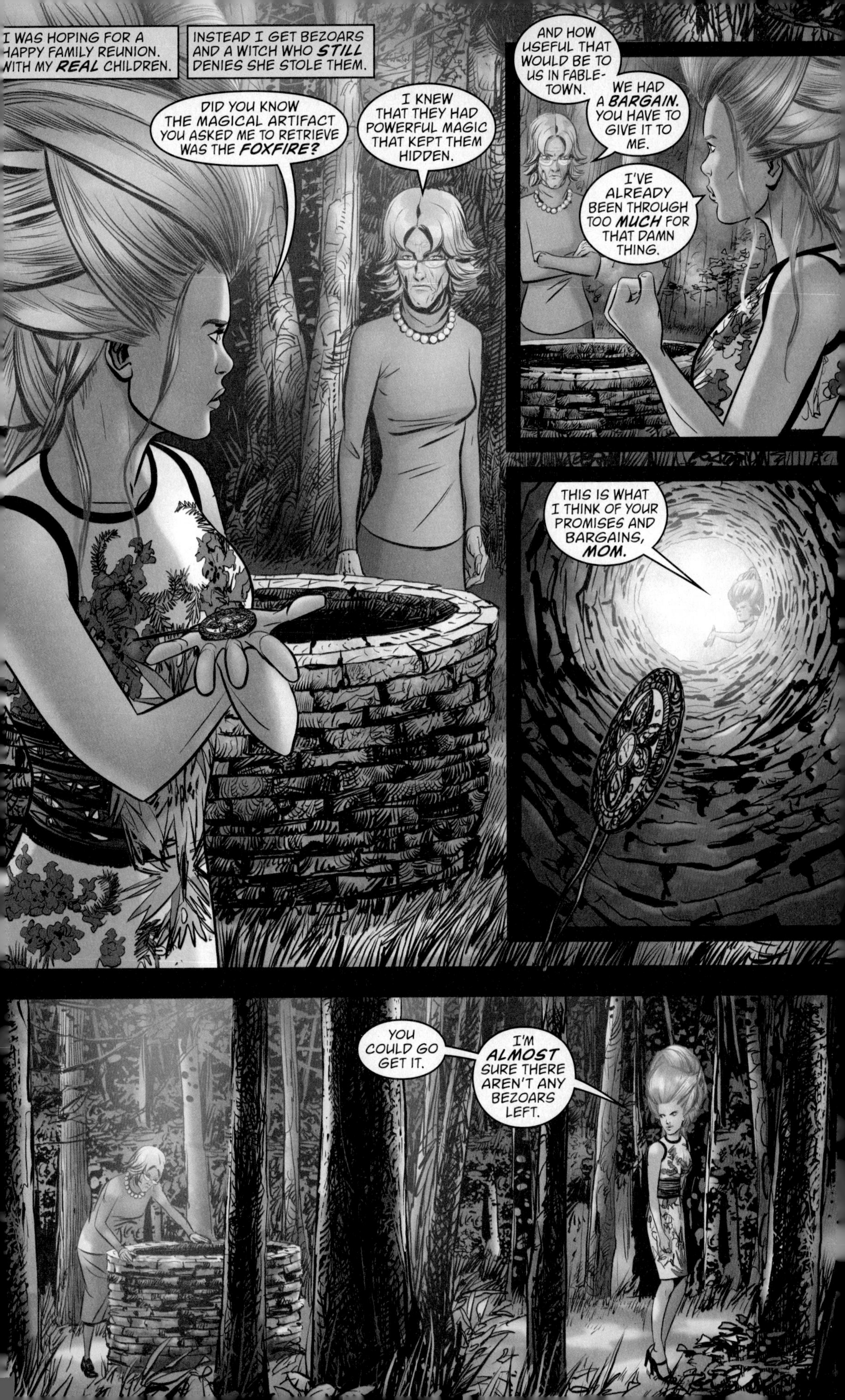

I WAS HOPING FOR A HAPPY FAMILY REUNION. WITH MY REAL CHILDREN.
INSTEAD I GET BEZOARS AND A WITCH WHO STILL DENIES SHE STOLE THEM.
DID YOU KNOW THE MAGICAL ARTIFACT YOU ASKED ME TO RETRIEVE WAS THE FOXFIRE?
I KNEW THAT THEY HAD POWERFUL MAGIC THAT KEPT THEM HIDDEN.
AND HOW USEFUL THAT WOULD BE TO US IN FABLE-TOWN.
WE HAD A BARGAIN. YOU HAVE TO GIVE IT TO ME.
I'VE ALREADY BEEN THROUGH TOO MUCH FOR THAT DAMN THING.
THIS IS WHAT I THINK OF YOUR PROMISES AND BARGAINS, MOM.
YOU COULD GO GET IT.
I'M ALMOST SURE THERE AREN'T ANY BEZOARS LEFT.

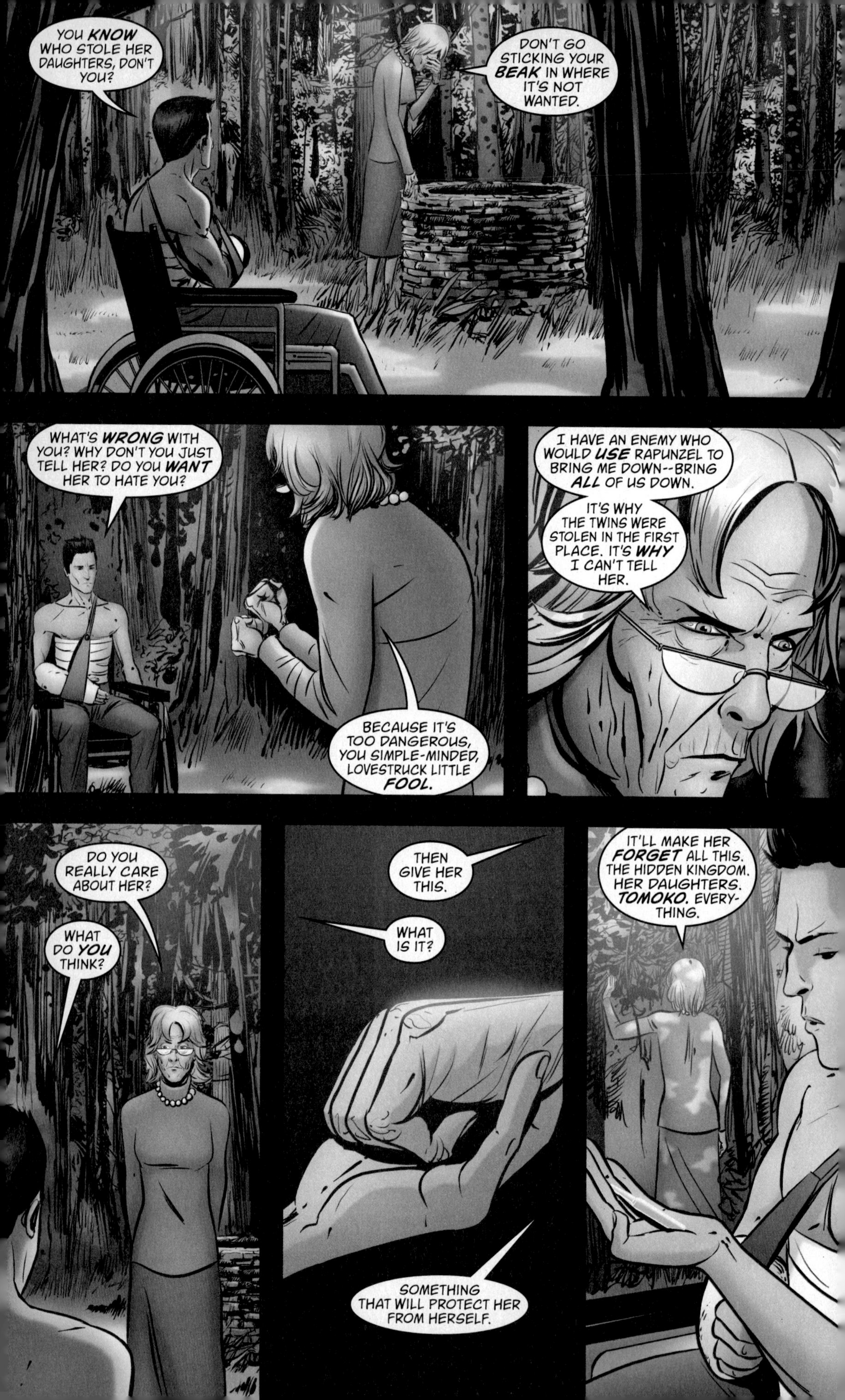
YOU KNOW WHO STOLE HER DAUGHTERS, DON'T YOU?
DON'T GO STICKING YOUR BEAK IN WHERE IT'S NOT WANTED.
WHAT'S WRONG WITH YOU? WHY DON'T YOU JUST TELL HER? DO YOU WANT HER TO HATE YOU?
BECAUSE IT'S TOO DANGEROUS, YOU SIMPLE-MINDED, LOVESTRUCK LITTLE FOOL.
I HAVE AN ENEMY WHO WOULD USE RAPUNZEL TO BRING ME DOWN--BRING ALL OF US DOWN.
IT'S WHY THE TWINS WERE STOLEN IN THE FIRST PLACE. IT'S WHY I CAN'T TELL HER.
DO YOU REALLY CARE ABOUT HER?
WHAT DO YOU THINK?
THEN GIVE HER THIS.
WHAT IS IT?
SOMETHING THAT WILL PROTECT HER FROM HERSELF.
IT'LL MAKE HER FORGET ALL THIS. THE HIDDEN KINGDOM. HER DAUGHTERS. TOMOKO. EVERYTHING.

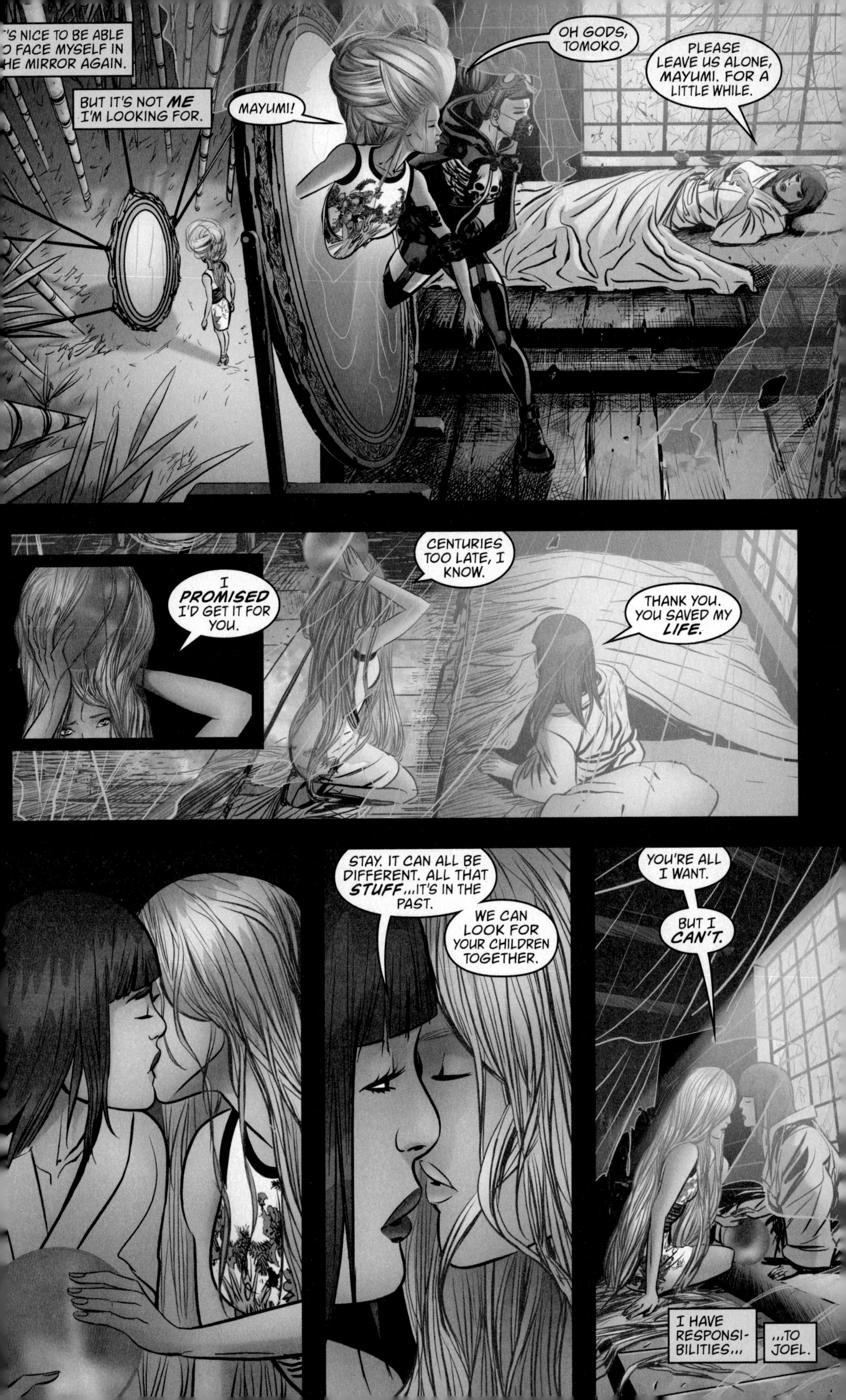
'S NICE TO BE ABLE
O FACE MYSELF IN
HE MIRROR AGAIN.
BUT IT'S NOT **ME** I'M LOOKING FOR.
MAYUMI!
OH GODS, TOMOKO.
PLEASE LEAVE US ALONE, MAYUMI. FOR A LITTLE WHILE.
I **PROMISED** I'D GET IT FOR YOU.
CENTURIES TOO LATE, I KNOW.
THANK YOU. YOU SAVED MY **LIFE**.
STAY. IT CAN ALL BE DIFFERENT. ALL THAT **STUFF**...IT'S IN THE PAST.
WE CAN LOOK FOR YOUR CHILDREN TOGETHER.
YOU'RE ALL I WANT.
BUT I **CAN'T**.
I HAVE RESPONSI- BILITIES...
...TO JOEL.

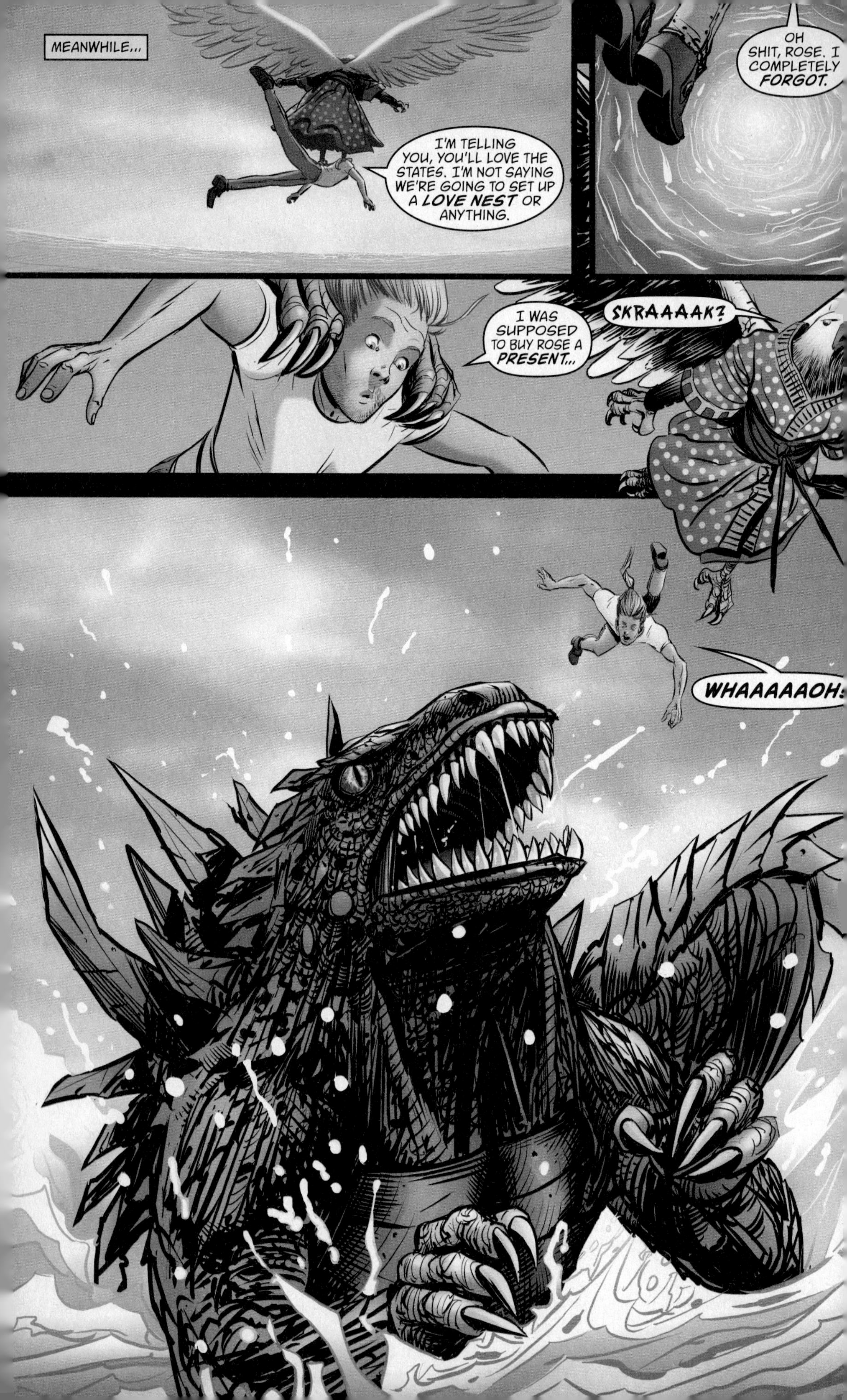
MEANWHILE...
I'M TELLING YOU, YOU'LL LOVE THE STATES. I'M NOT SAYING WE'RE GOING TO SET UP A **LOVE NEST** OR ANYTHING.
OH SHIT, ROSE. I COMPLETELY **FORGOT**.
I WAS SUPPOSED TO BUY ROSE A **PRESENT**...
SKRAAAAK?
WHAAAAAOH!

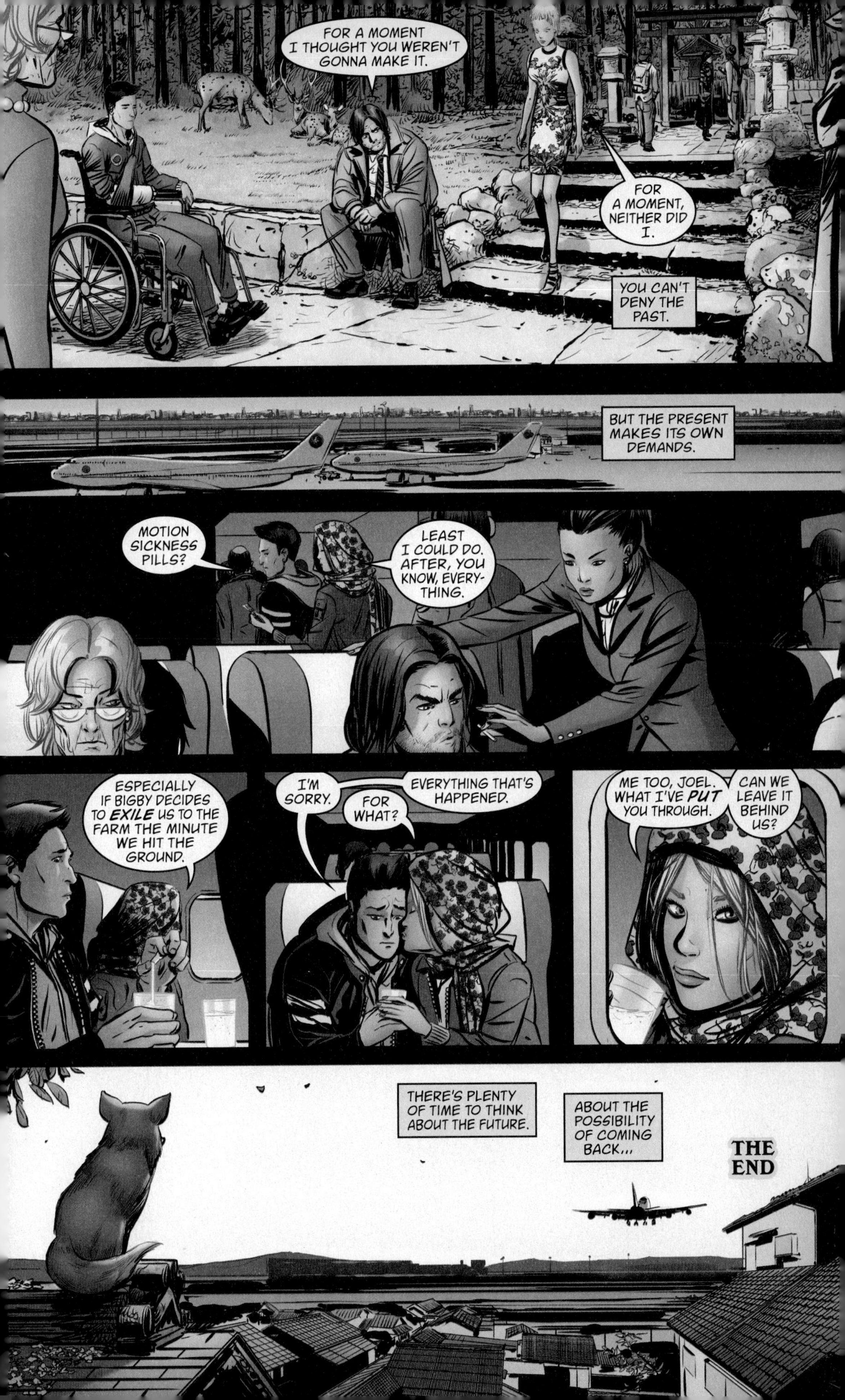
FOR A MOMENT I THOUGHT YOU WEREN'T GONNA MAKE IT.
FOR A MOMENT, NEITHER DID I.
YOU CAN'T DENY THE PAST.
BUT THE PRESENT MAKES ITS OWN DEMANDS.
MOTION SICKNESS PILLS?
LEAST I COULD DO. AFTER, YOU KNOW, EVERY-THING.
ESPECIALLY IF BIGBY DECIDES TO EXILE US TO THE FARM THE MINUTE WE HIT THE GROUND.
I'M SORRY.
FOR WHAT?
EVERYTHING THAT'S HAPPENED.
ME TOO, JOEL. WHAT I'VE PUT YOU THROUGH.
CAN WE LEAVE IT BEHIND US?
THERE'S PLENTY OF TIME TO THINK ABOUT THE FUTURE.
ABOUT THE POSSIBILITY OF COMING BACK...
THE END

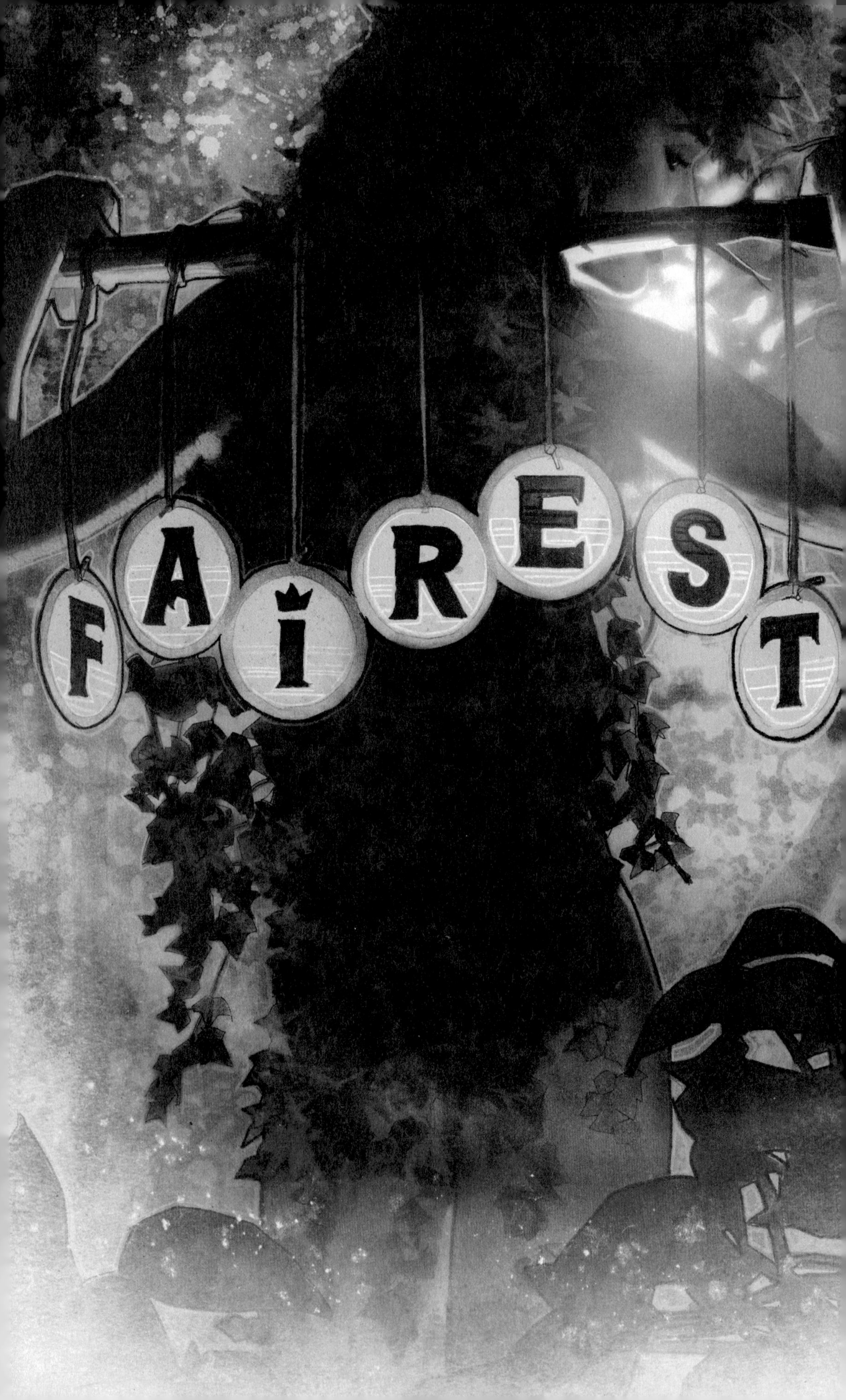
FAIREST

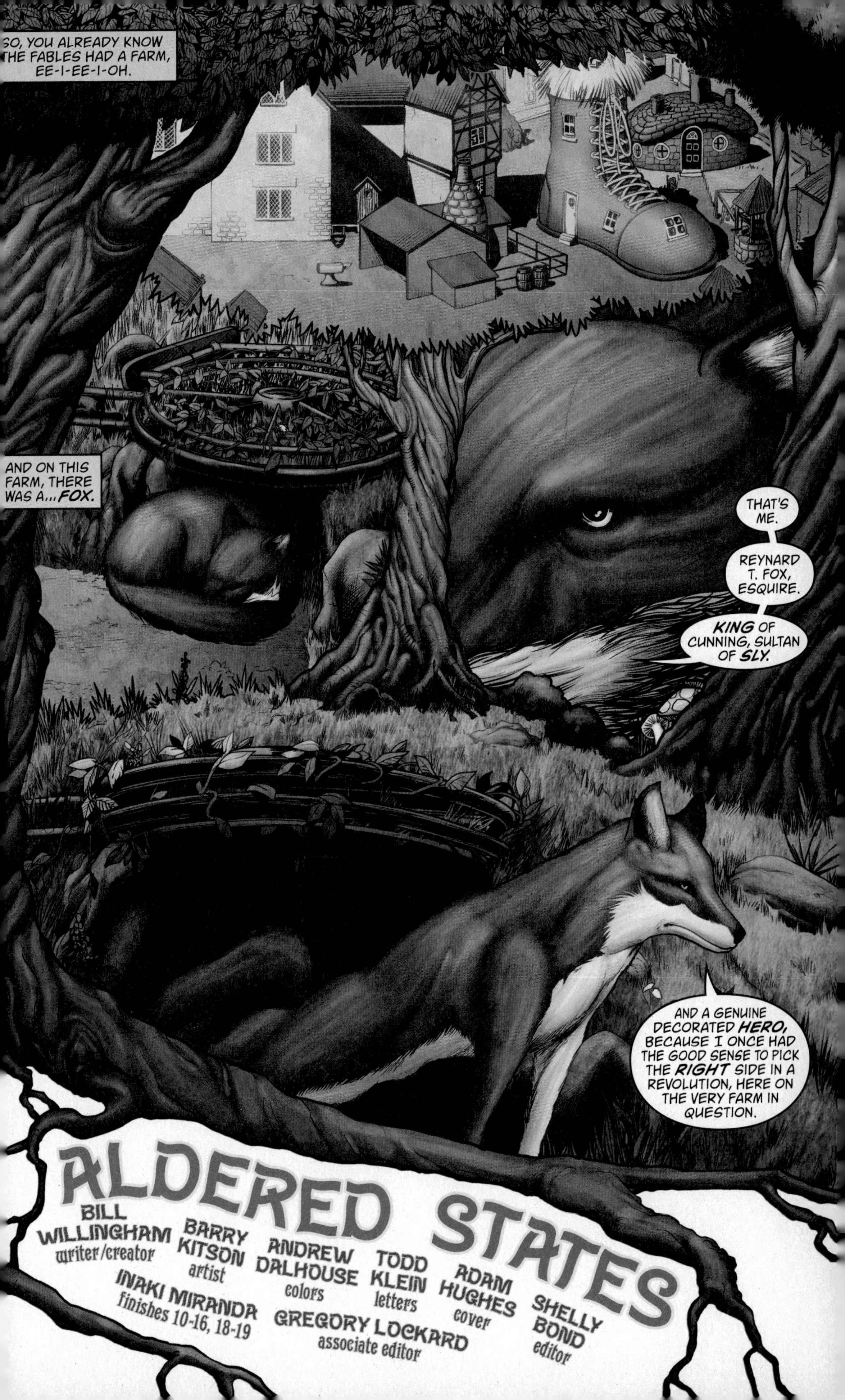
SO, YOU ALREADY KNOW THE FABLES HAD A FARM, EE-I-EE-I-OH.
AND ON THIS FARM, THERE WAS A...FOX.
THAT'S ME.
REYNARD T. FOX, ESQUIRE.
KING OF CUNNING, SULTAN OF SLY.
AND A GENUINE DECORATED HERO, BECAUSE I ONCE HAD THE GOOD SENSE TO PICK THE RIGHT SIDE IN A REVOLUTION, HERE ON THE VERY FARM IN QUESTION.
ALDERED STATES
BILL WILLINGHAM writer/creator
BARRY KITSON artist
ANDREW DALHOUSE colors
TODD KLEIN letters
ADAM HUGHES cover
SHELLY BOND editor
INAKI MIRANDA finishes 10-16, 18-19
GREGORY LOCKARD associate editor

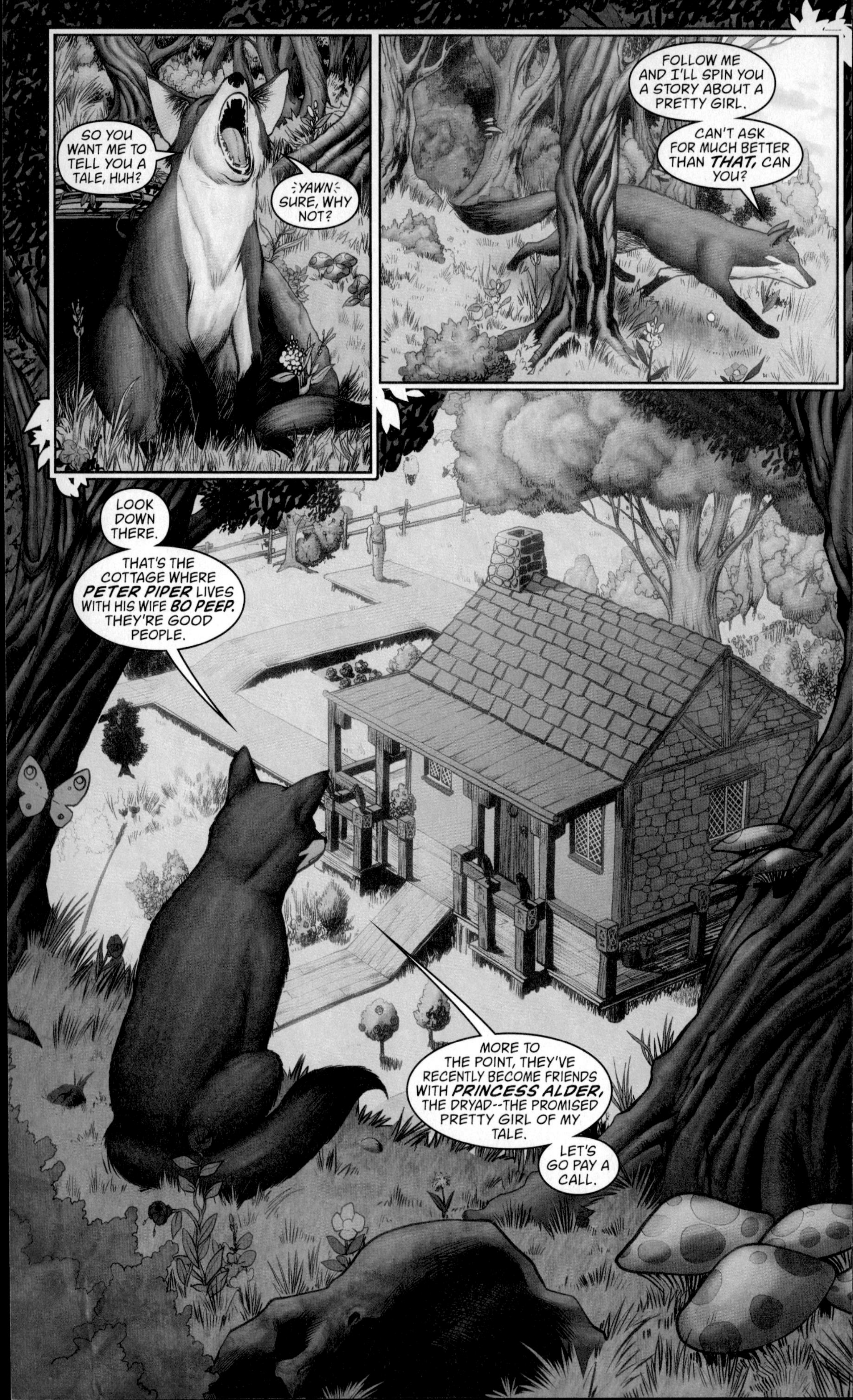
SO YOU WANT ME TO TELL YOU A TALE, HUH?
YAWN SURE, WHY NOT?
FOLLOW ME AND I'LL SPIN YOU A STORY ABOUT A PRETTY GIRL.
CAN'T ASK FOR MUCH BETTER THAN THAT, CAN YOU?
LOOK DOWN THERE.
THAT'S THE COTTAGE WHERE PETER PIPER LIVES WITH HIS WIFE BO PEEP. THEY'RE GOOD PEOPLE.
MORE TO THE POINT, THEY'VE RECENTLY BECOME FRIENDS WITH PRINCESS ALDER, THE DRYAD--THE PROMISED PRETTY GIRL OF MY TALE.
LET'S GO PAY A CALL.

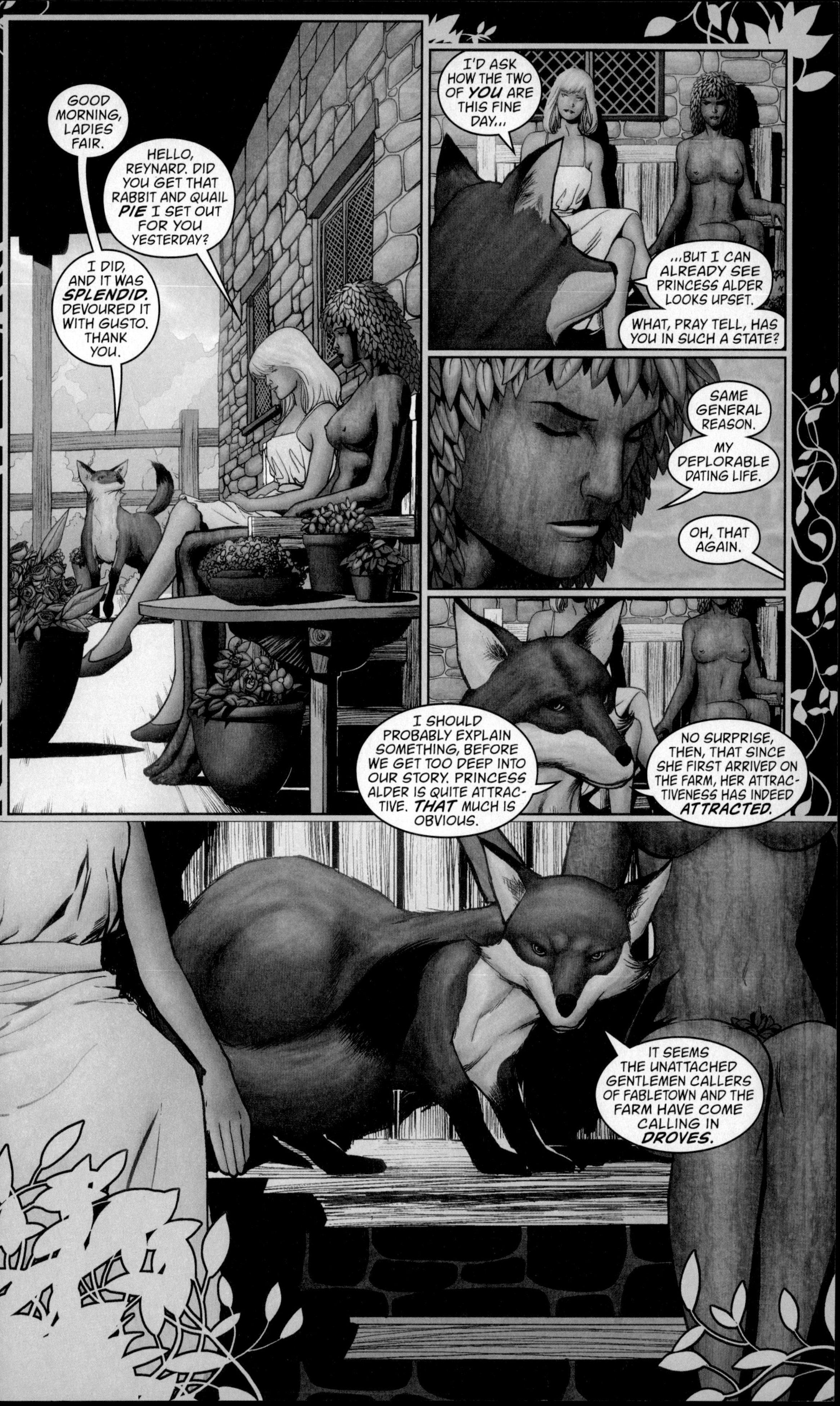
GOOD MORNING, LADIES FAIR.
HELLO, REYNARD. DID YOU GET THAT RABBIT AND QUAIL PIE I SET OUT FOR YOU YESTERDAY?
I DID, AND IT WAS SPLENDID. DEVOURED IT WITH GUSTO. THANK YOU.
I'D ASK HOW THE TWO OF YOU ARE THIS FINE DAY...
...BUT I CAN ALREADY SEE PRINCESS ALDER LOOKS UPSET.
WHAT, PRAY TELL, HAS YOU IN SUCH A STATE?
SAME GENERAL REASON. MY DEPLORABLE DATING LIFE.
OH, THAT AGAIN.
I SHOULD PROBABLY EXPLAIN SOMETHING, BEFORE WE GET TOO DEEP INTO OUR STORY. PRINCESS ALDER IS QUITE ATTRACTIVE. THAT MUCH IS OBVIOUS.
NO SURPRISE, THEN, THAT SINCE SHE FIRST ARRIVED ON THE FARM, HER ATTRACTIVENESS HAS INDEED ATTRACTED.
IT SEEMS THE UNATTACHED GENTLEMEN CALLERS OF FABLETOWN AND THE FARM HAVE COME CALLING IN DROVES.

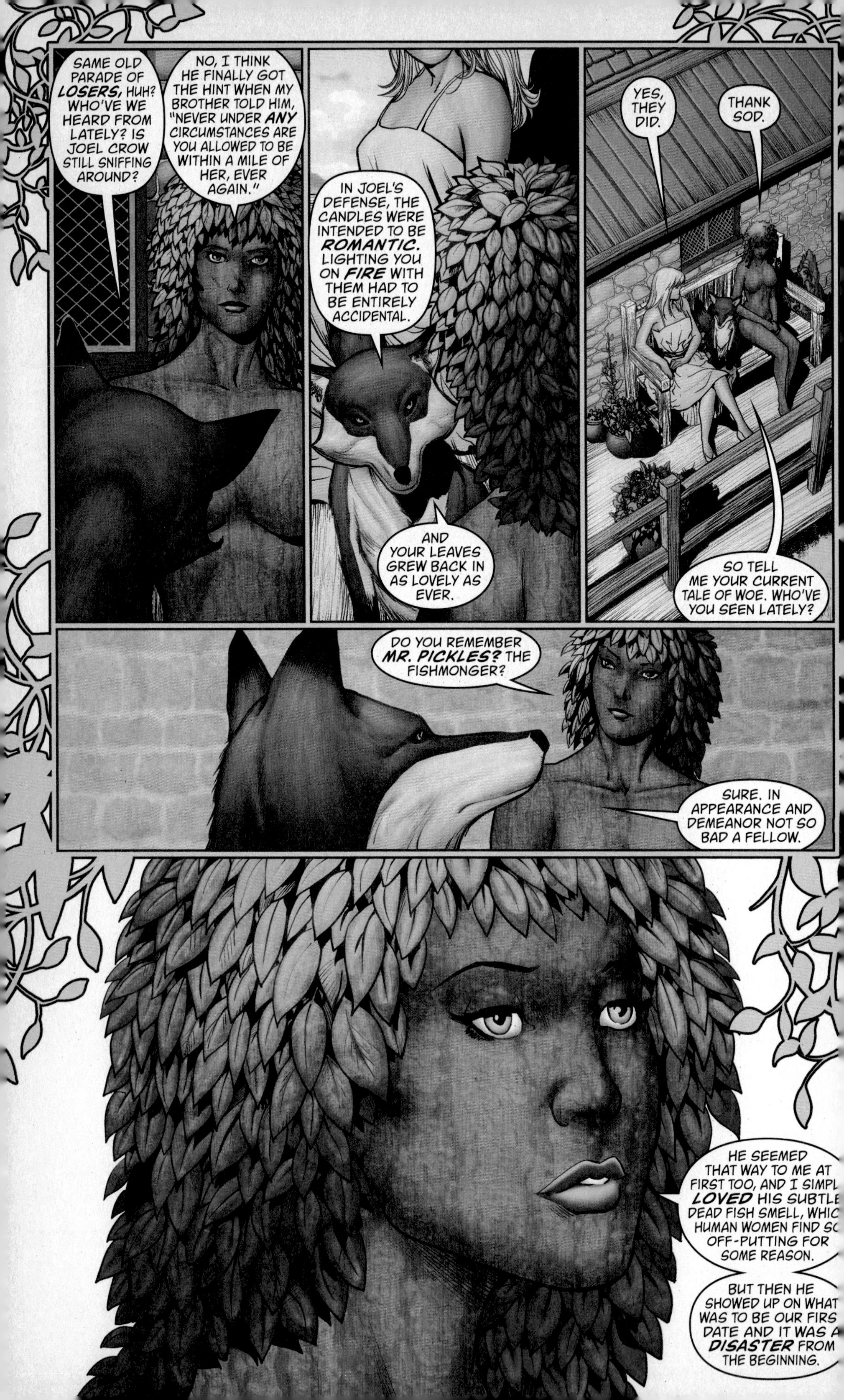
SAME OLD PARADE OF LOSERS, HUH? WHO'VE WE HEARD FROM LATELY? IS JOEL CROW STILL SNIFFING AROUND?
NO, I THINK HE FINALLY GOT THE HINT WHEN MY BROTHER TOLD HIM, "NEVER UNDER ANY CIRCUMSTANCES ARE YOU ALLOWED TO BE WITHIN A MILE OF HER, EVER AGAIN."
IN JOEL'S DEFENSE, THE CANDLES WERE INTENDED TO BE ROMANTIC. LIGHTING YOU ON FIRE WITH THEM HAD TO BE ENTIRELY ACCIDENTAL.
AND YOUR LEAVES GREW BACK IN AS LOVELY AS EVER.
YES, THEY DID.
THANK SOD.
SO TELL ME YOUR CURRENT TALE OF WOE. WHO'VE YOU SEEN LATELY?
DO YOU REMEMBER MR. PICKLES? THE FISHMONGER?
SURE. IN APPEARANCE AND DEMEANOR NOT SO BAD A FELLOW.
HE SEEMED THAT WAY TO ME AT FIRST TOO, AND I SIMPL LOVED HIS SUBTLE DEAD FISH SMELL, WHIC HUMAN WOMEN FIND SO OFF-PUTTING FOR SOME REASON.
BUT THEN HE SHOWED UP ON WHAT WAS TO BE OUR FIRS DATE AND IT WAS A DISASTER FROM THE BEGINNING.

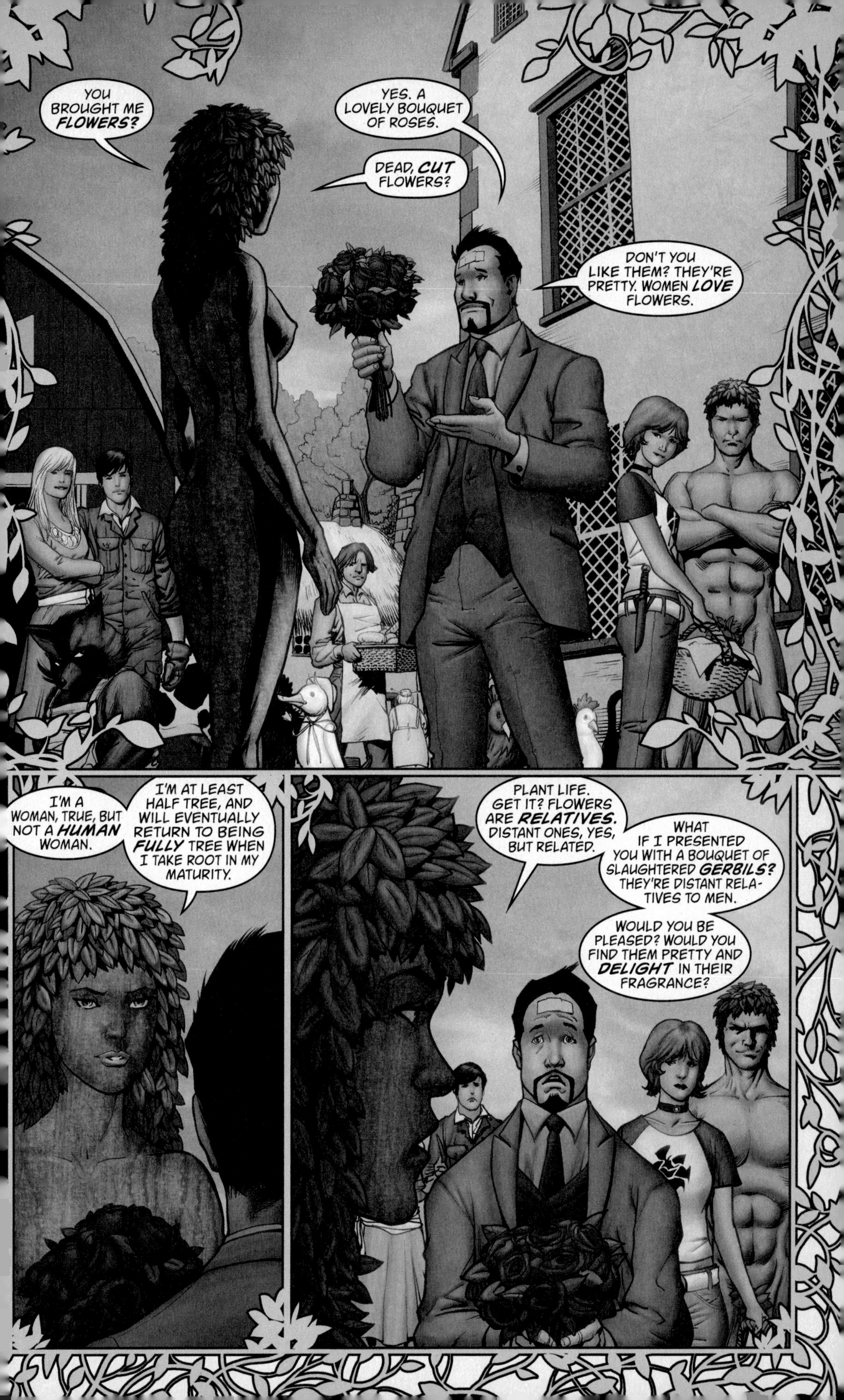
YOU BROUGHT ME FLOWERS?
YES. A LOVELY BOUQUET OF ROSES.
DEAD, CUT FLOWERS?
DON'T YOU LIKE THEM? THEY'RE PRETTY. WOMEN LOVE FLOWERS.
I'M A WOMAN, TRUE, BUT NOT A HUMAN WOMAN.
I'M AT LEAST HALF TREE, AND WILL EVENTUALLY RETURN TO BEING FULLY TREE WHEN I TAKE ROOT IN MY MATURITY.
PLANT LIFE. GET IT? FLOWERS ARE RELATIVES. DISTANT ONES, YES, BUT RELATED.
WHAT IF I PRESENTED YOU WITH A BOUQUET OF SLAUGHTERED GERBILS? THEY'RE DISTANT RELATIVES TO MEN.
WOULD YOU BE PLEASED? WOULD YOU FIND THEM PRETTY AND DELIGHT IN THEIR FRAGRANCE?

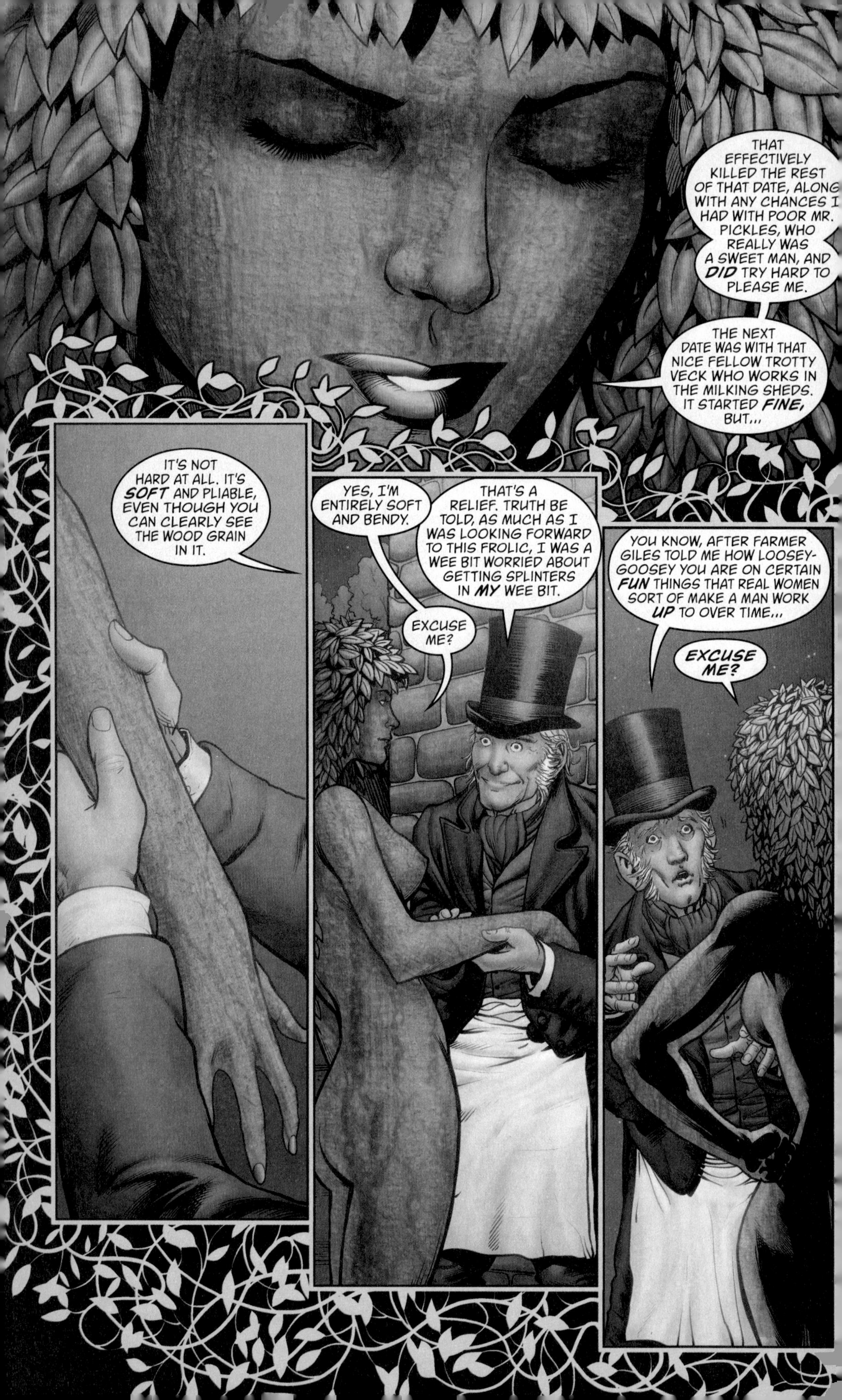
THAT EFFECTIVELY KILLED THE REST OF THAT DATE, ALONG WITH ANY CHANCES I HAD WITH POOR MR. PICKLES, WHO REALLY WAS A SWEET MAN, AND ***DID*** TRY HARD TO PLEASE ME.
THE NEXT DATE WAS WITH THAT NICE FELLOW TROTTY VECK WHO WORKS IN THE MILKING SHEDS. IT STARTED ***FINE,*** BUT...
IT'S NOT HARD AT ALL. IT'S ***SOFT*** AND PLIABLE, EVEN THOUGH YOU CAN CLEARLY SEE THE WOOD GRAIN IN IT.
YES, I'M ENTIRELY SOFT AND BENDY.
THAT'S A RELIEF. TRUTH BE TOLD, AS MUCH AS I WAS LOOKING FORWARD TO THIS FROLIC, I WAS A WEE BIT WORRIED ABOUT GETTING SPLINTERS IN ***MY*** WEE BIT.
EXCUSE ME?
YOU KNOW, AFTER FARMER GILES TOLD ME HOW LOOSEY-GOOSEY YOU ARE ON CERTAIN ***FUN*** THINGS THAT REAL WOMEN SORT OF MAKE A MAN WORK ***UP*** TO OVER TIME...
EXCUSE ME?

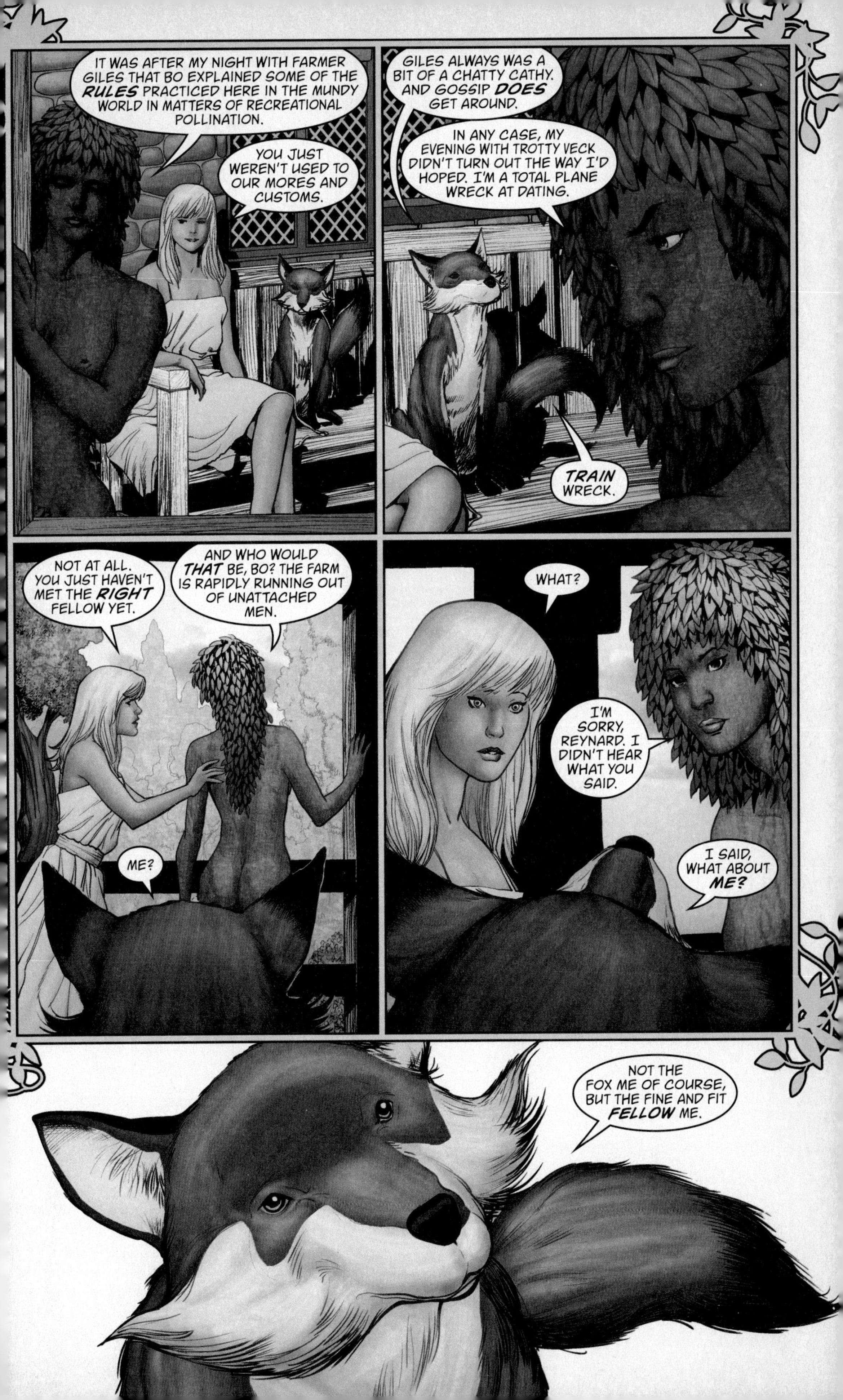
IT WAS AFTER MY NIGHT WITH FARMER GILES THAT BO EXPLAINED SOME OF THE RULES PRACTICED HERE IN THE MUNDY WORLD IN MATTERS OF RECREATIONAL POLLINATION.
YOU JUST WEREN'T USED TO OUR MORES AND CUSTOMS.
GILES ALWAYS WAS A BIT OF A CHATTY CATHY. AND GOSSIP DOES GET AROUND.
IN ANY CASE, MY EVENING WITH TROTTY VECK DIDN'T TURN OUT THE WAY I'D HOPED. I'M A TOTAL PLANE WRECK AT DATING.
TRAIN WRECK.
NOT AT ALL. YOU JUST HAVEN'T MET THE RIGHT FELLOW YET.
AND WHO WOULD THAT BE, BO? THE FARM IS RAPIDLY RUNNING OUT OF UNATTACHED MEN.
ME?
WHAT?
I'M SORRY, REYNARD. I DIDN'T HEAR WHAT YOU SAID.
I SAID, WHAT ABOUT ME?
NOT THE FOX ME OF COURSE, BUT THE FINE AND FIT FELLOW ME.

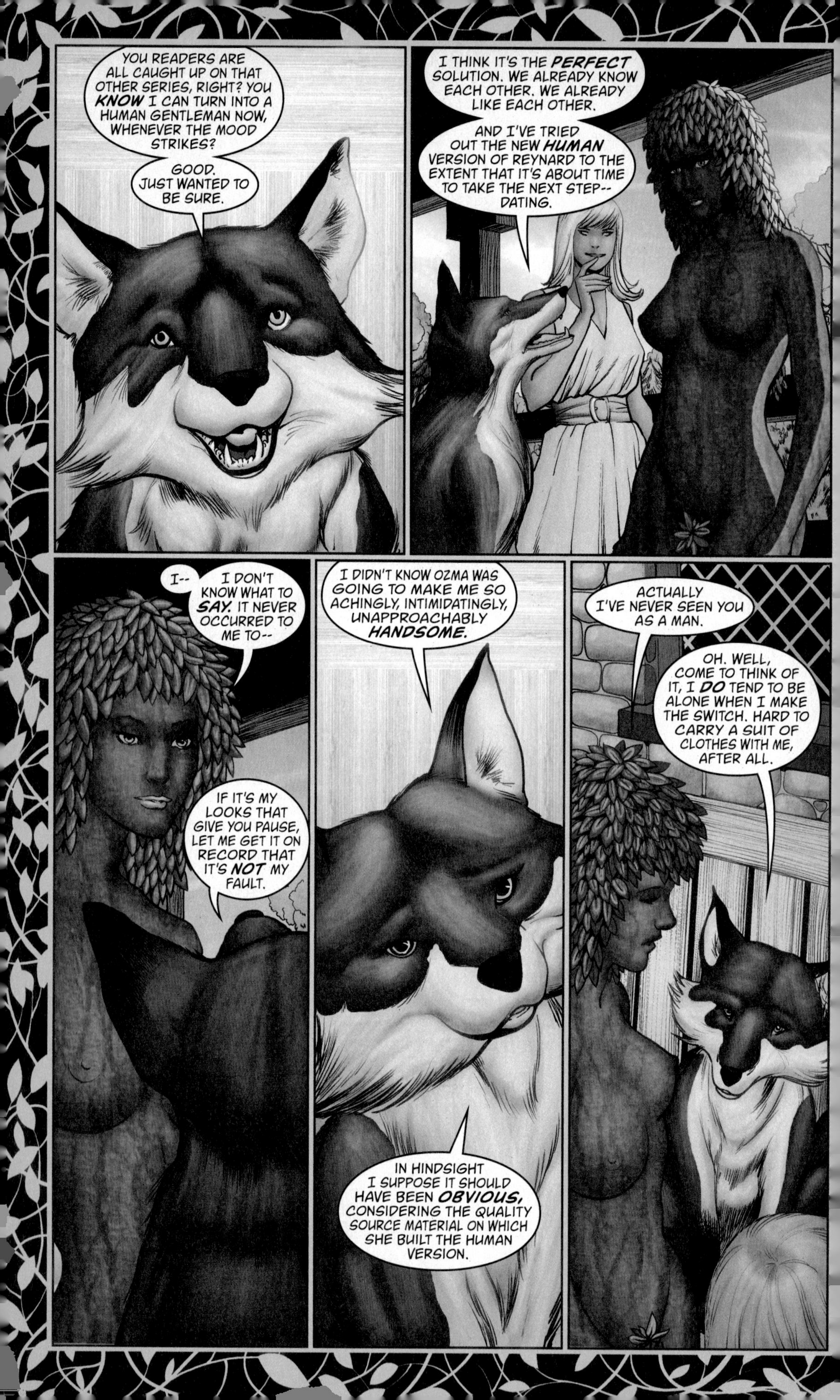

YOU READERS ARE ALL CAUGHT UP ON THAT OTHER SERIES, RIGHT? YOU KNOW I CAN TURN INTO A HUMAN GENTLEMAN NOW, WHENEVER THE MOOD STRIKES?
GOOD. JUST WANTED TO BE SURE.
I THINK IT'S THE PERFECT SOLUTION. WE ALREADY KNOW EACH OTHER. WE ALREADY LIKE EACH OTHER.
AND I'VE TRIED OUT THE NEW HUMAN VERSION OF REYNARD TO THE EXTENT THAT IT'S ABOUT TIME TO TAKE THE NEXT STEP-- DATING.
I--
I DON'T KNOW WHAT TO SAY. IT NEVER OCCURRED TO ME TO--
IF IT'S MY LOOKS THAT GIVE YOU PAUSE, LET ME GET IT ON RECORD THAT IT'S NOT MY FAULT.
I DIDN'T KNOW OZMA WAS GOING TO MAKE ME SO ACHINGLY, INTIMIDATINGLY, UNAPPROACHABLY HANDSOME.
IN HINDSIGHT I SUPPOSE IT SHOULD HAVE BEEN OBVIOUS, CONSIDERING THE QUALITY SOURCE MATERIAL ON WHICH SHE BUILT THE HUMAN VERSION.
ACTUALLY I'VE NEVER SEEN YOU AS A MAN.
OH. WELL, COME TO THINK OF IT, I DO TEND TO BE ALONE WHEN I MAKE THE SWITCH. HARD TO CARRY A SUIT OF CLOTHES WITH ME, AFTER ALL.

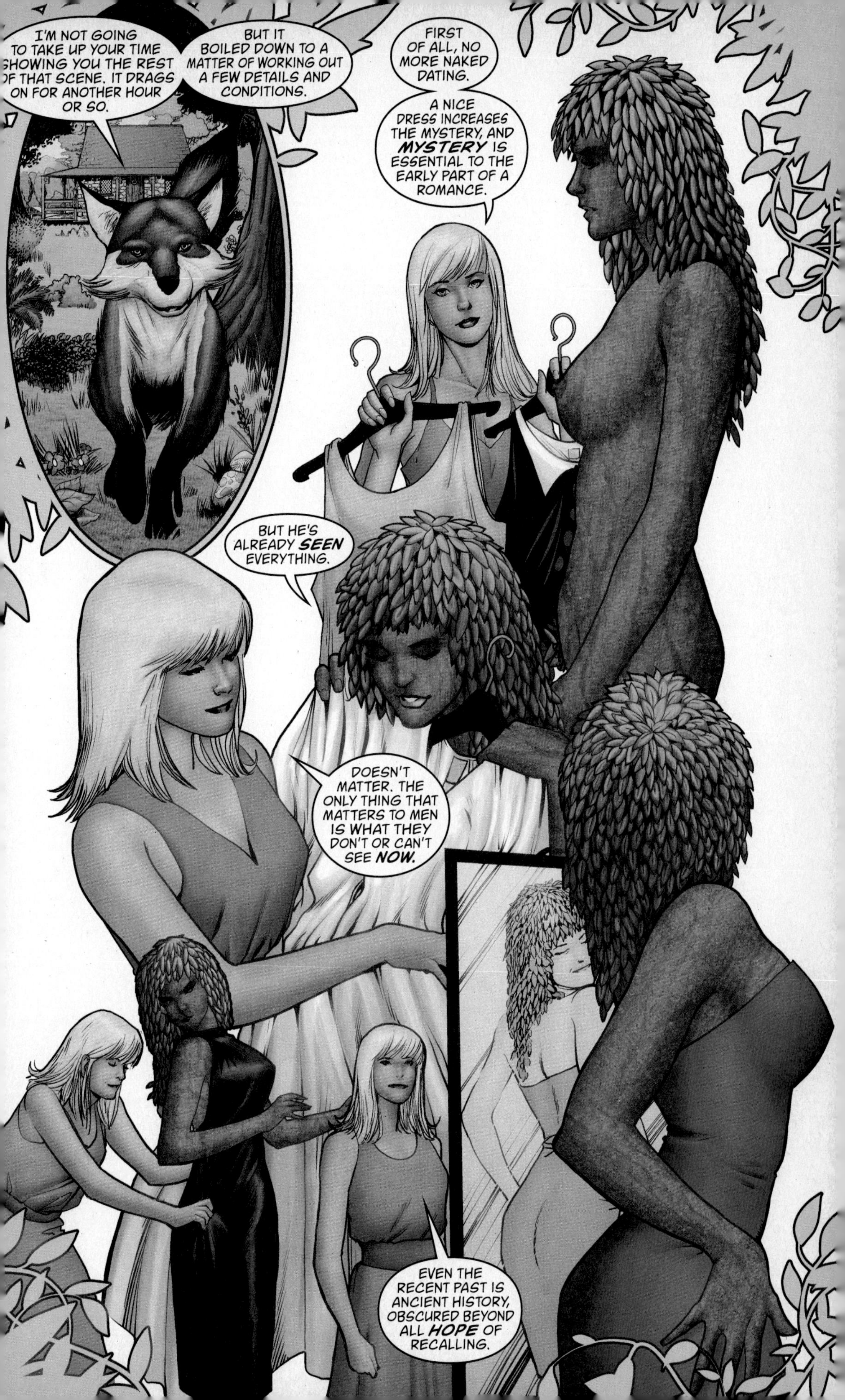
I'M NOT GOING TO TAKE UP YOUR TIME SHOWING YOU THE REST OF THAT SCENE. IT DRAGS ON FOR ANOTHER HOUR OR SO.
BUT IT BOILED DOWN TO A MATTER OF WORKING OUT A FEW DETAILS AND CONDITIONS.
FIRST OF ALL, NO MORE NAKED DATING.
A NICE DRESS INCREASES THE MYSTERY, AND **MYSTERY** IS ESSENTIAL TO THE EARLY PART OF A ROMANCE.
BUT HE'S ALREADY **SEEN** EVERYTHING.
DOESN'T MATTER. THE ONLY THING THAT MATTERS TO MEN IS WHAT THEY DON'T OR CAN'T SEE **NOW**.
EVEN THE RECENT PAST IS ANCIENT HISTORY, OBSCURED BEYOND ALL **HOPE** OF RECALLING.

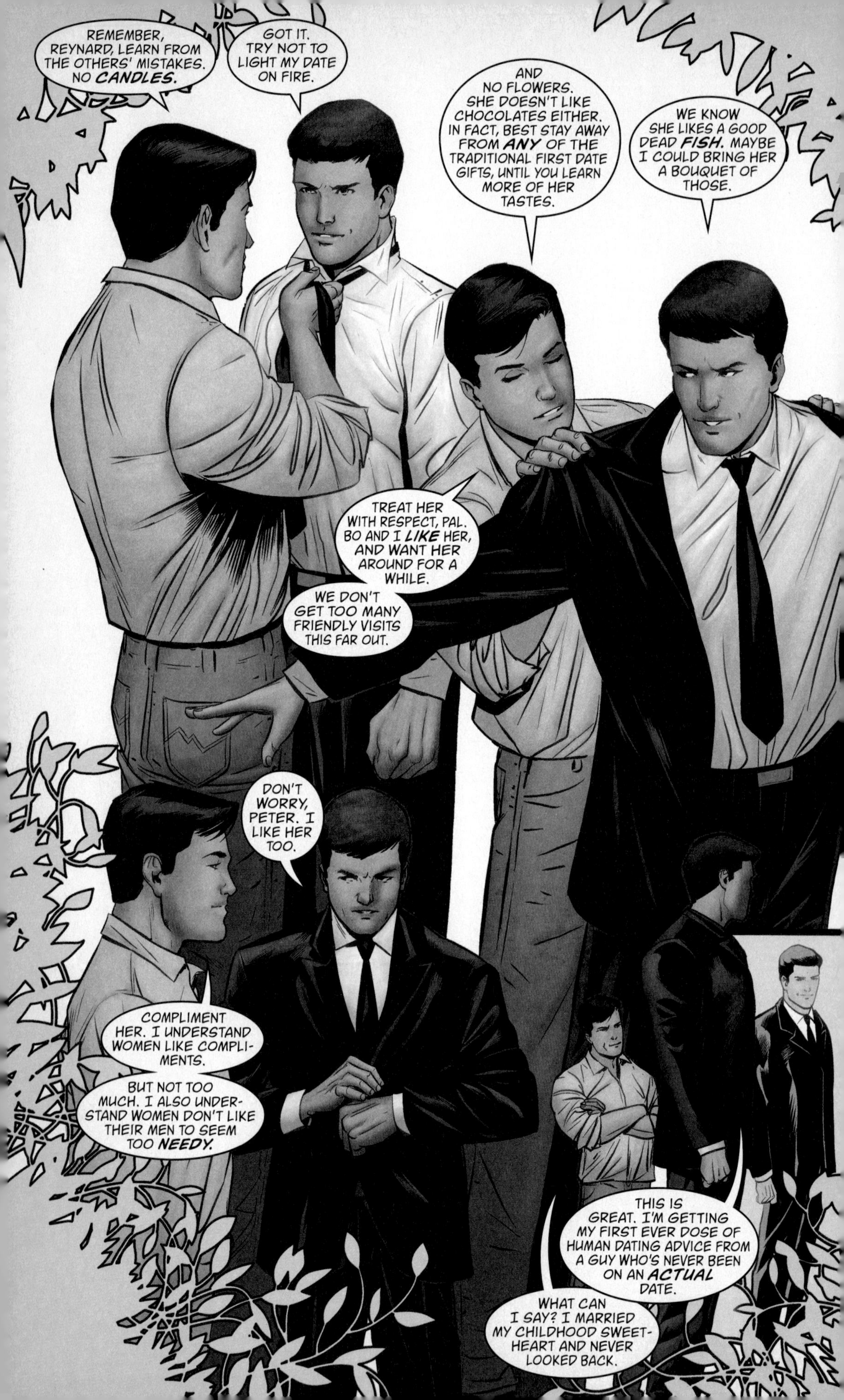
REMEMBER, REYNARD, LEARN FROM THE OTHERS' MISTAKES. NO CANDLES.
GOT IT. TRY NOT TO LIGHT MY DATE ON FIRE.
AND NO FLOWERS. SHE DOESN'T LIKE CHOCOLATES EITHER. IN FACT, BEST STAY AWAY FROM ANY OF THE TRADITIONAL FIRST DATE GIFTS, UNTIL YOU LEARN MORE OF HER TASTES.
WE KNOW SHE LIKES A GOOD DEAD FISH. MAYBE I COULD BRING HER A BOUQUET OF THOSE.
TREAT HER WITH RESPECT, PAL. BO AND I LIKE HER, AND WANT HER AROUND FOR A WHILE.
WE DON'T GET TOO MANY FRIENDLY VISITS THIS FAR OUT.
DON'T WORRY, PETER. I LIKE HER TOO.
COMPLIMENT HER. I UNDERSTAND WOMEN LIKE COMPLIMENTS.
BUT NOT TOO MUCH. I ALSO UNDERSTAND WOMEN DON'T LIKE THEIR MEN TO SEEM TOO NEEDY.
THIS IS GREAT. I'M GETTING MY FIRST EVER DOSE OF HUMAN DATING ADVICE FROM A GUY WHO'S NEVER BEEN ON AN ACTUAL DATE.
WHAT CAN I SAY? I MARRIED MY CHILDHOOD SWEETHEART AND NEVER LOOKED BACK.

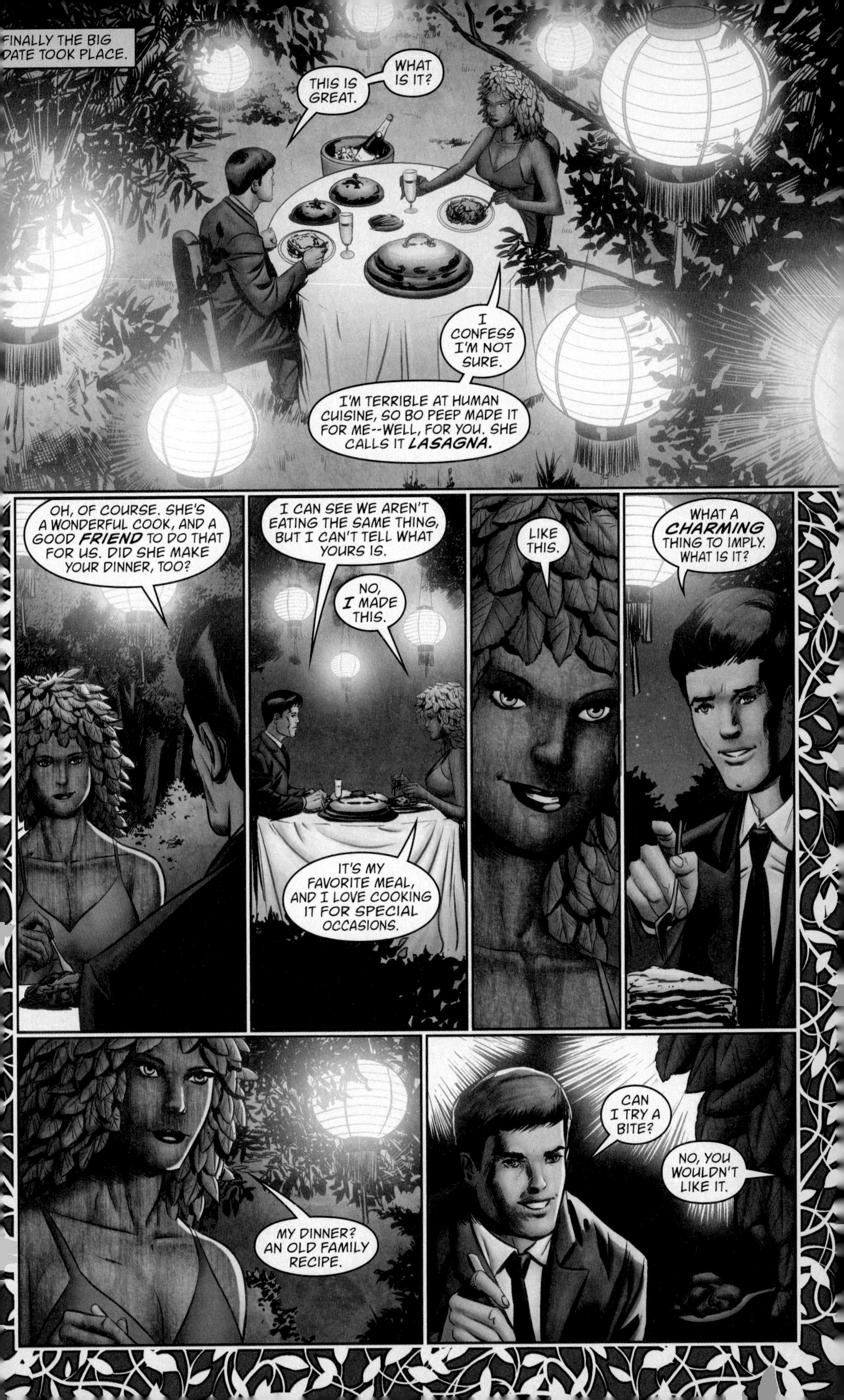

FINALLY THE BIG DATE TOOK PLACE.
THIS IS GREAT.
WHAT IS IT?
I CONFESS I'M NOT SURE.
I'M TERRIBLE AT HUMAN CUISINE, SO BO PEEP MADE IT FOR ME--WELL, FOR YOU. SHE CALLS IT LASAGNA.
OH, OF COURSE. SHE'S A WONDERFUL COOK, AND A GOOD FRIEND TO DO THAT FOR US. DID SHE MAKE YOUR DINNER, TOO?
I CAN SEE WE AREN'T EATING THE SAME THING, BUT I CAN'T TELL WHAT YOURS IS.
NO, I MADE THIS.
IT'S MY FAVORITE MEAL, AND I LOVE COOKING IT FOR SPECIAL OCCASIONS.
LIKE THIS.
WHAT A CHARMING THING TO IMPLY. WHAT IS IT?
MY DINNER? AN OLD FAMILY RECIPE.
CAN I TRY A BITE?
NO, YOU WOULDN'T LIKE IT.

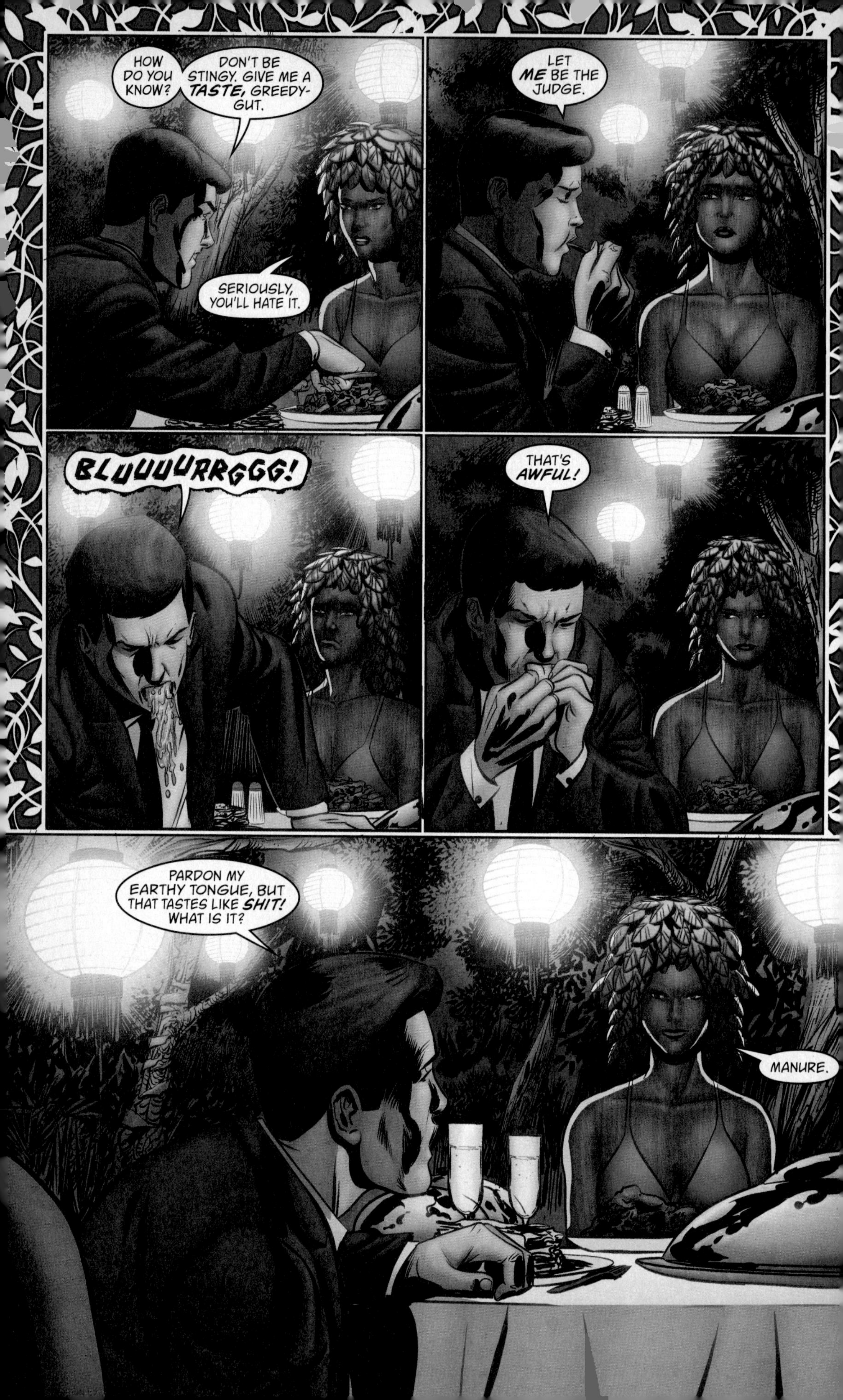
HOW DO YOU KNOW?
DON'T BE STINGY. GIVE ME A TASTE, GREEDY-GUT.
SERIOUSLY, YOU'LL HATE IT.
LET ME BE THE JUDGE.
BLUUUURRGGG!
THAT'S AWFUL!
PARDON MY EARTHY TONGUE, BUT THAT TASTES LIKE SHIT! WHAT IS IT?
MANURE.

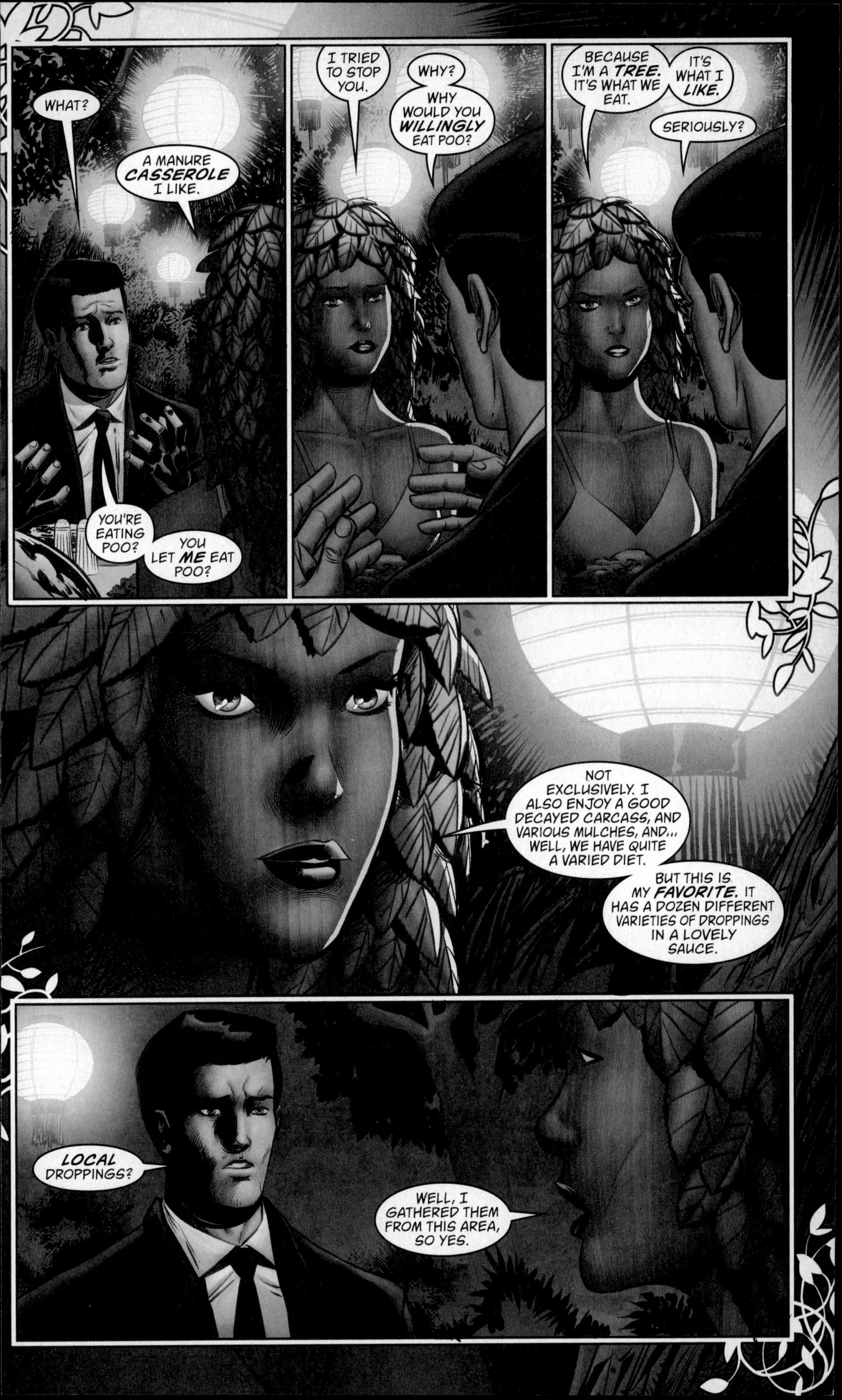
WHAT?
A MANURE CASSEROLE I LIKE.
YOU'RE EATING POO?
YOU LET ME EAT POO?
I TRIED TO STOP YOU.
WHY?
WHY WOULD YOU WILLINGLY EAT POO?
BECAUSE I'M A TREE. IT'S WHAT WE EAT.
IT'S WHAT I LIKE.
SERIOUSLY?
NOT EXCLUSIVELY. I ALSO ENJOY A GOOD DECAYED CARCASS, AND VARIOUS MULCHES, AND... WELL, WE HAVE QUITE A VARIED DIET.
BUT THIS IS MY FAVORITE. IT HAS A DOZEN DIFFERENT VARIETIES OF DROPPINGS IN A LOVELY SAUCE.
LOCAL DROPPINGS?
WELL, I GATHERED THEM FROM THIS AREA, SO YES.

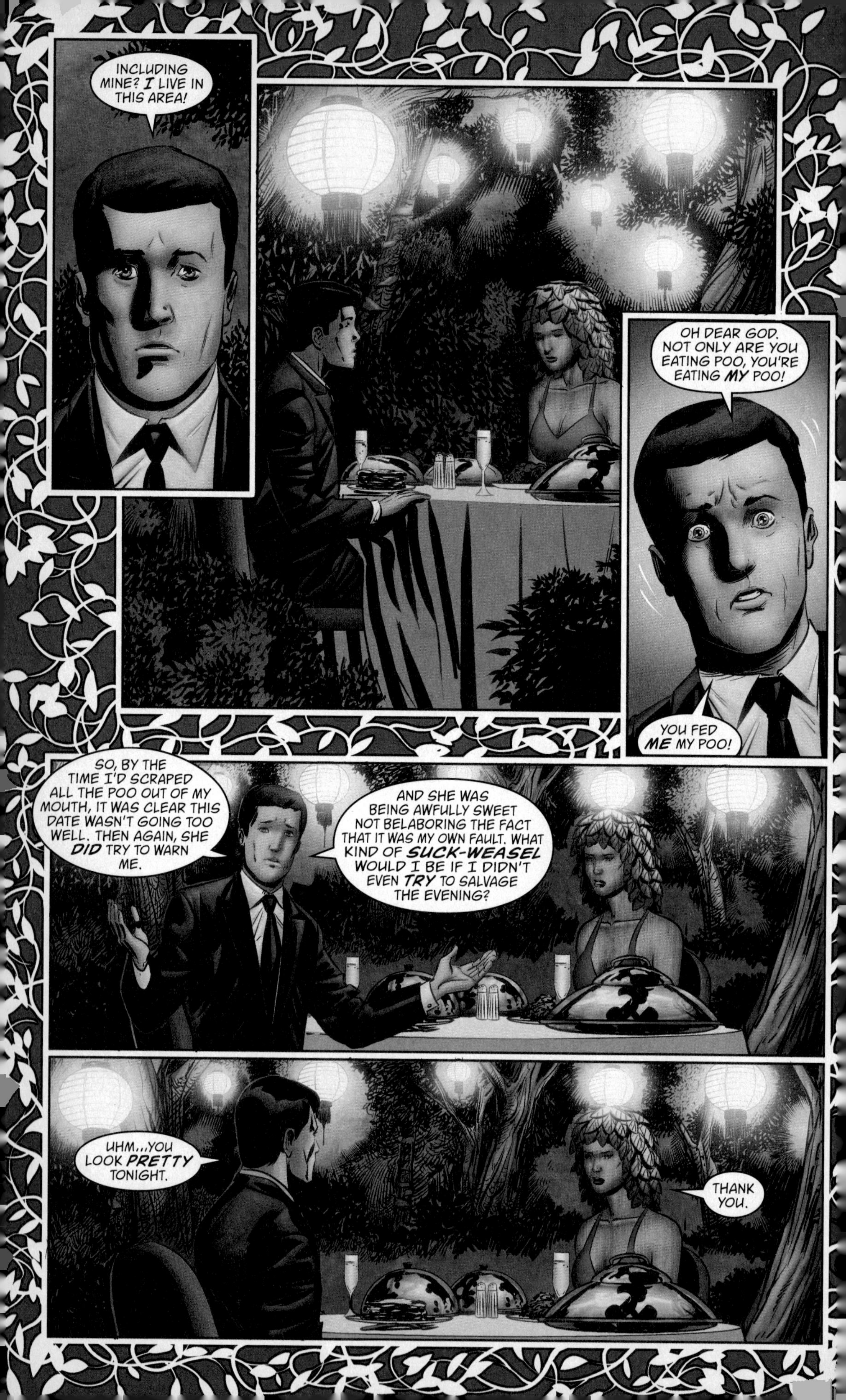
INCLUDING MINE? I LIVE IN THIS AREA!
OH DEAR GOD. NOT ONLY ARE YOU EATING POO, YOU'RE EATING MY POO!
YOU FED ME MY POO!
SO, BY THE TIME I'D SCRAPED ALL THE POO OUT OF MY MOUTH, IT WAS CLEAR THIS DATE WASN'T GOING TOO WELL. THEN AGAIN, SHE DID TRY TO WARN ME.
AND SHE WAS BEING AWFULLY SWEET NOT BELABORING THE FACT THAT IT WAS MY OWN FAULT. WHAT KIND OF SUCK-WEASEL WOULD I BE IF I DIDN'T EVEN TRY TO SALVAGE THE EVENING?
UHM...YOU LOOK PRETTY TONIGHT.
THANK YOU.

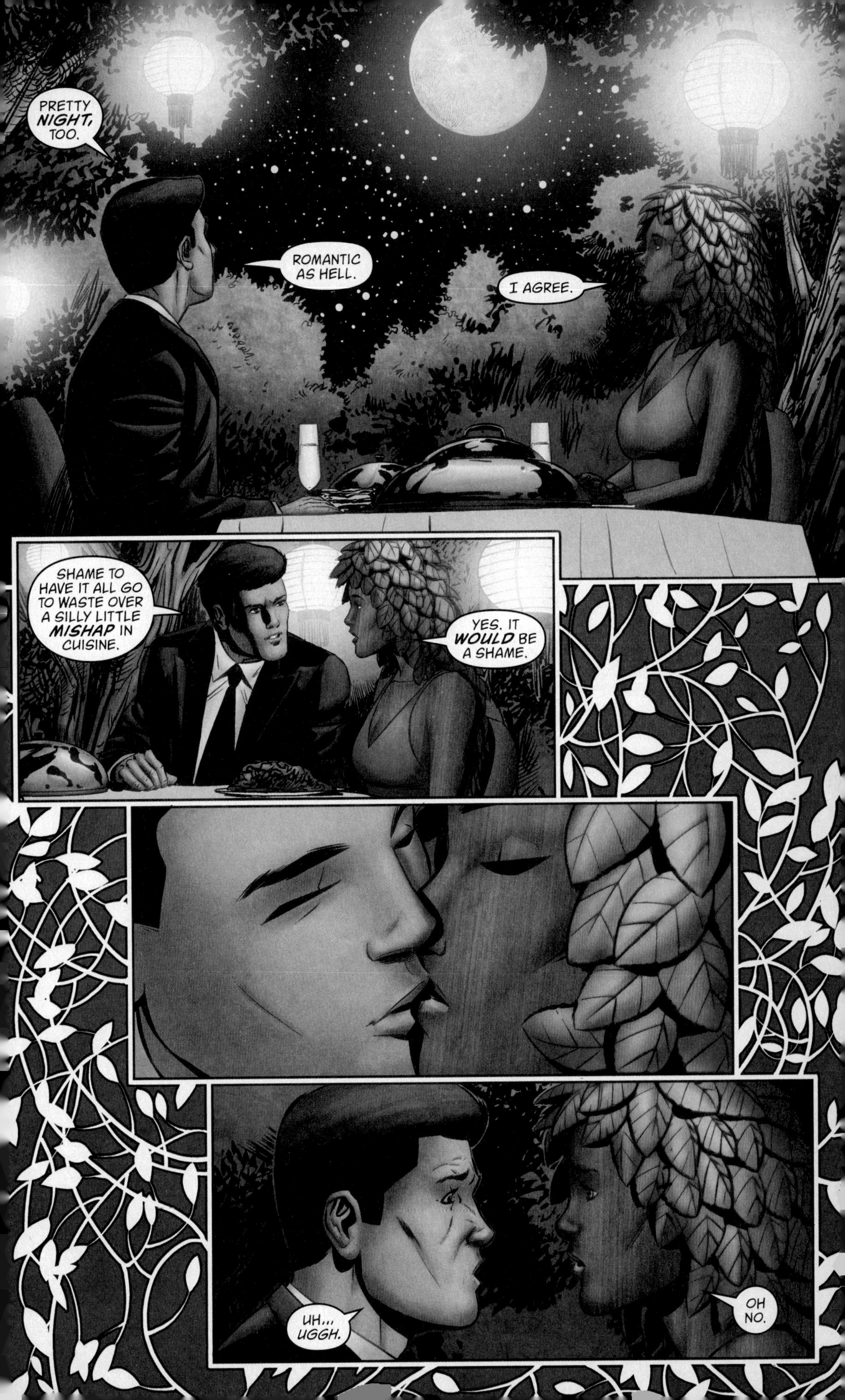
PRETTY NIGHT, TOO.
ROMANTIC AS HELL.
I AGREE.
SHAME TO HAVE IT ALL GO TO WASTE OVER A SILLY LITTLE MISHAP IN CUISINE.
YES. IT WOULD BE A SHAME.
UH... UGGH.
OH NO.

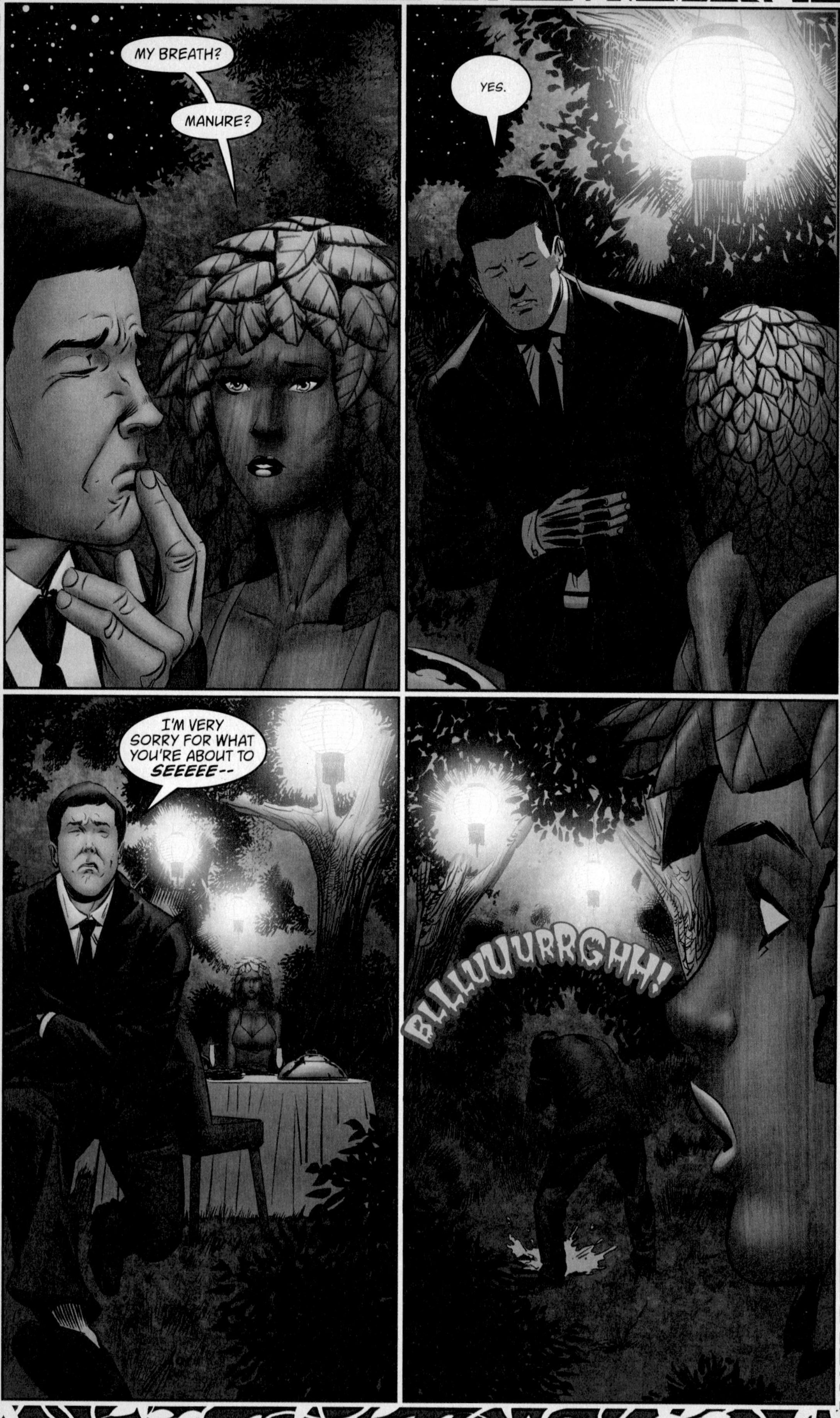
MY BREATH?
MANURE?
YES.
I'M VERY SORRY FOR WHAT YOU'RE ABOUT TO SEEEEE--
BLLUUUURRGHH!

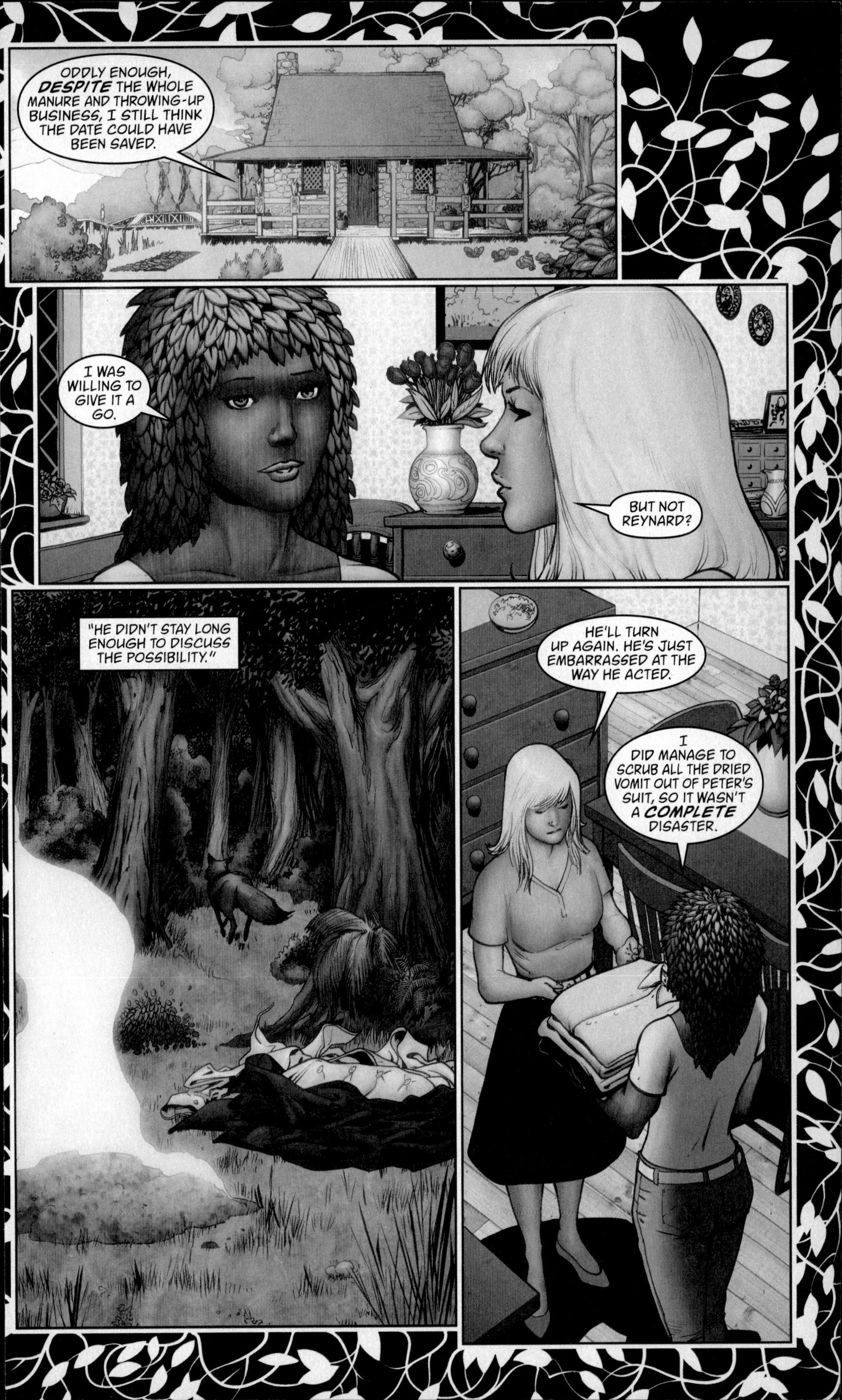
ODDLY ENOUGH, DESPITE THE WHOLE MANURE AND THROWING-UP BUSINESS, I STILL THINK THE DATE COULD HAVE BEEN SAVED.
I WAS WILLING TO GIVE IT A GO.
BUT NOT REYNARD?
"HE DIDN'T STAY LONG ENOUGH TO DISCUSS THE POSSIBILITY."
HE'LL TURN UP AGAIN. HE'S JUST EMBARRASSED AT THE WAY HE ACTED.
I DID MANAGE TO SCRUB ALL THE DRIED VOMIT OUT OF PETER'S SUIT, SO IT WASN'T A COMPLETE DISASTER.

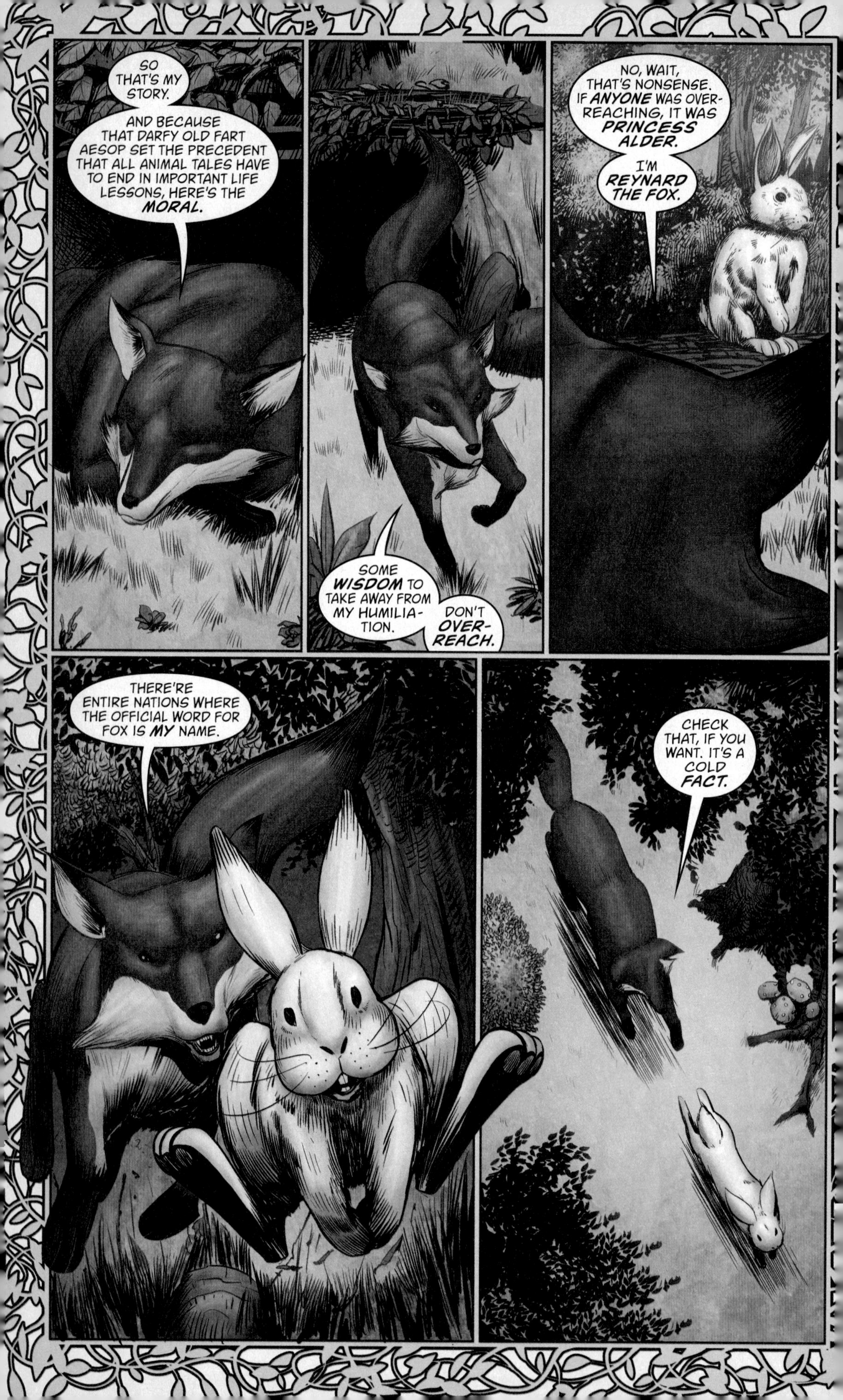
SO THAT'S MY STORY.
AND BECAUSE THAT DARFY OLD FART AESOP SET THE PRECEDENT THAT ALL ANIMAL TALES HAVE TO END IN IMPORTANT LIFE LESSONS, HERE'S THE MORAL.
SOME WISDOM TO TAKE AWAY FROM MY HUMILIATION.
DON'T OVER-REACH.
NO, WAIT, THAT'S NONSENSE. IF ANYONE WAS OVER-REACHING, IT WAS PRINCESS ALDER.
I'M REYNARD THE FOX.
THERE'RE ENTIRE NATIONS WHERE THE OFFICIAL WORD FOR FOX IS MY NAME.
CHECK THAT, IF YOU WANT. IT'S A COLD FACT.

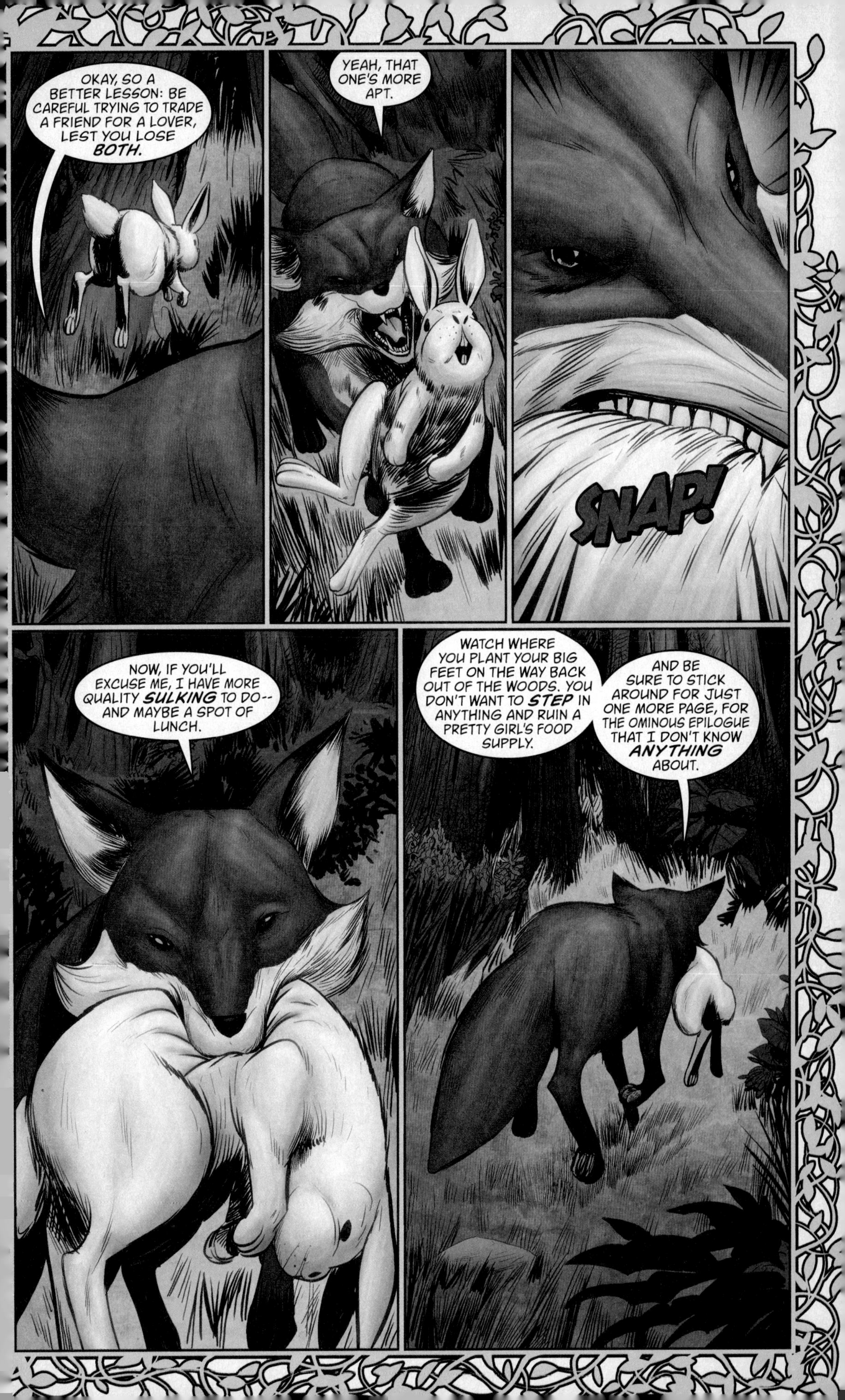
OKAY, SO A BETTER LESSON: BE CAREFUL TRYING TO TRADE A FRIEND FOR A LOVER, LEST YOU LOSE BOTH.
YEAH, THAT ONE'S MORE APT.
SNAP!
NOW, IF YOU'LL EXCUSE ME, I HAVE MORE QUALITY SULKING TO DO-- AND MAYBE A SPOT OF LUNCH.
WATCH WHERE YOU PLANT YOUR BIG FEET ON THE WAY BACK OUT OF THE WOODS. YOU DON'T WANT TO STEP IN ANYTHING AND RUIN A PRETTY GIRL'S FOOD SUPPLY.
AND BE SURE TO STICK AROUND FOR JUST ONE MORE PAGE, FOR THE OMINOUS EPILOGUE THAT I DON'T KNOW ANYTHING ABOUT.

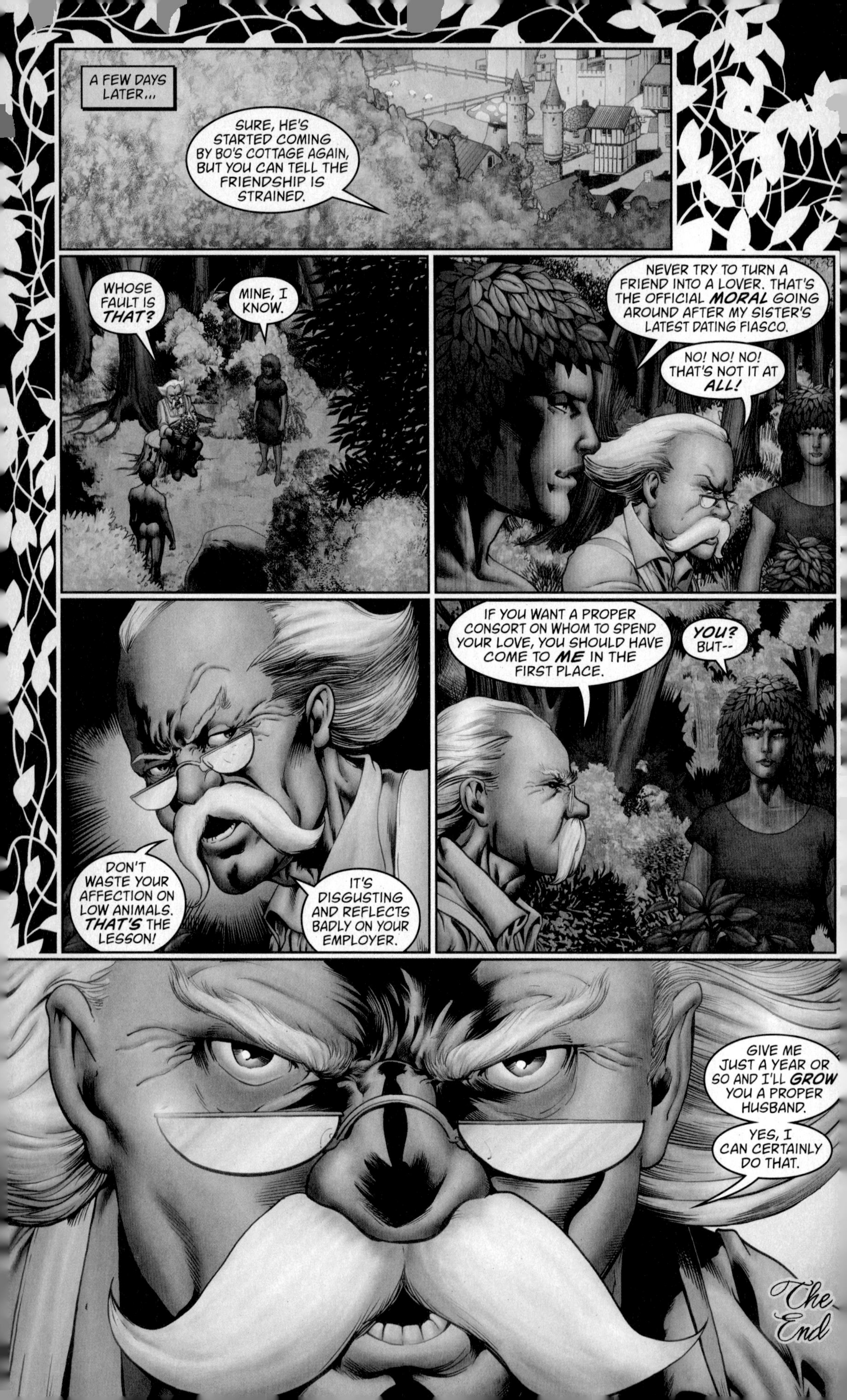
A FEW DAYS LATER...
SURE, HE'S STARTED COMING BY BO'S COTTAGE AGAIN, BUT YOU CAN TELL THE FRIENDSHIP IS STRAINED.
WHOSE FAULT IS THAT?
MINE, I KNOW.
NEVER TRY TO TURN A FRIEND INTO A LOVER. THAT'S THE OFFICIAL MORAL GOING AROUND AFTER MY SISTER'S LATEST DATING FIASCO.
NO! NO! NO! THAT'S NOT IT AT ALL!
DON'T WASTE YOUR AFFECTION ON LOW ANIMALS. THAT'S THE LESSON!
IT'S DISGUSTING AND REFLECTS BADLY ON YOUR EMPLOYER.
IF YOU WANT A PROPER CONSORT ON WHOM TO SPEND YOUR LOVE, YOU SHOULD HAVE COME TO ME IN THE FIRST PLACE.
YOU? BUT--
GIVE ME JUST A YEAR OR SO AND I'LL GROW YOU A PROPER HUSBAND.
YES, I CAN CERTAINLY DO THAT.
The End

BILL WILLINGHAM

FABLES VOL. 1: LEGENDS IN EXILE

FABLES VOL. 1:
LEGENDS IN EXILE

FABLES VOL. 2:
ANIMAL FARM

FABLES VOL. 3:
STORYBOOK LOVE

FABLES VOL. 4:
MARCH OF THE
WOODEN SOLDIERS

FABLES VOL. 5:
THE MEAN SEASONS

FABLES VOL. 6:
HOMELANDS

FABLES VOL. 7:
ARABIAN NIGHTS
(AND DAYS)

FABLES VOL. 8:
WOLVES

FABLES VOL. 9:
SONS OF EMPIRE

FABLES VOL. 10:
THE GOOD PRINCE

FABLES VOL. 11:
WAR AND PIECES

FABLES VOL. 12:
THE DARK AGES

FABLES VOL. 13:
THE GREAT FABLES
CROSSOVER

FABLES VOL. 14:
WITCHES

FABLES VOL. 15:
ROSE RED

FABLES VOL. 16:
SUPER TEAM

FABLES VOL. 17:
INHERIT THE WIND

FABLES: 1001 NIGHTS
OF SNOWFALL

FABLES: PETER & MAX

THE #1 NEW YORK TIMES BEST-SELLING SERIES

FABLES

Legends in Exile

"A top-notch fantasy comic that is on a par with SANDMAN." — *Variety*

DIRECTOR

BULLFINCH STREET

Bill Willingham
Lan Medina
Steve Leialoha
Craig Hamilton

VERTIGO